My pet dog Edu, who lives with my parents, is turning eighteen this year. That's right, eighteen. He's an old dog. Edu's been with me through a lot, but now he's blind and can barely walk. When I visit my parents, I want to spend as much time with him as I can. (My current weight is…72 kg!! Am I even serious about losing weight anymore?!)

–Mitsutoshi Shimabukuro, 2011

Mitsutoshi Shimabukuro made his debut in **Weekly Shonen Jump** in 1996. He is best known for **Seikimatsu Leader Den Takeshi!** for which he won the 46th Shogakukan Manga Award for children's manga in 2001. His current series, **Toriko**, began serialization in Japan in 2008.

TORIKO

TORIKO VOL. 13
SHONEN JUMP Manga Edition

STORY AND ART BY **MITSUTOSHI SHIMABUKURO**

Translation/Christine Dashiell
Adaptation/Hope Donovan
Touch-Up Art & Lettering/Maui Girl
Design/Matt Hinrichs
Editor/Hope Donovan

Printed in Canada

Published by VIZ Media, LLC
P.O. Box 77010
San Francisco, CA 94107

10 9 8 7 6 5 4 3 2 1
First printing, December 2012

PARENTAL ADVISORY
TORIKO is rated T for Teen and is recommended
for ages 13 and up. This volume contains
realistic and fantasy violence.
ratings.viz.com

www.viz.com

THE WORLD'S
MOST POPULAR MANGA
www.shonenjump.com

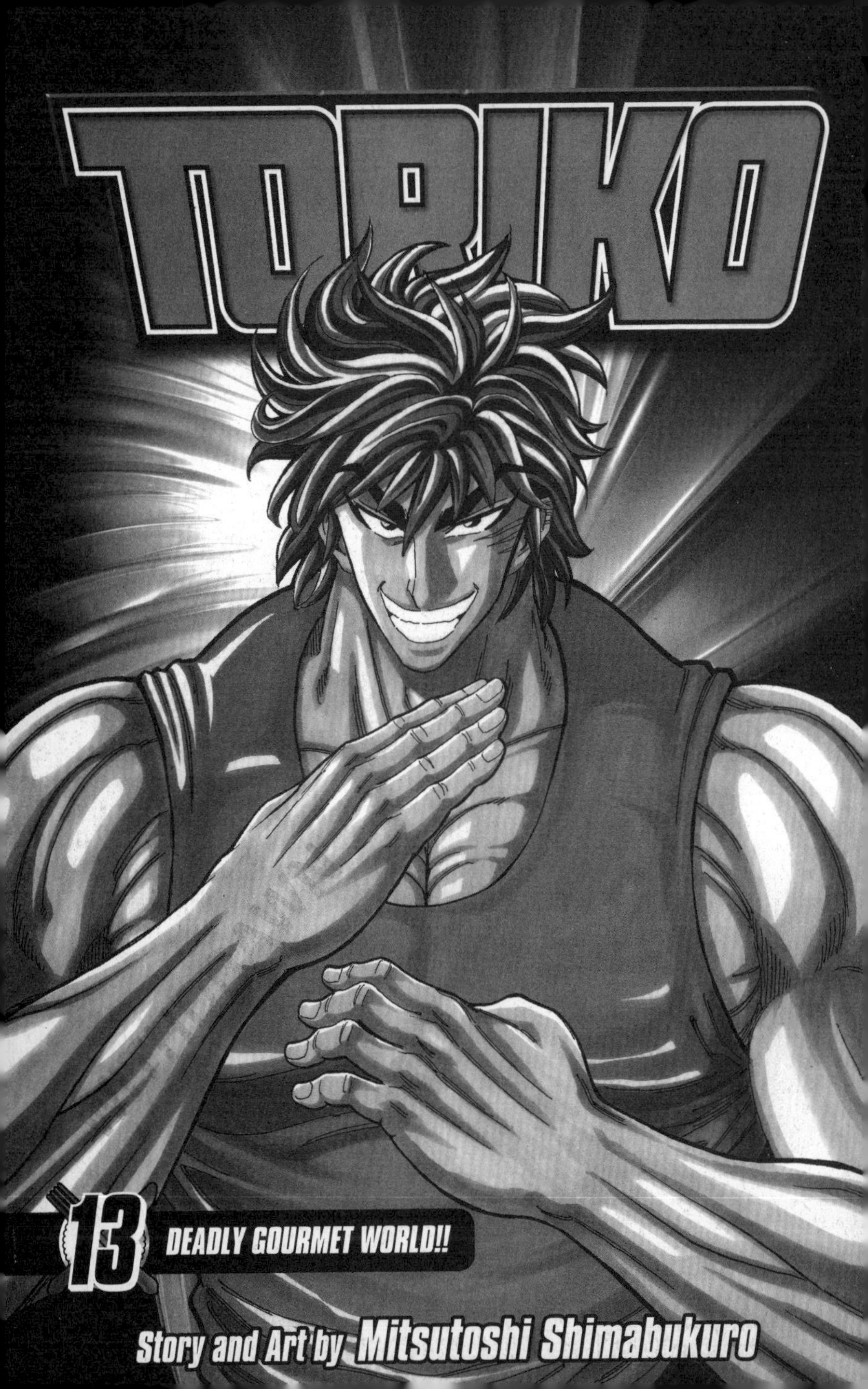
TORIKO
13
DEADLY GOURMET WORLD!!
Story and Art by Mitsutoshi Shimabukuro

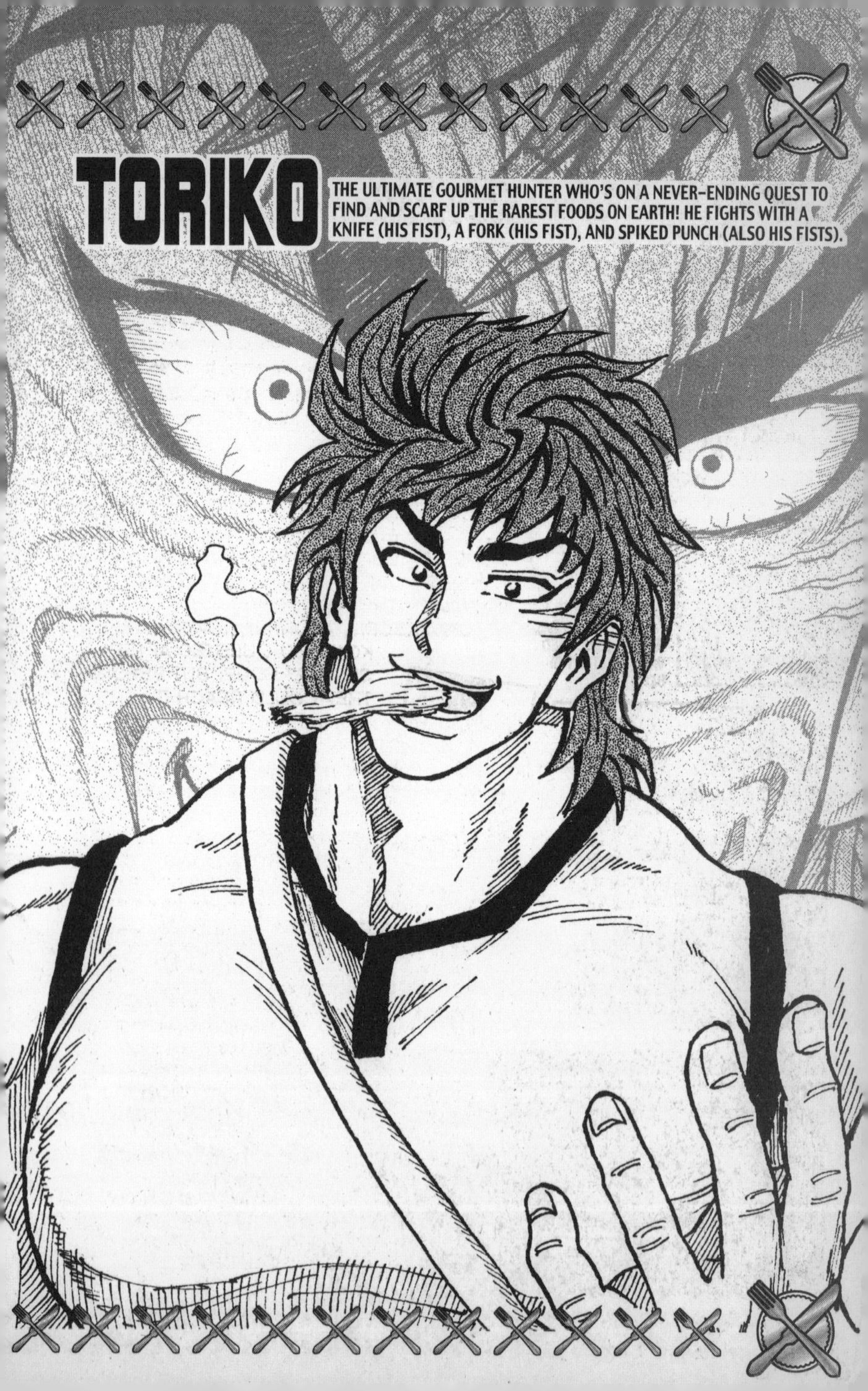
TORIKO
THE ULTIMATE GOURMET HUNTER WHO'S ON A NEVER-ENDING QUEST TO FIND AND SCARF UP THE RAREST FOODS ON EARTH! HE FIGHTS WITH A KNIFE (HIS FIST), A FORK (HIS FIST), AND SPIKED PUNCH (ALSO HIS FISTS).

WHAT'S FOR DINNER

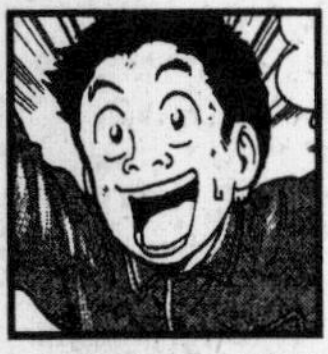

●KOMATSU
TALENTED IGO HOTEL CHEF AND TORIKO'S #1 FAN.

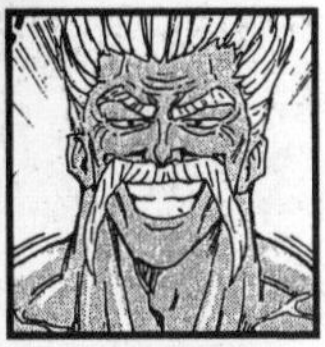

●ICHIRYU
FEISTY IGO PRESIDENT AND DISCIPLE OF GOURMET GOD ACACIA

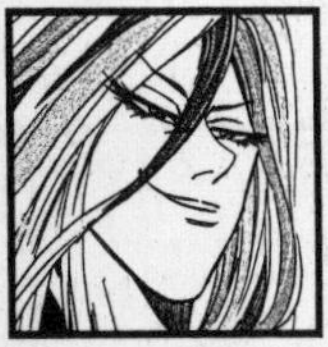

●SUNNY
ANOTHER OF THE FOUR KINGS. SENSORS IN HIS LONG HAIR ENABLE HIM TO "TASTE" THE WORLD. OBSESSED WITH ALL THAT IS BEAUTIFUL.

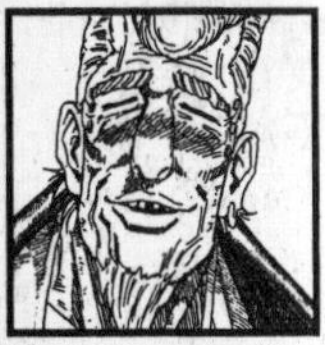

●JIRO
LEGENDARY GOURMET HUNTER WHO EARNED THE TITLE "KNOCKING MASTER." DISCIPLE OF ACACIA AND HEAVY DRINKER.

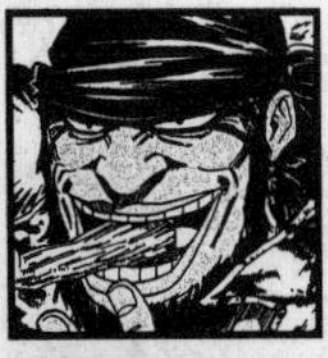

●YOSAKU
AKA "BLOOD-STAINED YOSAKU." A REVIVER WHO BREAKS THE RULES, BUT NOT HIS PROMISES.

GOURMET CORP.

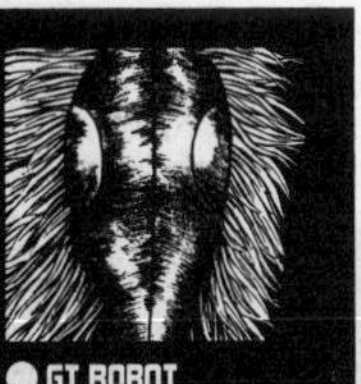

●GT ROBOT
GOURMET CORP.'S NEW ROBOT.

IT'S THE AGE OF GOURMET! KOMATSU, THE HEAD CHEF AT THE HOTEL OWNED BY THE IGO (INTERNATIONAL GOURMET ORGANIZATION), BECAME FAST FRIENDS WITH THE LEGENDARY GOURMET HUNTER TORIKO WHILE GATOR HUNTING. NOW KOMATSU ACCOMPANIES TORIKO ON HIS LIFELONG QUEST TO CREATE THE PERFECT FULL-COURSE MEAL.

TORIKO'S TREKS HAVE GOTTEN MORE INTERESTING SINCE THE IGO'S RIVAL, GOURMET CORP., HAS STARTING STIRRING UP TROUBLE. BUT TORIKO CONTINUES TO HUNT, TRAVEL THE WORLD, AND TAKE ON GOURMET CORP.'S NEFARIOUS AGENTS WHENEVER THEY INTERFERE.

ON A RECENT JOURNEY, TORIKO AND KOMATSU QUESTED AFTER CENTURY SOUP. BUT BEFORE THEY COULD REACH IT, GOURMET CORP. DREW TORIKO INTO A BATTLE SO BRUTAL THAT HE HAD TO SEEK MEDICAL TREATMENT IN LIFE, THE COUNTRY OF HEALING. MEANWHILE, AFTER PLENTY OF TRIAL AND ERROR KOMATSU COMPLETED THE RECIPE FOR CENTURY SOUP AND GAINED WORLD-WIDE ATTENTION!

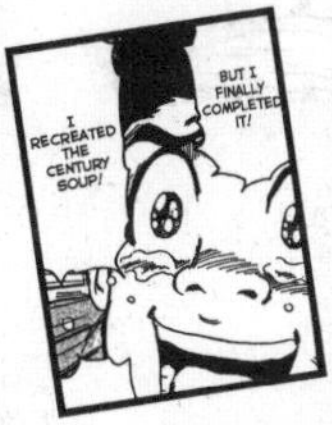
BUT I FINALLY COMPLETED IT!
I RECREATED THE CENTURY SOUP!

ONCE FULLY RECOVERED, TORIKO PAID A VISIT TO THE IGO PRESIDENT, WHO TOLD HIM TO CAPTURE THE KING OF VEGETABLES: OZONE GRASS! THE PRESIDENT ALSO TOLD TORIKO TO MAKE KOMATSU HIS CHEF PARTNER. THE DIFFICULT PATH TO OZONE GRASS HAS DRAWN TORIKO AND KOMATSU CLOSER THAN EVER, AND BOTH ARE ON THE VERGE OF BIG DISCOVERIES...

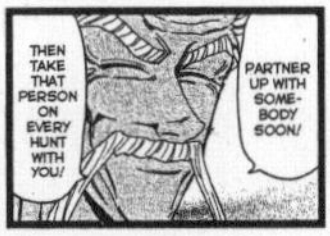
PARTNER UP WITH SOMEBODY SOON!
THEN TAKE THAT PERSON ON EVERY HUNT WITH YOU!

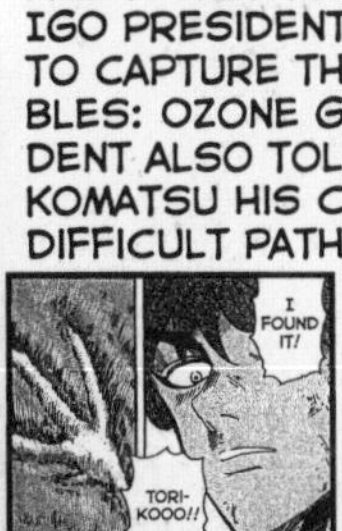
I FOUND IT!
TORI-KOOO!!

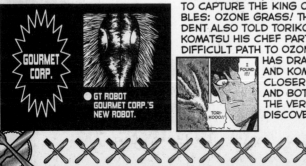

Contents

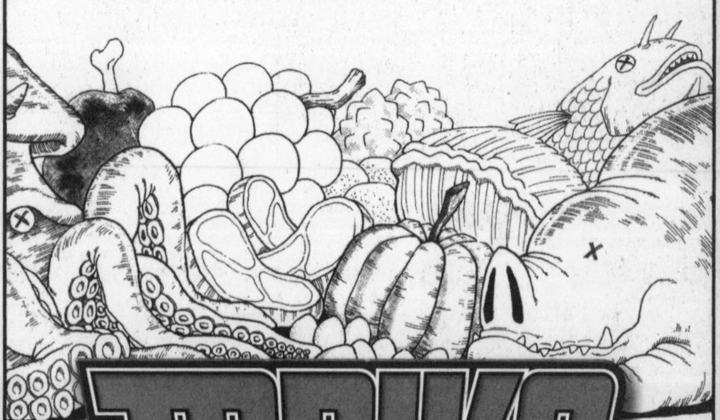

TORIKO

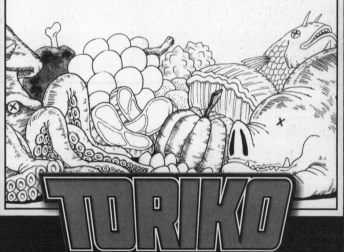

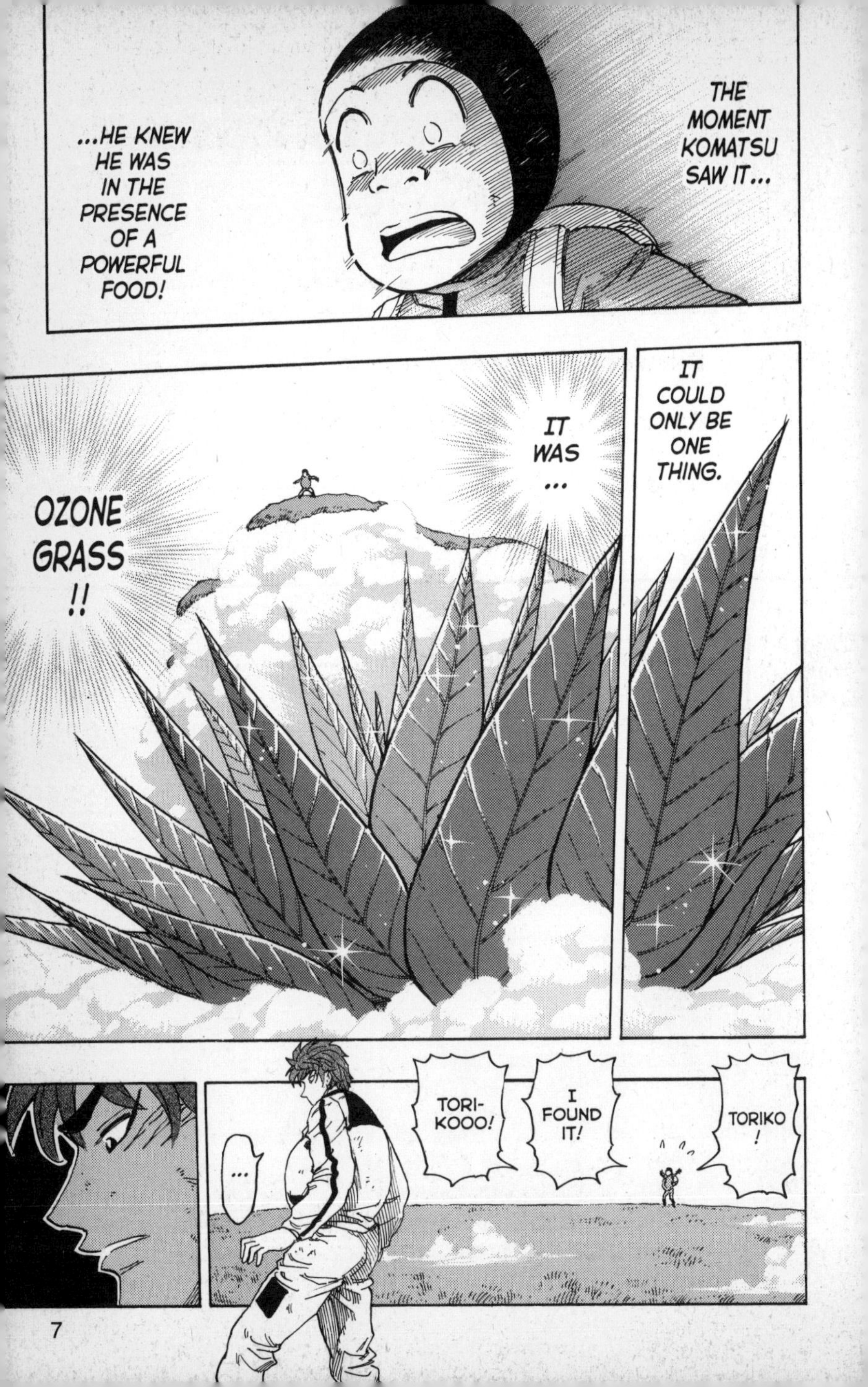
THE MOMENT KOMATSU SAW IT...
...HE KNEW HE WAS IN THE PRESENCE OF A POWERFUL FOOD!
IT COULD ONLY BE ONE THING.
IT WAS ...
OZONE GRASS !!
TORIKO!
I FOUND IT!
TORI-KOOO!
...

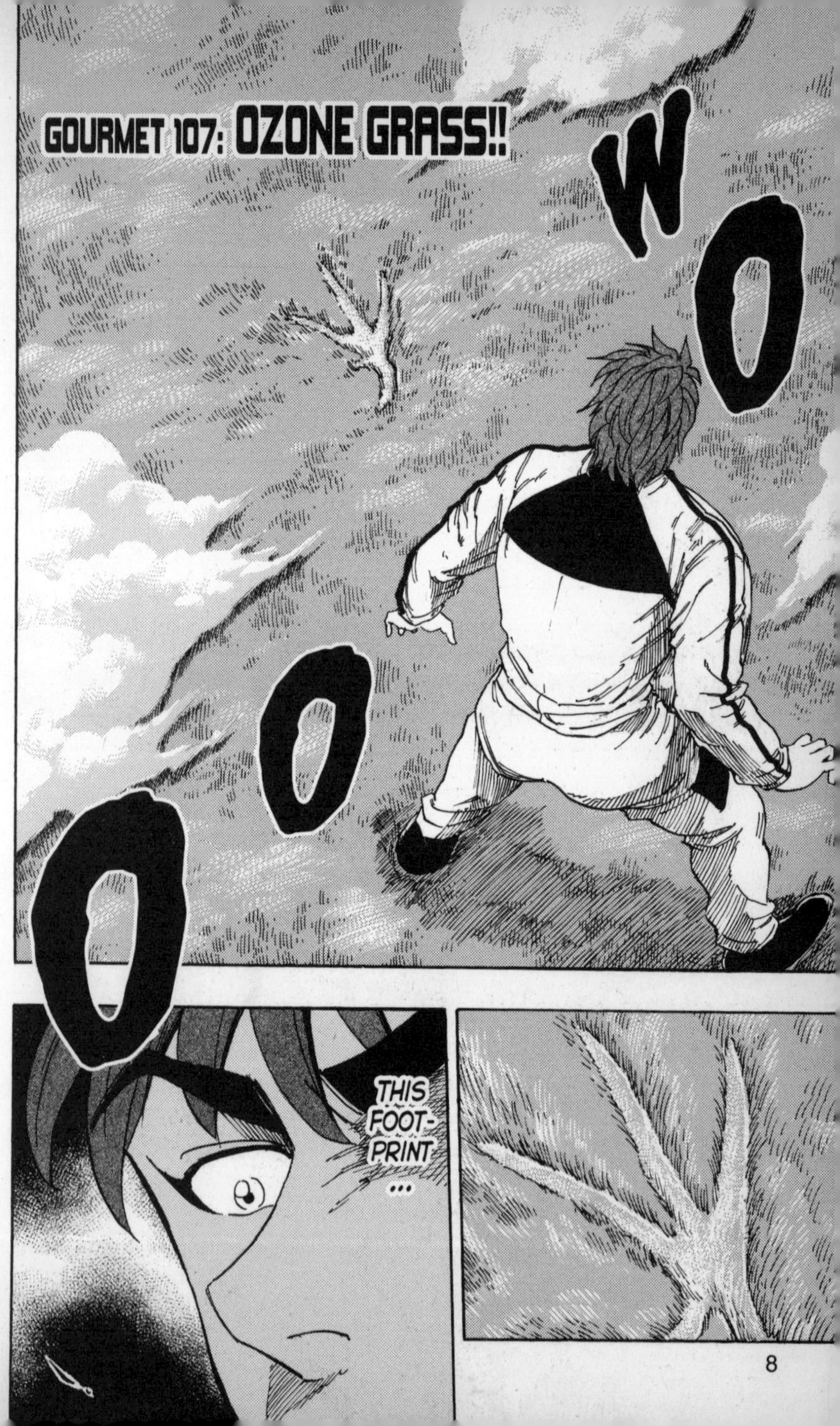
GOURMET 107: OZONE GRASS!!
WOOOO
THIS FOOT-PRINT...

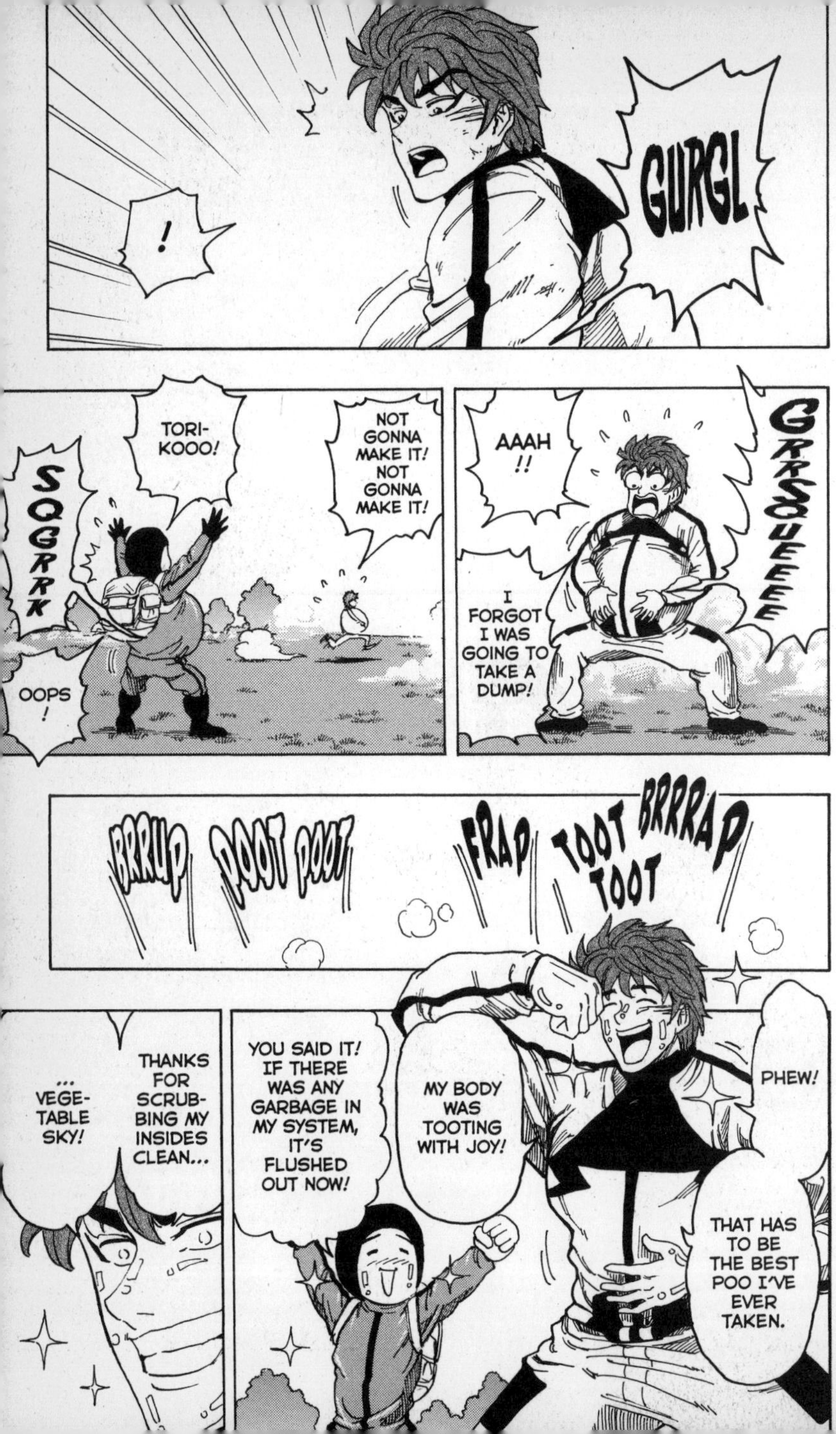
GURGL
!
GRRSQUEEEE
AAAH!!
I FORGOT I WAS GOING TO TAKE A DUMP!
NOT GONNA MAKE IT! NOT GONNA MAKE IT!
TORI-KOOO!
SQGRRK
OOPS!
BRRRAP
TOOT TOOT
FRAP
POOT POOT
BRRUP
PHEW!
THAT HAS TO BE THE BEST POO I'VE EVER TAKEN.
MY BODY WAS TOOTING WITH JOY!
YOU SAID IT! IF THERE WAS ANY GARBAGE IN MY SYSTEM, IT'S FLUSHED OUT NOW!
THANKS FOR SCRUB-BING MY INSIDES CLEAN...
...VEGE-TABLE SKY!

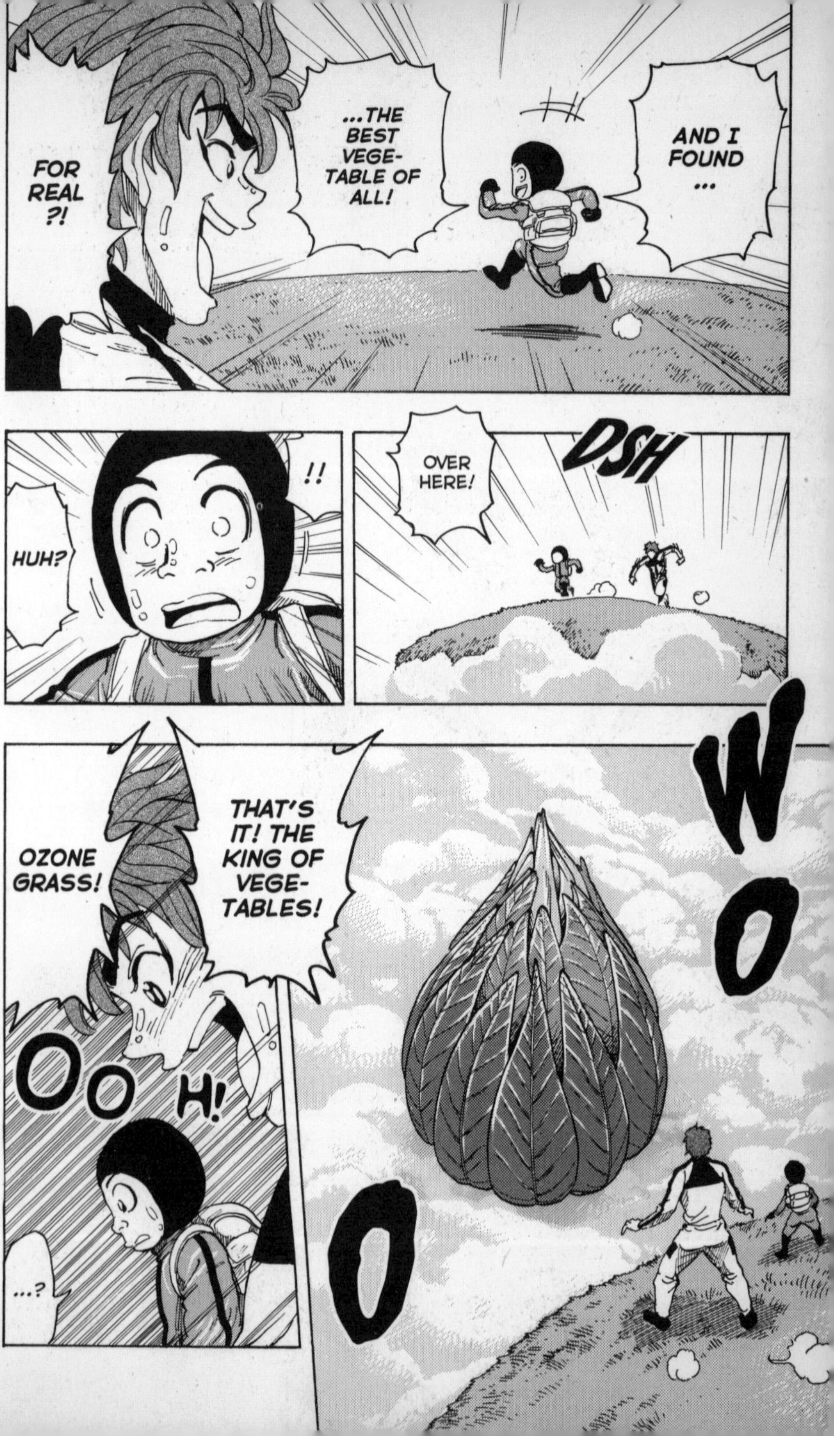
AND I FOUND ...
...THE BEST VEGE-TABLE OF ALL!
FOR REAL ?!
OVER HERE!
DSH
!!
HUH?
WO
THAT'S IT! THE KING OF VEGE-TABLES!
OZONE GRASS!
OOH!
O
...?

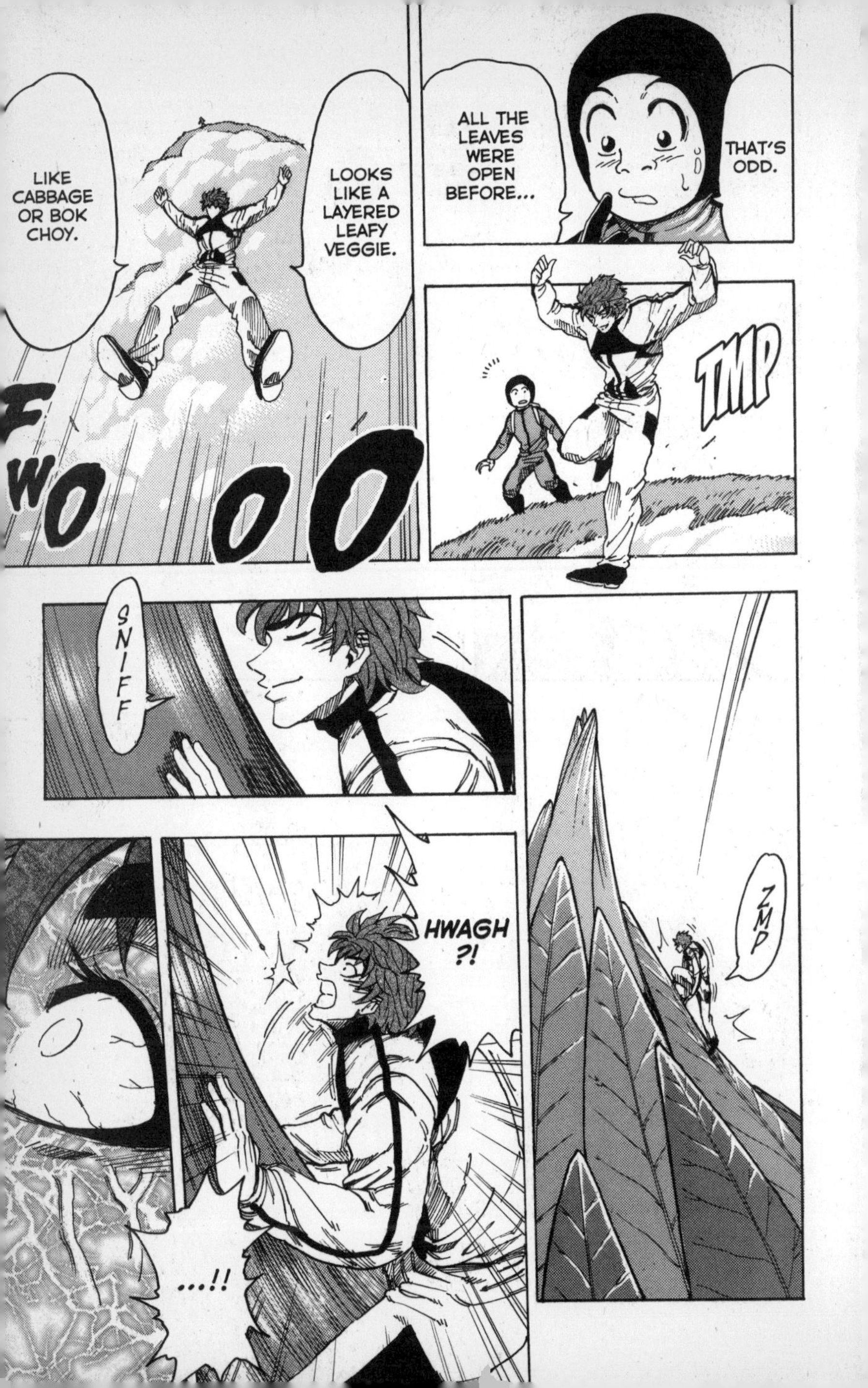
THAT'S ODD.
ALL THE LEAVES WERE OPEN BEFORE...
LOOKS LIKE A LAYERED LEAFY VEGGIE.
LIKE CABBAGE OR BOK CHOY.
FWOOOO
TMP
ZMP
SNIFF
HWAGH ?!
...!!

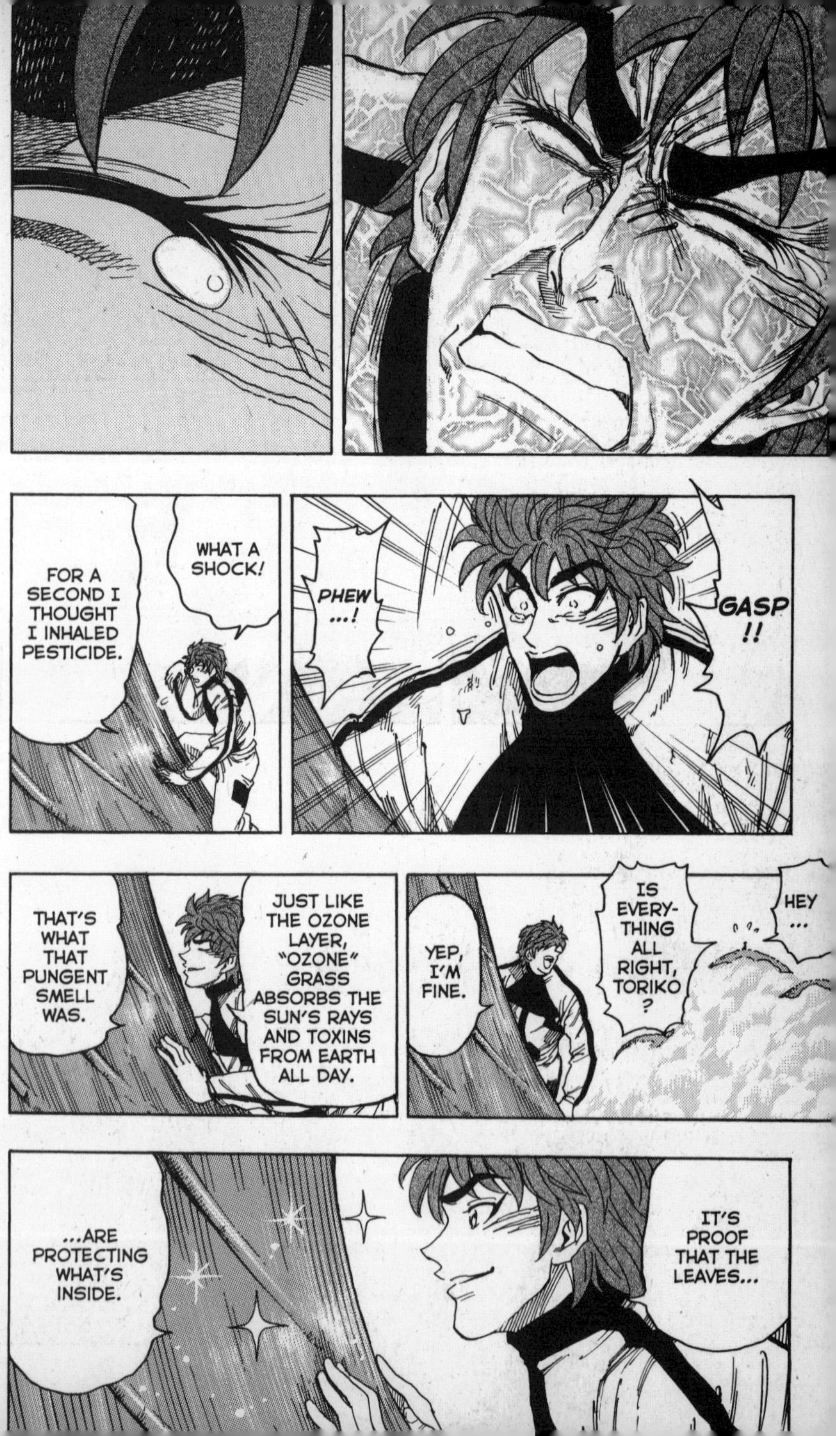
GASP!!
PHEW...!
WHAT A SHOCK!
FOR A SECOND I THOUGHT I INHALED PESTICIDE.
HEY...
IS EVERY-THING ALL RIGHT, TORIKO?
YEP, I'M FINE.
JUST LIKE THE OZONE LAYER, "OZONE" GRASS ABSORBS THE SUN'S RAYS AND TOXINS FROM EARTH ALL DAY.
THAT'S WHAT THAT PUNGENT SMELL WAS.
IT'S PROOF THAT THE LEAVES...
...ARE PROTECTING WHAT'S INSIDE.

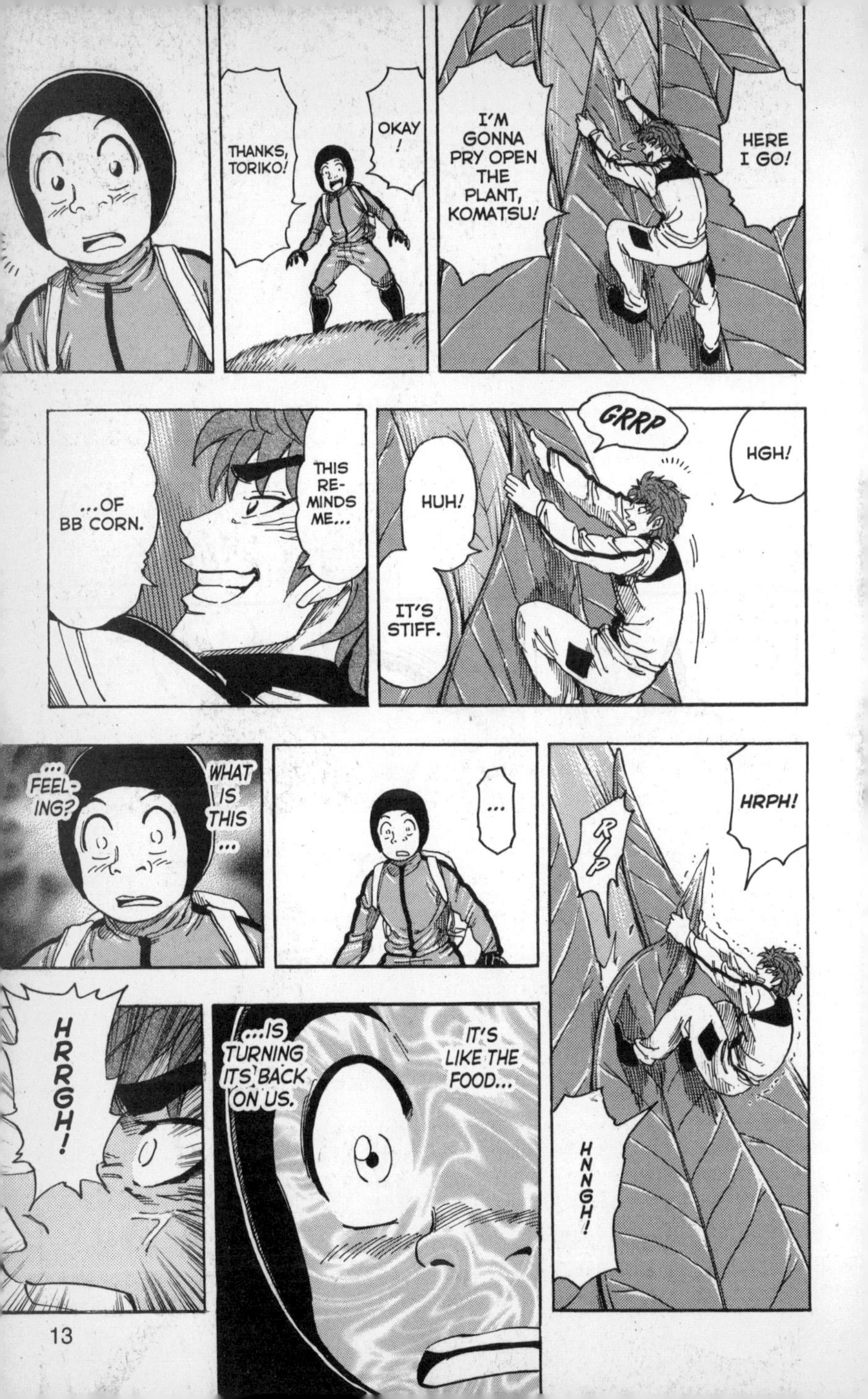
HERE I GO!
I'M GONNA PRY OPEN THE PLANT, KOMATSU!
OKAY!
THANKS, TORIKO!
HGH!
GRRP
HUH!
IT'S STIFF.
THIS RE-MINDS ME...
...OF BB CORN.
HRPH!
RIP
HNNGH!
...
WHAT IS THIS...
...FEEL-ING?
IT'S LIKE THE FOOD...
...IS TURNING ITS BACK ON US.
HRRGH!

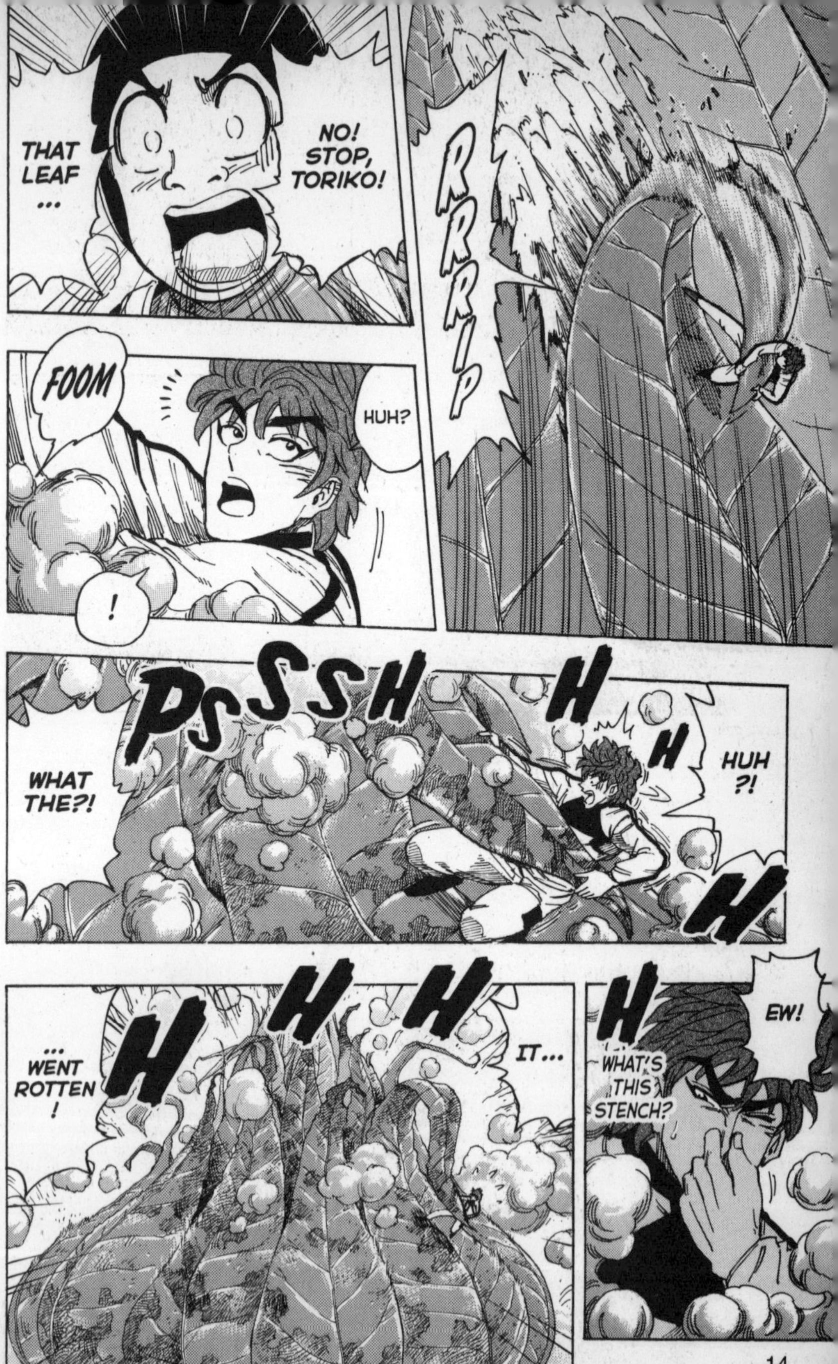
RRRIP
NO! STOP, TORIKO!
THAT LEAF ...
FOOM
HUH?
!
PSSSHHHHHHHHH
HUH ?!
WHAT THE?!
EW!
WHAT'S THIS STENCH?
IT...
... WENT ROTTEN !

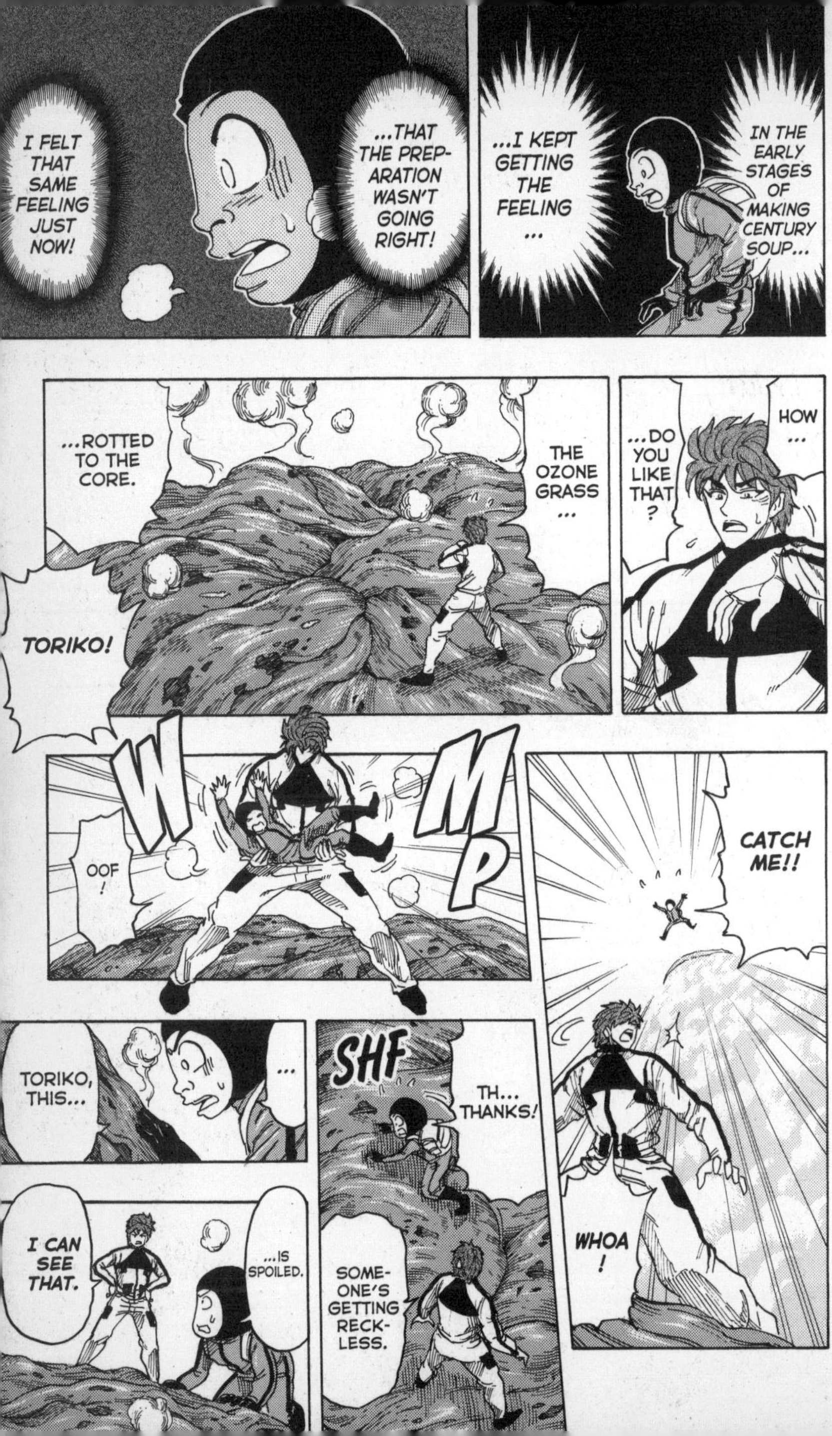
IN THE EARLY STAGES OF MAKING CENTURY SOUP...
...I KEPT GETTING THE FEELING ...
...THAT THE PREP-ARATION WASN'T GOING RIGHT!
I FELT THAT SAME FEELING JUST NOW!
HOW ...
...DO YOU LIKE THAT ?
THE OZONE GRASS ...
...ROTTED TO THE CORE.
TORIKO!
CATCH ME!!
WHOA !
WMP
OOF !
SHF
TH... THANKS!
...
TORIKO, THIS...
SOME-ONE'S GETTING RECK-LESS.
...IS SPOILED.
I CAN SEE THAT.

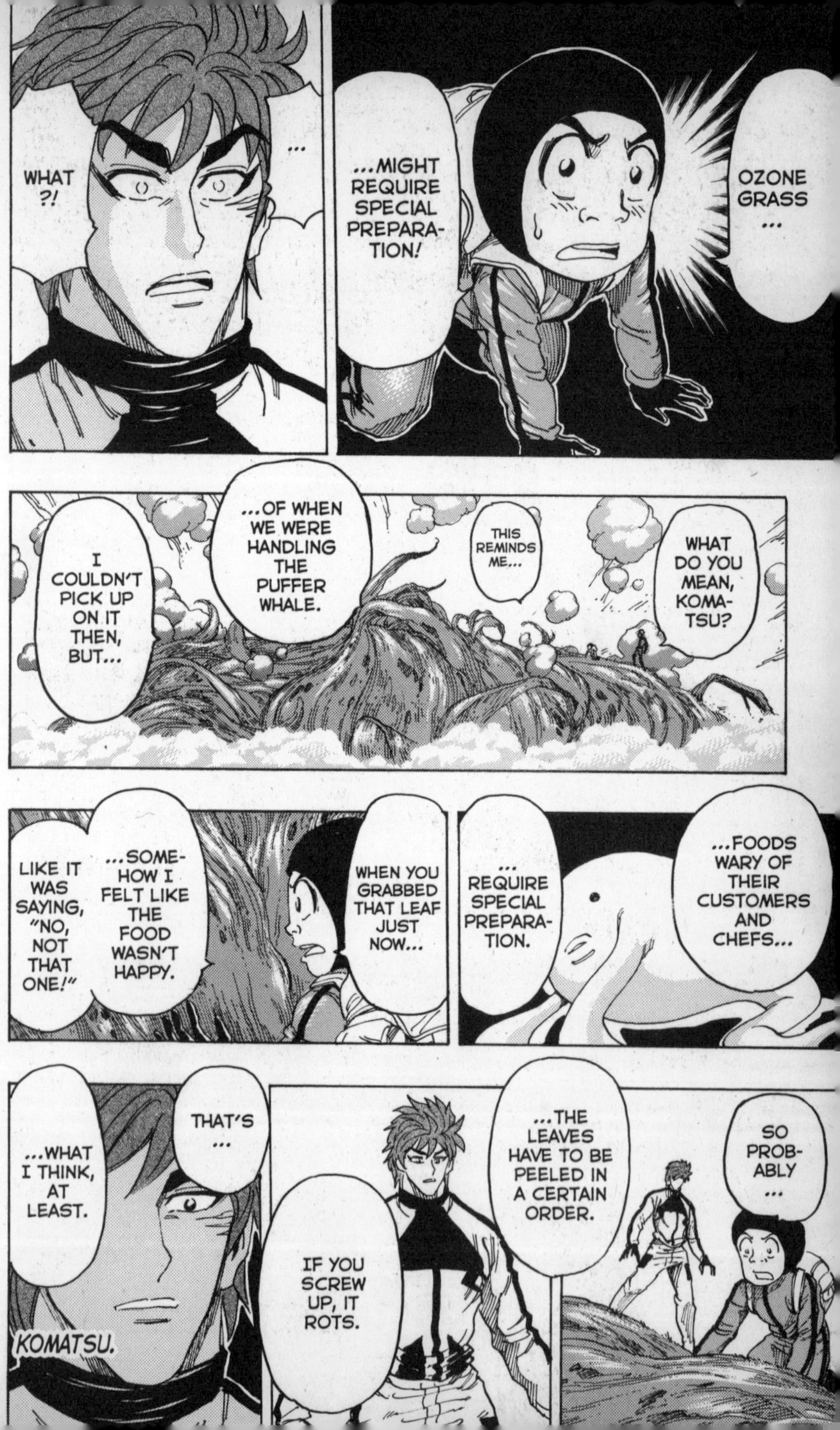
OZONE GRASS ...
...MIGHT REQUIRE SPECIAL PREPARATION!
...
WHAT ?!
WHAT DO YOU MEAN, KOMATSU?
THIS REMINDS ME...
...OF WHEN WE WERE HANDLING THE PUFFER WHALE.
I COULDN'T PICK UP ON IT THEN, BUT...
...FOODS WARY OF THEIR CUSTOMERS AND CHEFS...
...REQUIRE SPECIAL PREPARATION.
WHEN YOU GRABBED THAT LEAF JUST NOW...
...SOMEHOW I FELT LIKE THE FOOD WASN'T HAPPY.
LIKE IT WAS SAYING, "NO, NOT THAT ONE!"
SO PROBABLY ...
...THE LEAVES HAVE TO BE PEELED IN A CERTAIN ORDER.
IF YOU SCREW UP, IT ROTS.
THAT'S ...
...WHAT I THINK, AT LEAST.
KOMATSU.

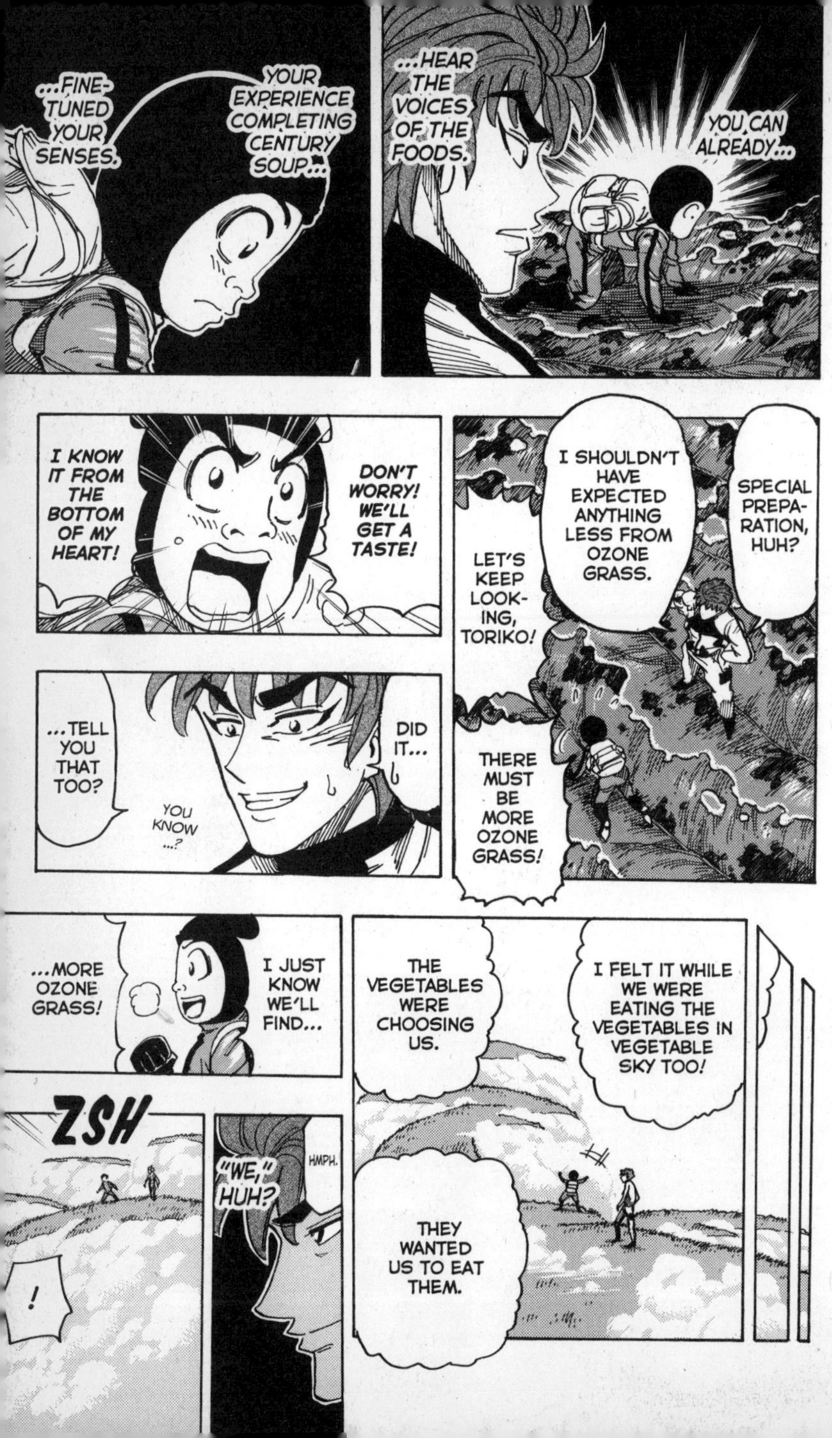
YOU CAN ALREADY...
...HEAR THE VOICES OF THE FOODS.
YOUR EXPERIENCE COMPLETING CENTURY SOUP...
...FINE-TUNED YOUR SENSES.
SPECIAL PREPA-RATION, HUH?
I SHOULDN'T HAVE EXPECTED ANYTHING LESS FROM OZONE GRASS.
LET'S KEEP LOOK-ING, TORIKO!
THERE MUST BE MORE OZONE GRASS!
DON'T WORRY! WE'LL GET A TASTE!
I KNOW IT FROM THE BOTTOM OF MY HEART!
DID IT...
YOU KNOW ...?
...TELL YOU THAT TOO?
I FELT IT WHILE WE WERE EATING THE VEGETABLES IN VEGETABLE SKY TOO!
THE VEGETABLES WERE CHOOSING US.
THEY WANTED US TO EAT THEM.
I JUST KNOW WE'LL FIND...
...MORE OZONE GRASS!
HMPH.
"WE," HUH?
ZSH
!

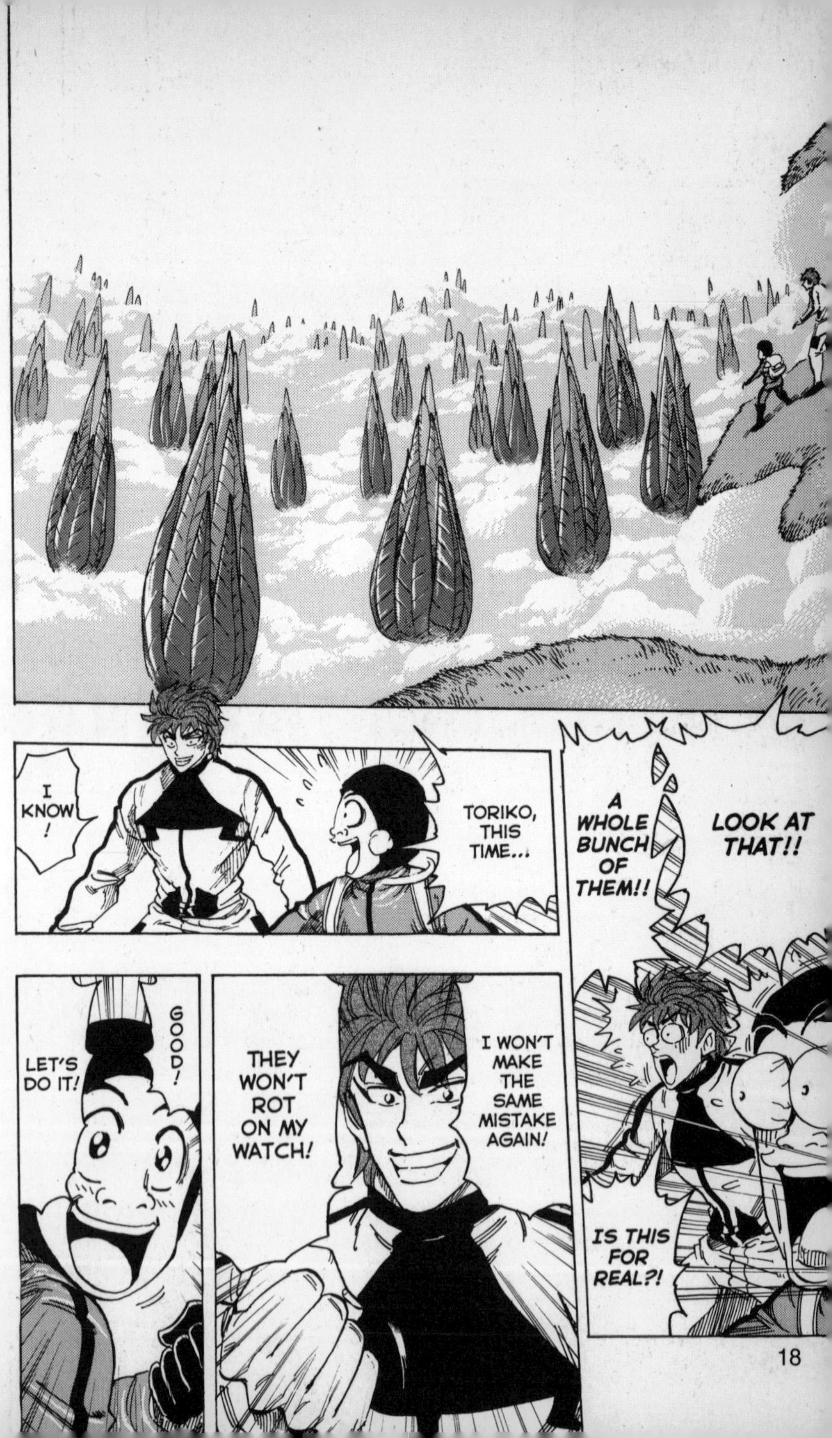
LOOK AT THAT!!
A WHOLE BUNCH OF THEM!!
IS THIS FOR REAL?!
TORIKO, THIS TIME...
I KNOW!
I WON'T MAKE THE SAME MISTAKE AGAIN!
THEY WON'T ROT ON MY WATCH!
GOOD!
LET'S DO IT!

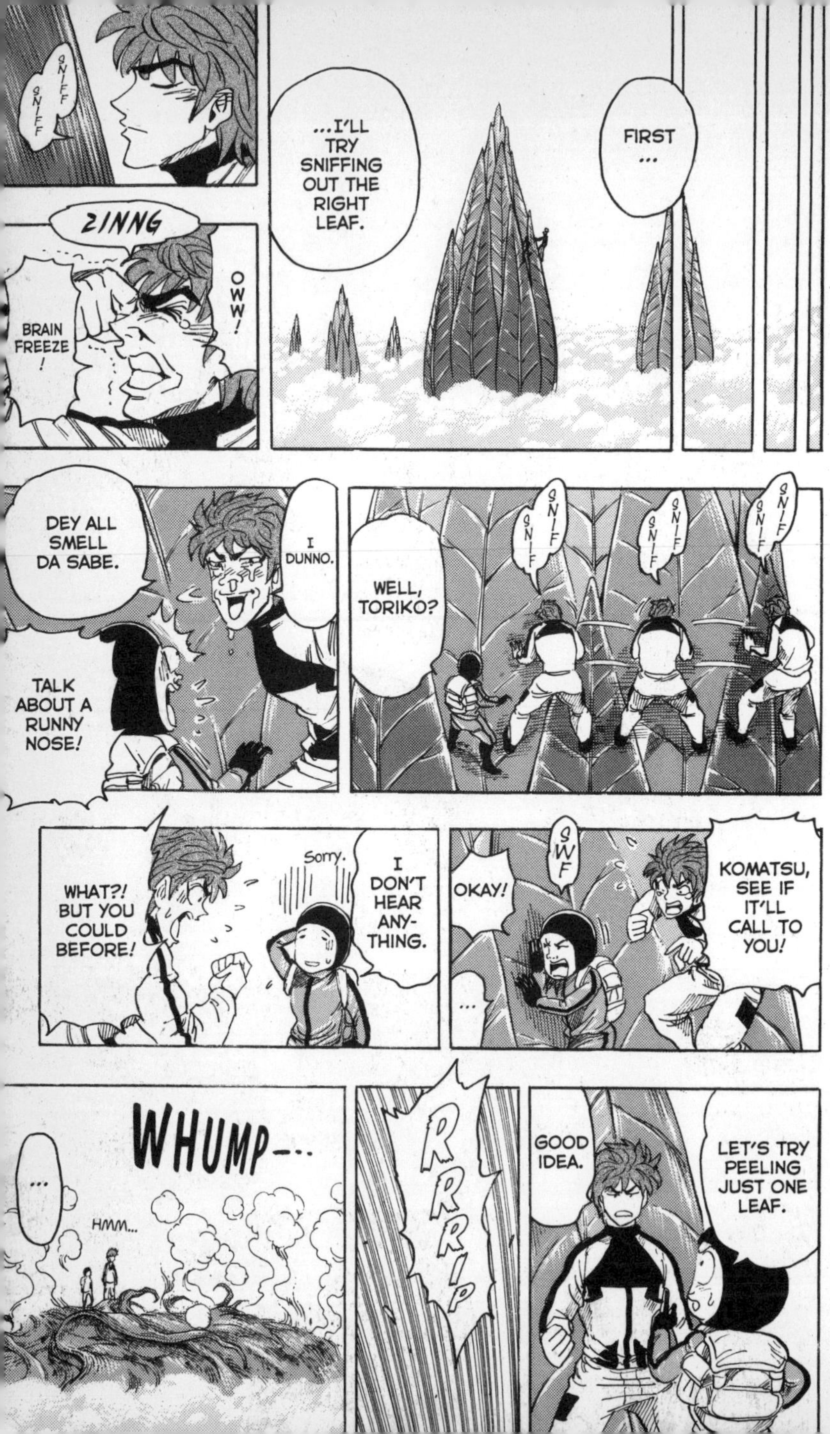
FIRST...
...I'LL TRY SNIFFING OUT THE RIGHT LEAF.
SNIFF SNIFF
ZINNG
OWW!
BRAIN FREEZE!
SNIF SNIF
SNIF SNIF
SNIF SNIF
WELL, TORIKO?
I DUNNO.
DEY ALL SMELL DA SABE.
TALK ABOUT A RUNNY NOSE!
KOMATSU, SEE IF IT'LL CALL TO YOU!
SWF
OKAY!
...
I DON'T HEAR ANY-THING.
Sorry.
WHAT?! BUT YOU COULD BEFORE!
LET'S TRY PEELING JUST ONE LEAF.
GOOD IDEA.
RRRIP
WHUMP...
...
HMM...

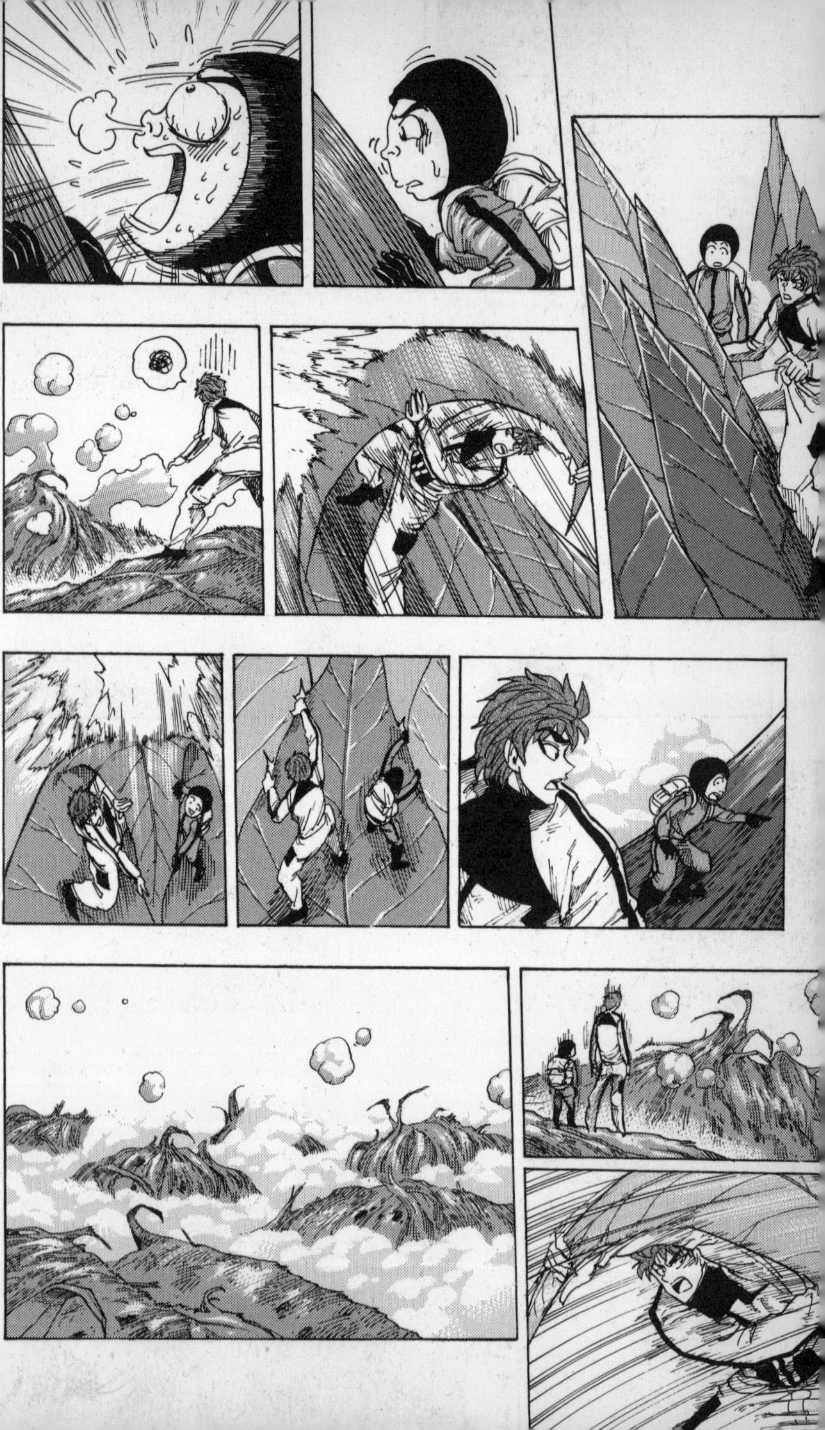

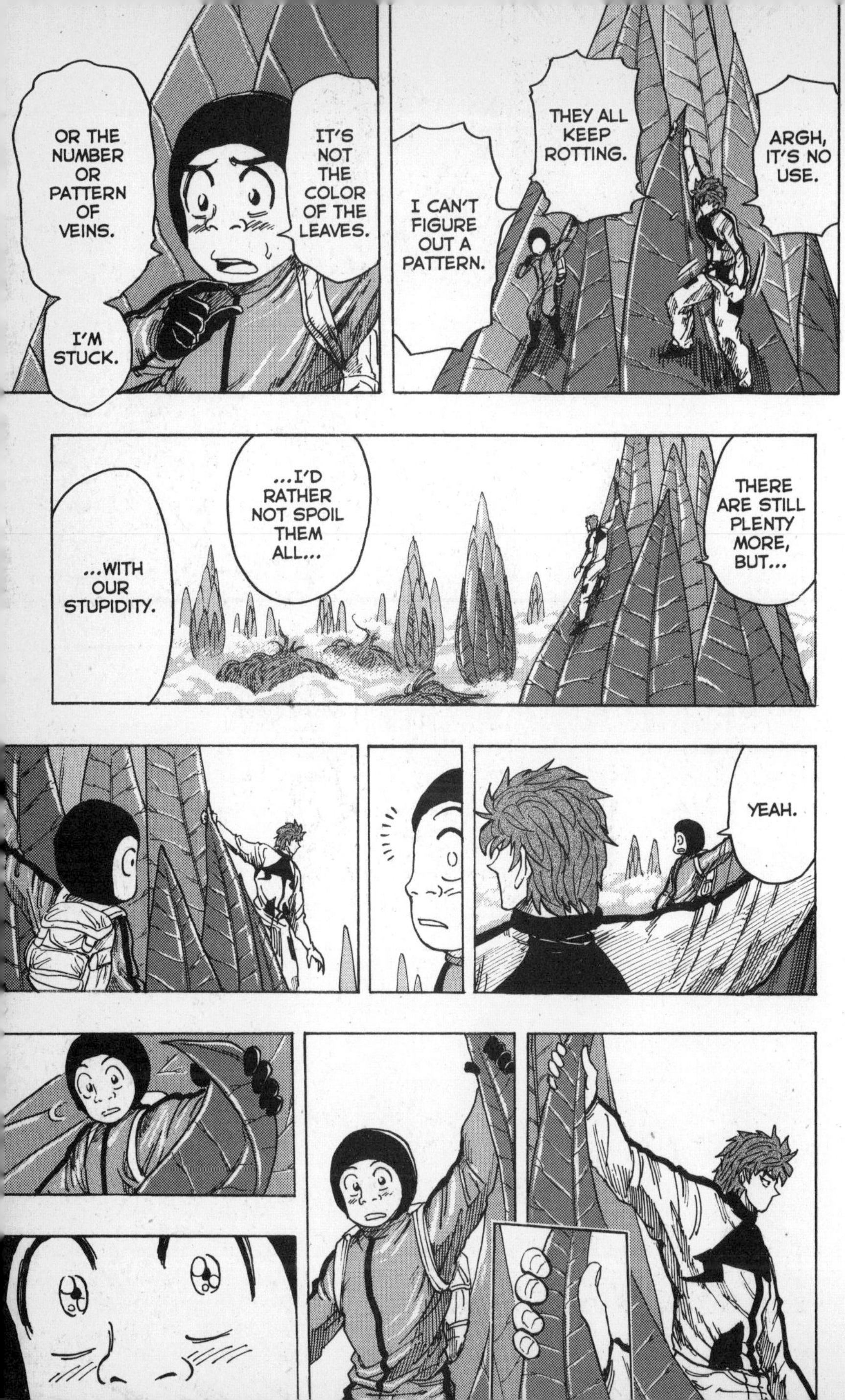
ARGH, IT'S NO USE.
THEY ALL KEEP ROTTING.
I CAN'T FIGURE OUT A PATTERN.
IT'S NOT THE COLOR OF THE LEAVES.
OR THE NUMBER OR PATTERN OF VEINS.
I'M STUCK.
THERE ARE STILL PLENTY MORE, BUT...
...I'D RATHER NOT SPOIL THEM ALL...
...WITH OUR STUPIDITY.
YEAH.

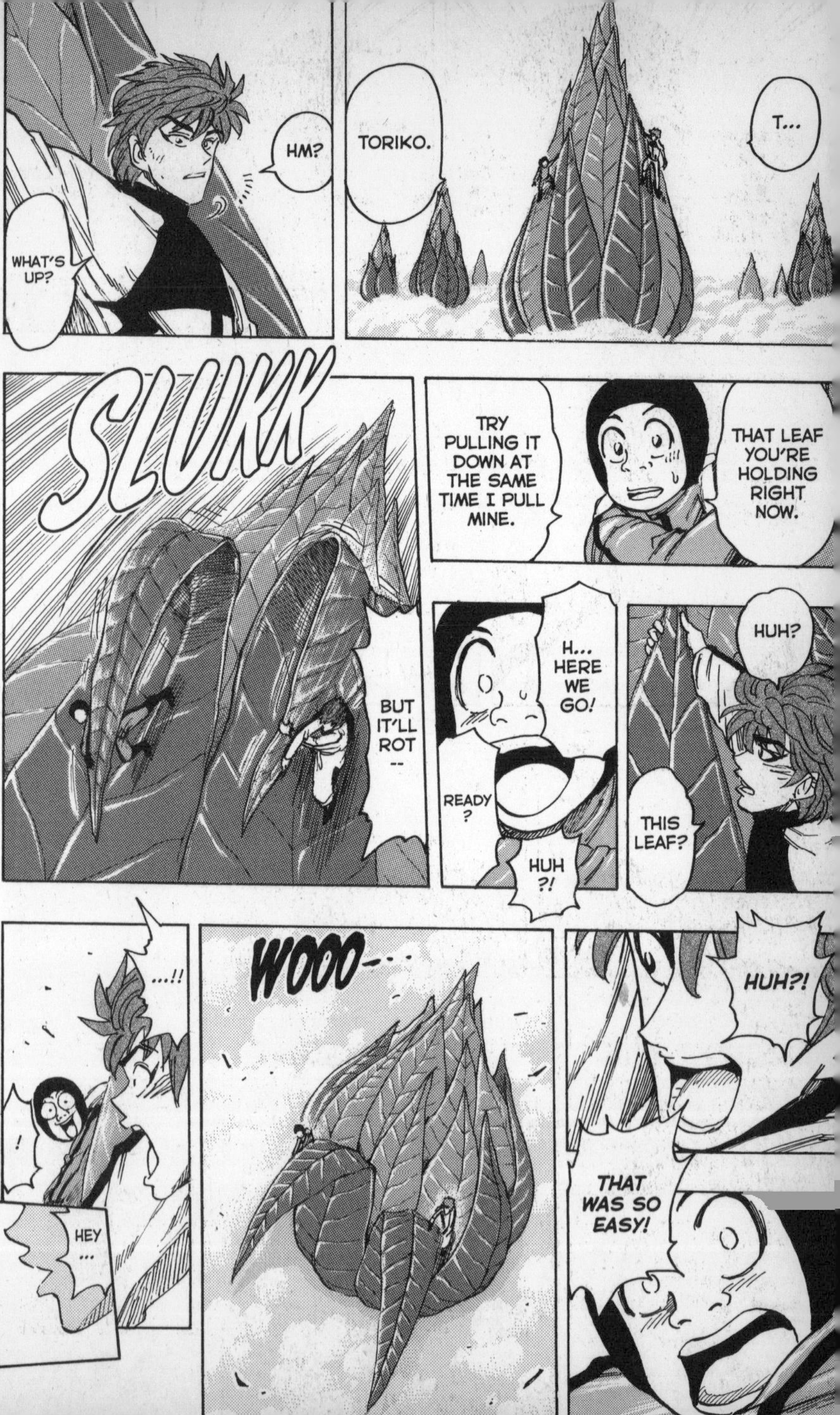
T...
TORIKO.
HM?
WHAT'S UP?
THAT LEAF YOU'RE HOLDING RIGHT NOW.
TRY PULLING IT DOWN AT THE SAME TIME I PULL MINE.
HUH?
THIS LEAF?
H... HERE WE GO!
READY?
HUH ?!
SLURK
BUT IT'LL ROT --
HUH?!
THAT WAS SO EASY!
WOOO---
...!!
HEY ...

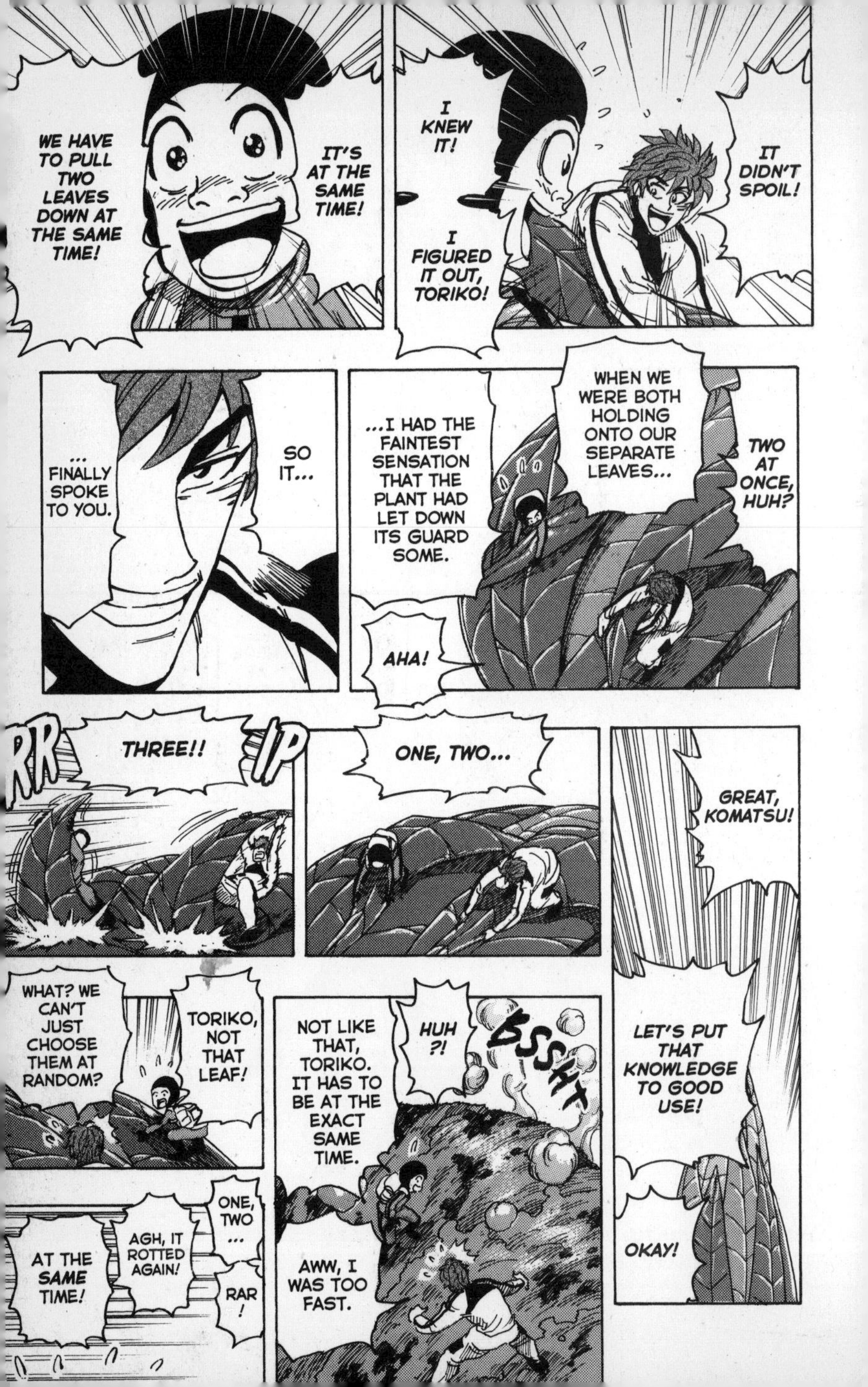
IT DIDN'T SPOIL!
I KNEW IT!
I FIGURED IT OUT, TORIKO!
IT'S AT THE SAME TIME!
WE HAVE TO PULL TWO LEAVES DOWN AT THE SAME TIME!
TWO AT ONCE, HUH?
WHEN WE WERE BOTH HOLDING ONTO OUR SEPARATE LEAVES...
...I HAD THE FAINTEST SENSATION THAT THE PLANT HAD LET DOWN ITS GUARD SOME.
AHA!
SO IT...
...FINALLY SPOKE TO YOU.
GREAT, KOMATSU!
LET'S PUT THAT KNOWLEDGE TO GOOD USE!
OKAY!
ONE, TWO...
THREE!!
RRIP
BSSHT
HUH ?!
NOT LIKE THAT, TORIKO. IT HAS TO BE AT THE EXACT SAME TIME.
AWW, I WAS TOO FAST.
TORIKO, NOT THAT LEAF!
WHAT? WE CAN'T JUST CHOOSE THEM AT RANDOM?
ONE, TWO ...
RAR !
AGH, IT ROTTED AGAIN!
AT THE SAME TIME!

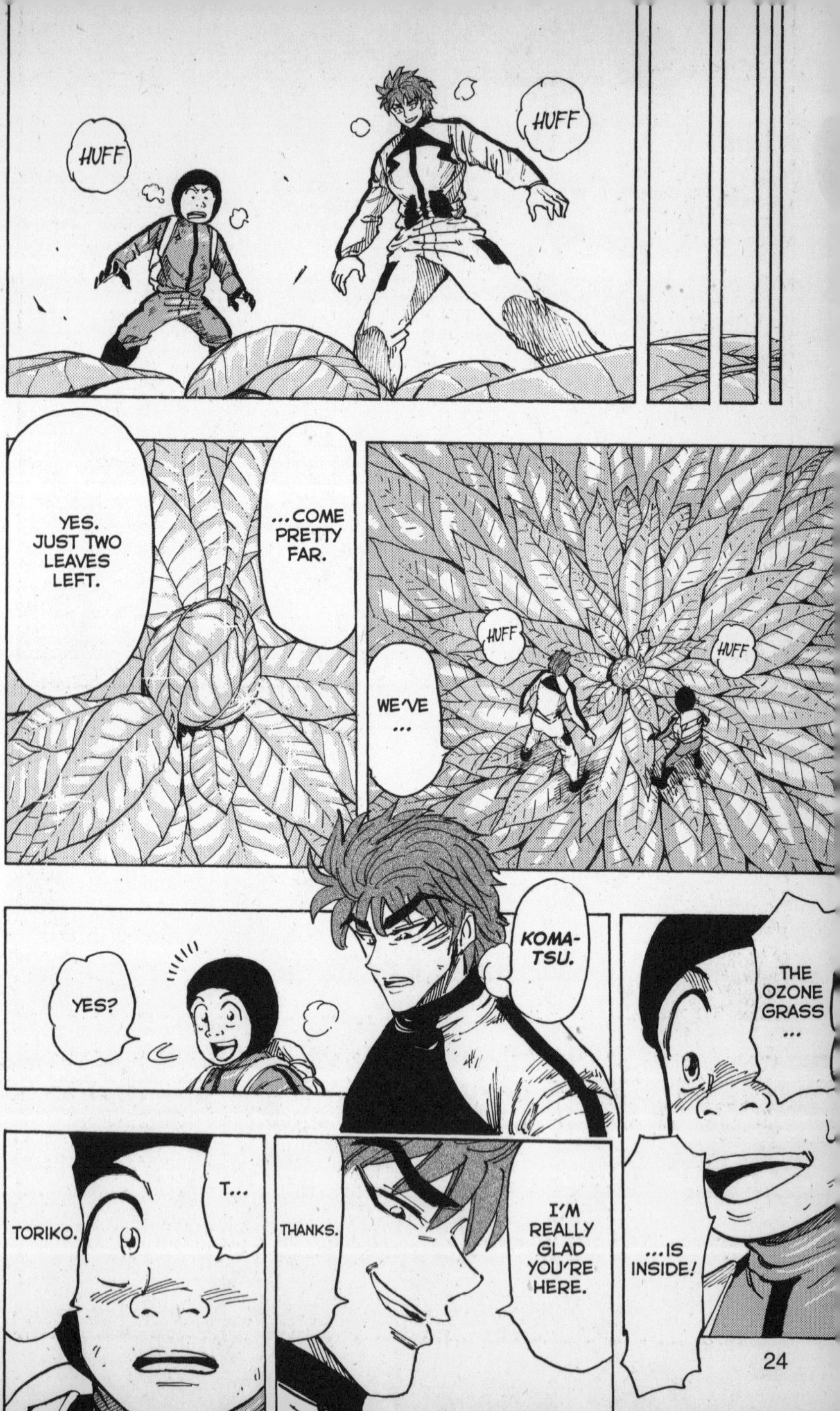
HUFF
HUFF
HUFF
HUFF
WE'VE ...
...COME PRETTY FAR.
YES. JUST TWO LEAVES LEFT.
THE OZONE GRASS ...
...IS INSIDE!
KOMA-TSU.
YES?
I'M REALLY GLAD YOU'RE HERE.
THANKS.
T...
TORIKO.

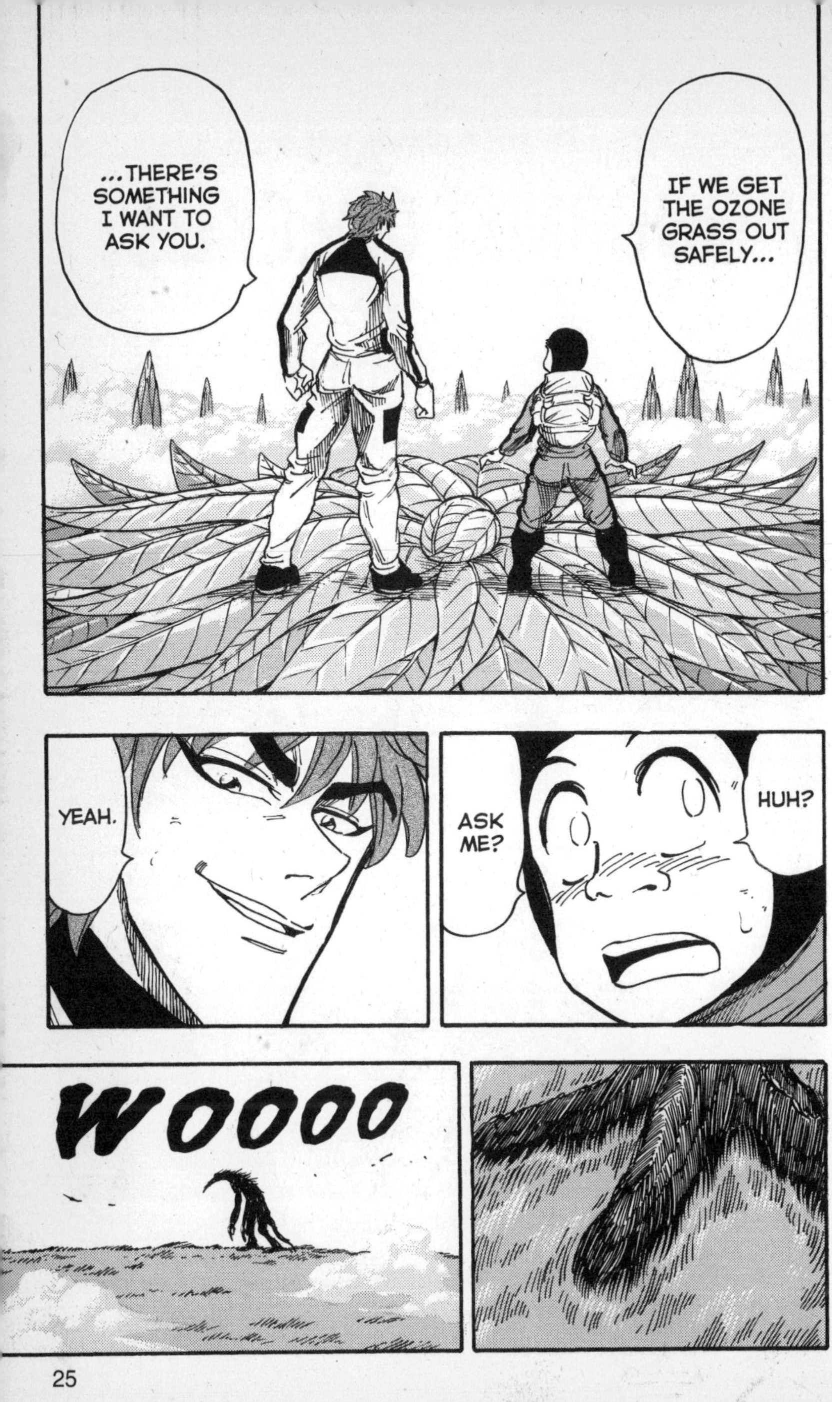
IF WE GET THE OZONE GRASS OUT SAFELY...
...THERE'S SOMETHING I WANT TO ASK YOU.
HUH?
ASK ME?
YEAH.
WOOOO

TORIKO

GOURMET CHECKLIST

Vol. 121

 ### THERAPY TULIP
(PLANT)

CAPTURE LEVEL: 49

HABITAT: NO SPECIFIC HABITAT

LENGTH: 2-50 METERS

HEIGHT: ---

WEIGHT: ---

PRICE: 20,000,000-100,000,000 YEN

PER FLOWER

SCALE

A RARE SPECIES OF PLANT THAT EATS THE INJURIES OF LIVING THINGS. SPEND JUST ONE MINUTE INSIDE THIS PLANT'S PETALS AND YOUR INJURIES WILL BE HEALED. BUT IF YOU FAINT, OR ENTER IT WHEN YOU'RE UNINJURED, THE THERAPY TULIP WILL GOBBLE YOU UP! CAUTION'S THE NAME OF THE GAME. IN SOME COUNTRIES, A MEDICAL LICENSE IS REQUIRED TO USE A THERAPY TULIP. IN THE NATURAL WORLD, GIANT THERAPY TULIPS HAVE BEEN KNOWN TO TOP 50 METERS IN HEIGHT, AND ARE CAPABLE OF HEALING GIANT BEASTS LIKE MAMMOTHS.

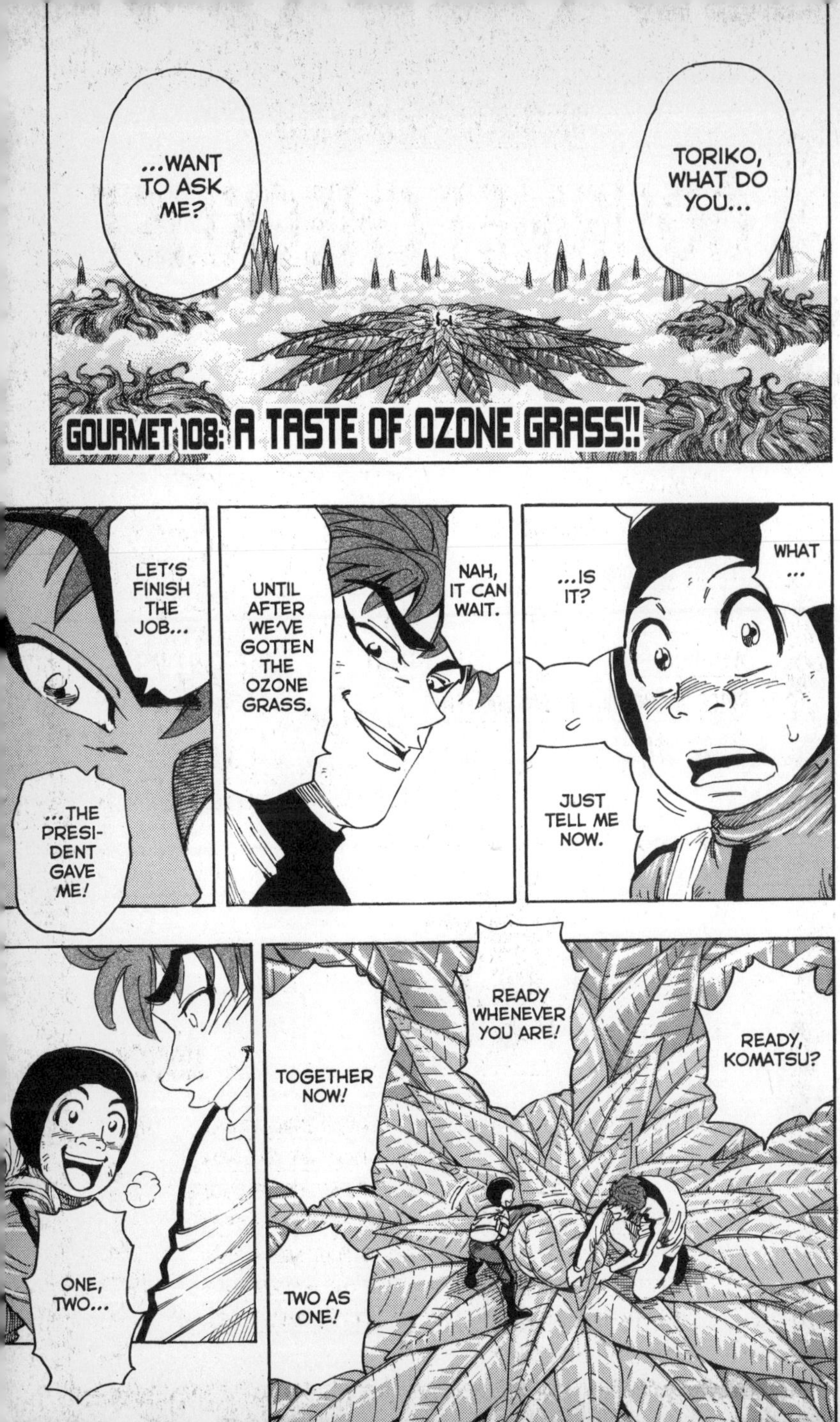
TORIKO, WHAT DO YOU...
...WANT TO ASK ME?
GOURMET 108: A TASTE OF OZONE GRASS!!
WHAT...
...IS IT?
JUST TELL ME NOW.
NAH, IT CAN WAIT.
UNTIL AFTER WE'VE GOTTEN THE OZONE GRASS.
LET'S FINISH THE JOB...
...THE PRESIDENT GAVE ME!
READY, KOMATSU?
READY WHENEVER YOU ARE!
TOGETHER NOW!
TWO AS ONE!
ONE, TWO...

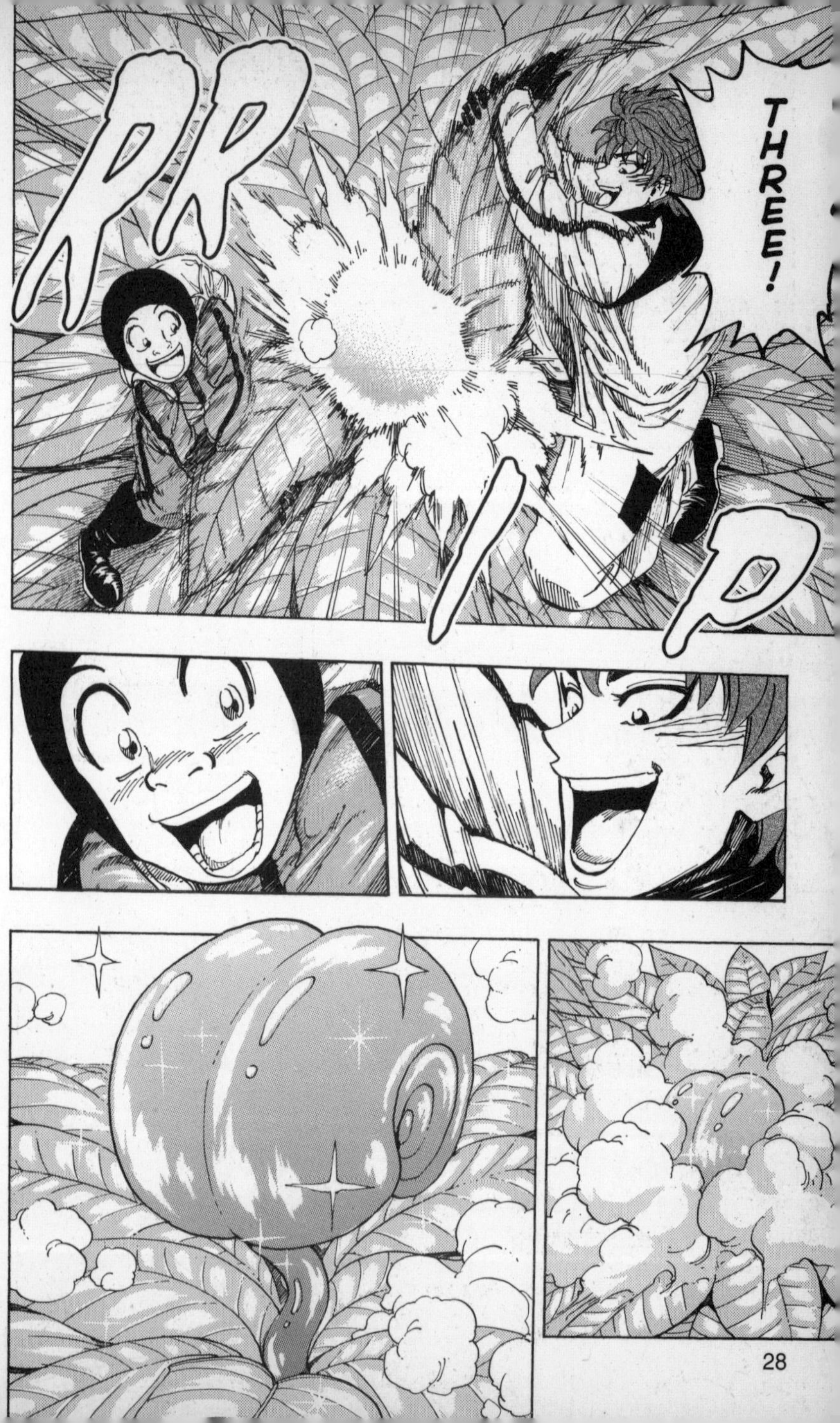
THREE!
RRIP

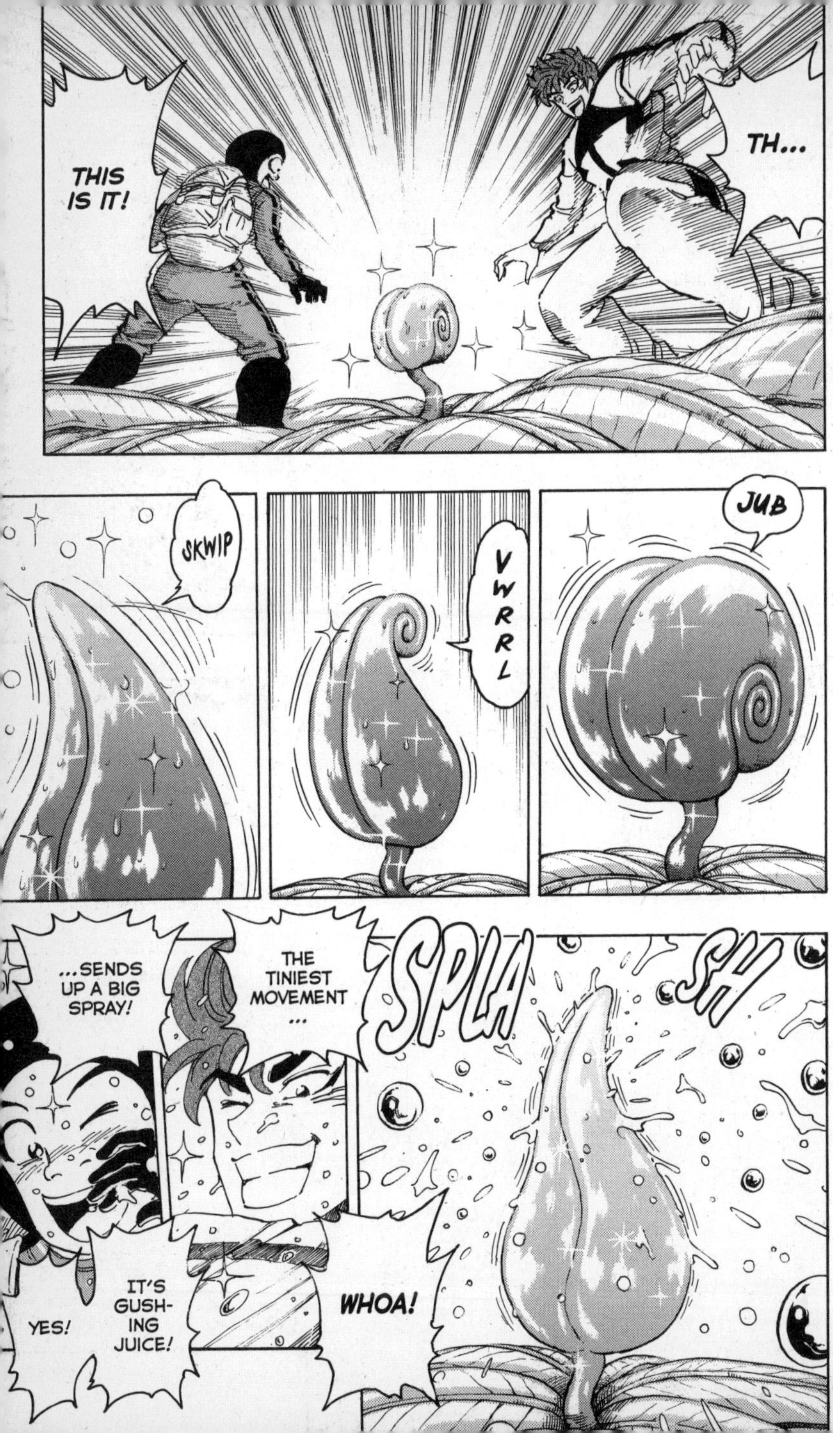
TH...
THIS IS IT!
JUB
VWRRL
SKWIP
SPLASH
WHOA!
THE TINIEST MOVEMENT ...
...SENDS UP A BIG SPRAY!
IT'S GUSH-ING JUICE!
YES!

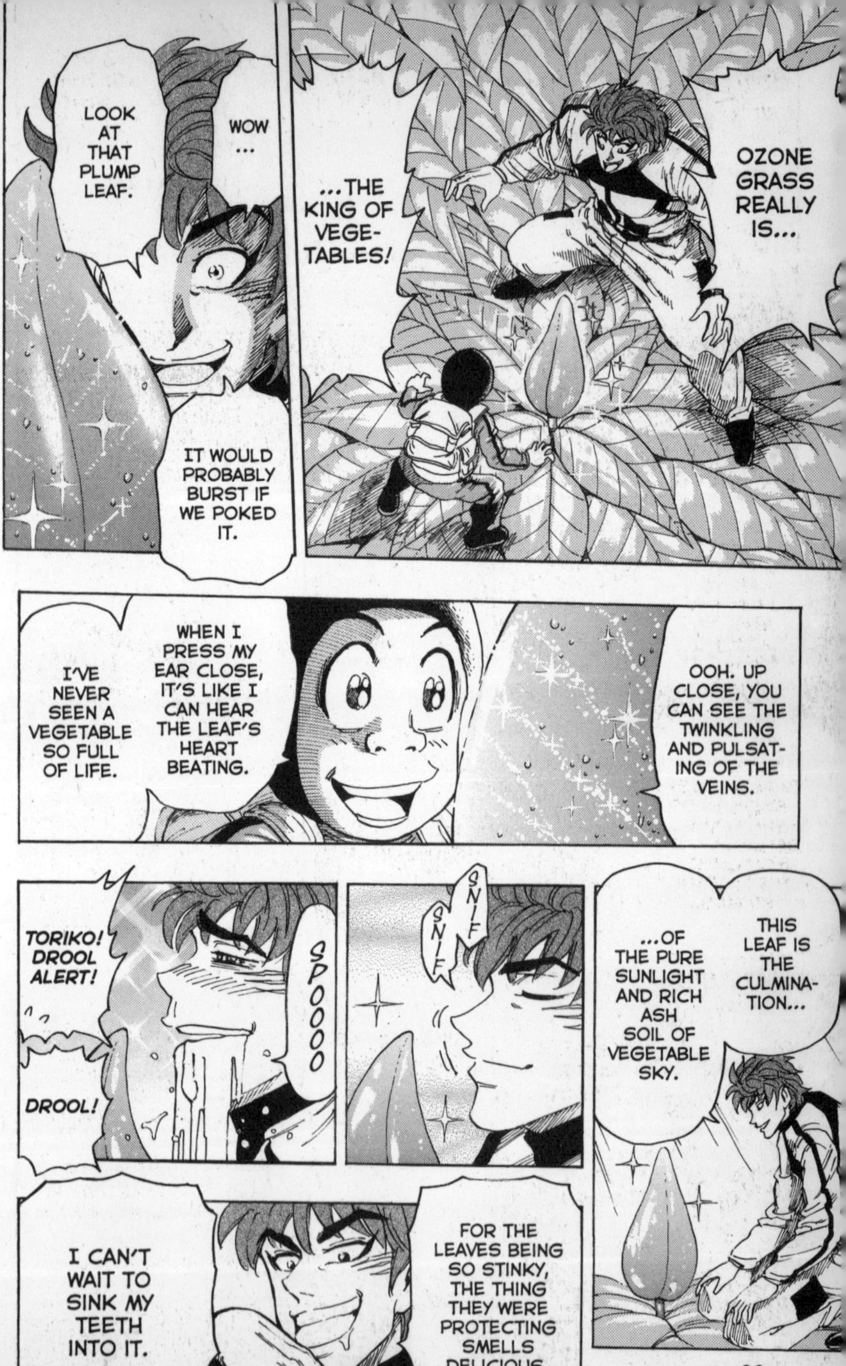
OZONE GRASS REALLY IS...
...THE KING OF VEGE-TABLES!
WOW...
LOOK AT THAT PLUMP LEAF.
IT WOULD PROBABLY BURST IF WE POKED IT.
OOH. UP CLOSE, YOU CAN SEE THE TWINKLING AND PULSAT-ING OF THE VEINS.
WHEN I PRESS MY EAR CLOSE, IT'S LIKE I CAN HEAR THE LEAF'S HEART BEATING.
I'VE NEVER SEEN A VEGETABLE SO FULL OF LIFE.
THIS LEAF IS THE CULMINA-TION...
...OF THE PURE SUNLIGHT AND RICH ASH SOIL OF VEGETABLE SKY.
SNIF
SNIF
SPOOOOO
TORIKO! DROOL ALERT!
DROOL!
FOR THE LEAVES BEING SO STINKY, THE THING THEY WERE PROTECTING SMELLS DELICIOUS.
I CAN'T WAIT TO SINK MY TEETH INTO IT.

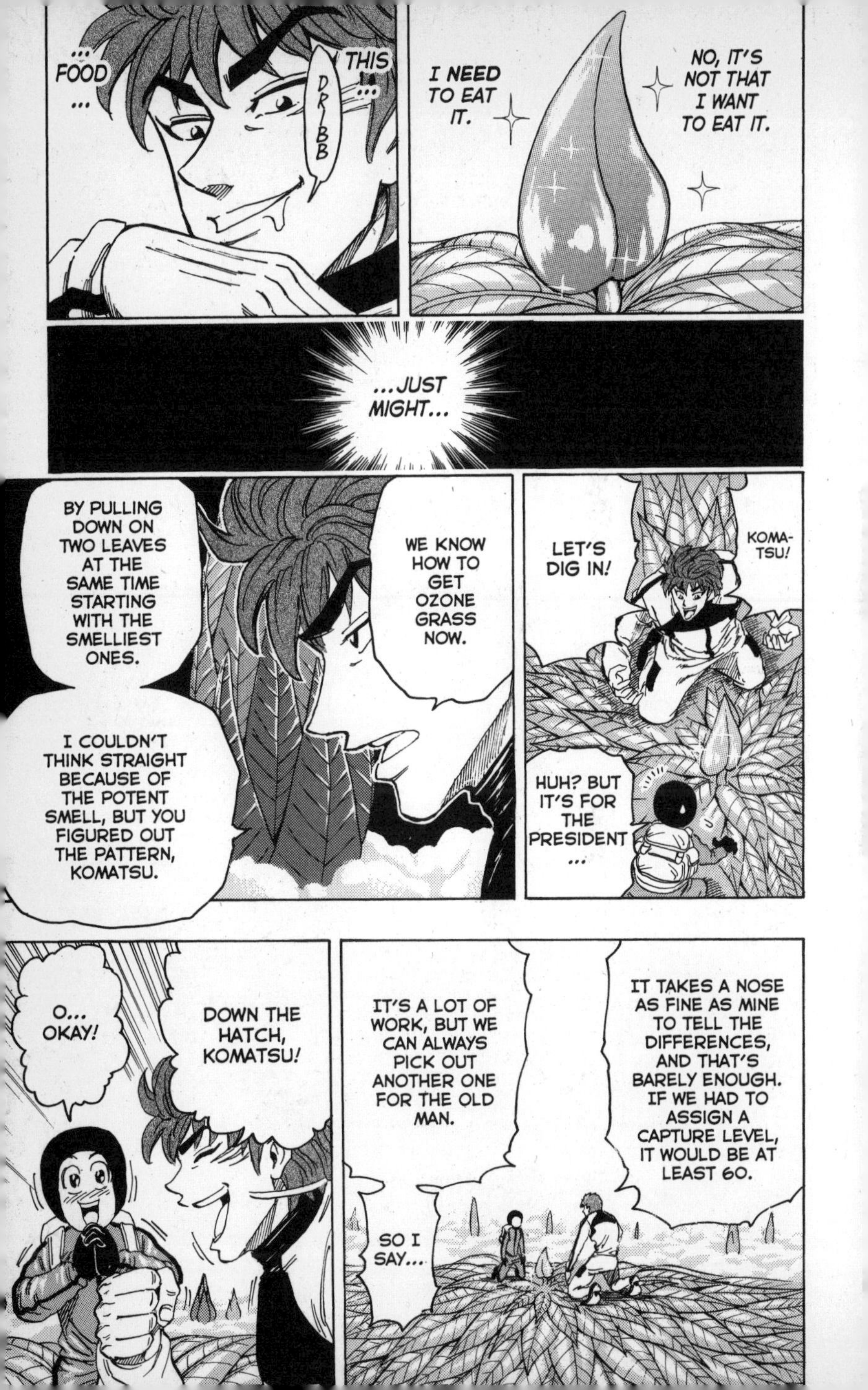
NO, IT'S NOT THAT I WANT TO EAT IT.
I NEED TO EAT IT.
THIS...
DRIBB
...FOOD...
...JUST MIGHT...
KOMA-TSU!
LET'S DIG IN!
HUH? BUT IT'S FOR THE PRESIDENT...
WE KNOW HOW TO GET OZONE GRASS NOW.
BY PULLING DOWN ON TWO LEAVES AT THE SAME TIME STARTING WITH THE SMELLIEST ONES.
I COULDN'T THINK STRAIGHT BECAUSE OF THE POTENT SMELL, BUT YOU FIGURED OUT THE PATTERN, KOMATSU.
IT TAKES A NOSE AS FINE AS MINE TO TELL THE DIFFERENCES, AND THAT'S BARELY ENOUGH. IF WE HAD TO ASSIGN A CAPTURE LEVEL, IT WOULD BE AT LEAST 60.
IT'S A LOT OF WORK, BUT WE CAN ALWAYS PICK OUT ANOTHER ONE FOR THE OLD MAN.
SO I SAY...
DOWN THE HATCH, KOMATSU!
O... OKAY!

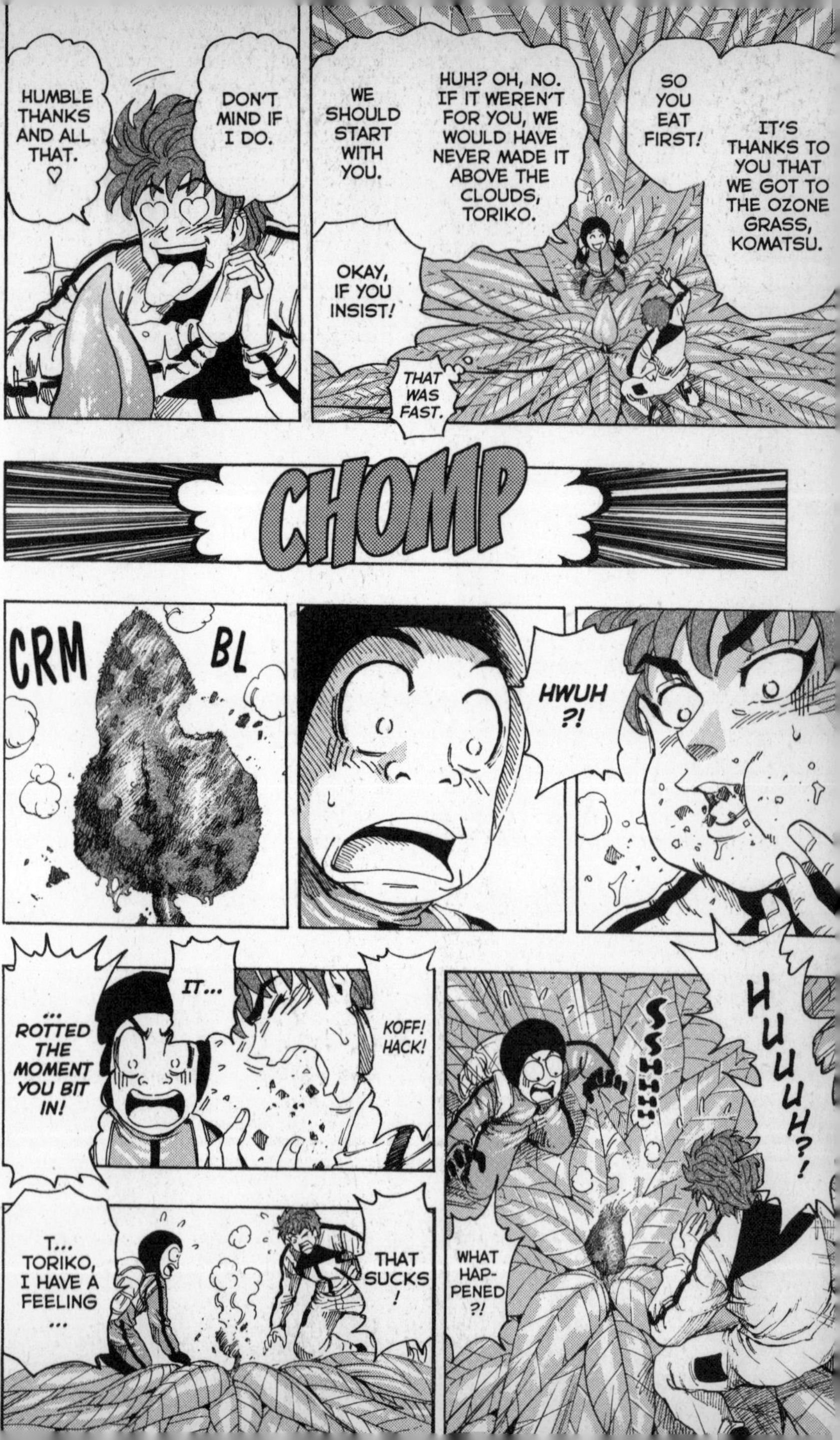
IT'S THANKS TO YOU THAT WE GOT TO THE OZONE GRASS, KOMATSU.
SO YOU EAT FIRST!
HUH? OH, NO. IF IT WEREN'T FOR YOU, WE WOULD HAVE NEVER MADE IT ABOVE THE CLOUDS, TORIKO.
WE SHOULD START WITH YOU.
OKAY, IF YOU INSIST!
THAT WAS FAST.
DON'T MIND IF I DO.
HUMBLE THANKS AND ALL THAT. ♡
CHOMP
HWUH ?!
BL
CRM
IT...
KOFF! HACK!
... ROTTED THE MOMENT YOU BIT IN!
HUUUH?!
SSHHHH
WHAT HAP-PENED ?!
THAT SUCKS !
T... TORIKO, I HAVE A FEELING ...

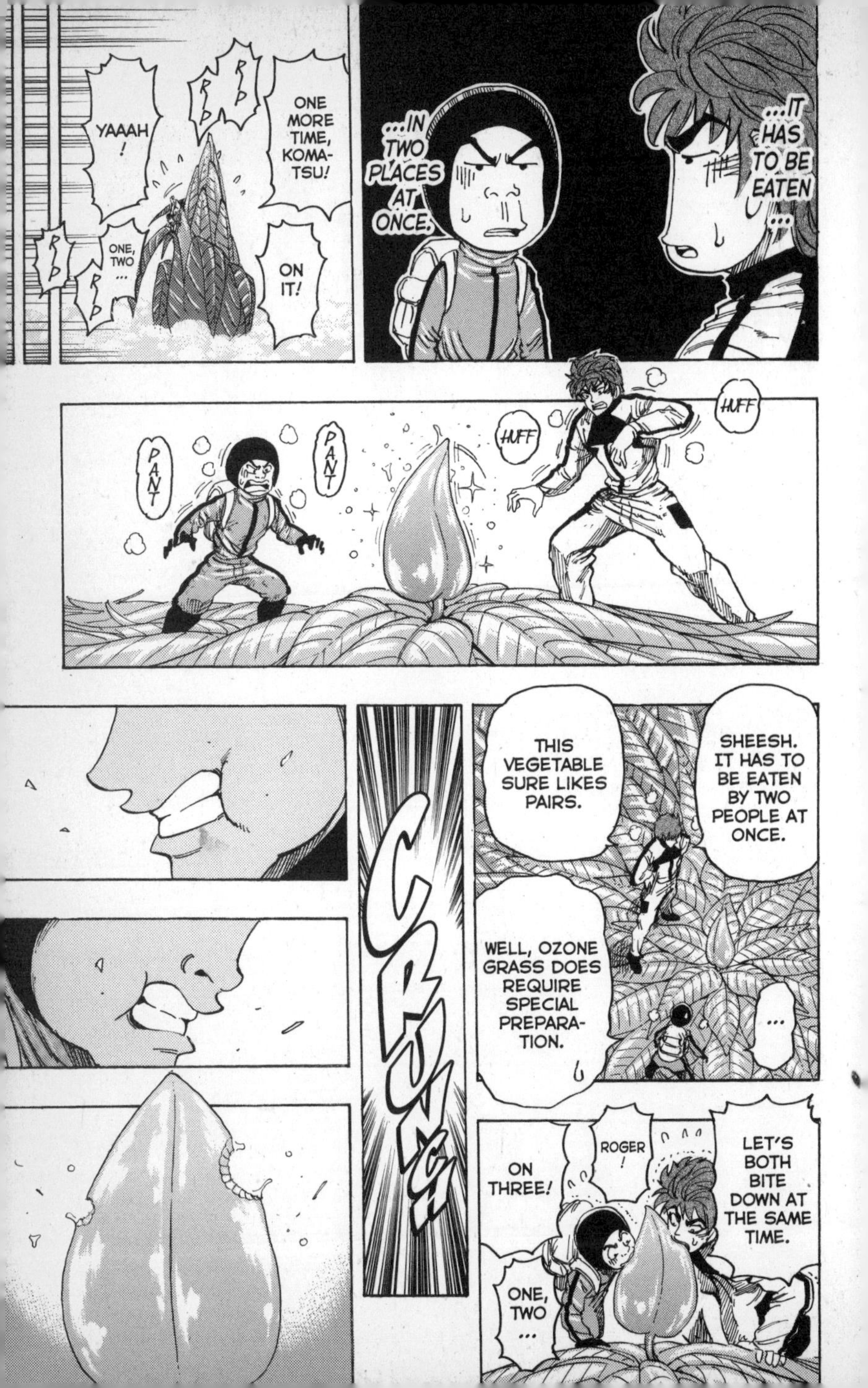
...IT HAS TO BE EATEN...
...IN TWO PLACES AT ONCE.
ONE MORE TIME, KOMATSU!
RIP RIP
YAAAH!
ON IT!
ONE, TWO...
RIP RIP
HUFF
HUFF
PANT
PANT
SHEESH. IT HAS TO BE EATEN BY TWO PEOPLE AT ONCE.
THIS VEGETABLE SURE LIKES PAIRS.
...
WELL, OZONE GRASS DOES REQUIRE SPECIAL PREPARA-TION.
LET'S BOTH BITE DOWN AT THE SAME TIME.
ROGER!
ON THREE!
ONE, TWO...
CRUNCH

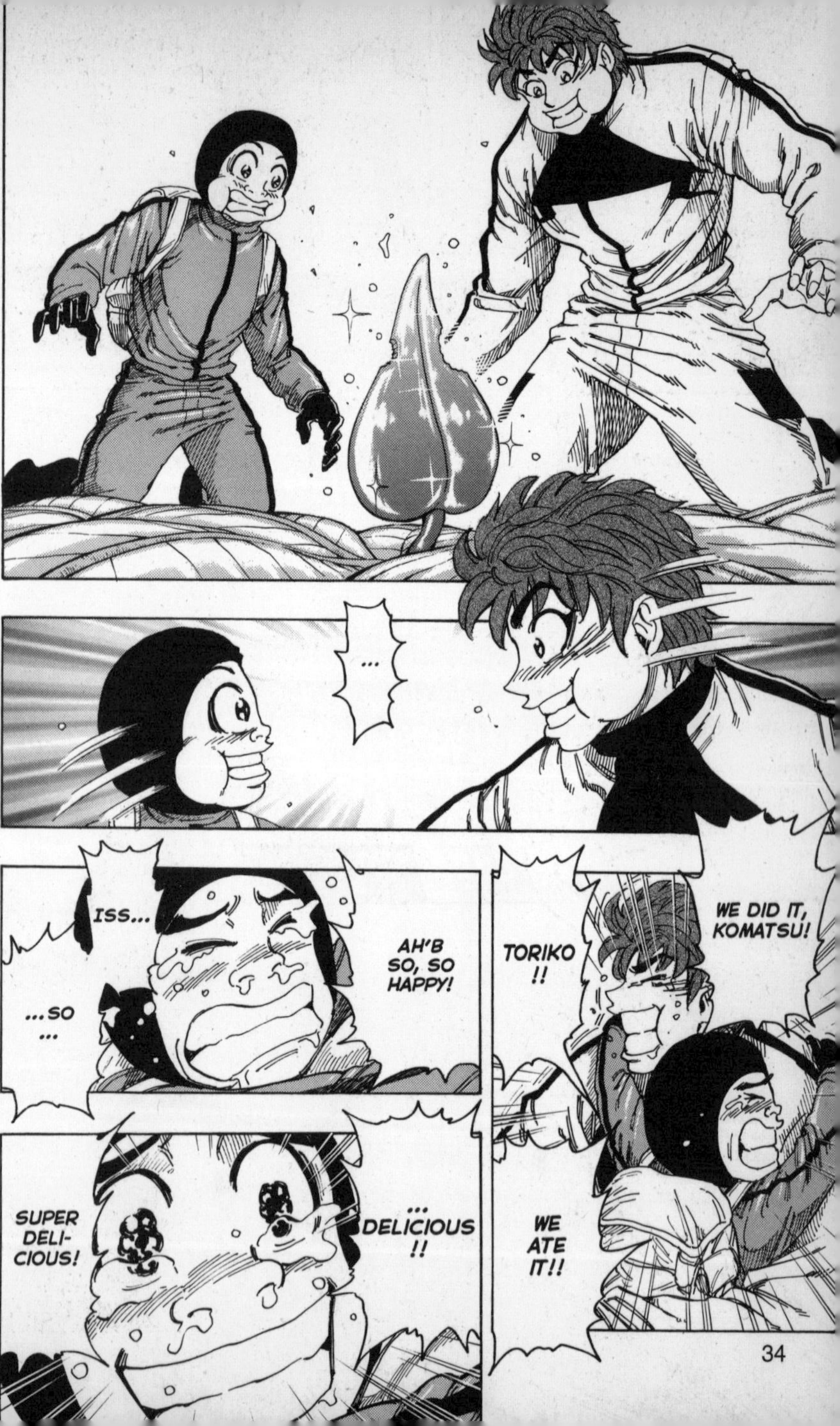
...
WE DID IT, KOMATSU!
TORIKO!!
WE ATE IT!!
ISS...
...SO ...
AH'B SO, SO HAPPY!
... DELICIOUS!!
SUPER DELI-CIOUS!

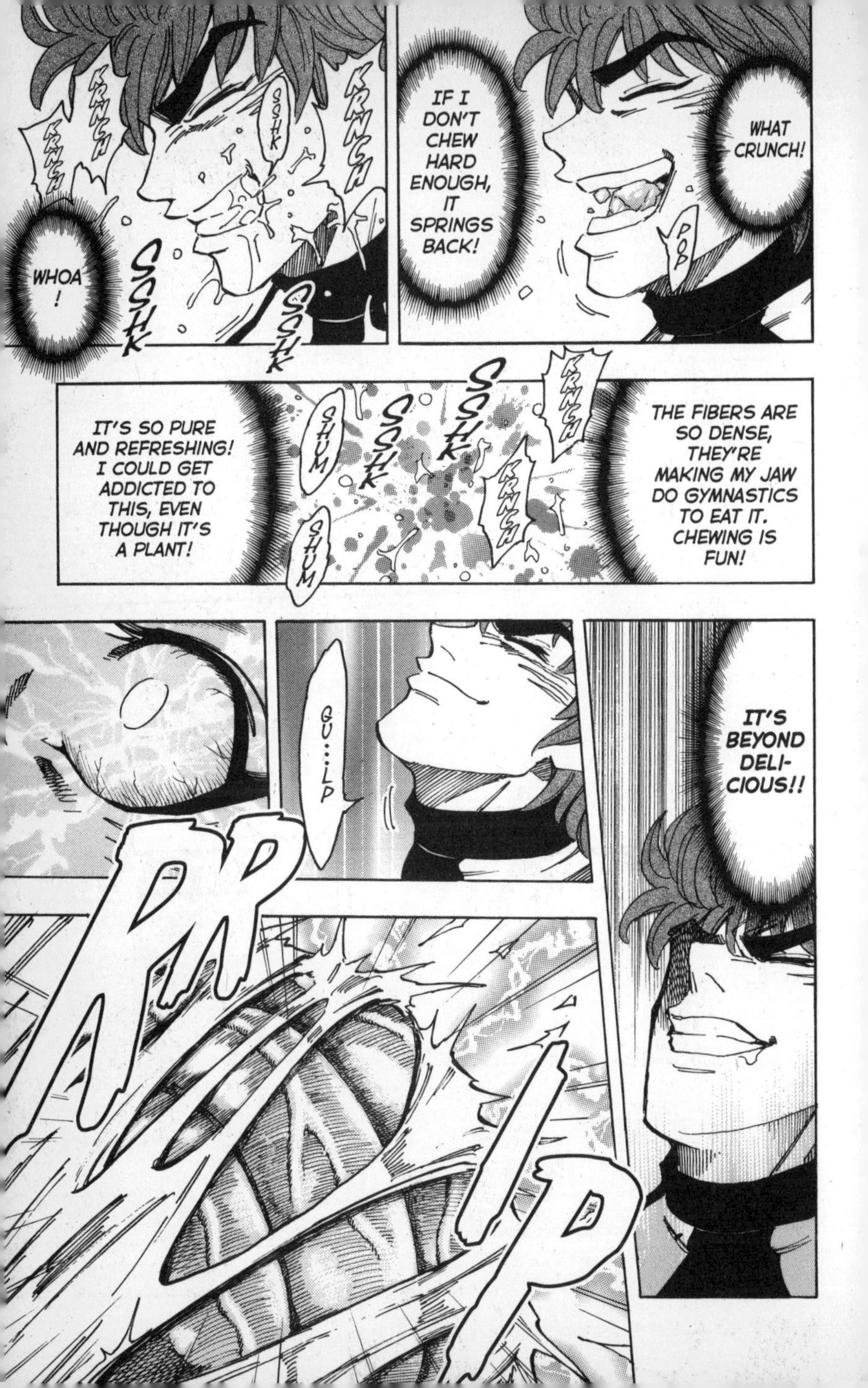
WHAT CRUNCH!
IF I DON'T CHEW HARD ENOUGH, IT SPRINGS BACK!
POP
KRNCH
SSHK
KRNCH
KRNCH
WHOA!
SSHK
SSHK
THE FIBERS ARE SO DENSE, THEY'RE MAKING MY JAW DO GYMNASTICS TO EAT IT. CHEWING IS FUN!
KRNCH
KRNCH
SSHK
SSHK
SHUM
SHUM
IT'S SO PURE AND REFRESHING! I COULD GET ADDICTED TO THIS, EVEN THOUGH IT'S A PLANT!
IT'S BEYOND DELI-CIOUS!!
GU...LP

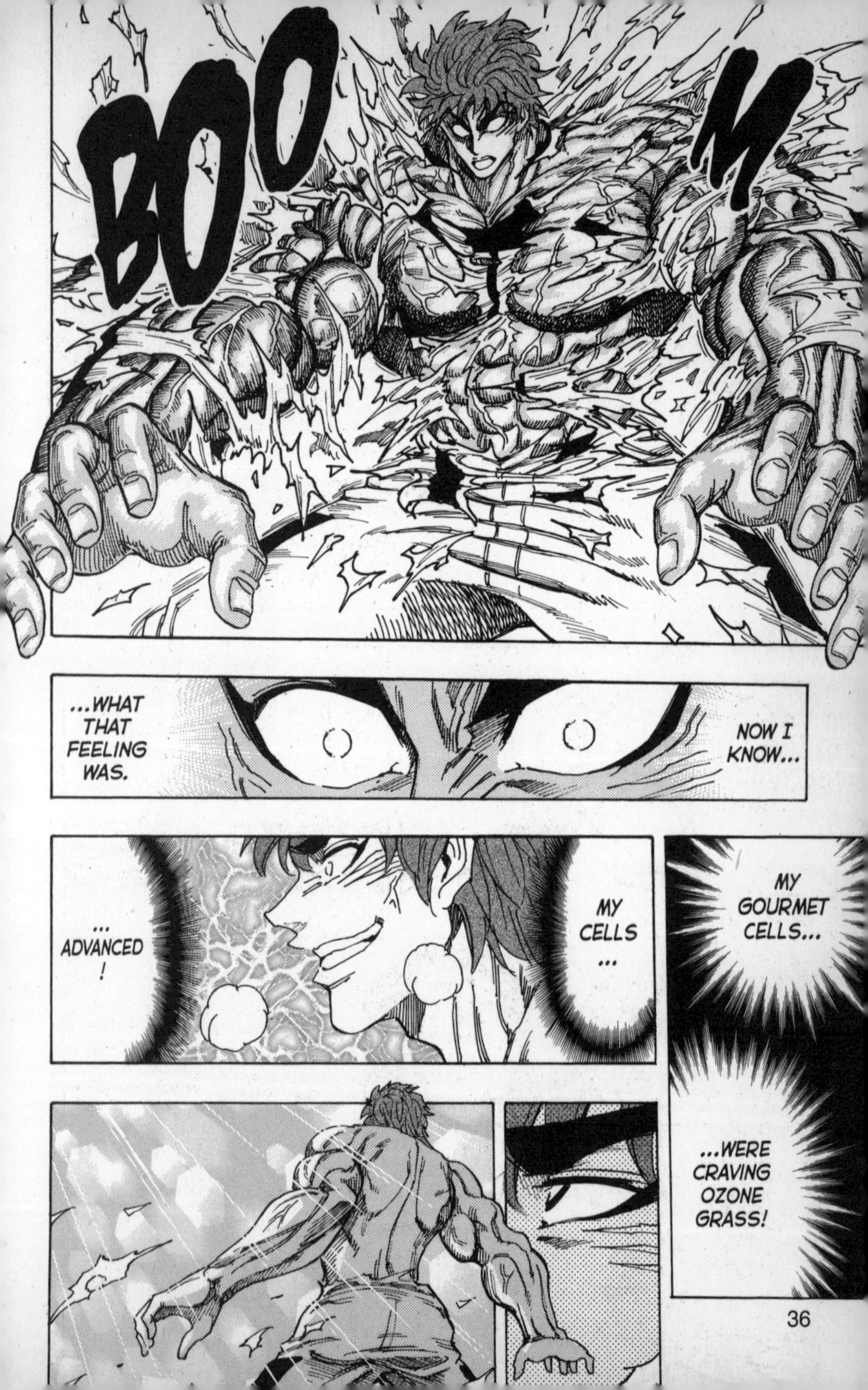
BOOOM
NOW I KNOW...
...WHAT THAT FEELING WAS.
MY GOURMET CELLS...
...WERE CRAVING OZONE GRASS!
MY CELLS...
...ADVANCED!

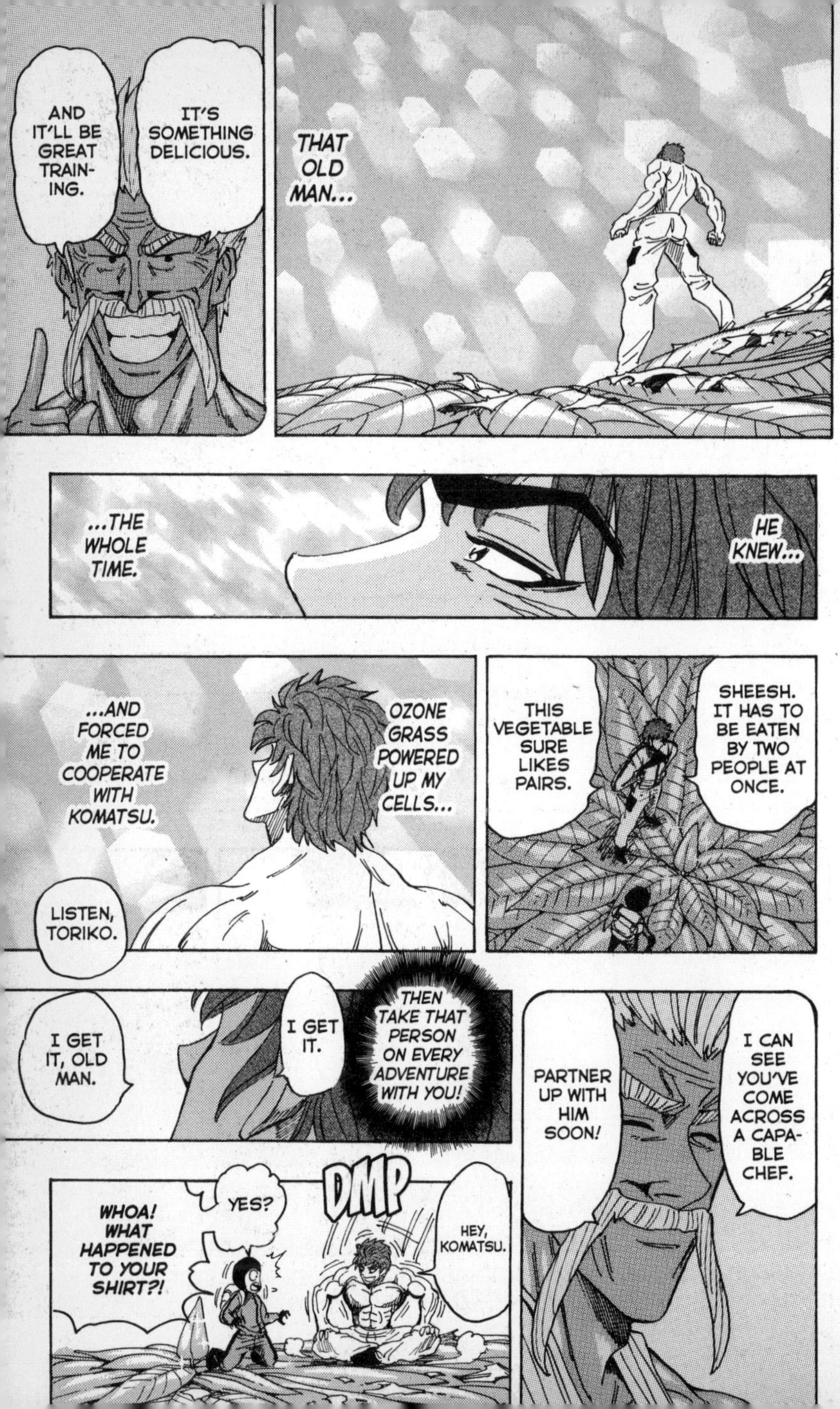
THAT OLD MAN...
IT'S SOMETHING DELICIOUS.
AND IT'LL BE GREAT TRAIN-ING.
HE KNEW...
...THE WHOLE TIME.
SHEESH. IT HAS TO BE EATEN BY TWO PEOPLE AT ONCE.
THIS VEGETABLE SURE LIKES PAIRS.
OZONE GRASS POWERED UP MY CELLS...
...AND FORCED ME TO COOPERATE WITH KOMATSU.
LISTEN, TORIKO.
I CAN SEE YOU'VE COME ACROSS A CAPA-BLE CHEF.
PARTNER UP WITH HIM SOON!
THEN TAKE THAT PERSON ON EVERY ADVENTURE WITH YOU!
I GET IT.
I GET IT, OLD MAN.
HEY, KOMATSU.
DMP
YES?
WHOA! WHAT HAPPENED TO YOUR SHIRT?!

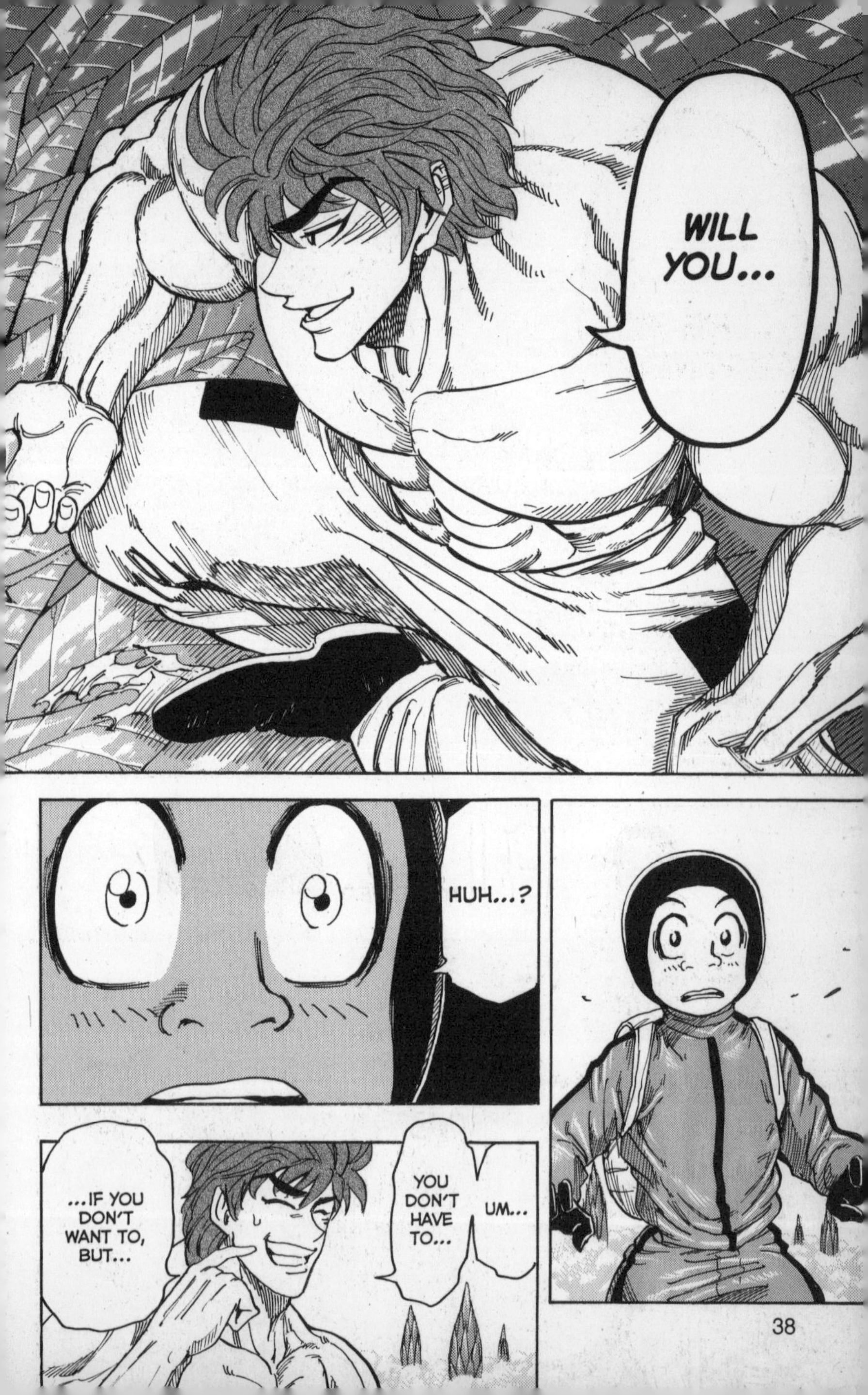
WILL YOU...
HUH...?
UM...
YOU DON'T HAVE TO...
...IF YOU DON'T WANT TO, BUT...

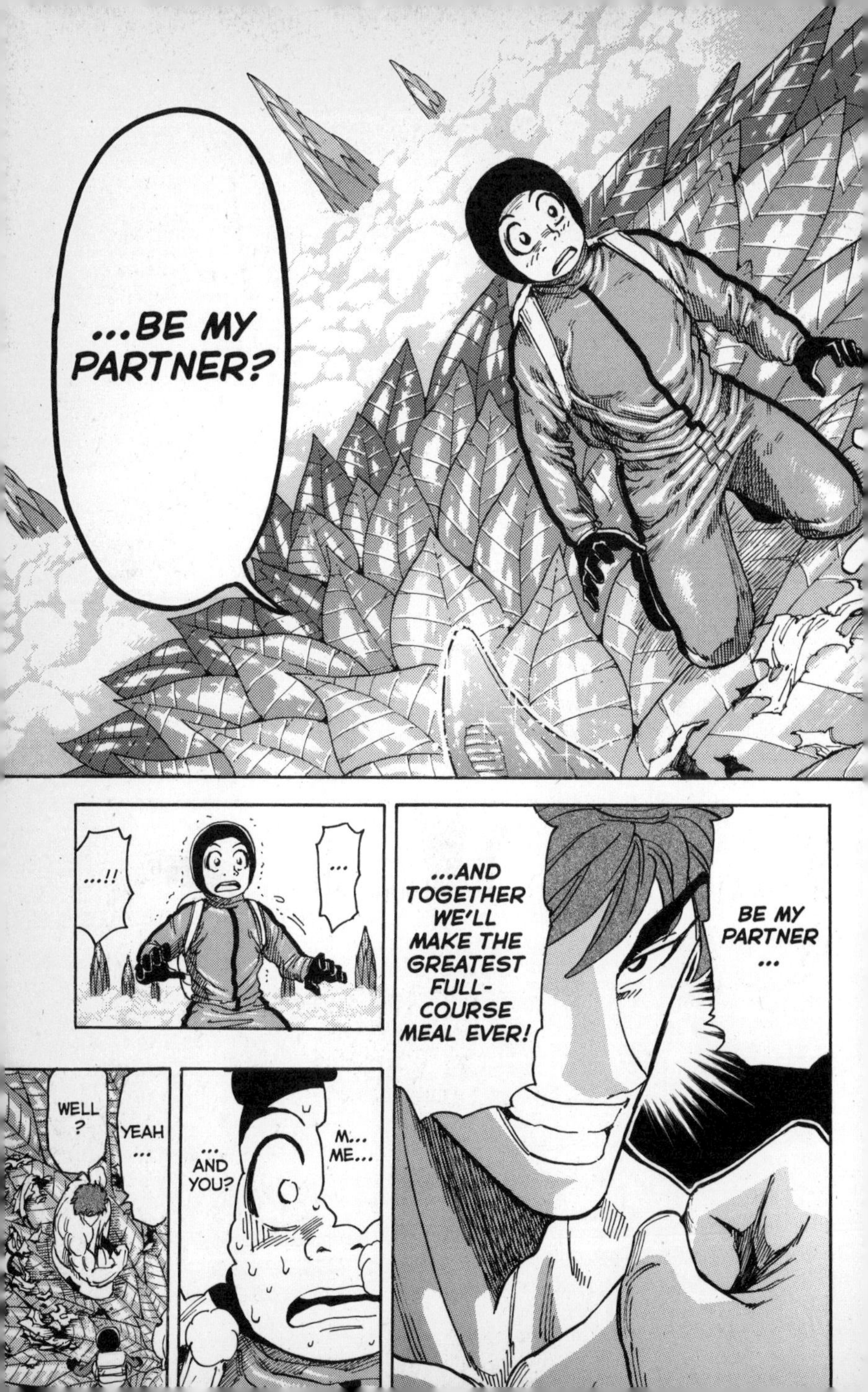
...BE MY PARTNER?
BE MY PARTNER ...
...AND TOGETHER WE'LL MAKE THE GREATEST FULL-COURSE MEAL EVER!
...
...!!
M... ME...
... AND YOU?
WELL ?
YEAH ...

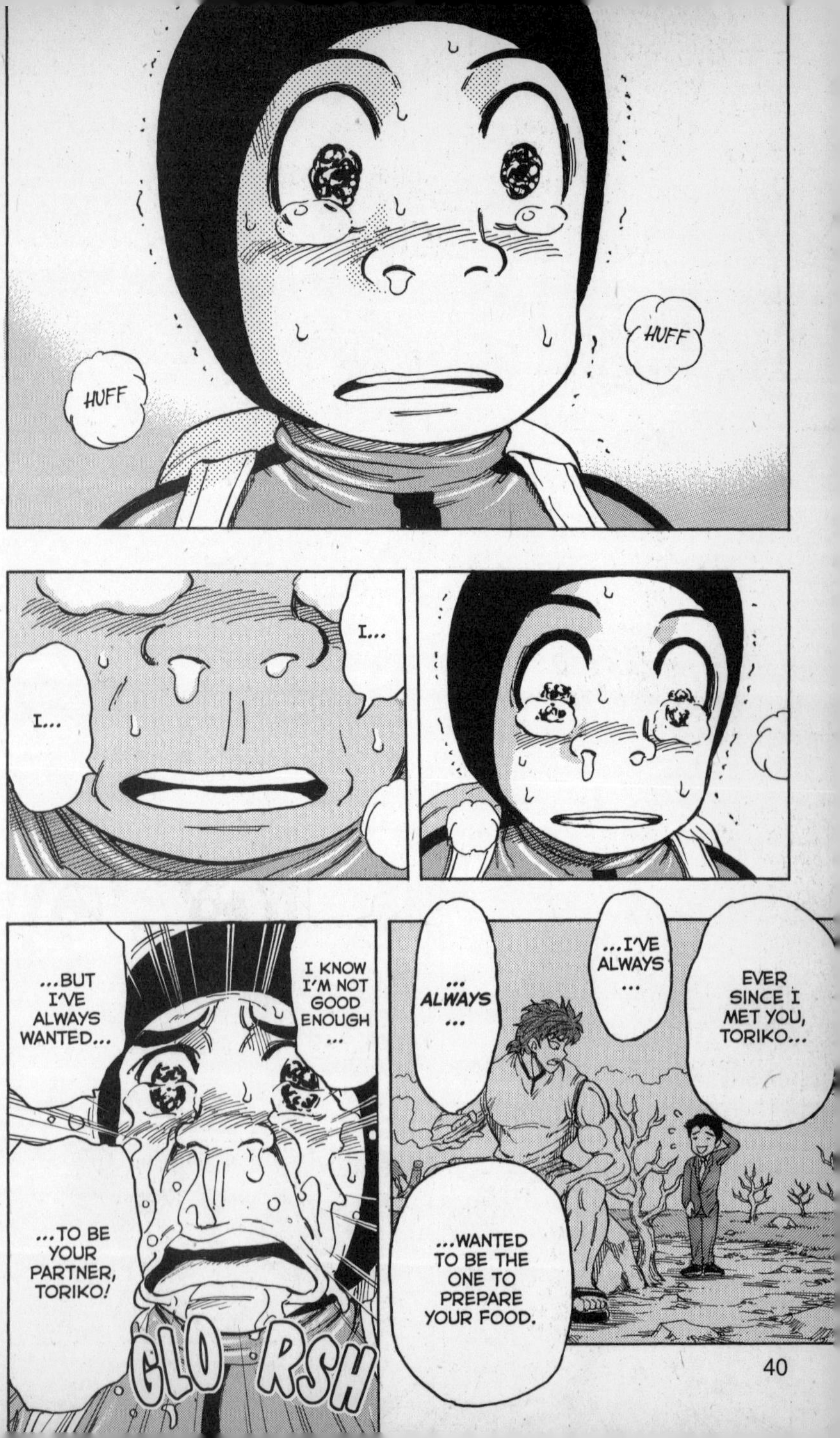
HUFF
HUFF
I...
I...
EVER SINCE I MET YOU, TORIKO...
...I'VE ALWAYS ...
... ALWAYS ...
...WANTED TO BE THE ONE TO PREPARE YOUR FOOD.
I KNOW I'M NOT GOOD ENOUGH ...
...BUT I'VE ALWAYS WANTED...
...TO BE YOUR PARTNER, TORIKO!
GLO RSH

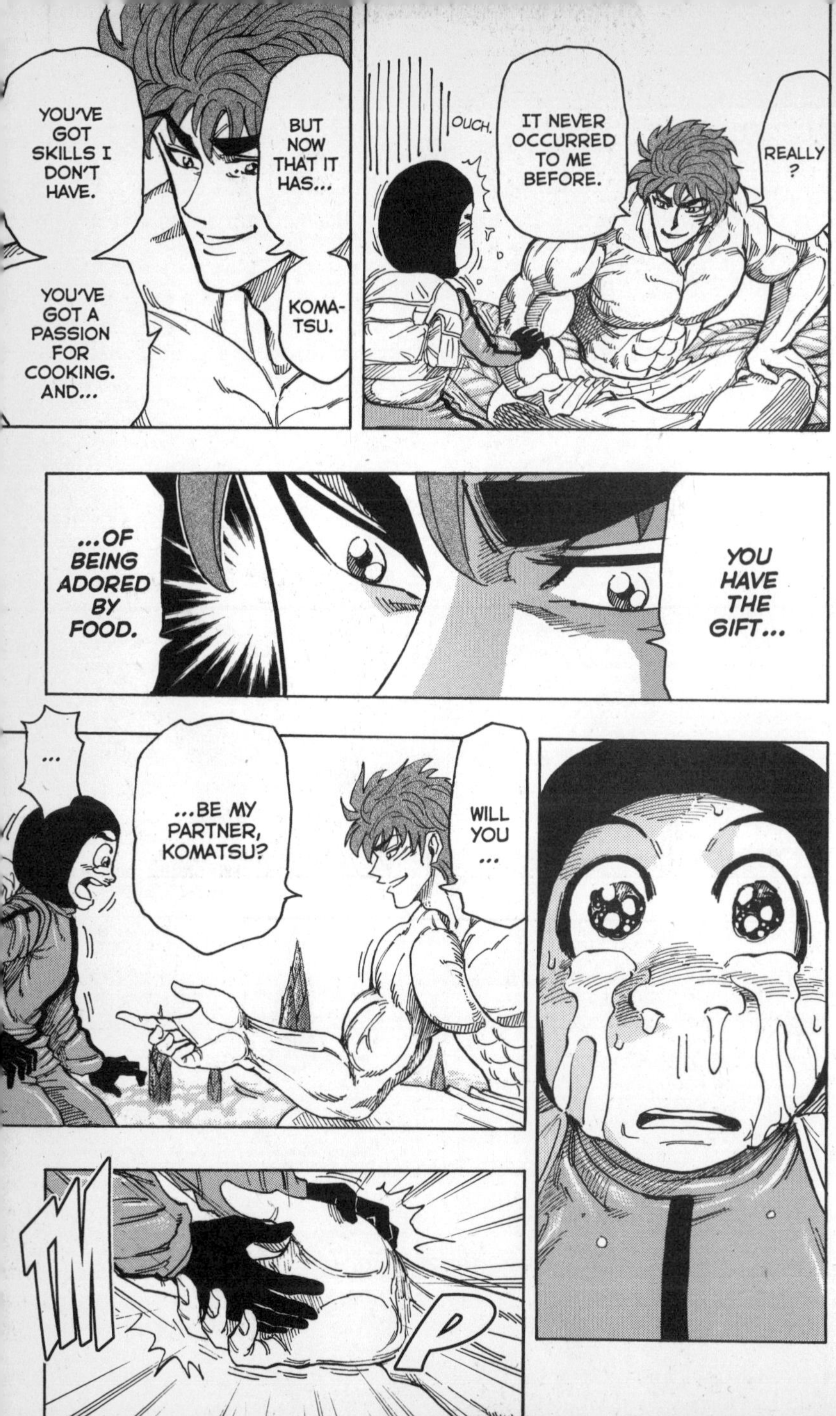
REALLY?
IT NEVER OCCURRED TO ME BEFORE.
OUCH.
BUT NOW THAT IT HAS...
KOMA-TSU.
YOU'VE GOT SKILLS I DON'T HAVE.
YOU'VE GOT A PASSION FOR COOKING. AND...
YOU HAVE THE GIFT...
...OF BEING ADORED BY FOOD.
WILL YOU...
...BE MY PARTNER, KOMATSU?
...
TMP

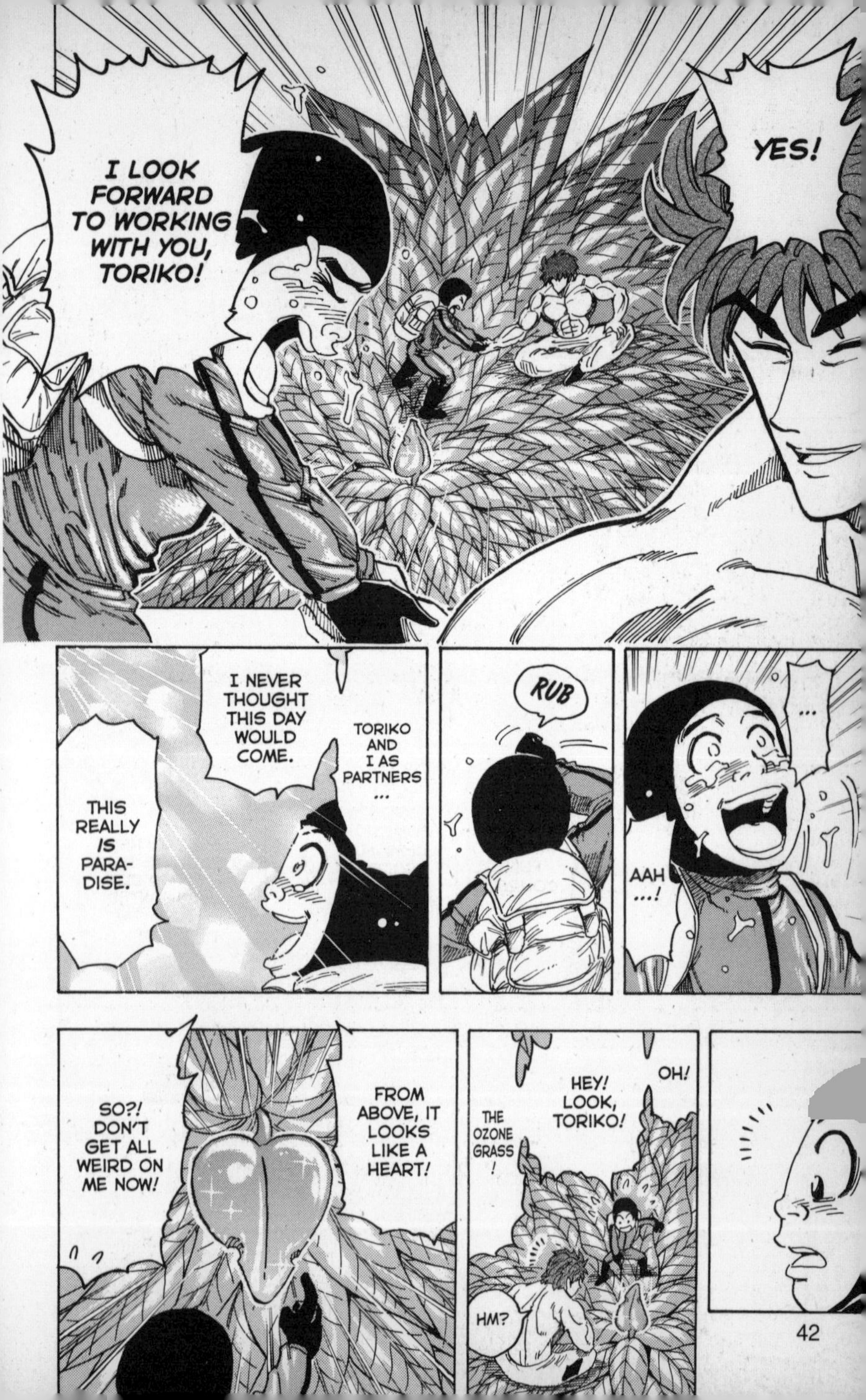
YES!
I LOOK FORWARD TO WORKING WITH YOU, TORIKO!
...
AAH ...!
RUB
I NEVER THOUGHT THIS DAY WOULD COME.
TORIKO AND I AS PARTNERS ...
THIS REALLY IS PARADISE.
OH!
HEY! LOOK, TORIKO!
THE OZONE GRASS !
HM?
FROM ABOVE, IT LOOKS LIKE A HEART!
SO?! DON'T GET ALL WEIRD ON ME NOW!

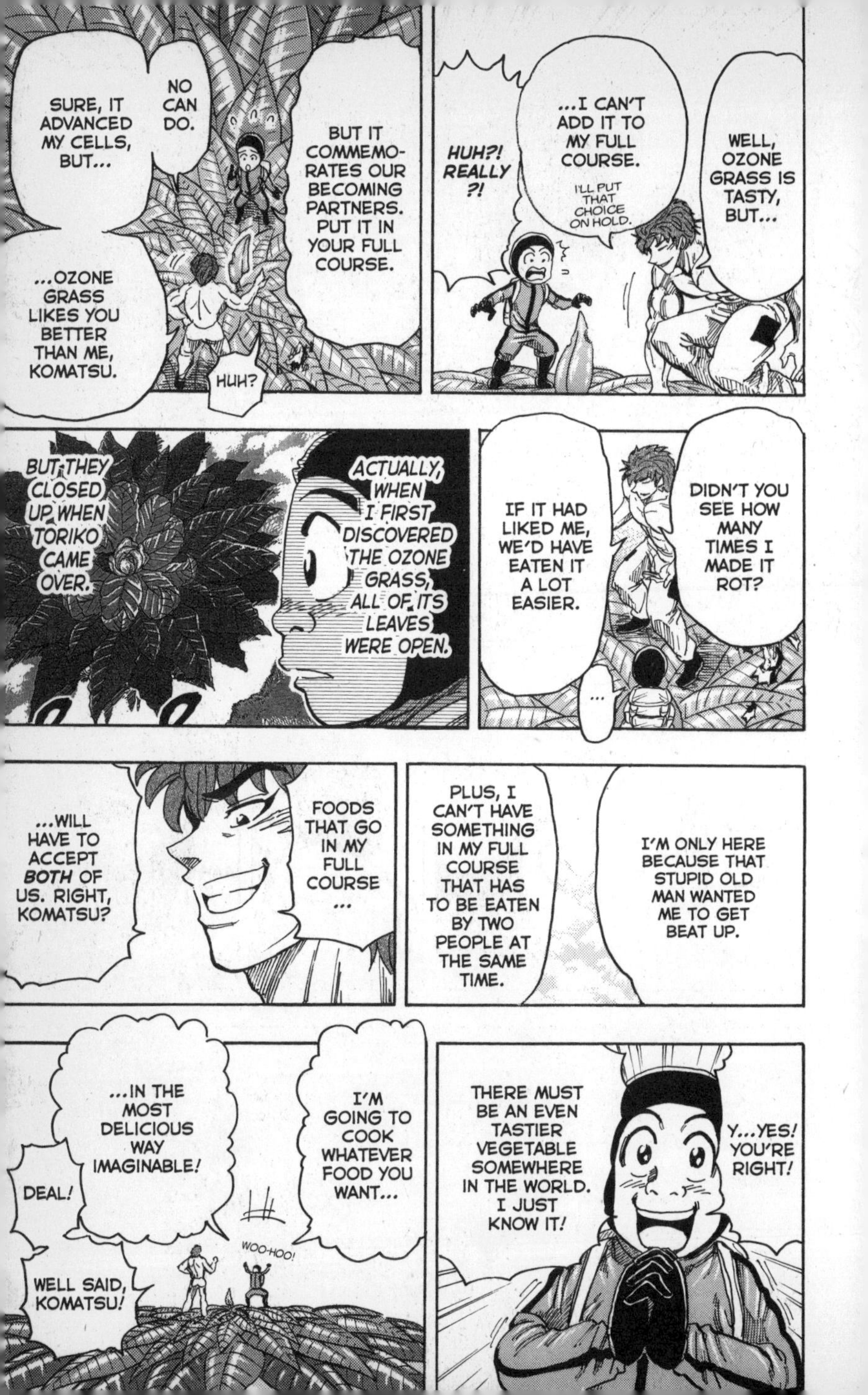
WELL, OZONE GRASS IS TASTY, BUT...
...I CAN'T ADD IT TO MY FULL COURSE.
I'LL PUT THAT CHOICE ON HOLD.
HUH?! REALLY?!
BUT IT COMMEMORATES OUR BECOMING PARTNERS. PUT IT IN YOUR FULL COURSE.
NO CAN DO.
SURE, IT ADVANCED MY CELLS, BUT...
...OZONE GRASS LIKES YOU BETTER THAN ME, KOMATSU.
HUH?
DIDN'T YOU SEE HOW MANY TIMES I MADE IT ROT?
IF IT HAD LIKED ME, WE'D HAVE EATEN IT A LOT EASIER.
...
ACTUALLY, WHEN I FIRST DISCOVERED THE OZONE GRASS, ALL OF ITS LEAVES WERE OPEN.
BUT THEY CLOSED UP WHEN TORIKO CAME OVER.
I'M ONLY HERE BECAUSE THAT STUPID OLD MAN WANTED ME TO GET BEAT UP.
PLUS, I CAN'T HAVE SOMETHING IN MY FULL COURSE THAT HAS TO BE EATEN BY TWO PEOPLE AT THE SAME TIME.
FOODS THAT GO IN MY FULL COURSE...
...WILL HAVE TO ACCEPT *BOTH* OF US. RIGHT, KOMATSU?
Y...YES! YOU'RE RIGHT!
THERE MUST BE AN EVEN TASTIER VEGETABLE SOMEWHERE IN THE WORLD. I JUST KNOW IT!
I'M GOING TO COOK WHATEVER FOOD YOU WANT...
...IN THE MOST DELICIOUS WAY IMAGINABLE!
DEAL!
WOO-HOO!
WELL SAID, KOMATSU!

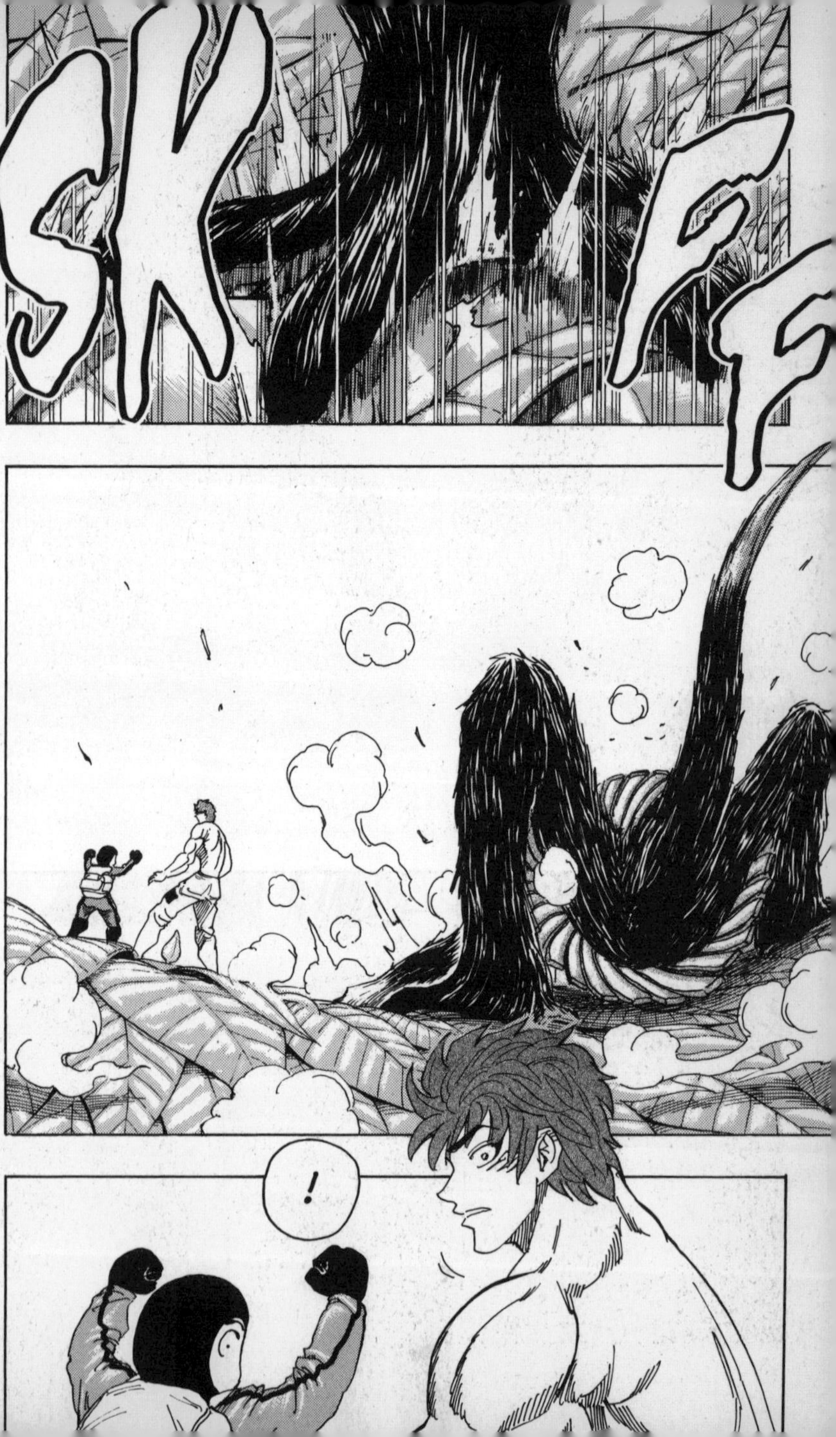
SKWAP
!

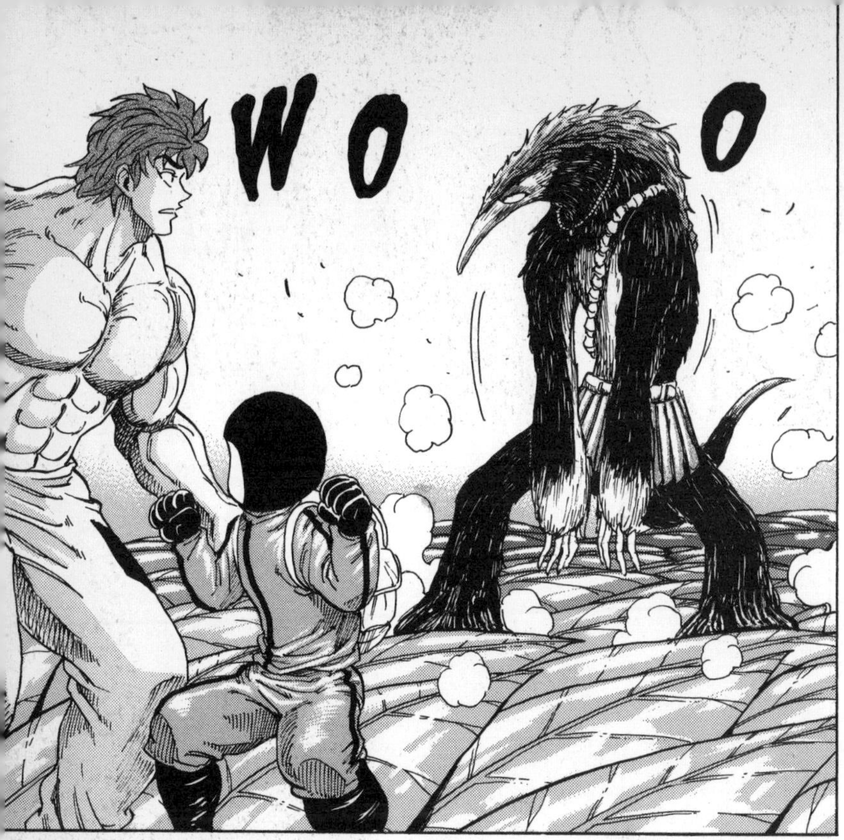
WOOO

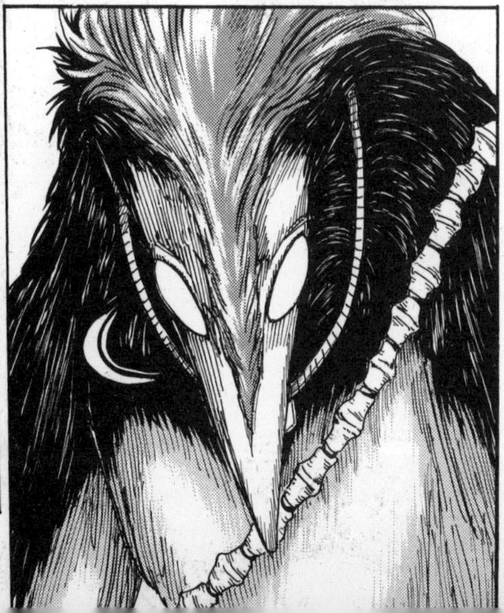

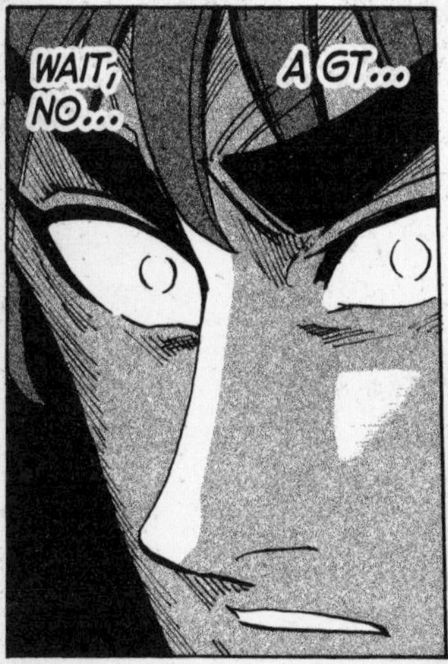
A GT...
WAIT, NO...

TORIKO

GOURMET CHECKLIST

Vol. 122

GOLDEN CARROT
(VEGETABLE)

CAPTURE LEVEL: LESS THAN 1 (CAN BE CULTIVATED)

HABITAT: ANYWHERE THE RIGHT CONDITIONS
ARE MET

LENGTH: 20 CM

HEIGHT: ---

WEIGHT: 200 G

PRICE: 7,000 YEN PER CARROT

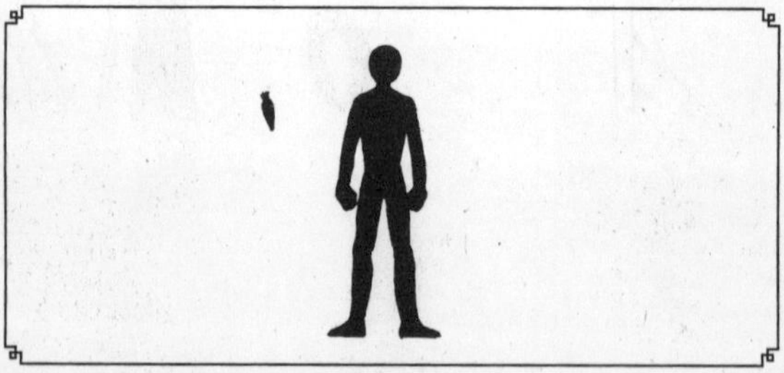

SCALE

DID THIS END UP IN KOMATSU'S RECIPE FOR CENTURY
SOUP? THIS TWINKLING TUBER IS THE RAREST OF ALL
CARROTS. GOLDEN CARROTS ARE SUPPLE AND JUICY, NOT
TO MENTION SUPER SWEET. IT'S NO SURPRISE GOLDEN
CARROT JUICE SELLS FOR A PRETTY PENNY!

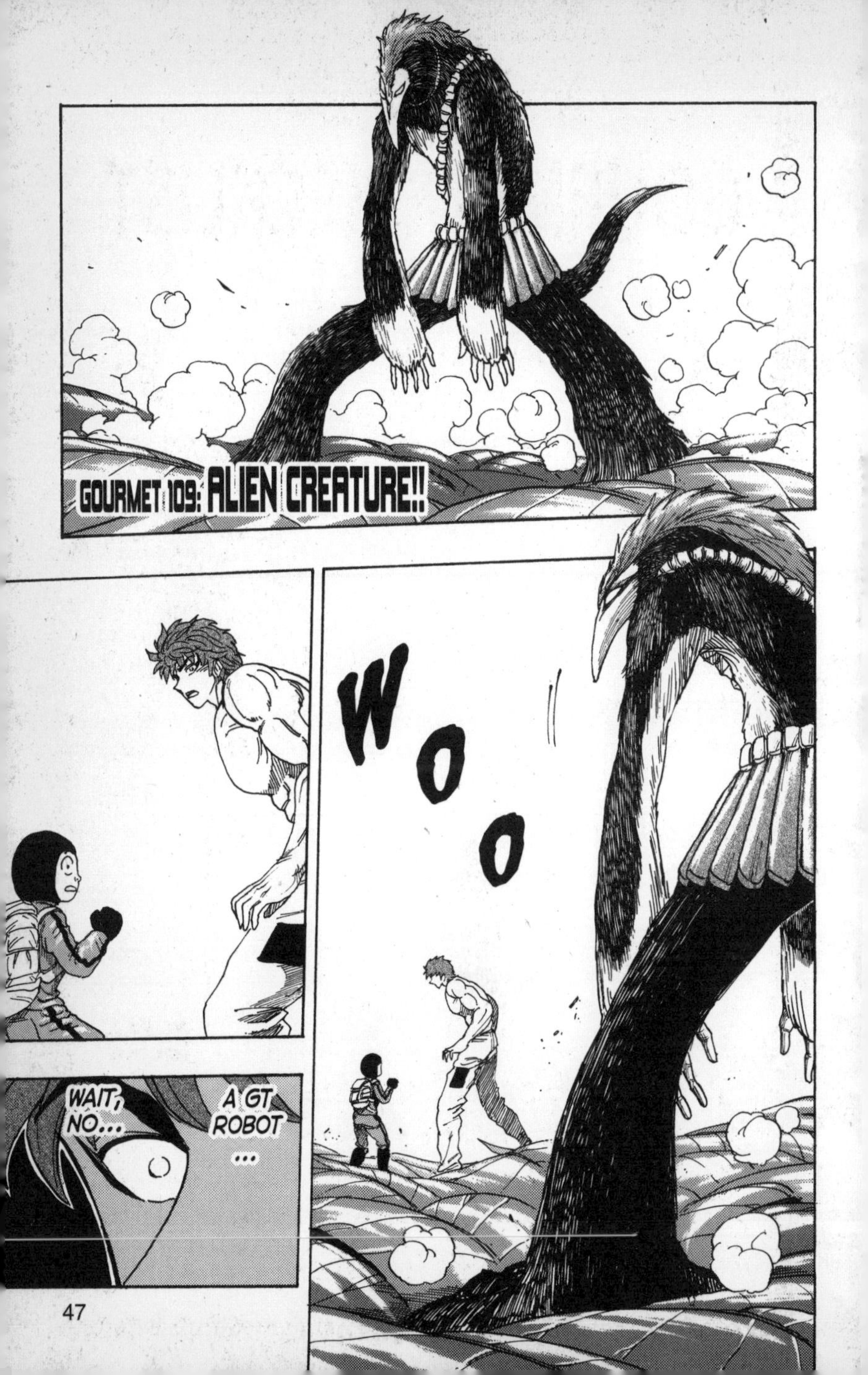
GOURMET 109: ALIEN CREATURE!!
WOOO
A GT ROBOT ...
WAIT, NO...

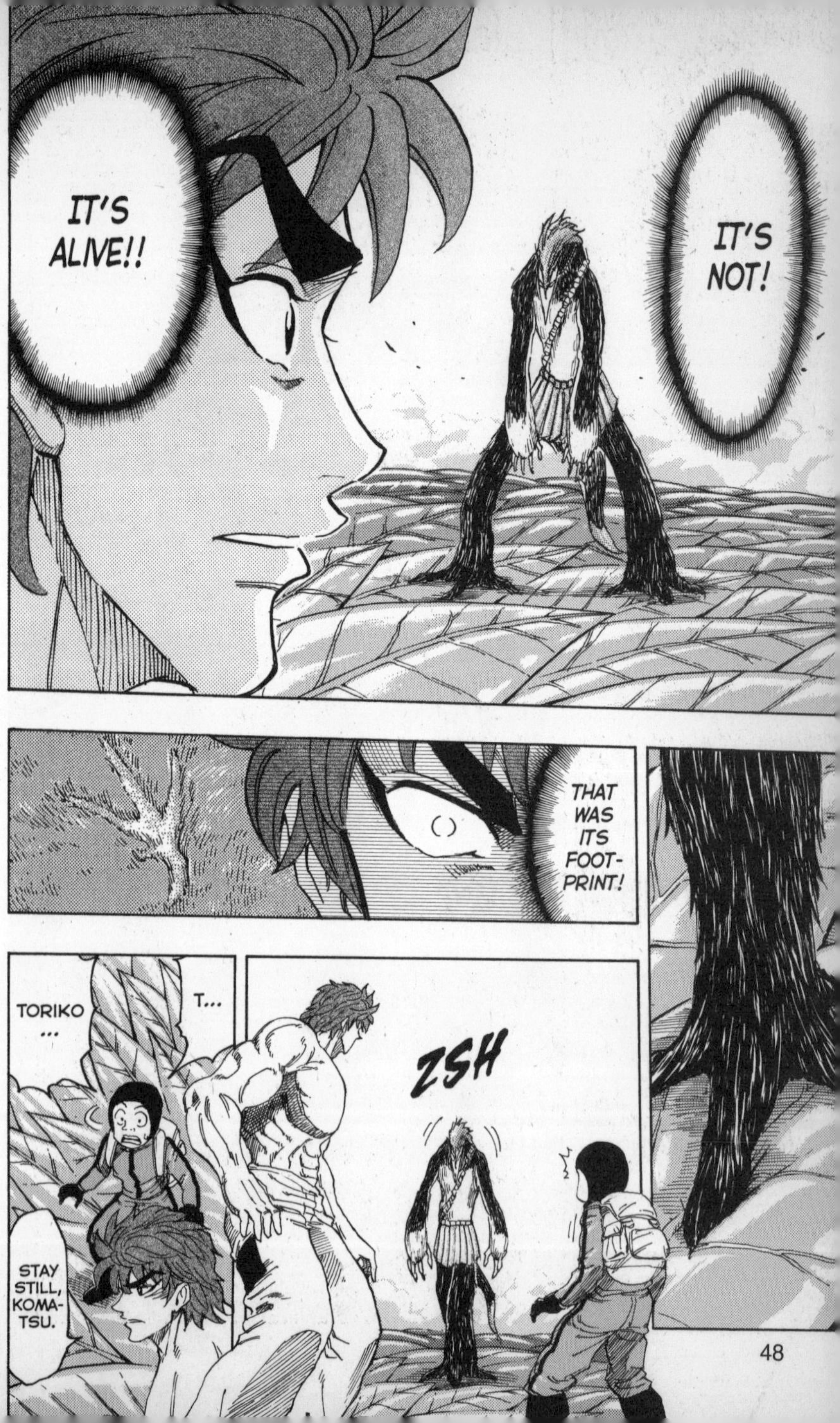
IT'S NOT!
IT'S ALIVE!!
THAT WAS ITS FOOT-PRINT!
T...
ZSH
TORIKO ...
STAY STILL, KOMA-TSU.

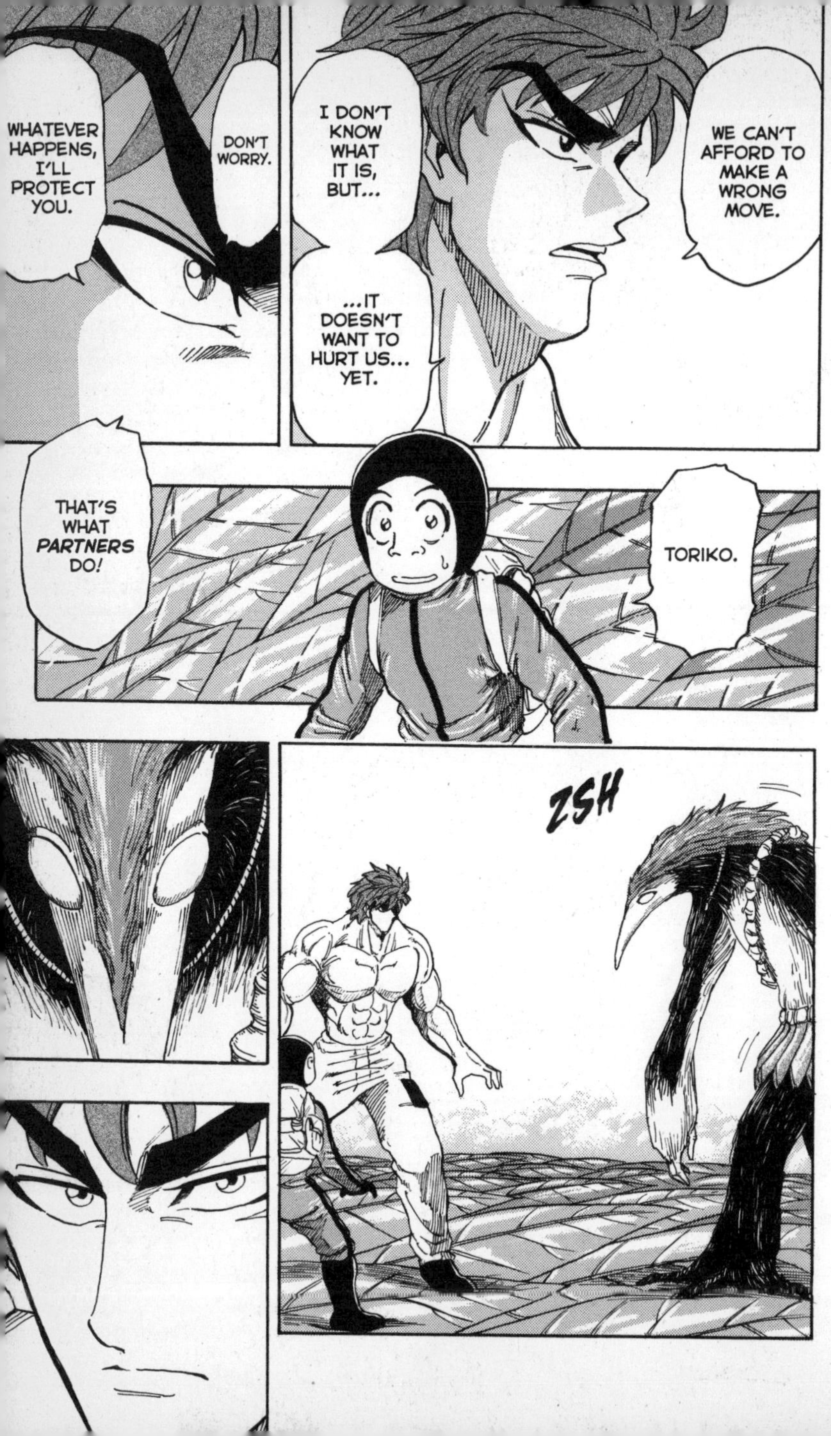
WE CAN'T AFFORD TO MAKE A WRONG MOVE.
I DON'T KNOW WHAT IT IS, BUT...
...IT DOESN'T WANT TO HURT US... YET.
DON'T WORRY.
WHATEVER HAPPENS, I'LL PROTECT YOU.
TORIKO.
THAT'S WHAT *PARTNERS* DO!
ZSH

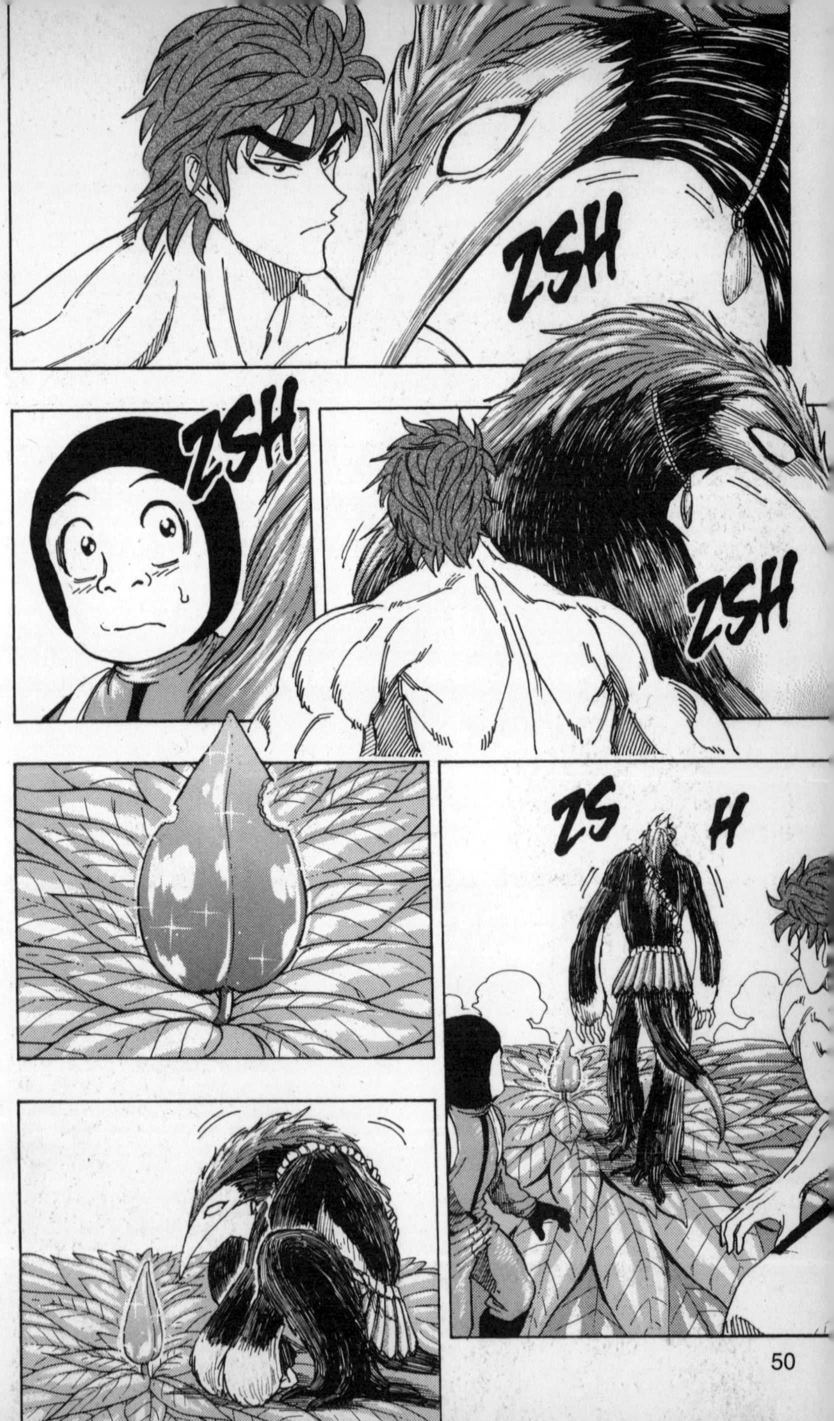
ZSH
ZSH
ZSH
ZS H

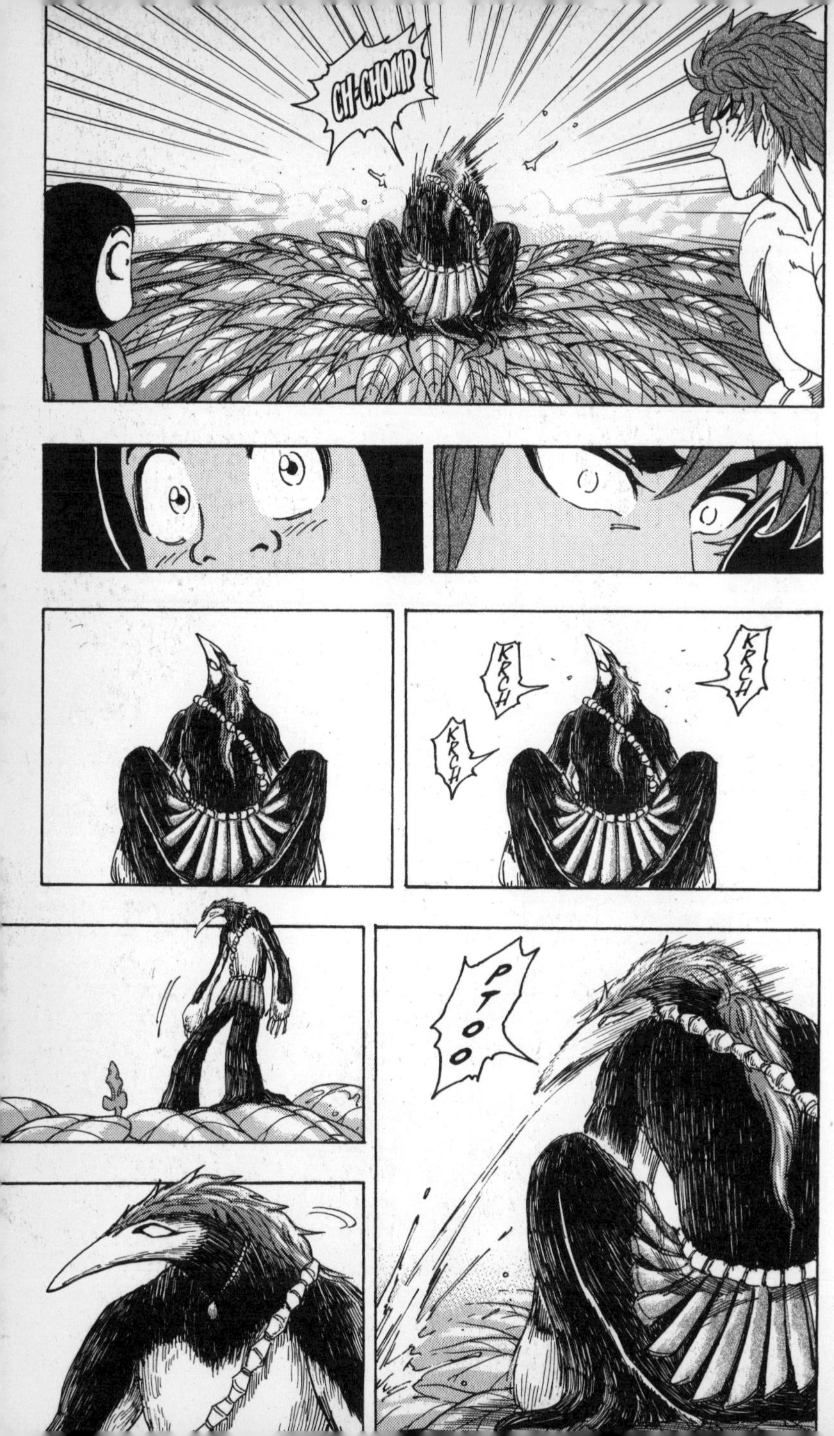
CH-CHOMP
KRCH
KRCH
KRCH
PTOOO

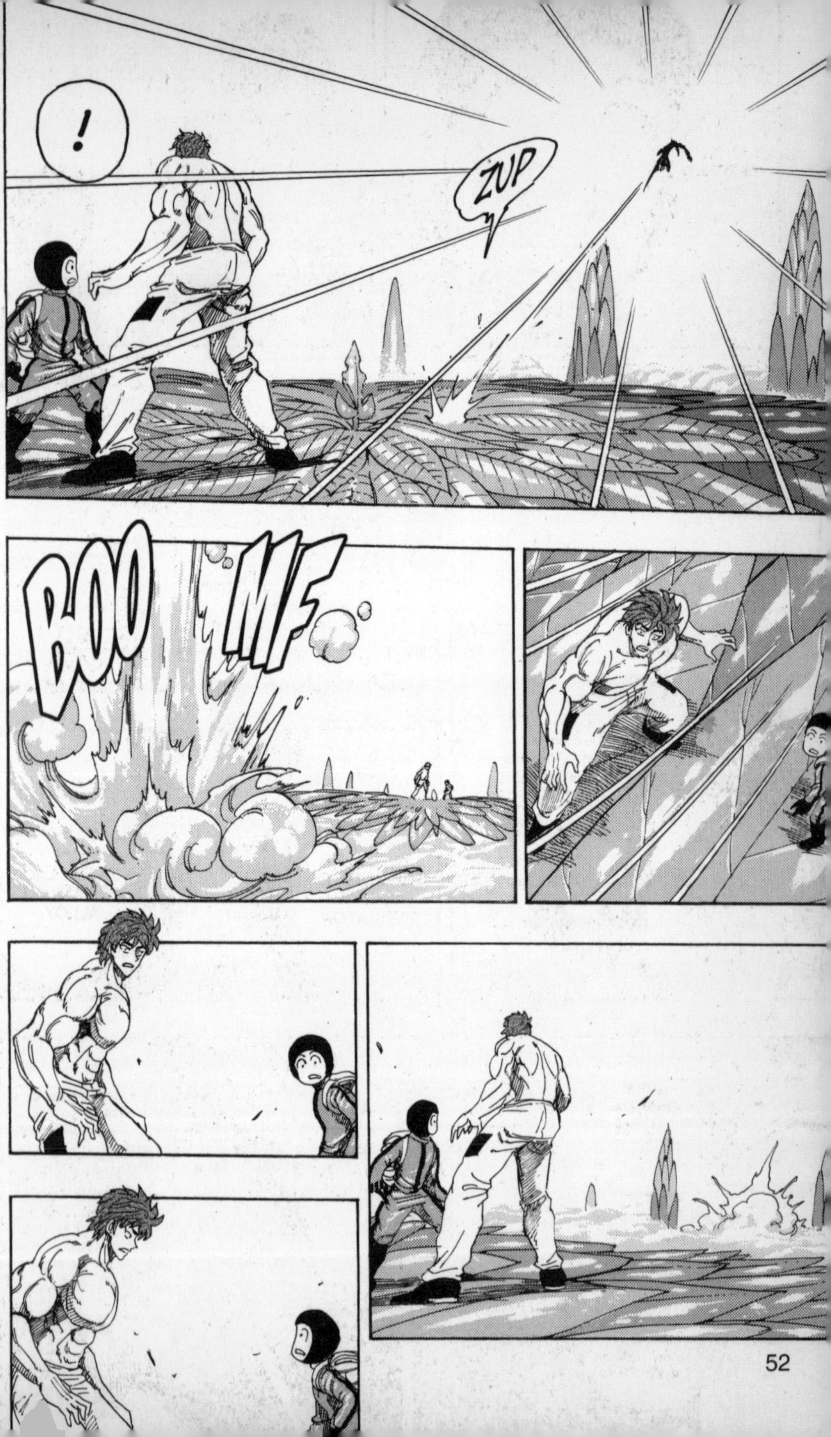
!
ZUP
BOOMF

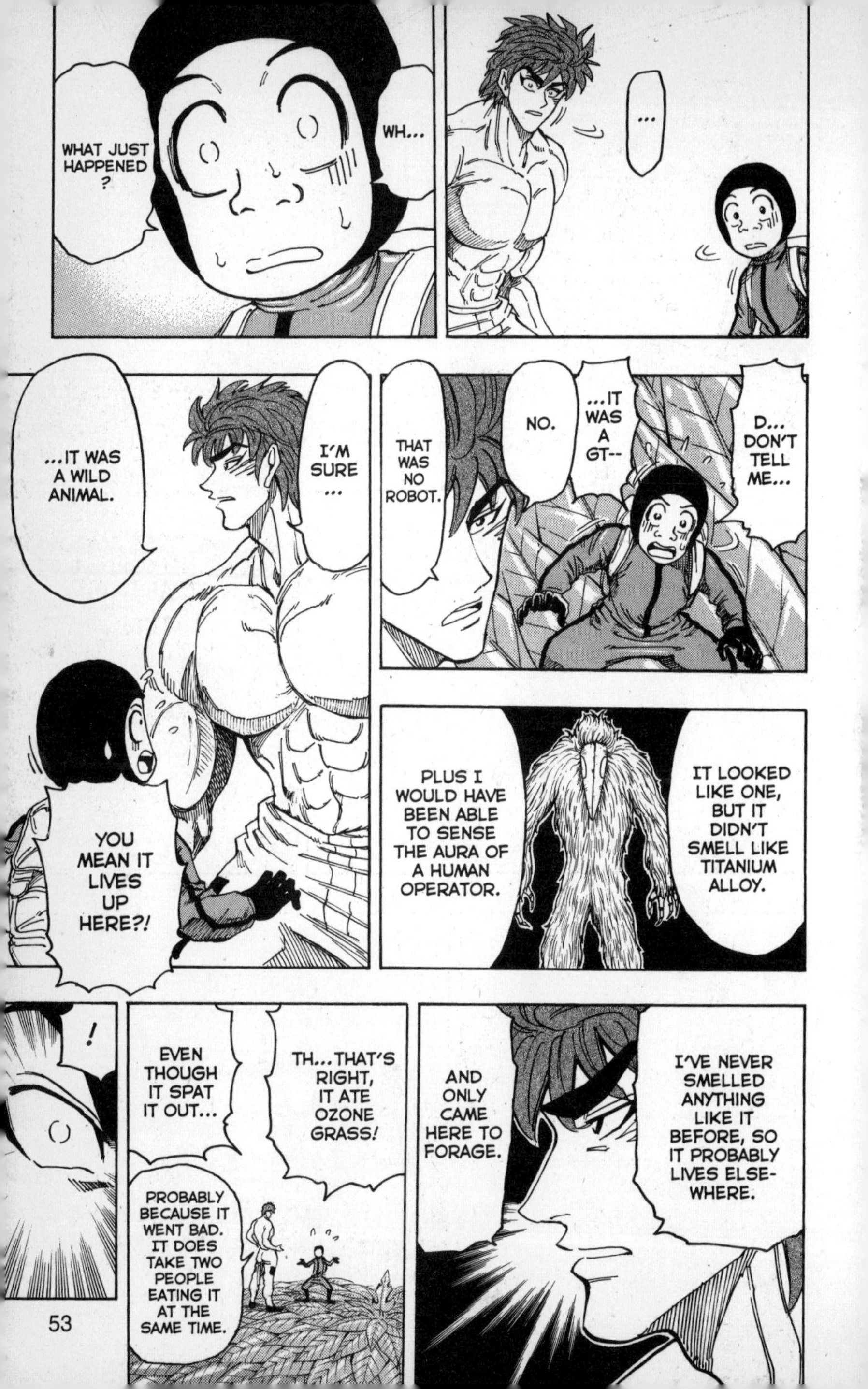
...
WH...
WHAT JUST HAPPENED ?
D... DON'T TELL ME...
...IT WAS A GT--
NO.
THAT WAS NO ROBOT.
IT LOOKED LIKE ONE, BUT IT DIDN'T SMELL LIKE TITANIUM ALLOY.
PLUS I WOULD HAVE BEEN ABLE TO SENSE THE AURA OF A HUMAN OPERATOR.
I'M SURE ...
...IT WAS A WILD ANIMAL.
YOU MEAN IT LIVES UP HERE?!
I'VE NEVER SMELLED ANYTHING LIKE IT BEFORE, SO IT PROBABLY LIVES ELSE-WHERE.
AND ONLY CAME HERE TO FORAGE.
TH...THAT'S RIGHT, IT ATE OZONE GRASS!
EVEN THOUGH IT SPAT IT OUT...
PROBABLY BECAUSE IT WENT BAD. IT DOES TAKE TWO PEOPLE EATING IT AT THE SAME TIME.
!

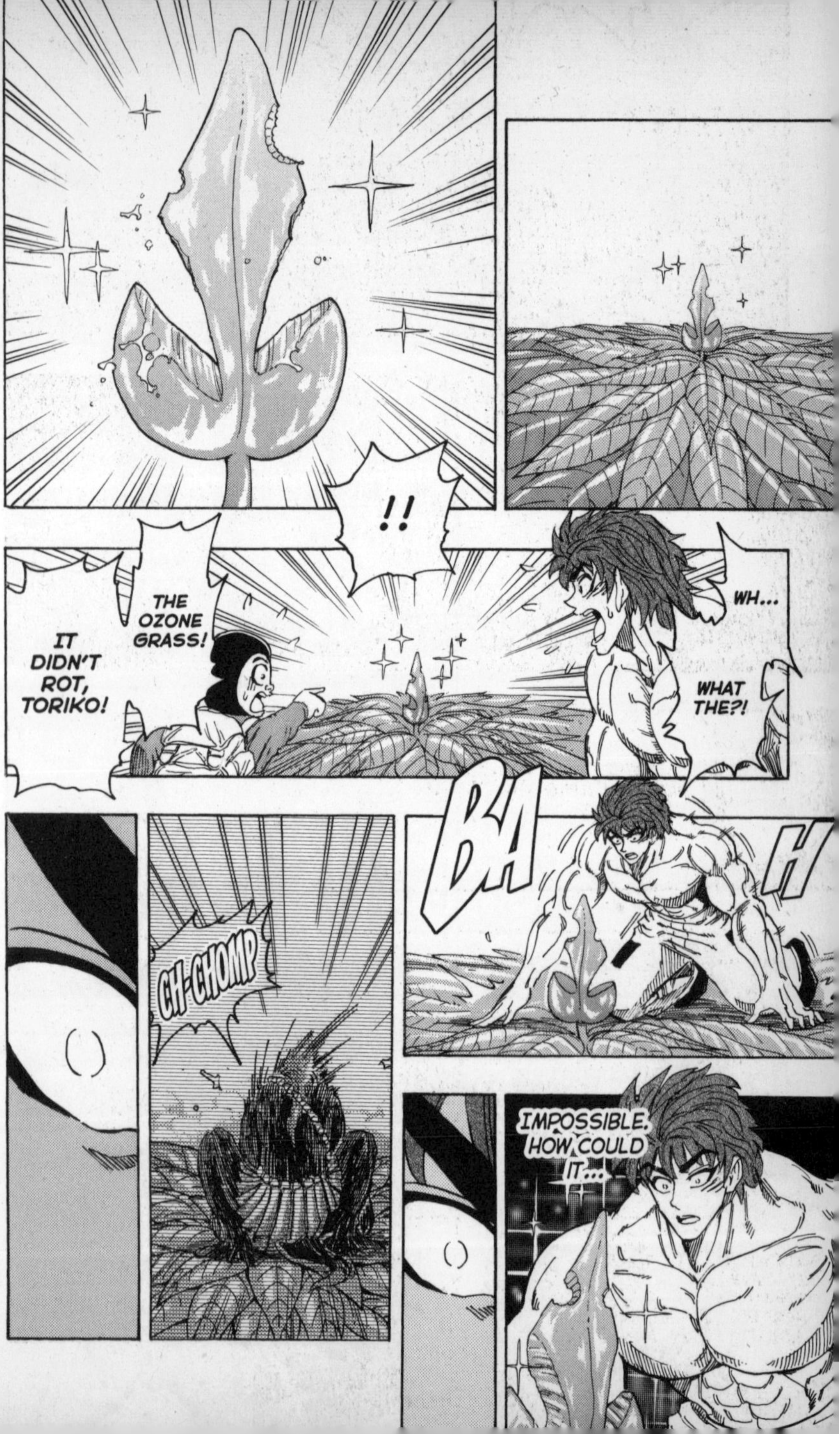
!!
WH... WHAT THE?!
THE OZONE GRASS!
IT DIDN'T ROT, TORIKO!
BAH
CH-CHOMP
IMPOSSIBLE. HOW COULD IT...

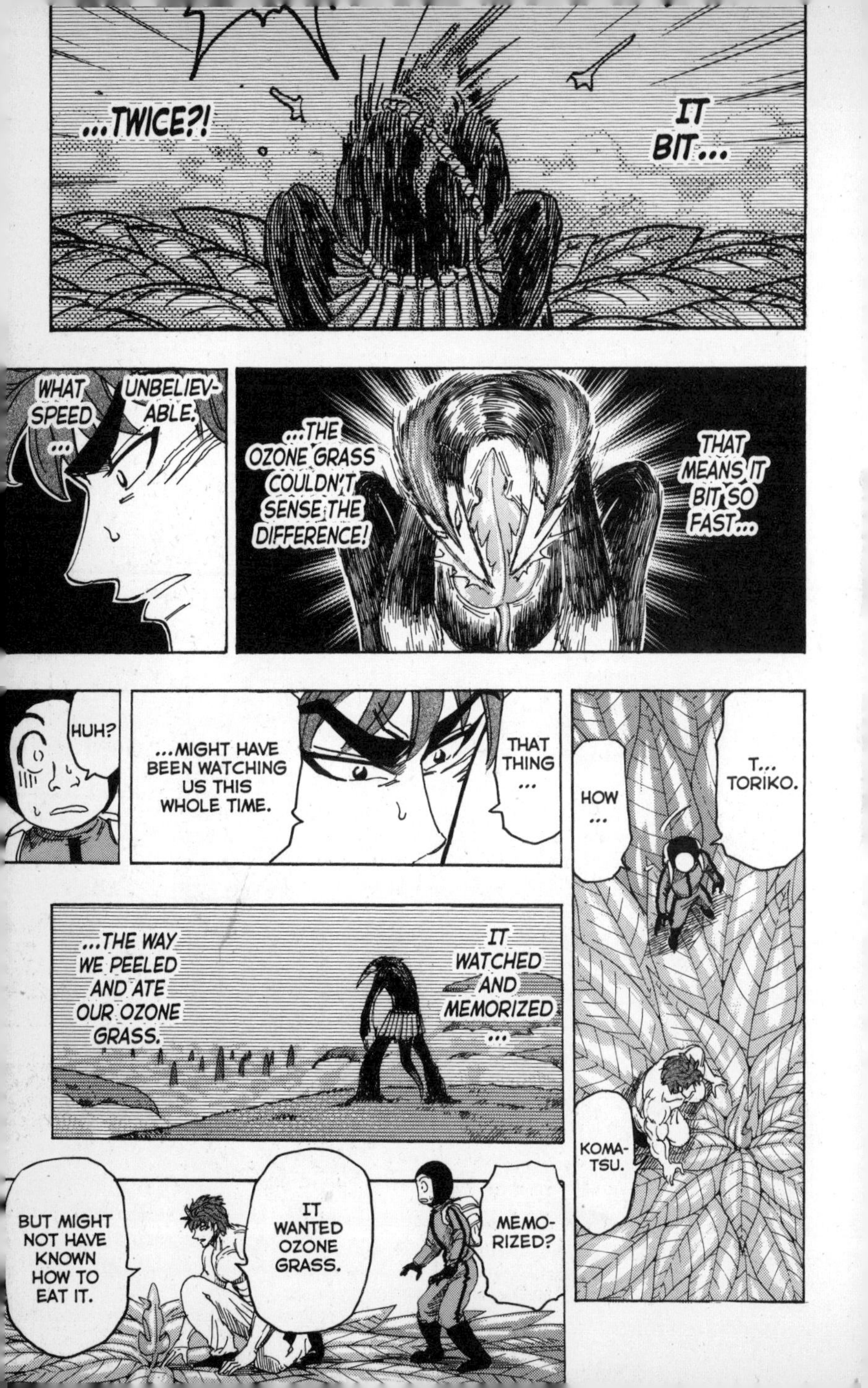
IT BIT...
...TWICE?!
THAT MEANS IT BIT SO FAST...
...THE OZONE GRASS COULDN'T SENSE THE DIFFERENCE!
UNBELIEV-ABLE.
WHAT SPEED...
T... TORIKO.
HOW...
KOMA-TSU.
THAT THING...
...MIGHT HAVE BEEN WATCHING US THIS WHOLE TIME.
HUH?
IT WATCHED AND MEMORIZED...
...THE WAY WE PEELED AND ATE OUR OZONE GRASS.
MEMO-RIZED?
IT WANTED OZONE GRASS.
BUT MIGHT NOT HAVE KNOWN HOW TO EAT IT.

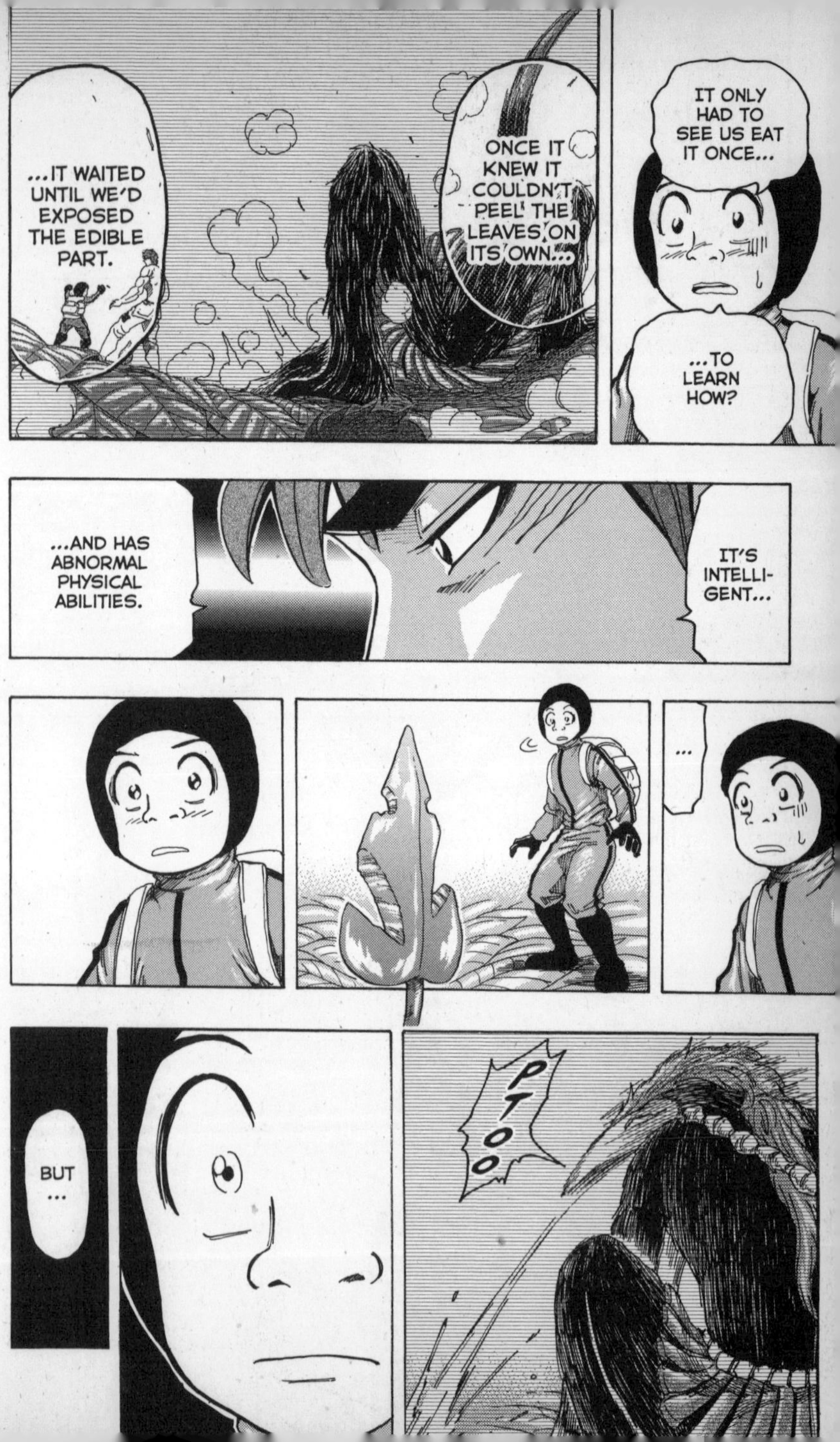
IT ONLY HAD TO SEE US EAT IT ONCE...
...TO LEARN HOW?
ONCE IT KNEW IT COULDN'T PEEL THE LEAVES ON ITS OWN...
...IT WAITED UNTIL WE'D EXPOSED THE EDIBLE PART.
IT'S INTELLI- GENT...
...AND HAS ABNORMAL PHYSICAL ABILITIES.
...
PTOOO
BUT ...

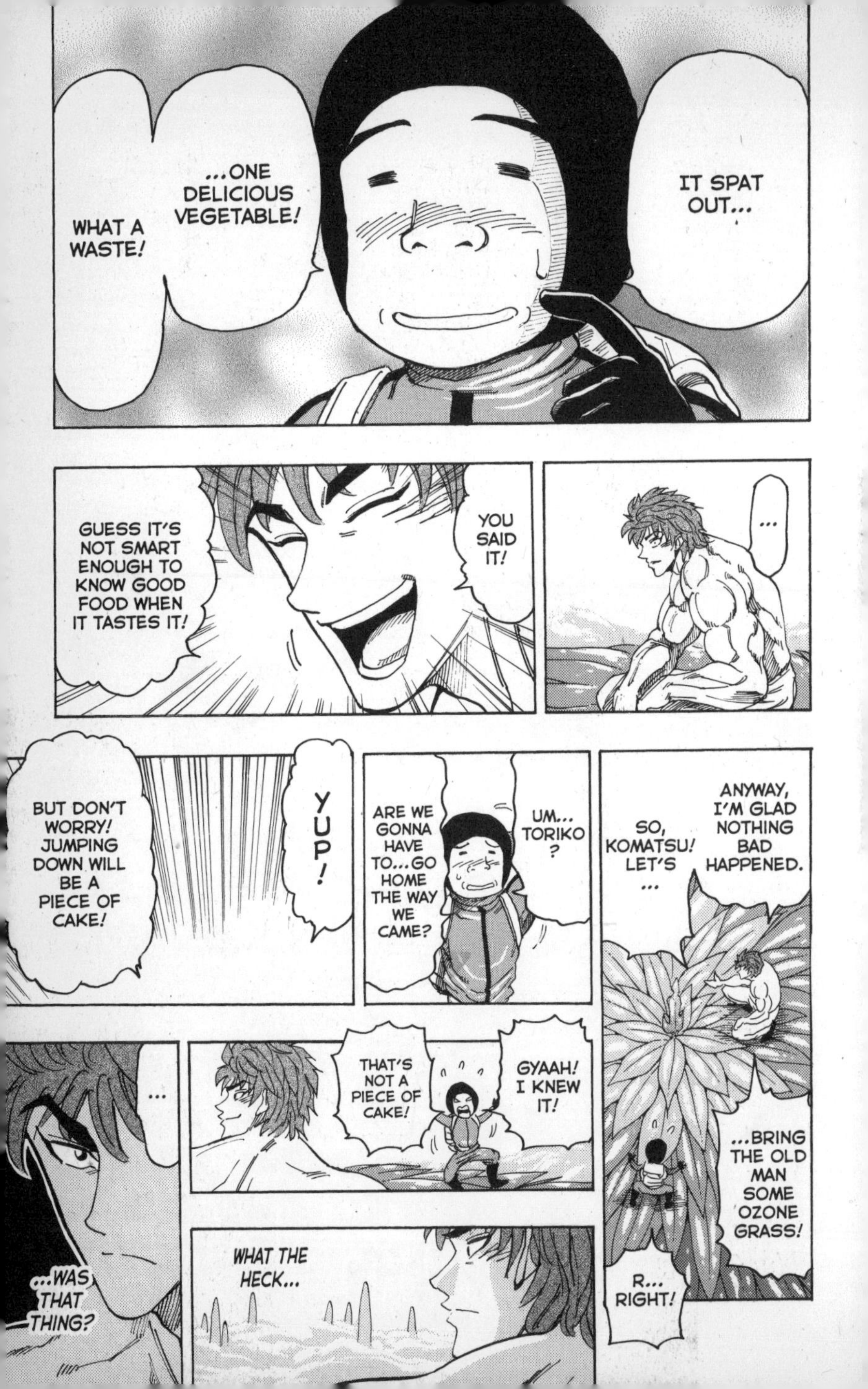
IT SPAT OUT...
...ONE DELICIOUS VEGETABLE!
WHAT A WASTE!
...
YOU SAID IT!
GUESS IT'S NOT SMART ENOUGH TO KNOW GOOD FOOD WHEN IT TASTES IT!
ANYWAY, I'M GLAD NOTHING BAD HAPPENED.
SO, KOMATSU! LET'S ...
...BRING THE OLD MAN SOME OZONE GRASS!
R... RIGHT!
UM... TORIKO?
ARE WE GONNA HAVE TO...GO HOME THE WAY WE CAME?
YUP!
BUT DON'T WORRY! JUMPING DOWN WILL BE A PIECE OF CAKE!
GYAAH! I KNEW IT!
THAT'S NOT A PIECE OF CAKE!
WHAT THE HECK...
...
...WAS THAT THING?

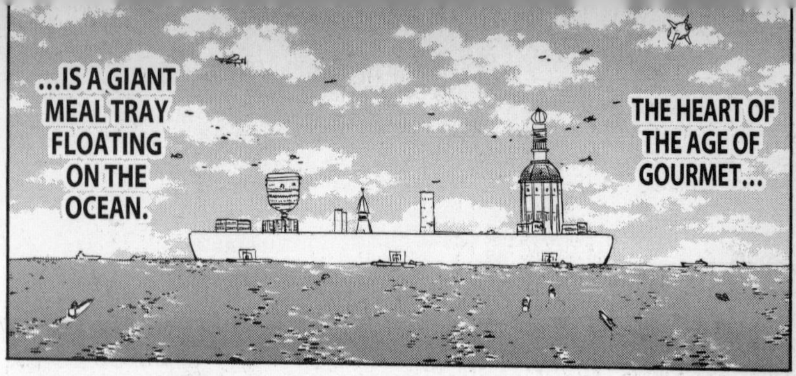
THE HEART OF THE AGE OF GOURMET...
...IS A GIANT MEAL TRAY FLOATING ON THE OCEAN.
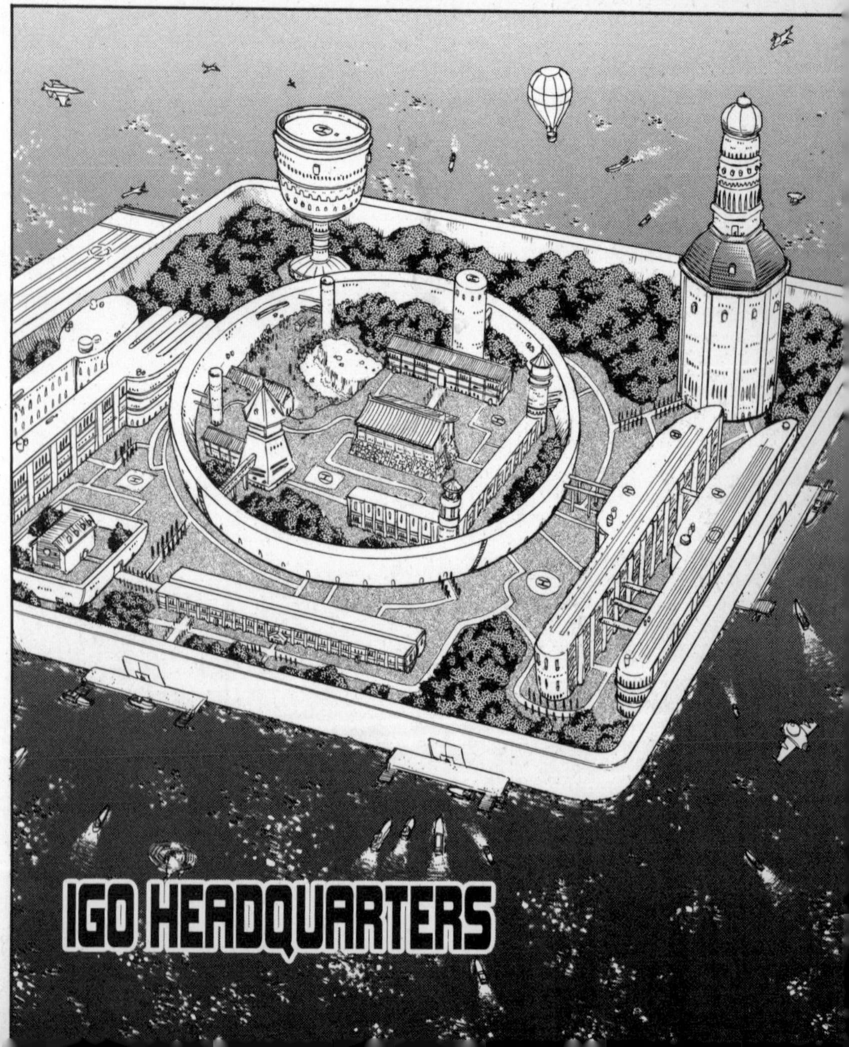
IGO HEADQUARTERS

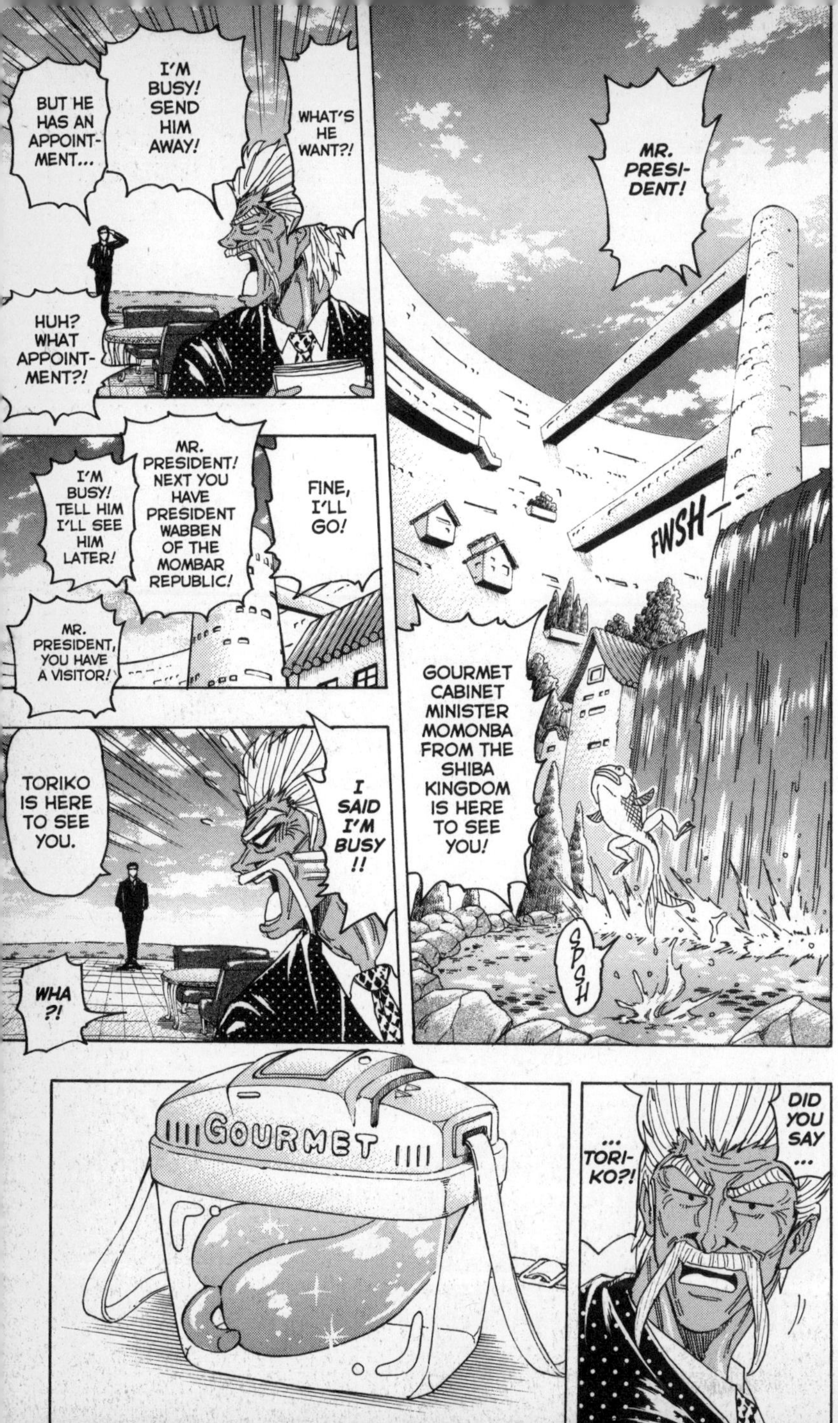
MR. PRESIDENT!
FWSH
GOURMET CABINET MINISTER MOMONBA FROM THE SHIBA KINGDOM IS HERE TO SEE YOU!
SPSH
WHAT'S HE WANT?!
I'M BUSY! SEND HIM AWAY!
BUT HE HAS AN APPOINTMENT...
HUH? WHAT APPOINTMENT?!
FINE, I'LL GO!
MR. PRESIDENT! NEXT YOU HAVE PRESIDENT WABBEN OF THE MOMBAR REPUBLIC!
I'M BUSY! TELL HIM I'LL SEE HIM LATER!
MR. PRESIDENT, YOU HAVE A VISITOR!
I SAID I'M BUSY!!
TORIKO IS HERE TO SEE YOU.
WHA?!
DID YOU SAY ...
... TORI-KO?!
GOURMET

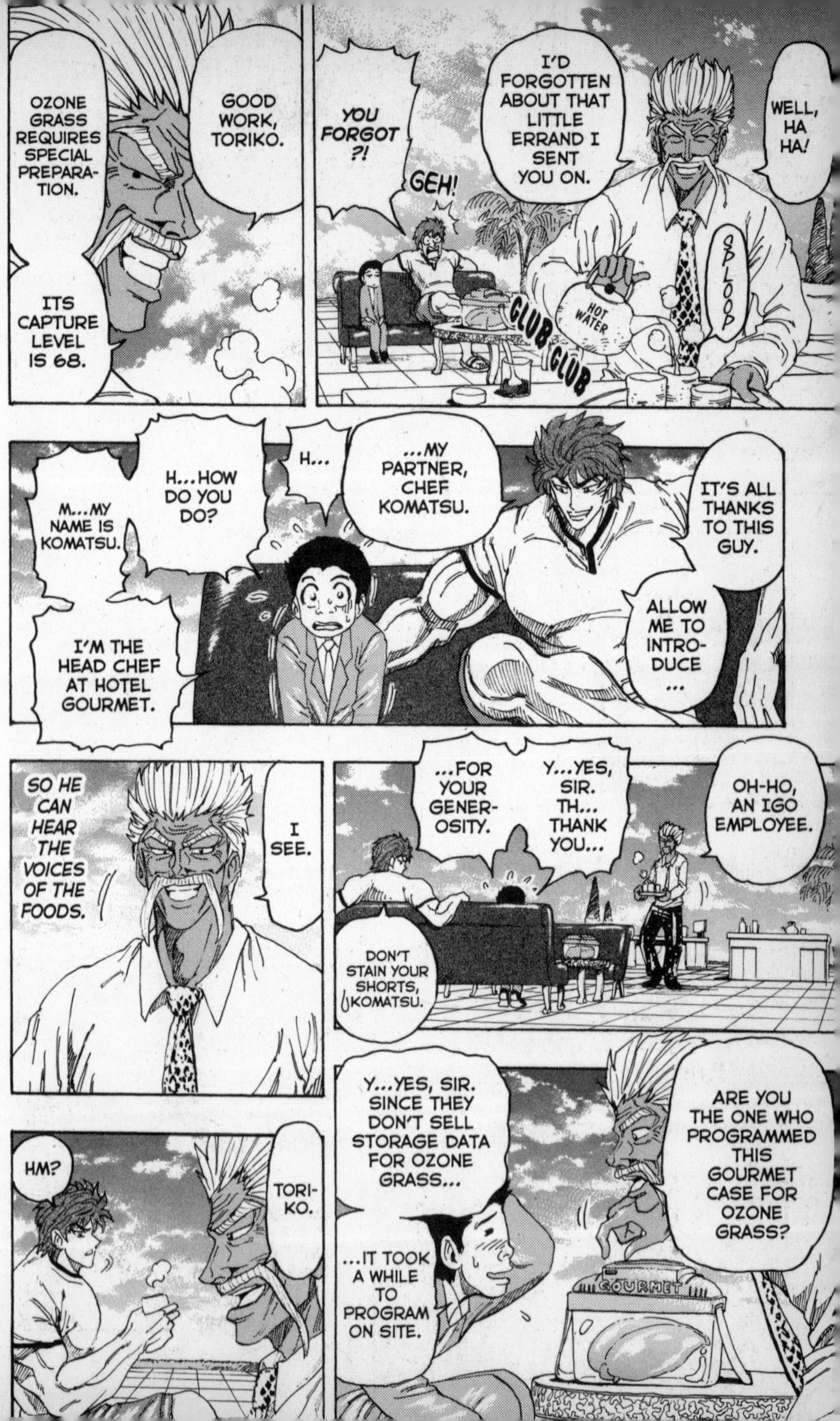
WELL, HA HA!
I'D FORGOTTEN ABOUT THAT LITTLE ERRAND I SENT YOU ON.
SPLOOP
HOT WATER
GEH!
YOU FORGOT ?!
GLUB GLUB GLUB
GOOD WORK, TORIKO.
OZONE GRASS REQUIRES SPECIAL PREPARATION.
ITS CAPTURE LEVEL IS 68.
IT'S ALL THANKS TO THIS GUY.
ALLOW ME TO INTRODUCE...
...MY PARTNER, CHEF KOMATSU.
H...
H...HOW DO YOU DO?
M...MY NAME IS KOMATSU.
I'M THE HEAD CHEF AT HOTEL GOURMET.
OH-HO, AN IGO EMPLOYEE.
Y...YES, SIR. TH... THANK YOU...
...FOR YOUR GENEROSITY.
DON'T STAIN YOUR SHORTS, KOMATSU.
I SEE.
SO HE CAN HEAR THE VOICES OF THE FOODS.
ARE YOU THE ONE WHO PROGRAMMED THIS GOURMET CASE FOR OZONE GRASS?
GOURMET
Y...YES, SIR. SINCE THEY DON'T SELL STORAGE DATA FOR OZONE GRASS...
...IT TOOK A WHILE TO PROGRAM ON SITE.
TORIKO.
HM?

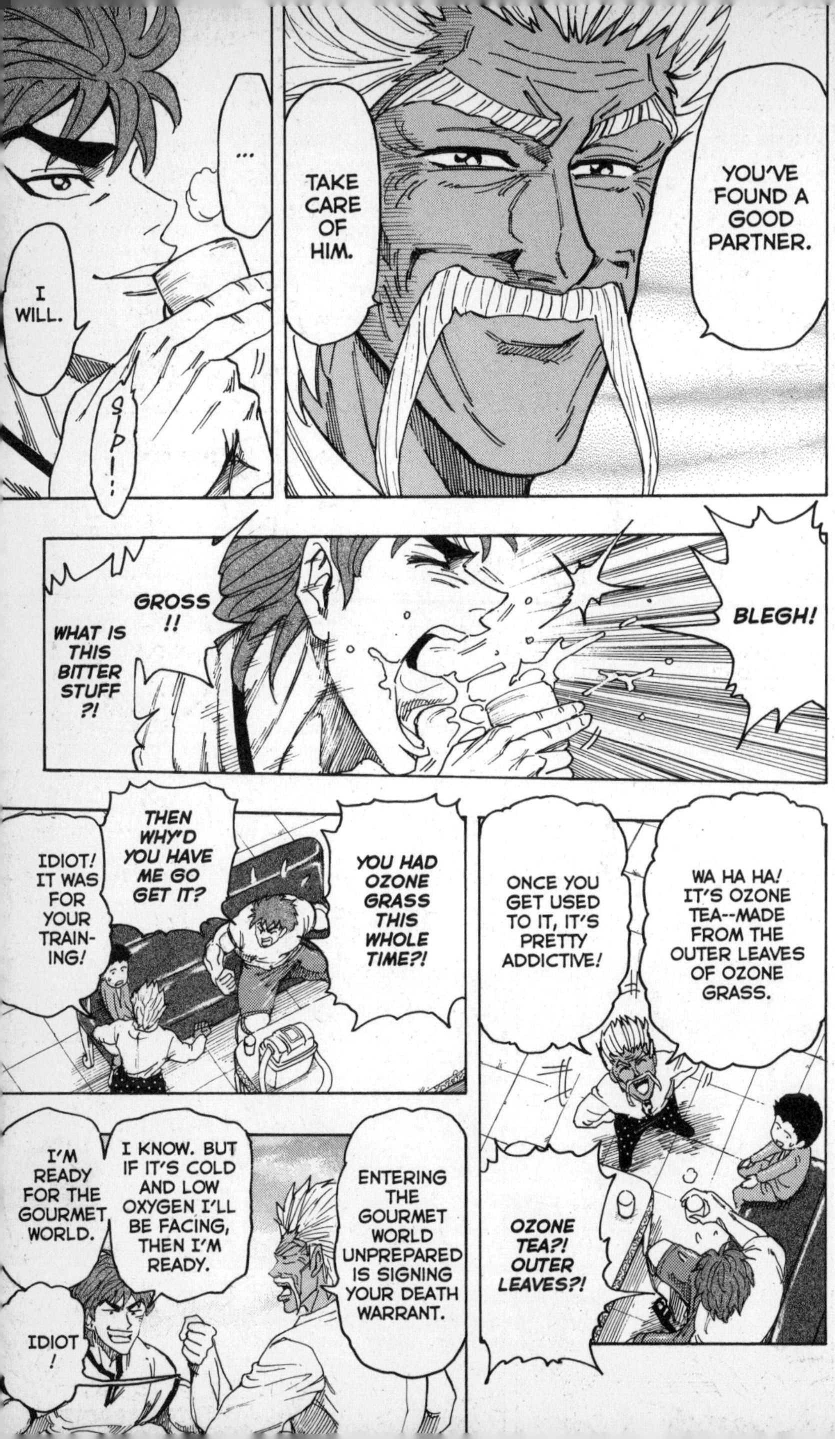
YOU'VE FOUND A GOOD PARTNER.
TAKE CARE OF HIM.
...
I WILL.
SIP!!
BLEGH!
GROSS!!
WHAT IS THIS BITTER STUFF?!
WA HA HA! IT'S OZONE TEA--MADE FROM THE OUTER LEAVES OF OZONE GRASS.
ONCE YOU GET USED TO IT, IT'S PRETTY ADDICTIVE!
OZONE TEA?! OUTER LEAVES?!
YOU HAD OZONE GRASS THIS WHOLE TIME?!
THEN WHY'D YOU HAVE ME GO GET IT?
IDIOT! IT WAS FOR YOUR TRAINING!
I'M READY FOR THE GOURMET WORLD.
ENTERING THE GOURMET WORLD UNPREPARED IS SIGNING YOUR DEATH WARRANT.
I KNOW. BUT IF IT'S COLD AND LOW OXYGEN I'LL BE FACING, THEN I'M READY.
IDIOT!

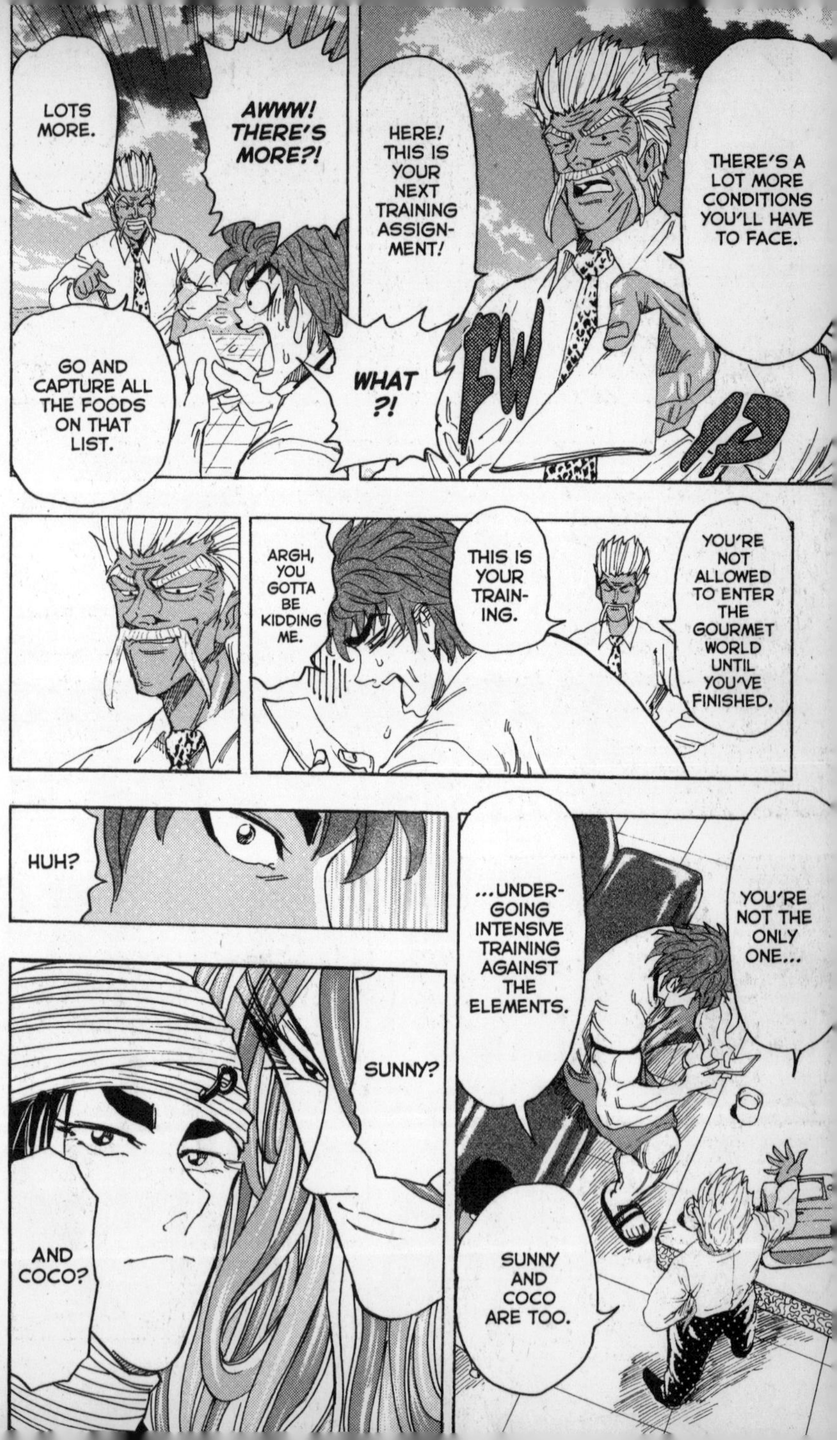
THERE'S A LOT MORE CONDITIONS YOU'LL HAVE TO FACE.
HERE! THIS IS YOUR NEXT TRAINING ASSIGNMENT!
FWIP
WHAT ?!
AWWW! THERE'S MORE?!
LOTS MORE.
GO AND CAPTURE ALL THE FOODS ON THAT LIST.
YOU'RE NOT ALLOWED TO ENTER THE GOURMET WORLD UNTIL YOU'VE FINISHED.
THIS IS YOUR TRAINING.
ARGH, YOU GOTTA BE KIDDING ME.
YOU'RE NOT THE ONLY ONE...
...UNDERGOING INTENSIVE TRAINING AGAINST THE ELEMENTS.
SUNNY AND COCO ARE TOO.
HUH?
SUNNY?
AND COCO?

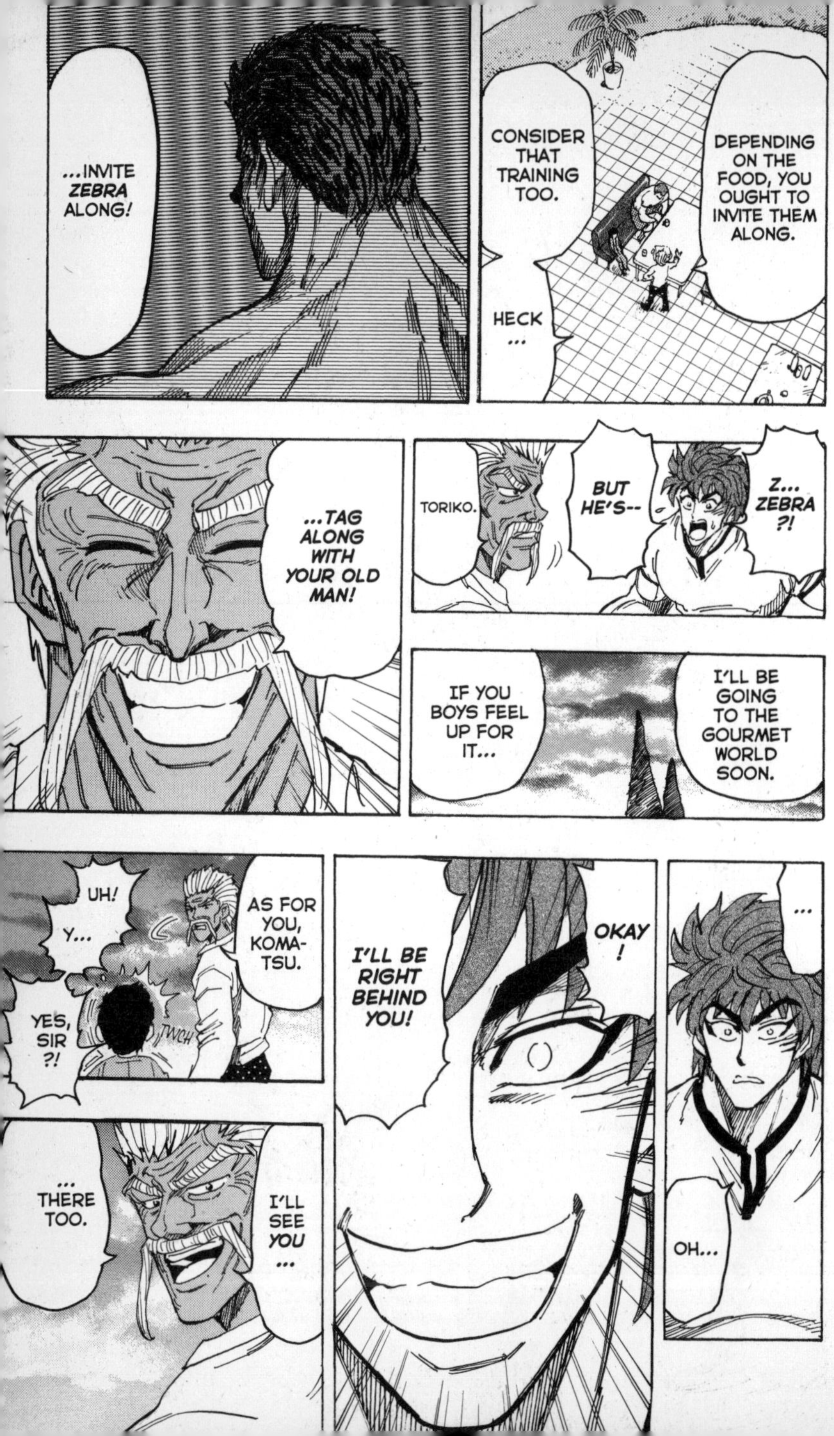
DEPENDING ON THE FOOD, YOU OUGHT TO INVITE THEM ALONG.
CONSIDER THAT TRAINING TOO.
HECK...
...INVITE ZEBRA ALONG!
Z... ZEBRA?!
BUT HE'S--
TORIKO.
I'LL BE GOING TO THE GOURMET WORLD SOON.
IF YOU BOYS FEEL UP FOR IT...
...TAG ALONG WITH YOUR OLD MAN!
...
OH...
OKAY!
I'LL BE RIGHT BEHIND YOU!
AS FOR YOU, KOMATSU.
UH!
Y...
YES, SIR?!
TWCH
I'LL SEE YOU...
...THERE TOO.

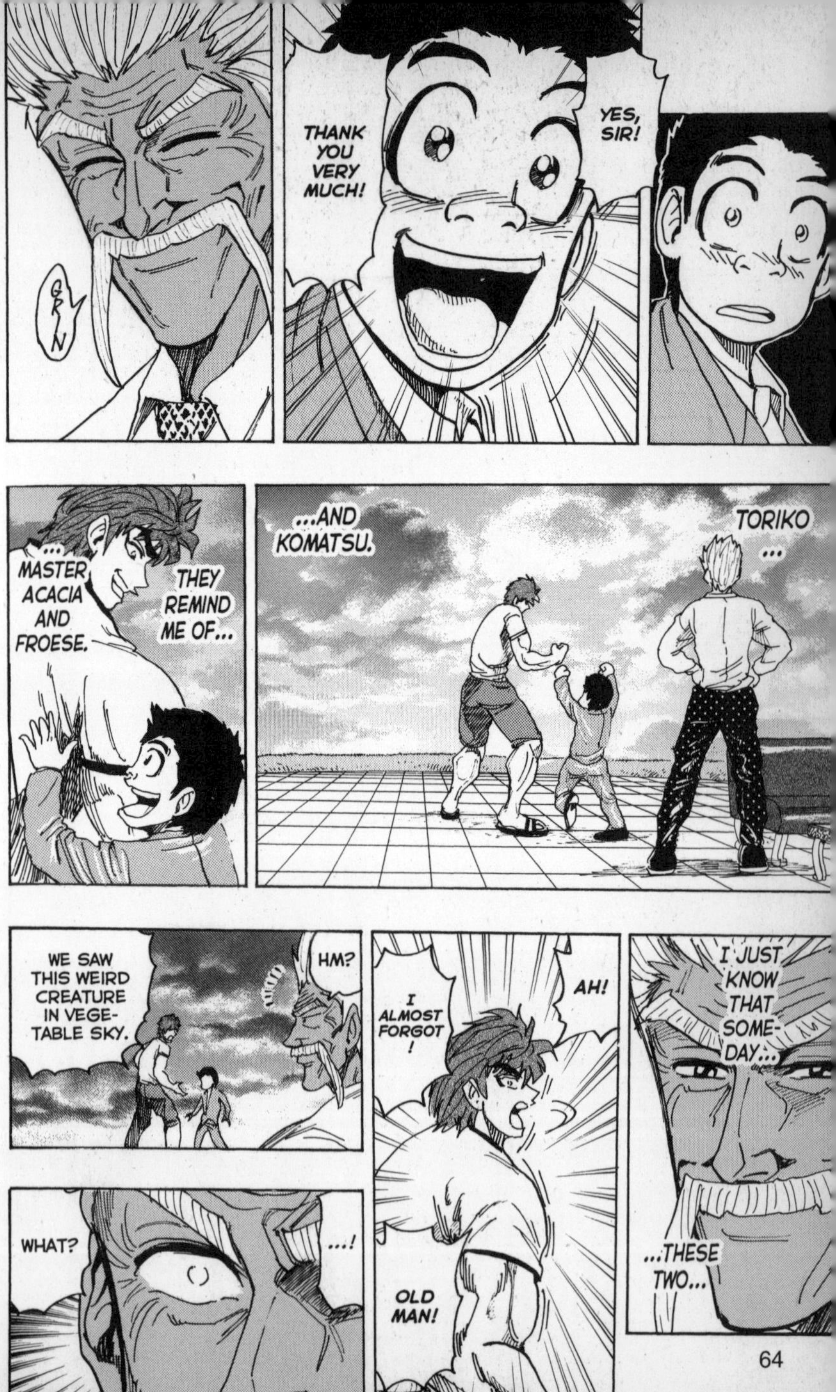
YES, SIR!
THANK YOU VERY MUCH!
GRIN
TORIKO...
...AND KOMATSU.
THEY REMIND ME OF...
...MASTER ACACIA AND FROESE.
I JUST KNOW THAT SOMEDAY...
...THESE TWO...
AH!
I ALMOST FORGOT!
OLD MAN!
HM?
WE SAW THIS WEIRD CREATURE IN VEGETABLE SKY.
...!
WHAT?

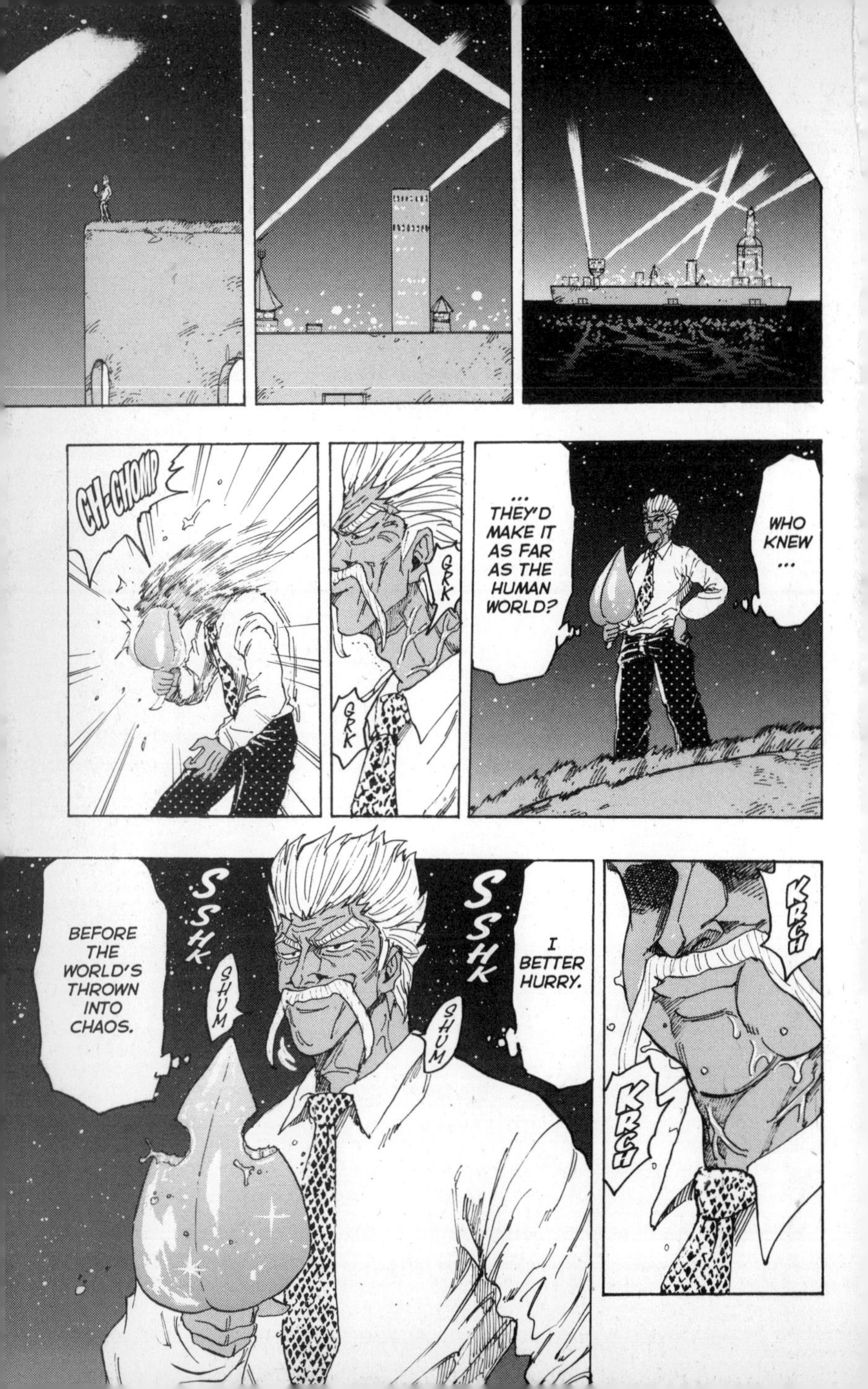
WHO KNEW ...
... THEY'D MAKE IT AS FAR AS THE HUMAN WORLD?
GRK
GRK
CH-CHOMP
KRCH
KRCH
SSHK
SHUM
I BETTER HURRY.
SSHK
SHUM
BEFORE THE WORLD'S THROWN INTO CHAOS.

GOURMET CHECKLIST

Vol. 123

SUSHI SALT

(SEASONING)

CAPTURE LEVEL: 7

HABITAT: MOUNTAIN SLOPES ABOVE 3,000 METERS

LENGTH: ---

HEIGHT: ---

WEIGHT: ---

PRICE: 1 KG / 20,000 YEN

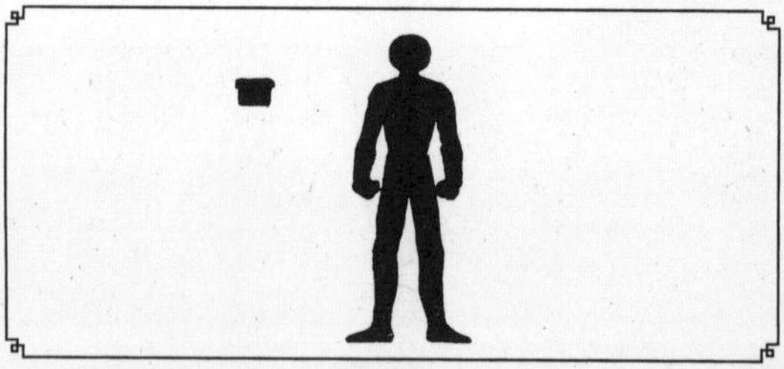

SCALE

DID THIS END UP IN KOMATSU'S RECIPE FOR CENTURY SOUP? SUSHI SALT IS TYPICALLY REFINED FROM ROCK SALTS FOUND ON MOUNTAIN SLOPES ABOVE 3,000 METERS. IT HAS A RELATIVELY LOW SODIUM CHLORIDE CONCENTRATION, SO THIS SALT TENDS TO COMPLEMENT THE FLAVOR OF WHATEVER IT'S COOKED WITH RATHER THAN OVERWHELM IT. THESE DAYS, MORE PEOPLE EAT THEIR SUSHI WITH SUSHI SALT THAN THE MORE TRADITIONAL SOY SAUCE.

GOURMET 110: TO THE GOURMET WORLD!!

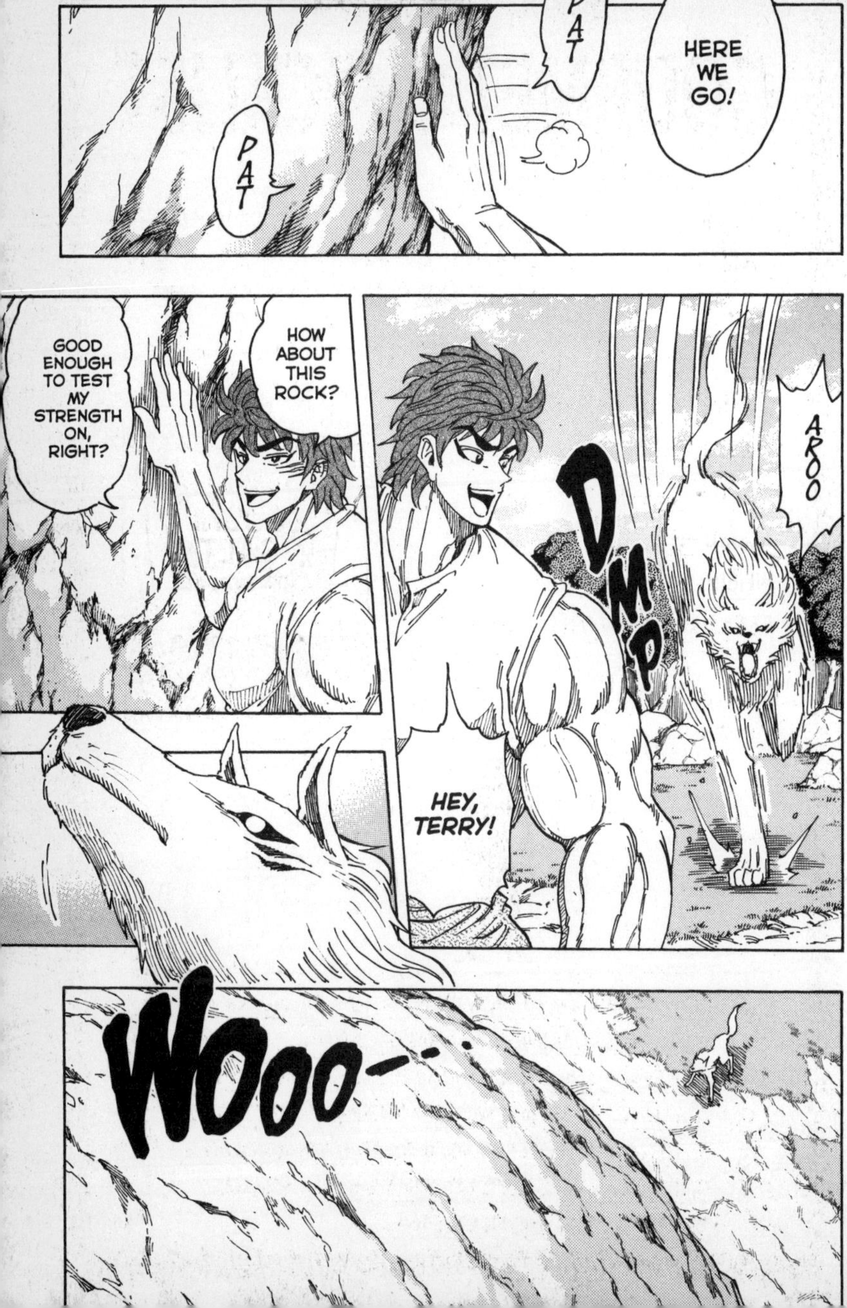
HERE WE GO!
PAT
PAT
AROO
DMP
HEY, TERRY!
HOW ABOUT THIS ROCK?
GOOD ENOUGH TO TEST MY STRENGTH ON, RIGHT?
WOOO-

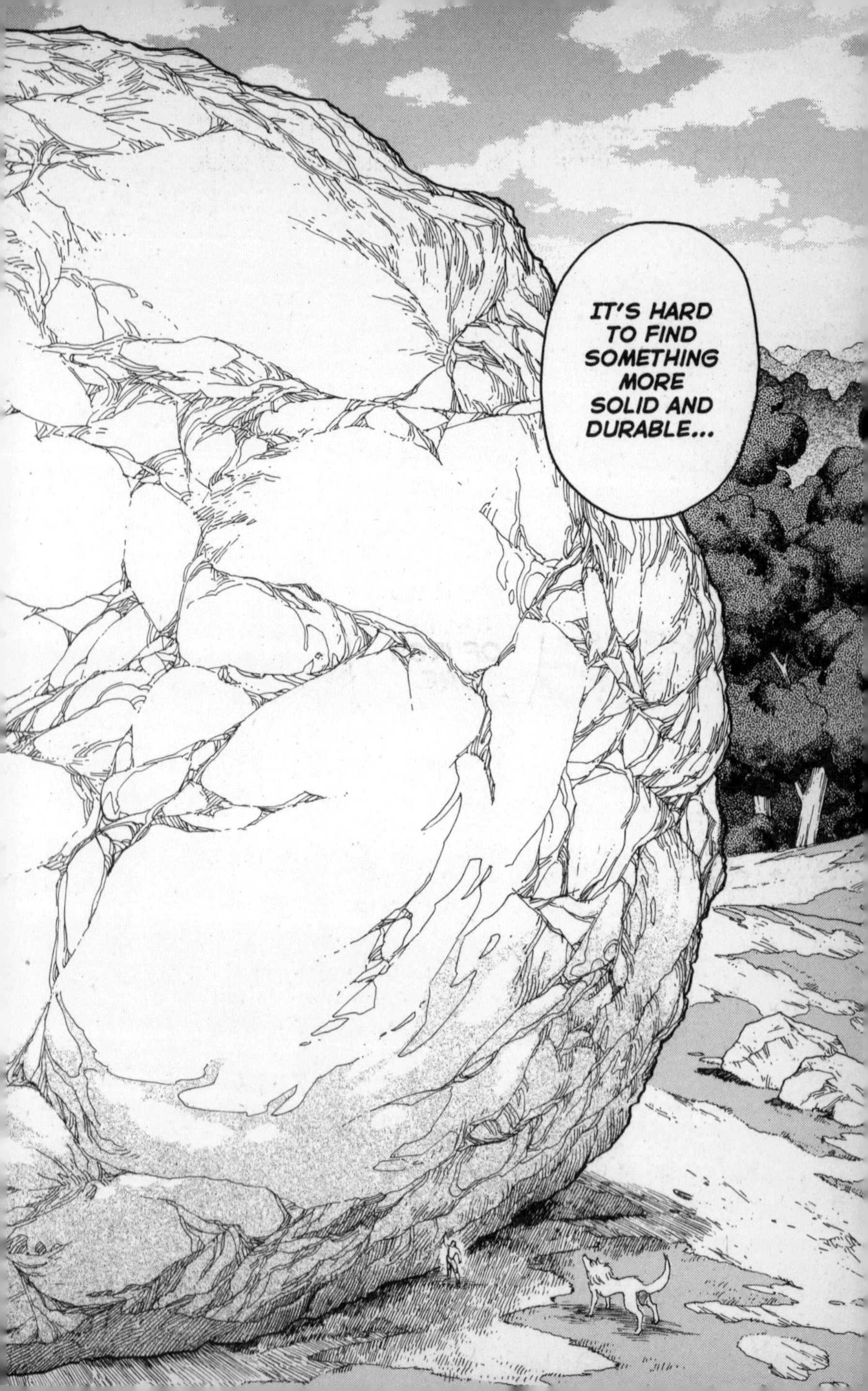
IT'S HARD TO FIND SOMETHING MORE SOLID AND DURABLE...

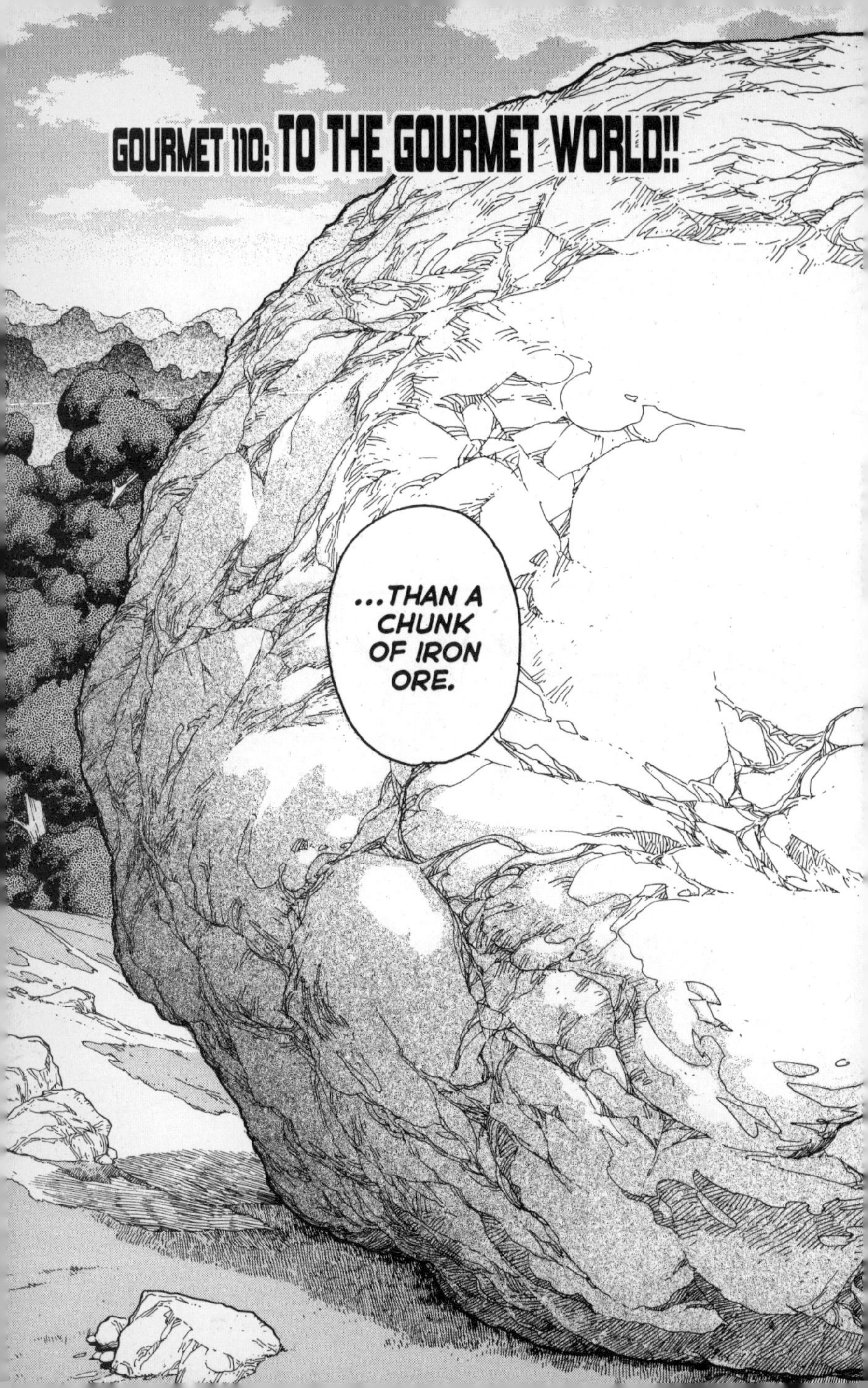
GOURMET 110: TO THE GOURMET WORLD!!
...THAN A CHUNK OF IRON ORE.

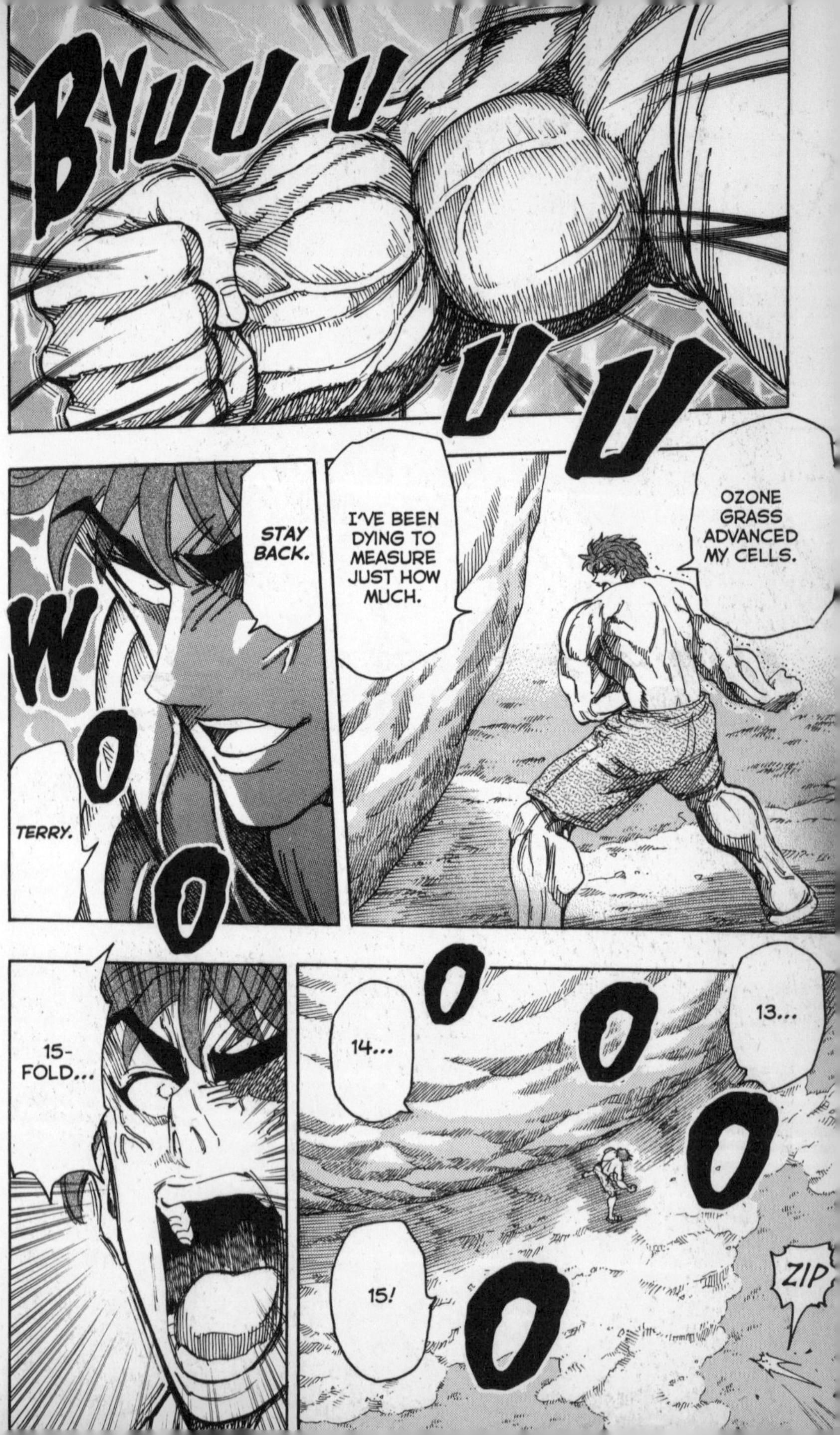
BYUUUUU
OZONE GRASS ADVANCED MY CELLS.
I'VE BEEN DYING TO MEASURE JUST HOW MUCH.
STAY BACK.
TERRY.
WOOO
13...
14...
OOOOOO
ZIP
15!
15-FOLD...

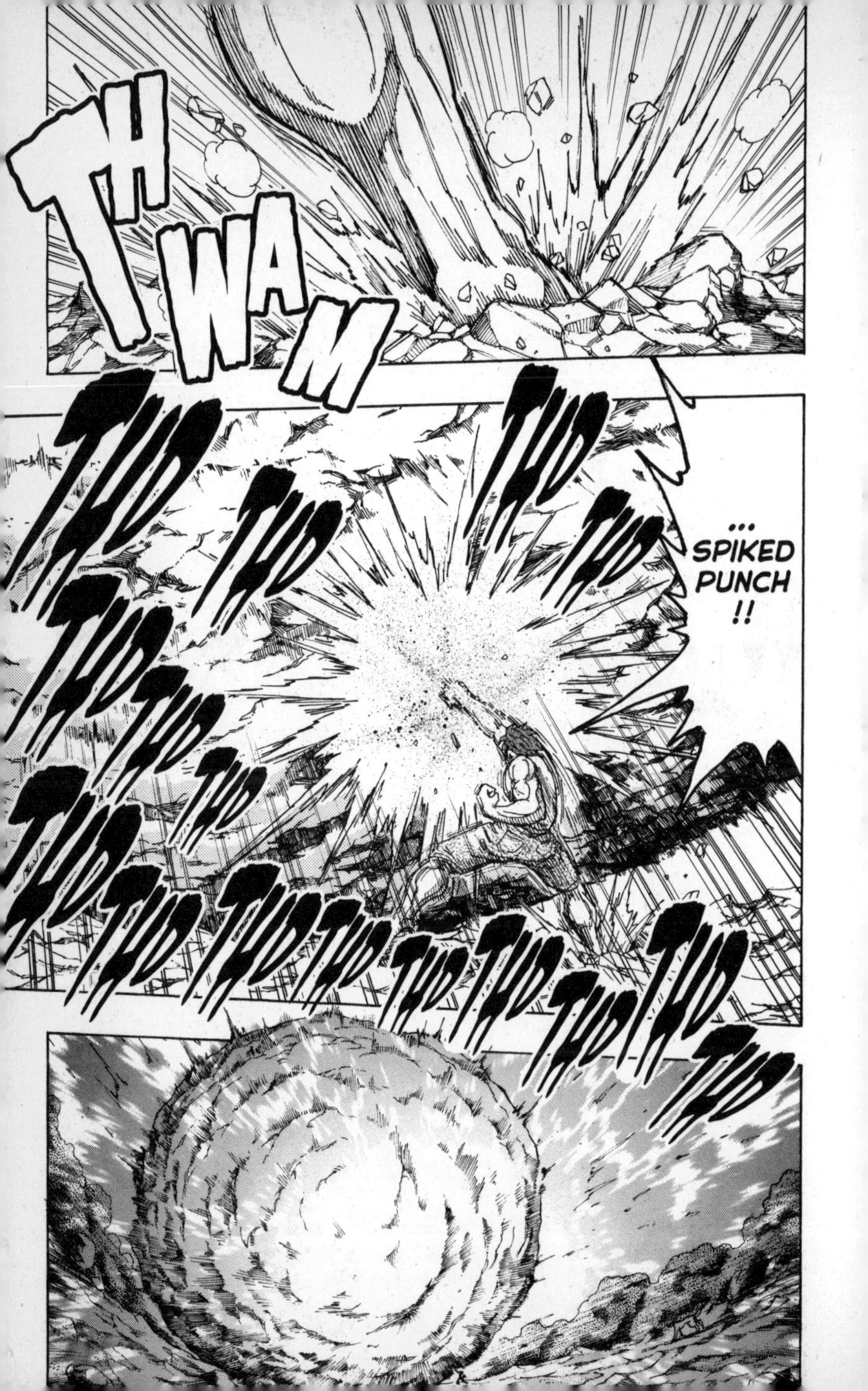
THWAM
... SPIKED PUNCH !!

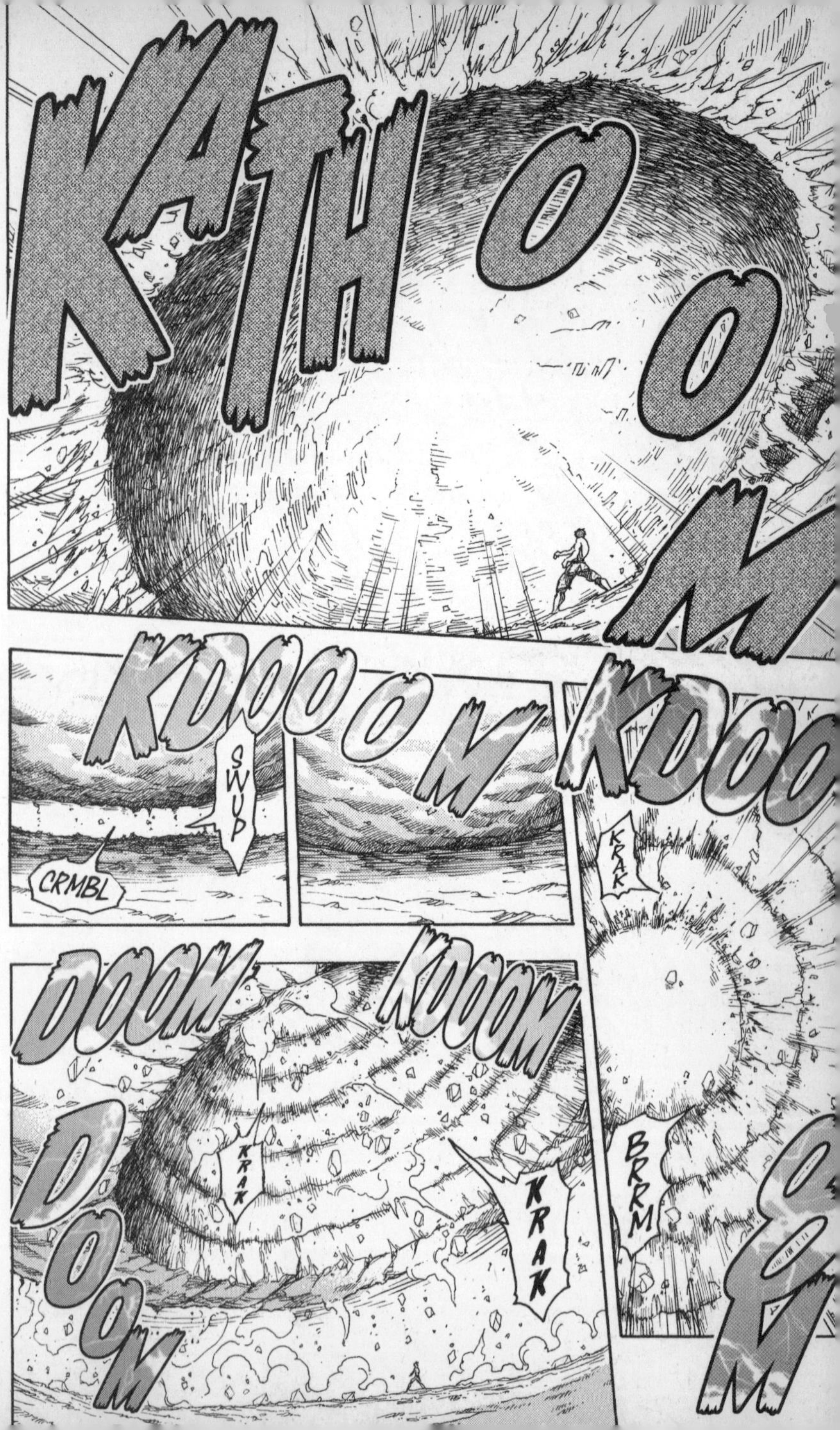
KATHOOOM
KDOOO
KRAK
BRRM
OOM
KDOOOOM
SWUP
CRMBL
KOOOM
DOOM
KRAK
KRAK
DOOOOM

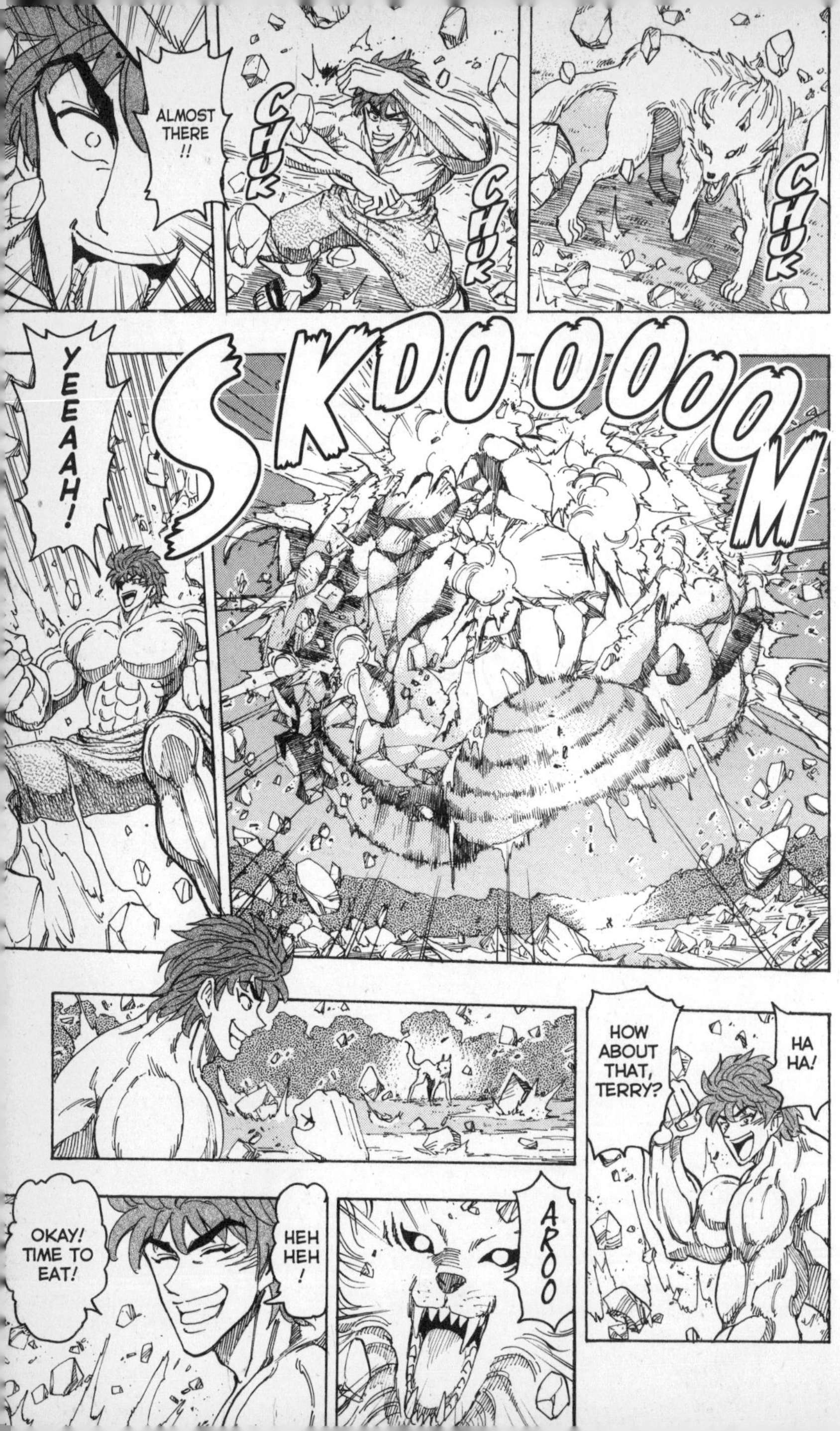
CHUK
CHUK
CHUK
ALMOST THERE!!
SKDOOOOOM
YEEAAAH!
HA HA!
HOW ABOUT THAT, TERRY?
AROO
HEH HEH!
OKAY! TIME TO EAT!

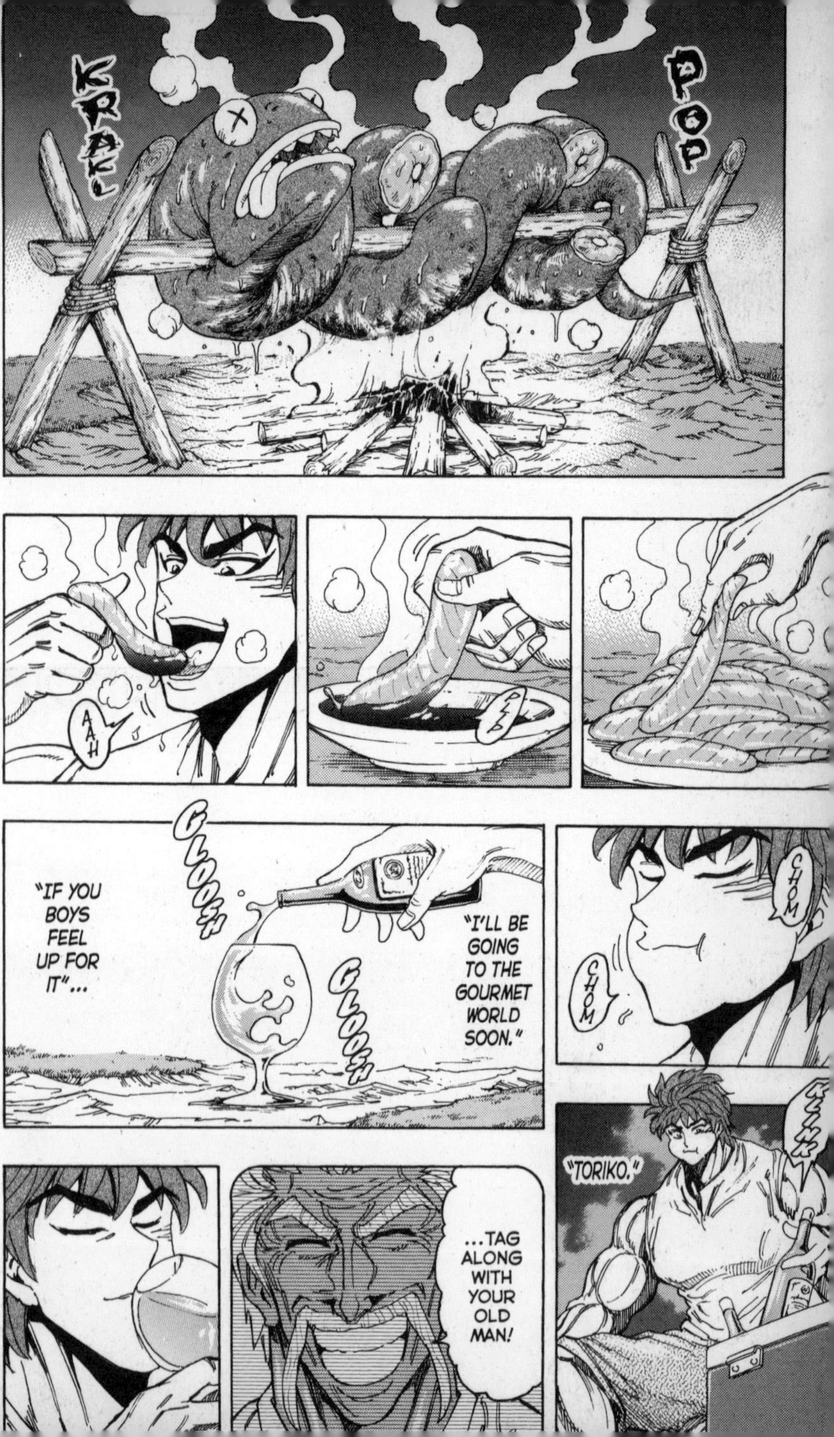
POP
KRAKL
PLIP
AAH
CHOM
CHOM
GLOOSH
"I'LL BE GOING TO THE GOURMET WORLD SOON."
GLOOSH
"IF YOU BOYS FEEL UP FOR IT"...
KLINK
"TORIKO."
...TAG ALONG WITH YOUR OLD MAN!

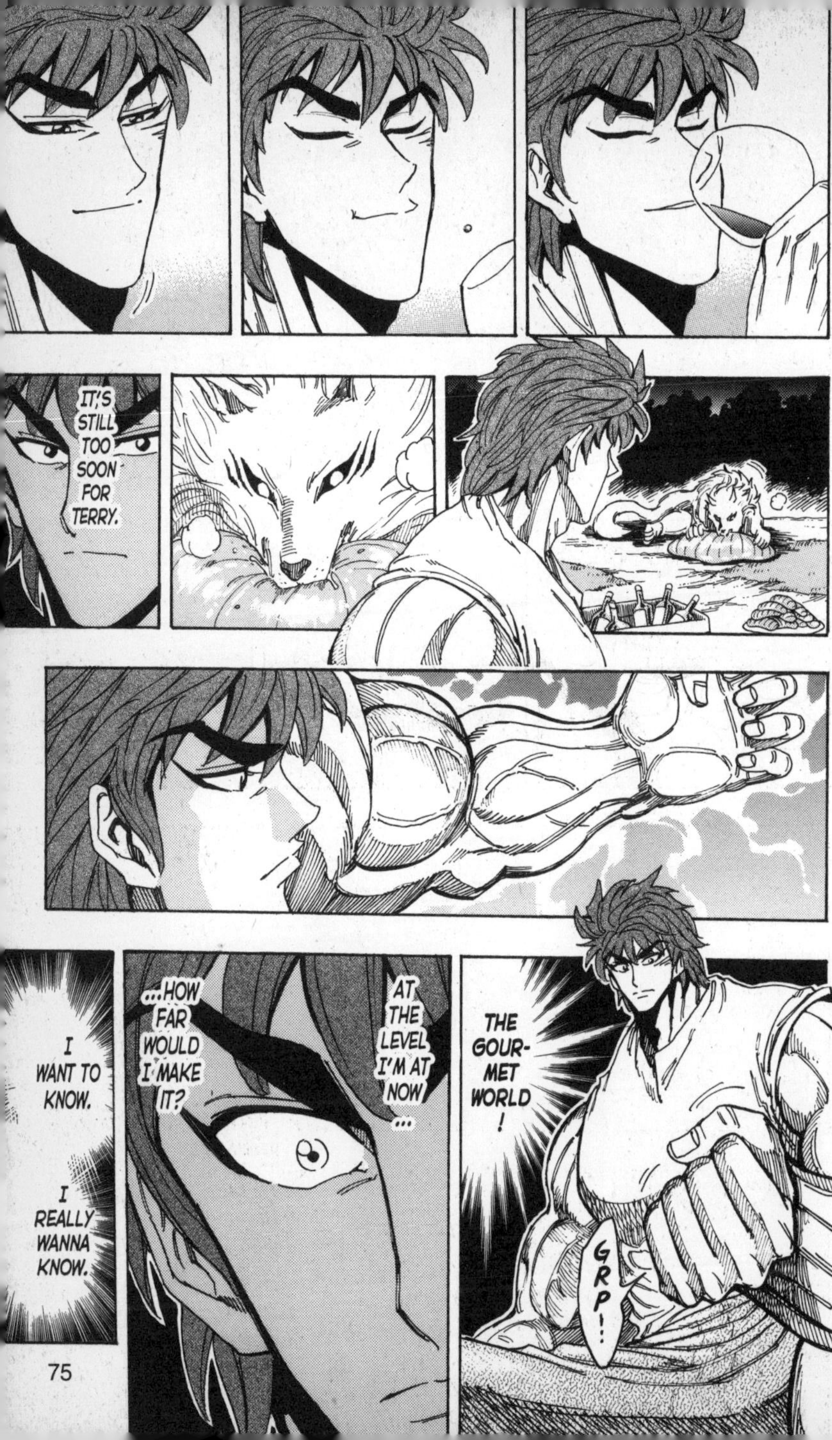
IT'S STILL TOO SOON FOR TERRY.
THE GOURMET WORLD!
GRP!!
AT THE LEVEL I'M AT NOW...
...HOW FAR WOULD I MAKE IT?
I WANT TO KNOW.
I REALLY WANNA KNOW.

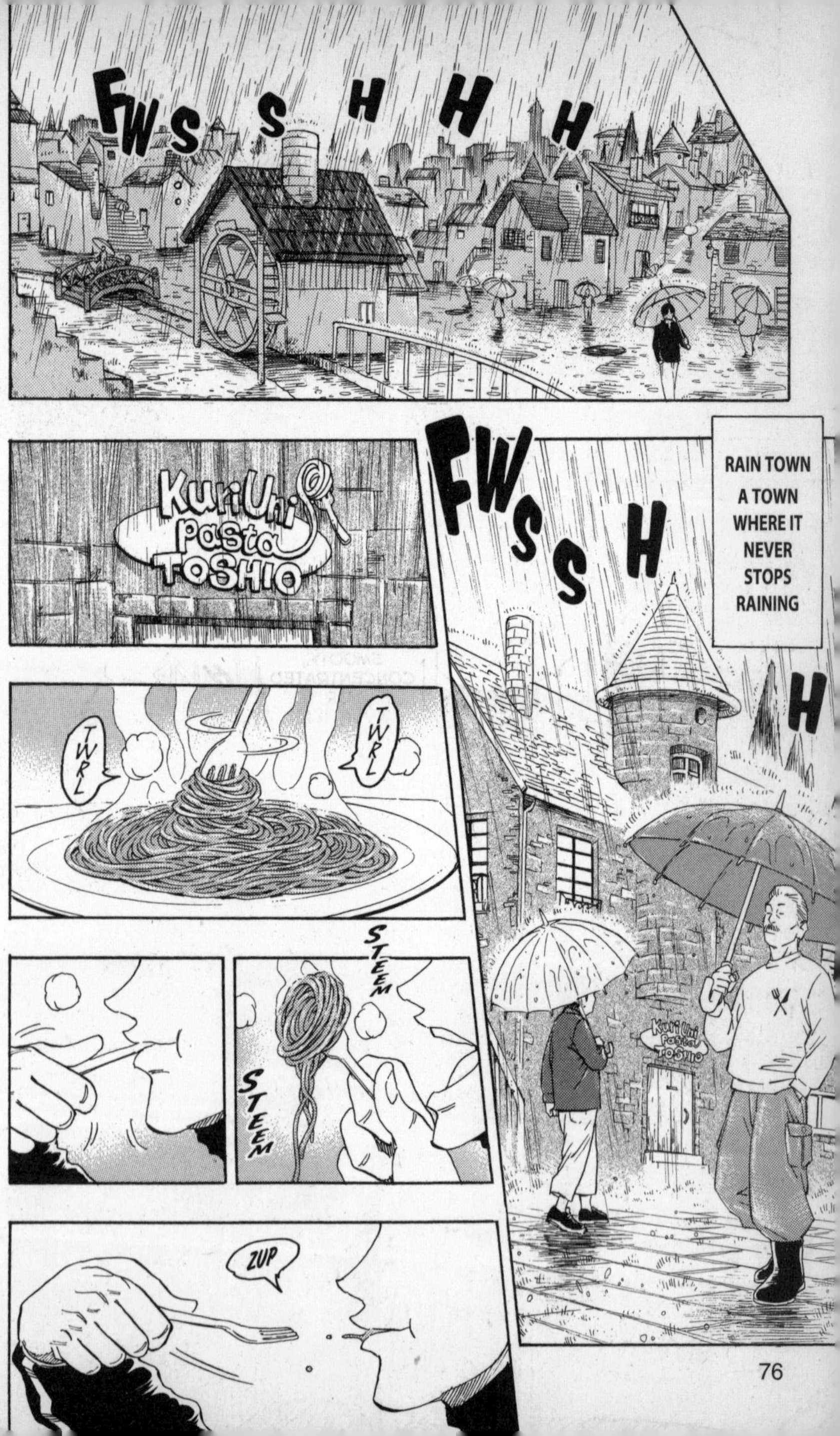
FWSSHHHH
FWSSHH
RAIN TOWN
A TOWN WHERE IT NEVER STOPS RAINING
KuriUni pasta TOSHIO
TWRL
TWRL
STEEM
STEEM
ZUP

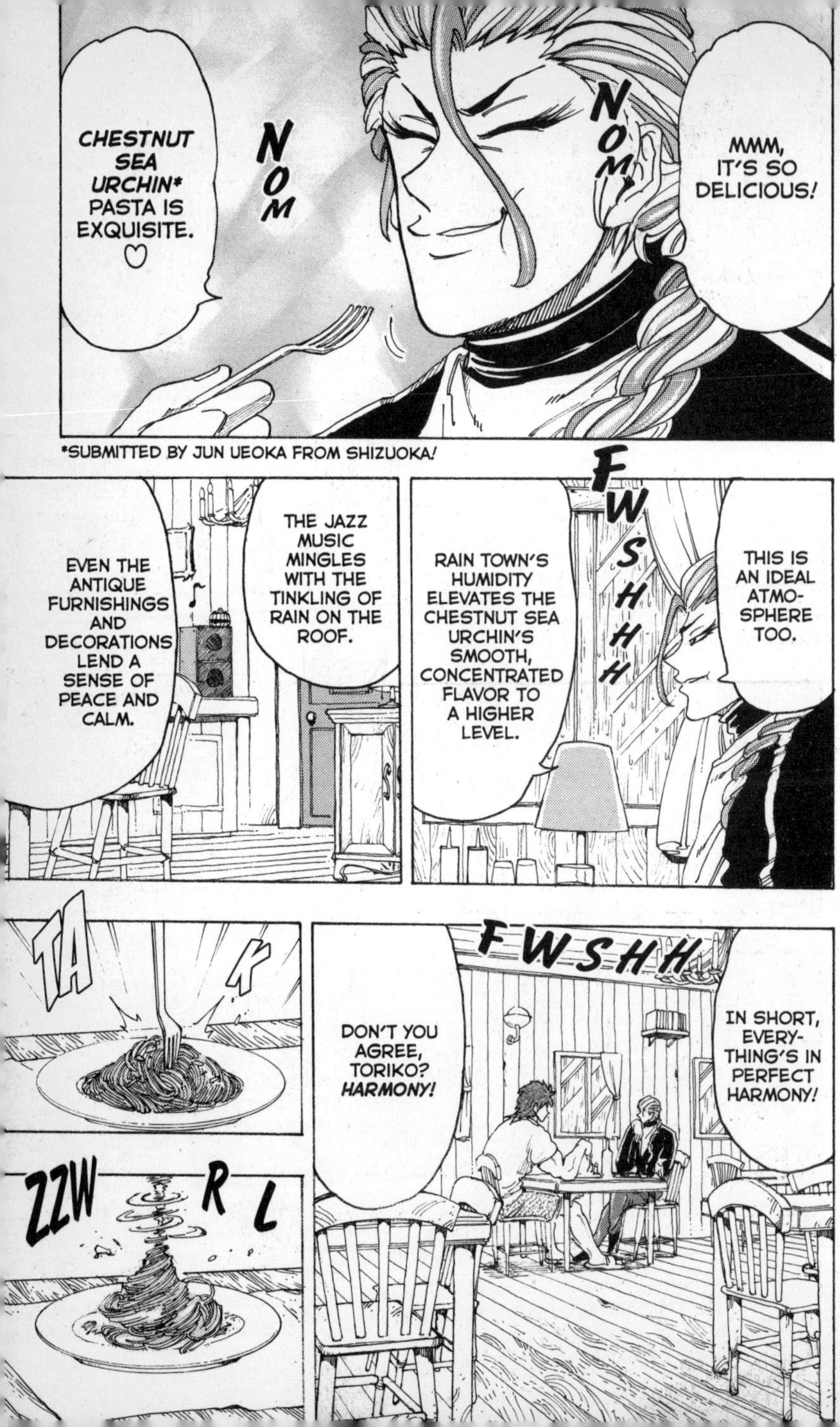
MMM, IT'S SO DELICIOUS!
NOM
NOM
CHESTNUT SEA URCHIN* PASTA IS EXQUISITE. ♡
THIS IS AN IDEAL ATMO-SPHERE TOO.
FWSHHH
RAIN TOWN'S HUMIDITY ELEVATES THE CHESTNUT SEA URCHIN'S SMOOTH, CONCENTRATED FLAVOR TO A HIGHER LEVEL.
THE JAZZ MUSIC MINGLES WITH THE TINKLING OF RAIN ON THE ROOF.
EVEN THE ANTIQUE FURNISHINGS AND DECORATIONS LEND A SENSE OF PEACE AND CALM.
FWSHH
IN SHORT, EVERY-THING'S IN PERFECT HARMONY!
DON'T YOU AGREE, TORIKO? *HARMONY!*
TAK
ZZWRL

*SUBMITTED BY JUN UEOKA FROM SHIZUOKA!

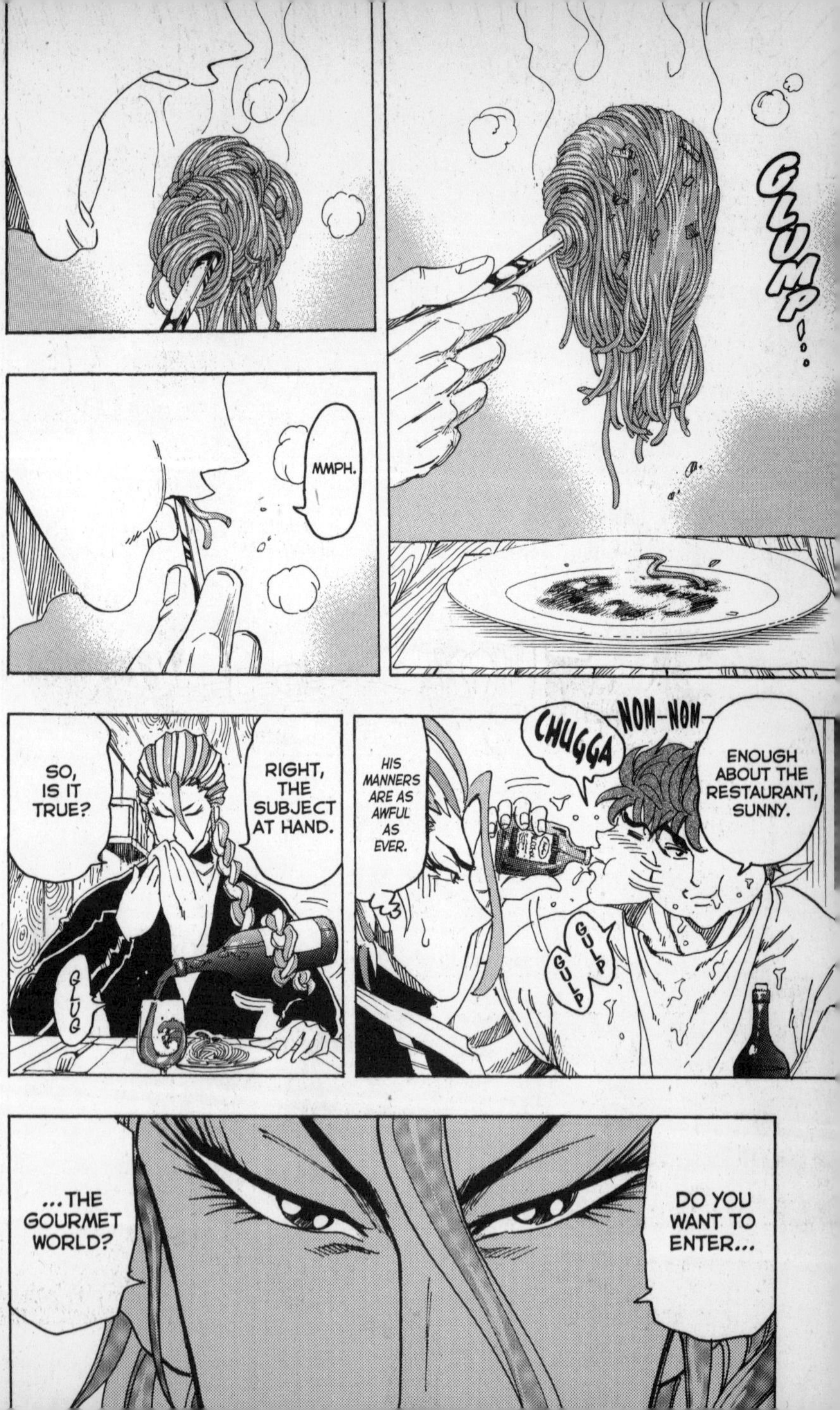
GLUMP!..
MMPH.
ENOUGH ABOUT THE RESTAURANT, SUNNY.
NOM-NOM
CHUGGA
HIS MANNERS ARE AS AWFUL AS EVER.
GULP GULP
RIGHT, THE SUBJECT AT HAND.
SO, IS IT TRUE?
GLUG
DO YOU WANT TO ENTER...
...THE GOURMET WORLD?

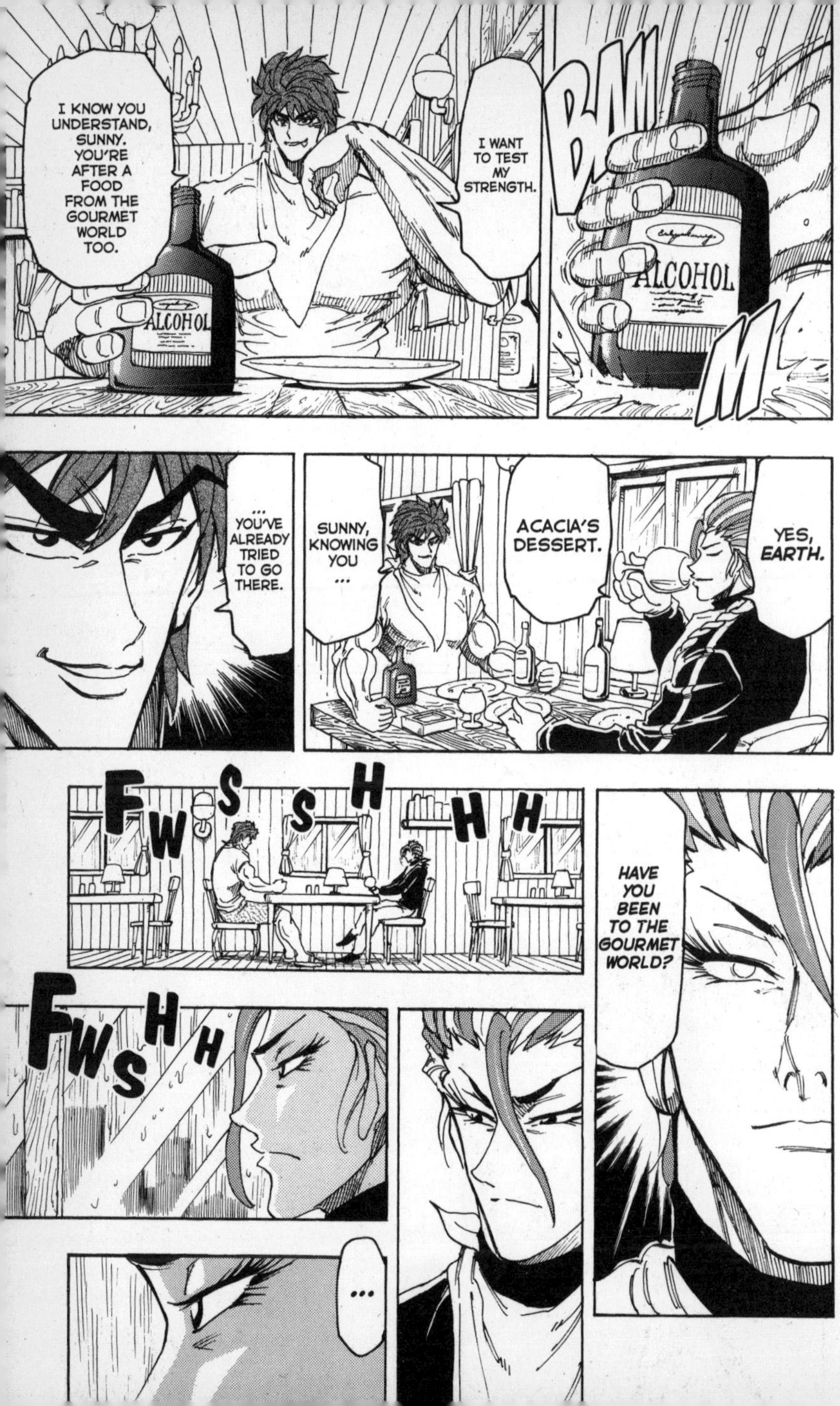
BAMM
I WANT TO TEST MY STRENGTH.
I KNOW YOU UNDERSTAND, SUNNY. YOU'RE AFTER A FOOD FROM THE GOURMET WORLD TOO.
YES, EARTH.
ACACIA'S DESSERT.
SUNNY, KNOWING YOU ...
... YOU'VE ALREADY TRIED TO GO THERE.
HAVE YOU BEEN TO THE GOURMET WORLD?
FWSSHHH
FWSHH
...

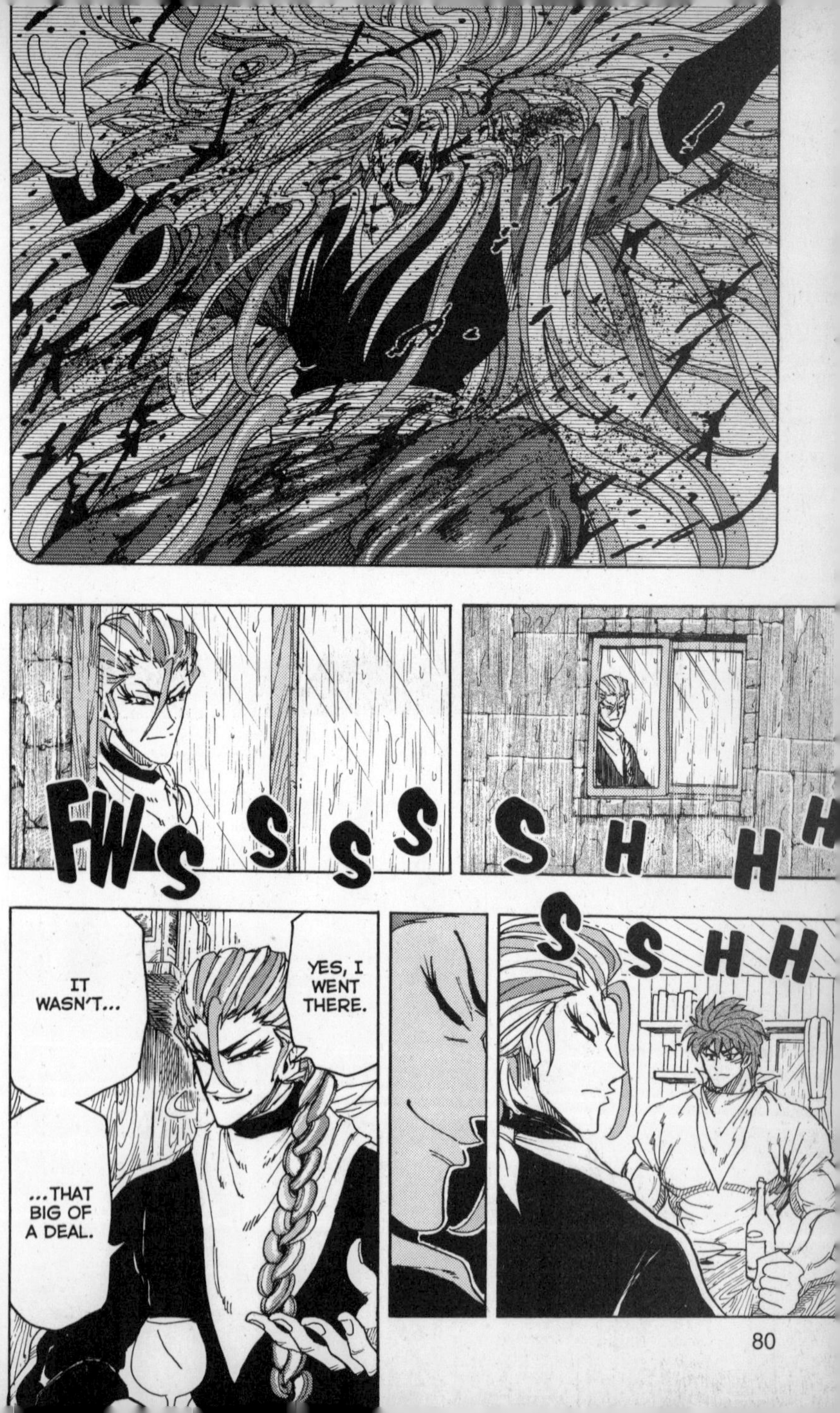
FWSSSSSSHHH
SSSHHH
YES, I WENT THERE.
IT WASN'T...
...THAT BIG OF A DEAL.

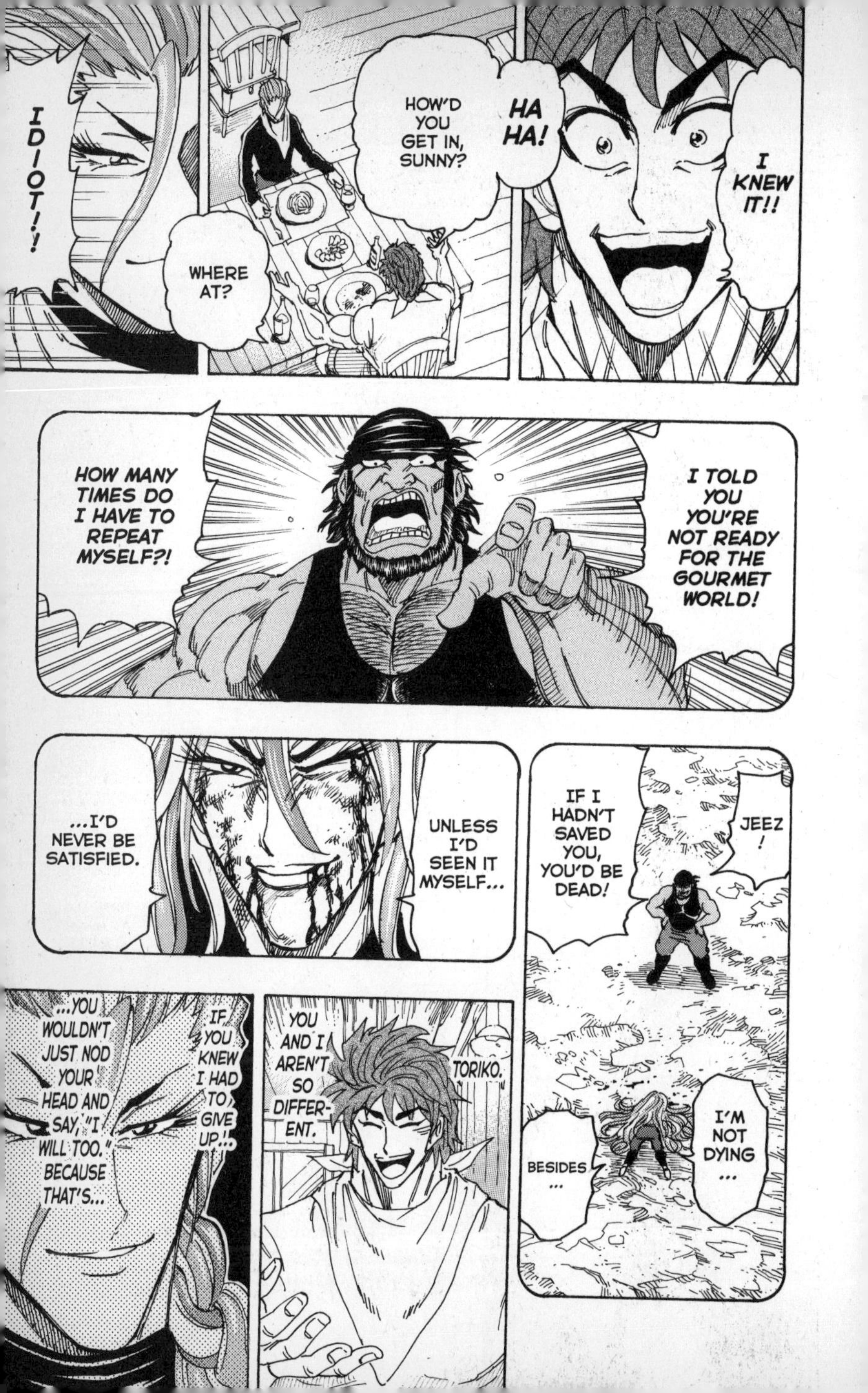
I KNEW IT!!
HA HA!
HOW'D YOU GET IN, SUNNY?
WHERE AT?
IDIOT!!
I TOLD YOU YOU'RE NOT READY FOR THE GOURMET WORLD!
HOW MANY TIMES DO I HAVE TO REPEAT MYSELF?!
JEEZ!
IF I HADN'T SAVED YOU, YOU'D BE DEAD!
I'M NOT DYING...
BESIDES...
UNLESS I'D SEEN IT MYSELF...
...I'D NEVER BE SATISFIED.
TORIKO.
YOU AND I AREN'T SO DIFFER-ENT.
IF YOU KNEW I HAD TO GIVE UP...
...YOU WOULDN'T JUST NOD YOUR HEAD AND SAY, "I WILL TOO." BECAUSE THAT'S...

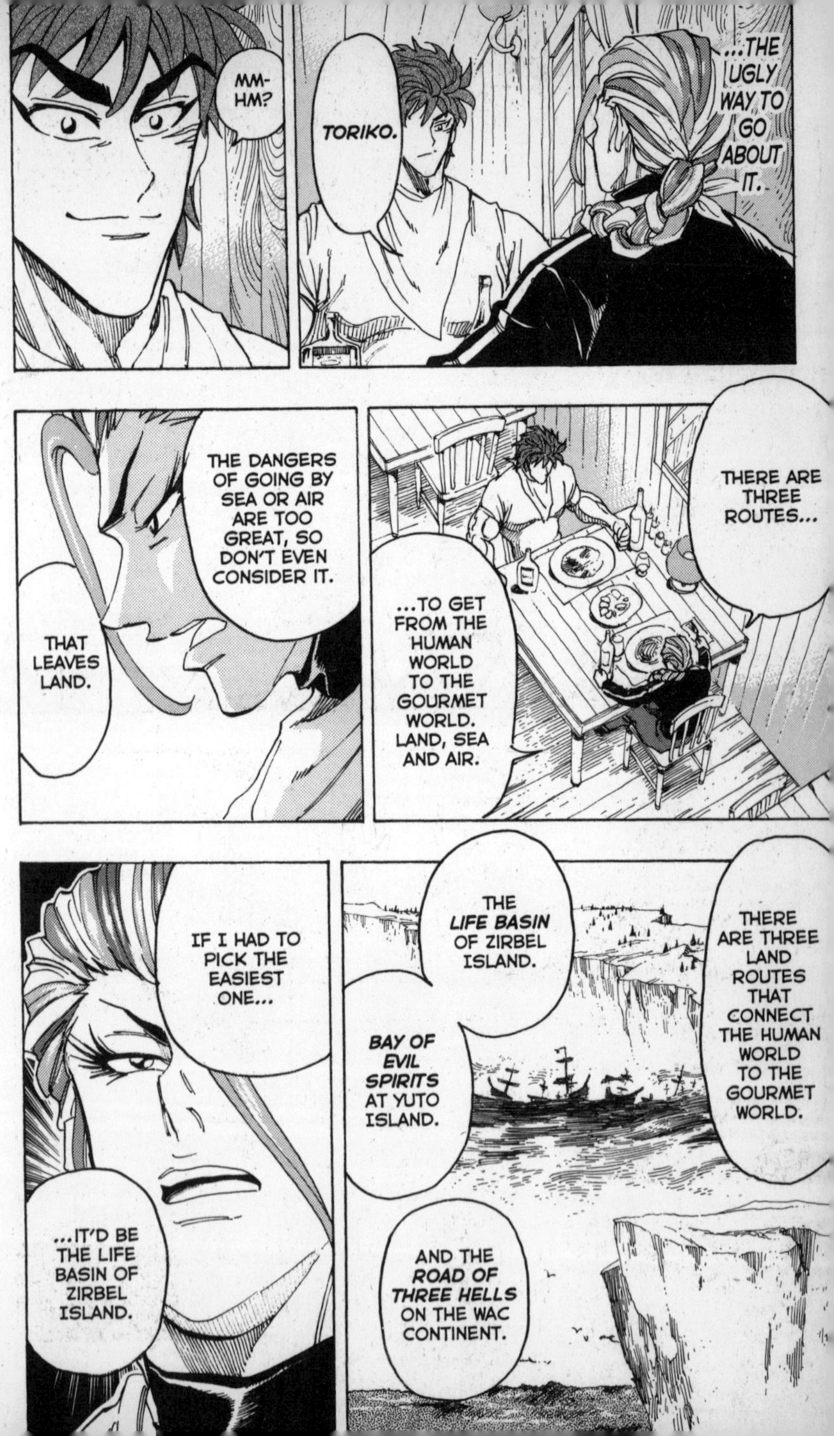
...THE UGLY WAY TO GO ABOUT IT.
TORIKO.
MM-HM?
THERE ARE THREE ROUTES...
...TO GET FROM THE HUMAN WORLD TO THE GOURMET WORLD. LAND, SEA AND AIR.
THE DANGERS OF GOING BY SEA OR AIR ARE TOO GREAT, SO DON'T EVEN CONSIDER IT.
THAT LEAVES LAND.
THERE ARE THREE LAND ROUTES THAT CONNECT THE HUMAN WORLD TO THE GOURMET WORLD.
THE LIFE BASIN OF ZIRBEL ISLAND.
BAY OF EVIL SPIRITS AT YUTO ISLAND.
AND THE ROAD OF THREE HELLS ON THE WAC CONTINENT.
IF I HAD TO PICK THE EASIEST ONE...
...IT'D BE THE LIFE BASIN OF ZIRBEL ISLAND.

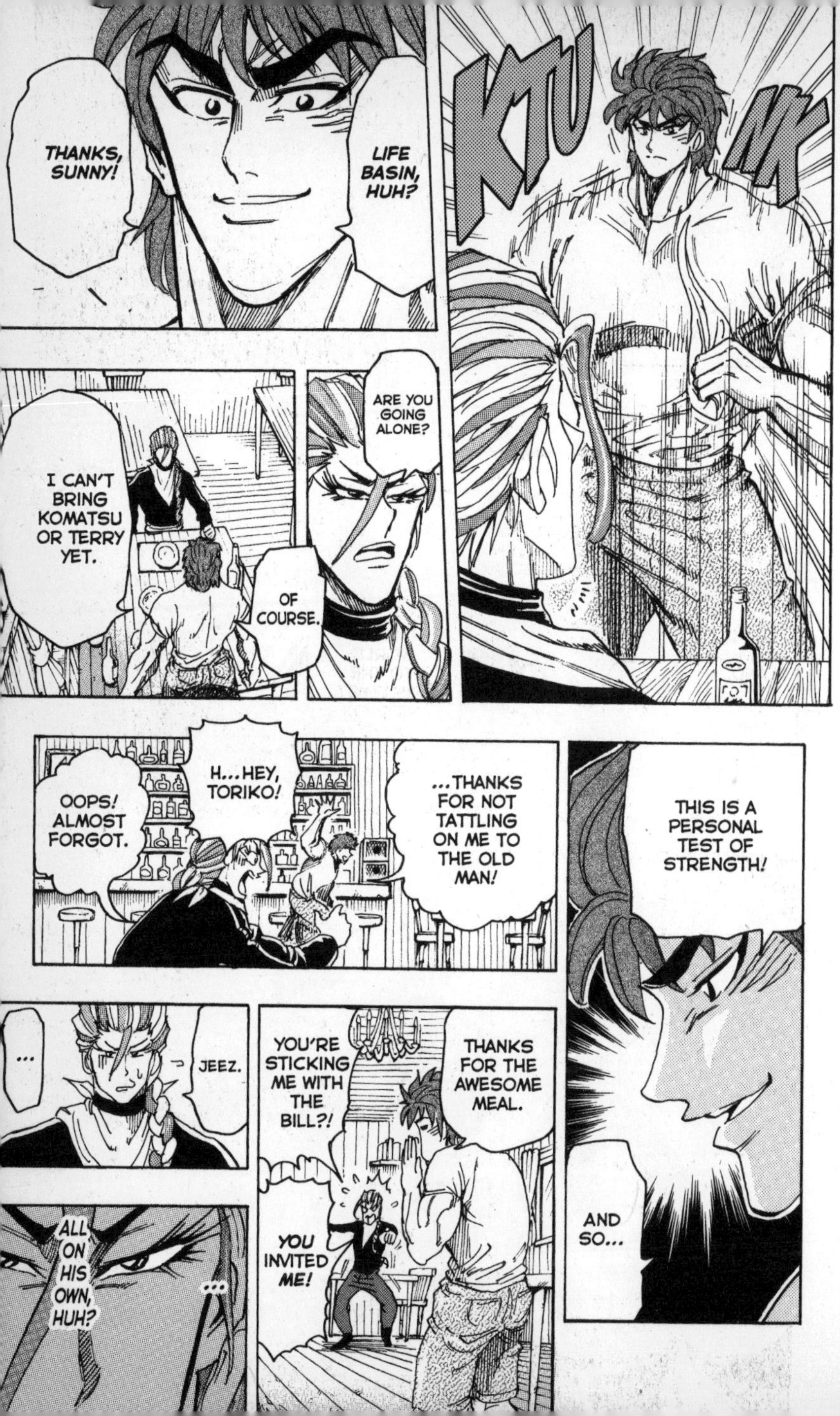
KTUNK
LIFE BASIN, HUH?
THANKS, SUNNY!
ARE YOU GOING ALONE?
OF COURSE.
I CAN'T BRING KOMATSU OR TERRY YET.
THIS IS A PERSONAL TEST OF STRENGTH!
AND SO...
...THANKS FOR NOT TATTLING ON ME TO THE OLD MAN!
H...HEY, TORIKO!
OOPS! ALMOST FORGOT.
THANKS FOR THE AWESOME MEAL.
YOU'RE STICKING ME WITH THE BILL?!
YOU INVITED ME!
JEEZ.
...
...
ALL ON HIS OWN, HUH?

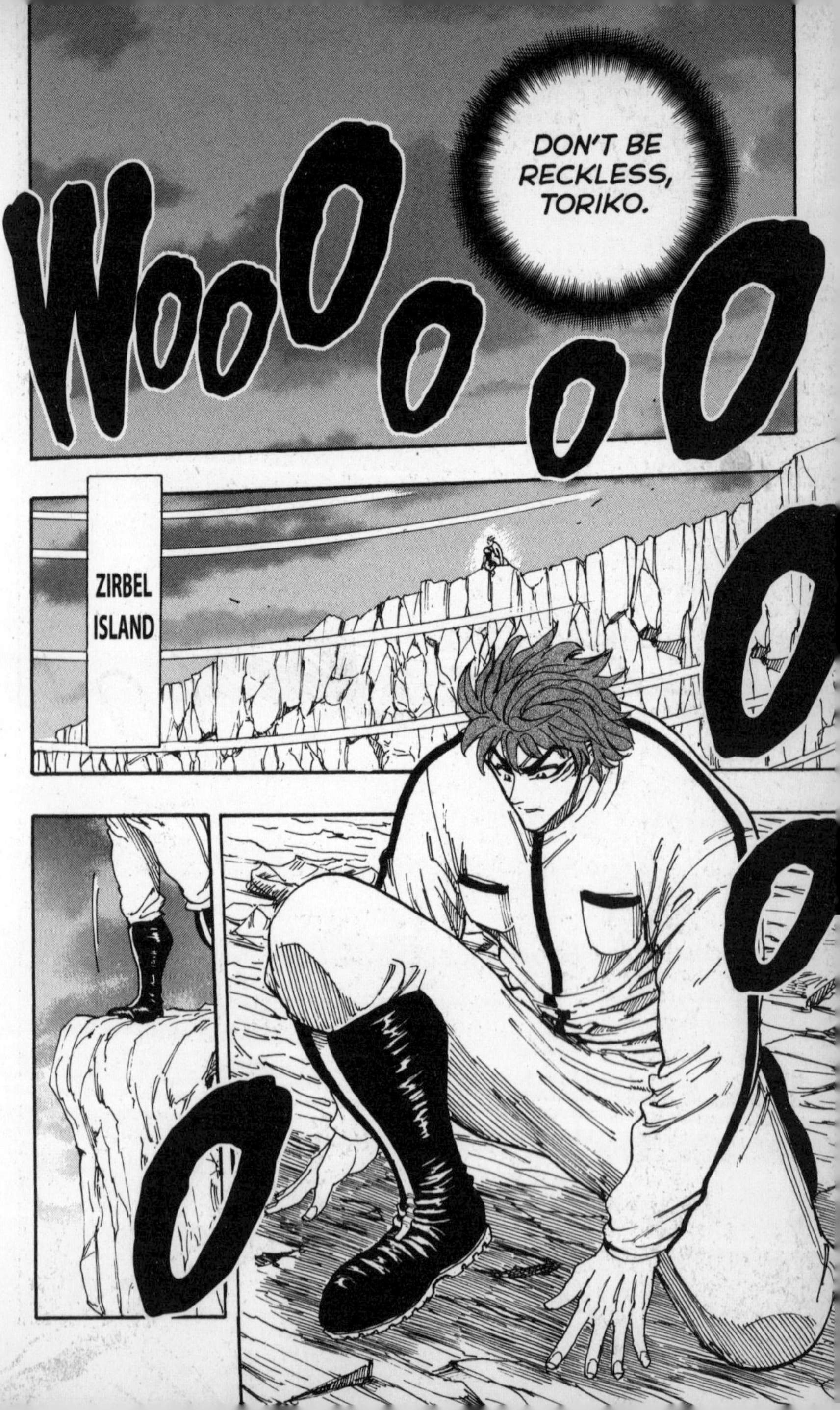
DON'T BE RECKLESS, TORIKO.
WOOOOOOOOOO
ZIRBEL ISLAND

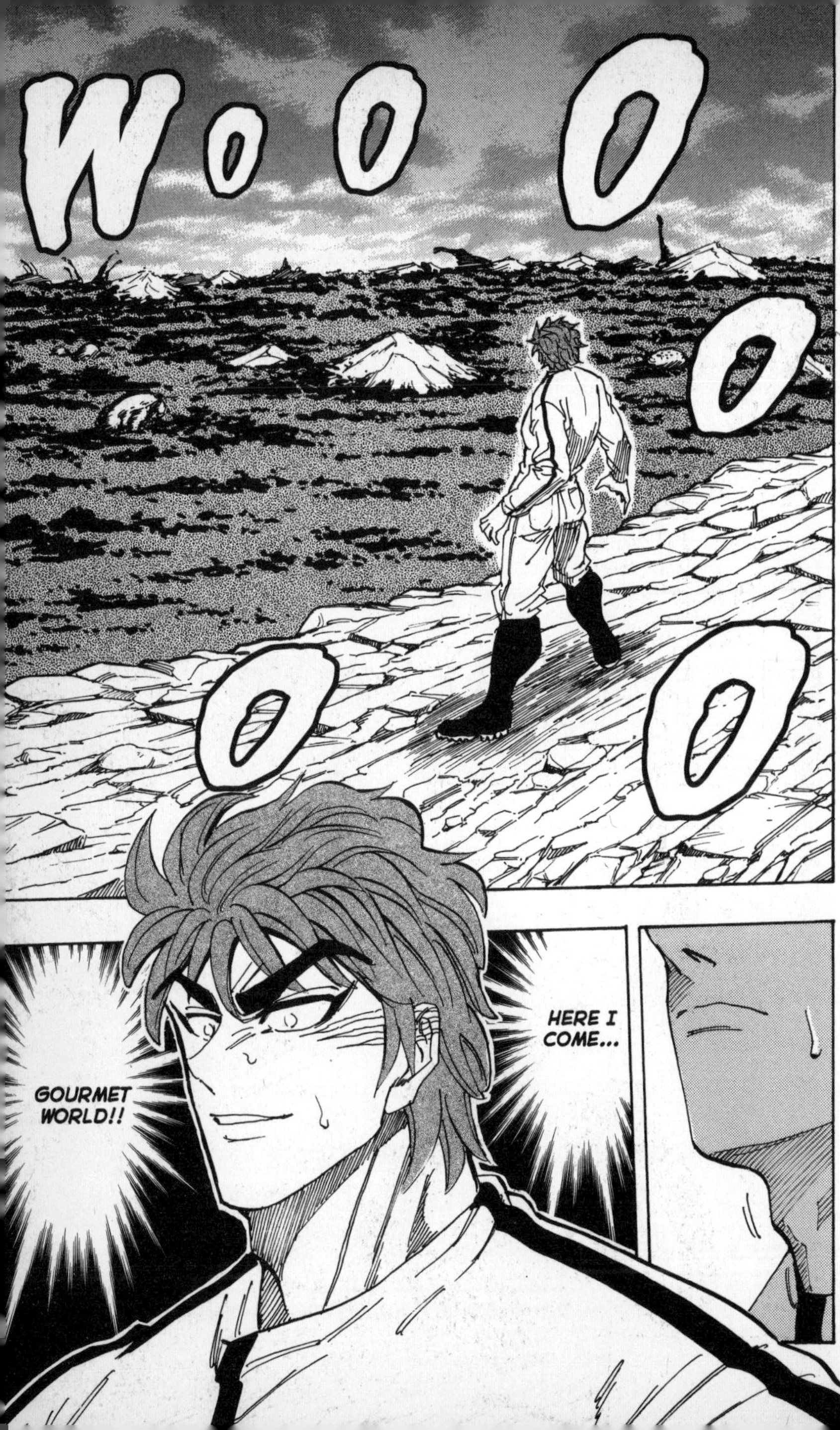
WOOOOOO
HERE I COME...
GOURMET WORLD!!

TORIKO

GOURMET CHECKLIST

Vol. 124

SEVEN-FLAVOR SAKE

(SEASONING)

AND THEN TO RATCHET UP THE FLAVOR ...
BLOOP
CHRK
...I'LL ADD SOME SEVEN-FLAVOR SAKE.

CAPTURE LEVEL: LESS THAN 1

HABITAT: HOUSEHOLD ITEM

LENGTH: ---

HEIGHT: ---

WEIGHT: ---

PRICE: 20,000 YEN PER BOTTLE

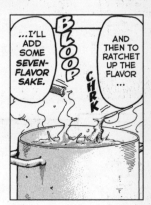

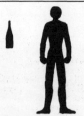

SCALE

DID THIS END UP IN KOMATSU'S RECIPE FOR CENTURY SOUP? A RICE-MALT SAKE, SEVEN-FLAVOR SAKE'S RICH FLAVOR MAKES IT POPULAR BOTH AS A SEASONING AND A BEVERAGE. APPARENTLY, PLENTY OF CHEFS ARE KNOWN TO SLIP AWAY TO THE CORNER OF THE KITCHEN AND TAKE NIPS FROM THEIR SEVEN-FLAVOR SAKE.

GOURMET 111: DEADLY GOURMET WORLD!!

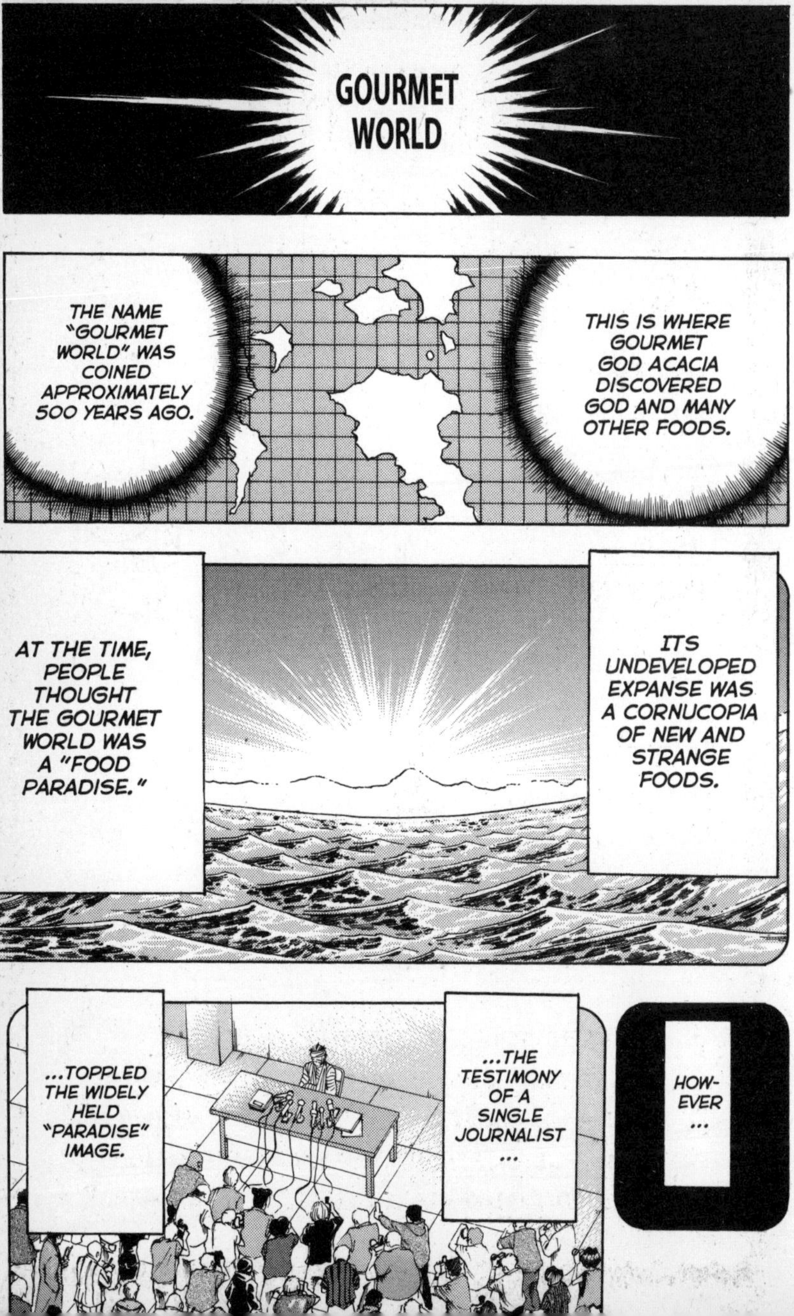
GOURMET WORLD
THIS IS WHERE GOURMET GOD ACACIA DISCOVERED GOD AND MANY OTHER FOODS.
THE NAME "GOURMET WORLD" WAS COINED APPROXIMATELY 500 YEARS AGO.
ITS UNDEVELOPED EXPANSE WAS A CORNUCOPIA OF NEW AND STRANGE FOODS.
AT THE TIME, PEOPLE THOUGHT THE GOURMET WORLD WAS A "FOOD PARADISE."
HOW-EVER...
...THE TESTIMONY OF A SINGLE JOURNALIST...
...TOPPLED THE WIDELY HELD "PARADISE" IMAGE.

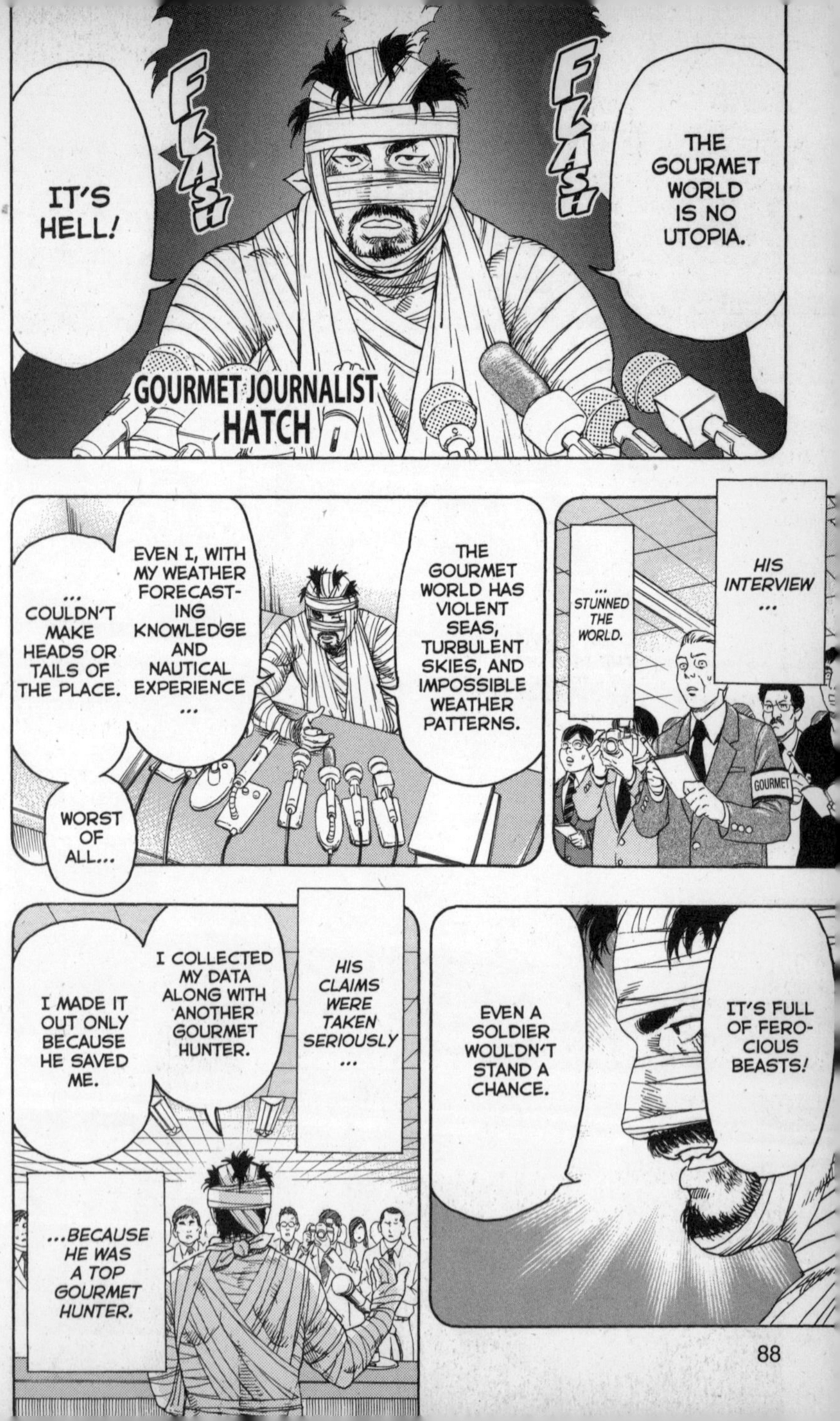
THE GOURMET WORLD IS NO UTOPIA.
FLASH
FLASH
IT'S HELL!
GOURMET JOURNALIST HATCH
HIS INTERVIEW ...
... STUNNED THE WORLD.
GOURMET
THE GOURMET WORLD HAS VIOLENT SEAS, TURBULENT SKIES, AND IMPOSSIBLE WEATHER PATTERNS.
EVEN I, WITH MY WEATHER FORECAST-ING KNOWLEDGE AND NAUTICAL EXPERIENCE ...
... COULDN'T MAKE HEADS OR TAILS OF THE PLACE.
WORST OF ALL...
IT'S FULL OF FERO-CIOUS BEASTS!
EVEN A SOLDIER WOULDN'T STAND A CHANCE.
HIS CLAIMS WERE TAKEN SERIOUSLY ...
I COLLECTED MY DATA ALONG WITH ANOTHER GOURMET HUNTER.
I MADE IT OUT ONLY BECAUSE HE SAVED ME.
...BECAUSE HE WAS A TOP GOURMET HUNTER.

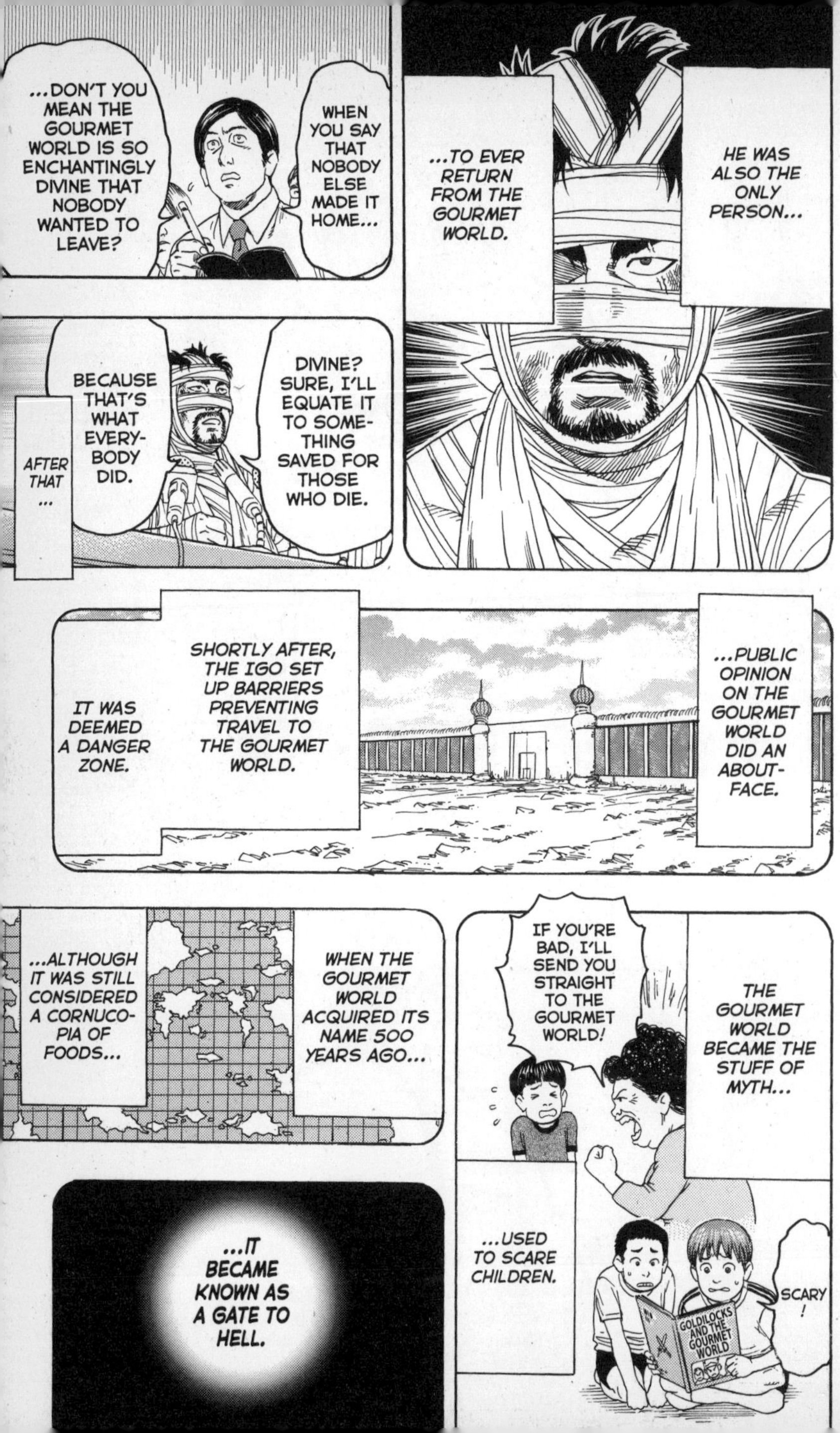
HE WAS ALSO THE ONLY PERSON...
...TO EVER RETURN FROM THE GOURMET WORLD.
WHEN YOU SAY THAT NOBODY ELSE MADE IT HOME...
...DON'T YOU MEAN THE GOURMET WORLD IS SO ENCHANTINGLY DIVINE THAT NOBODY WANTED TO LEAVE?
DIVINE? SURE, I'LL EQUATE IT TO SOME-THING SAVED FOR THOSE WHO DIE.
BECAUSE THAT'S WHAT EVERY-BODY DID.
AFTER THAT...
...PUBLIC OPINION ON THE GOURMET WORLD DID AN ABOUT-FACE.
SHORTLY AFTER, THE IGO SET UP BARRIERS PREVENTING TRAVEL TO THE GOURMET WORLD.
IT WAS DEEMED A DANGER ZONE.
THE GOURMET WORLD BECAME THE STUFF OF MYTH...
IF YOU'RE BAD, I'LL SEND YOU STRAIGHT TO THE GOURMET WORLD!
...USED TO SCARE CHILDREN.
SCARY!
GOLDILOCKS AND THE GOURMET WORLD
WHEN THE GOURMET WORLD ACQUIRED ITS NAME 500 YEARS AGO...
...ALTHOUGH IT WAS STILL CONSIDERED A CORNUCOPIA OF FOODS...
...IT BECAME KNOWN AS A GATE TO HELL.

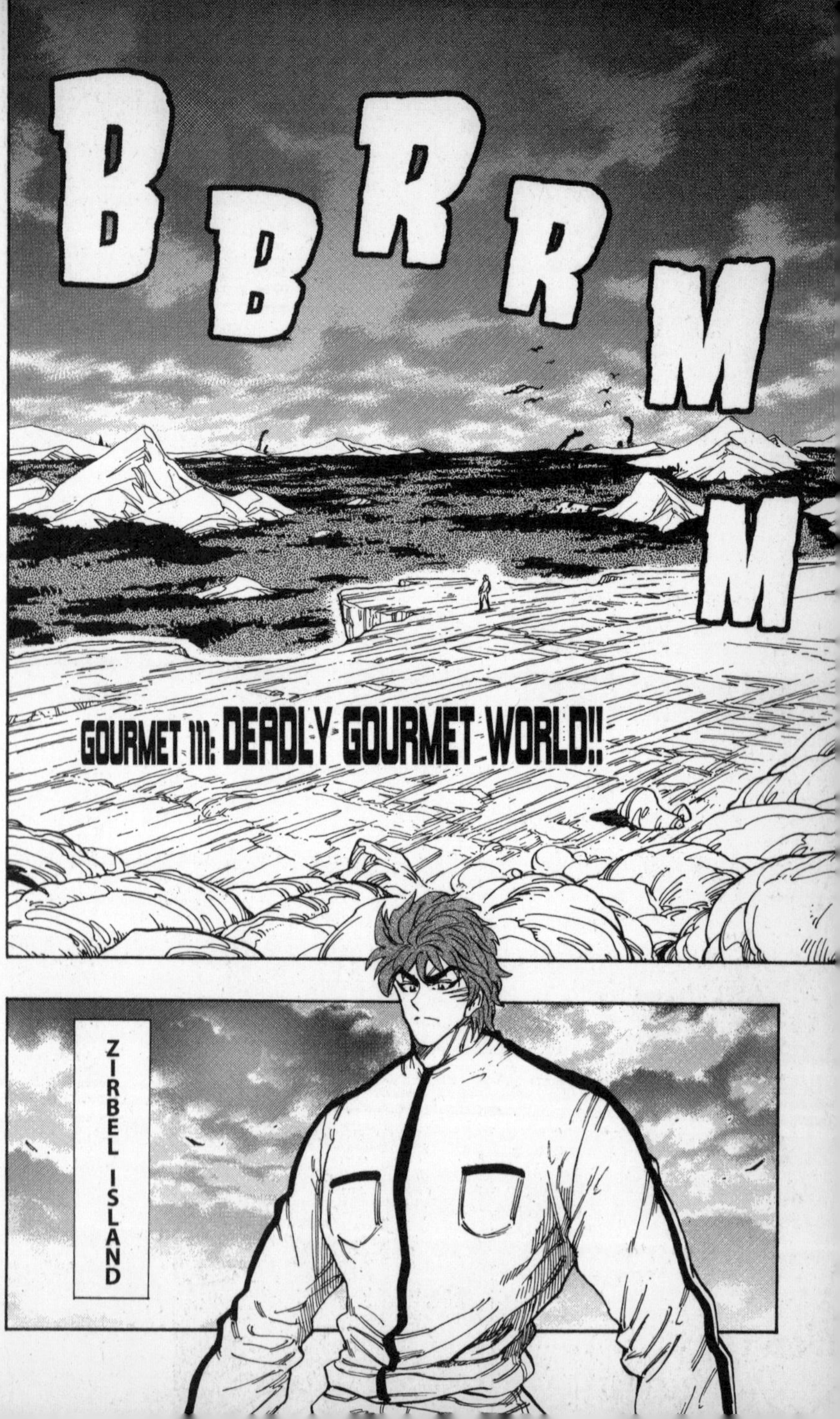
BBRRRMM
GOURMET 111: DEADLY GOURMET WORLD!!
ZIRBEL ISLAND

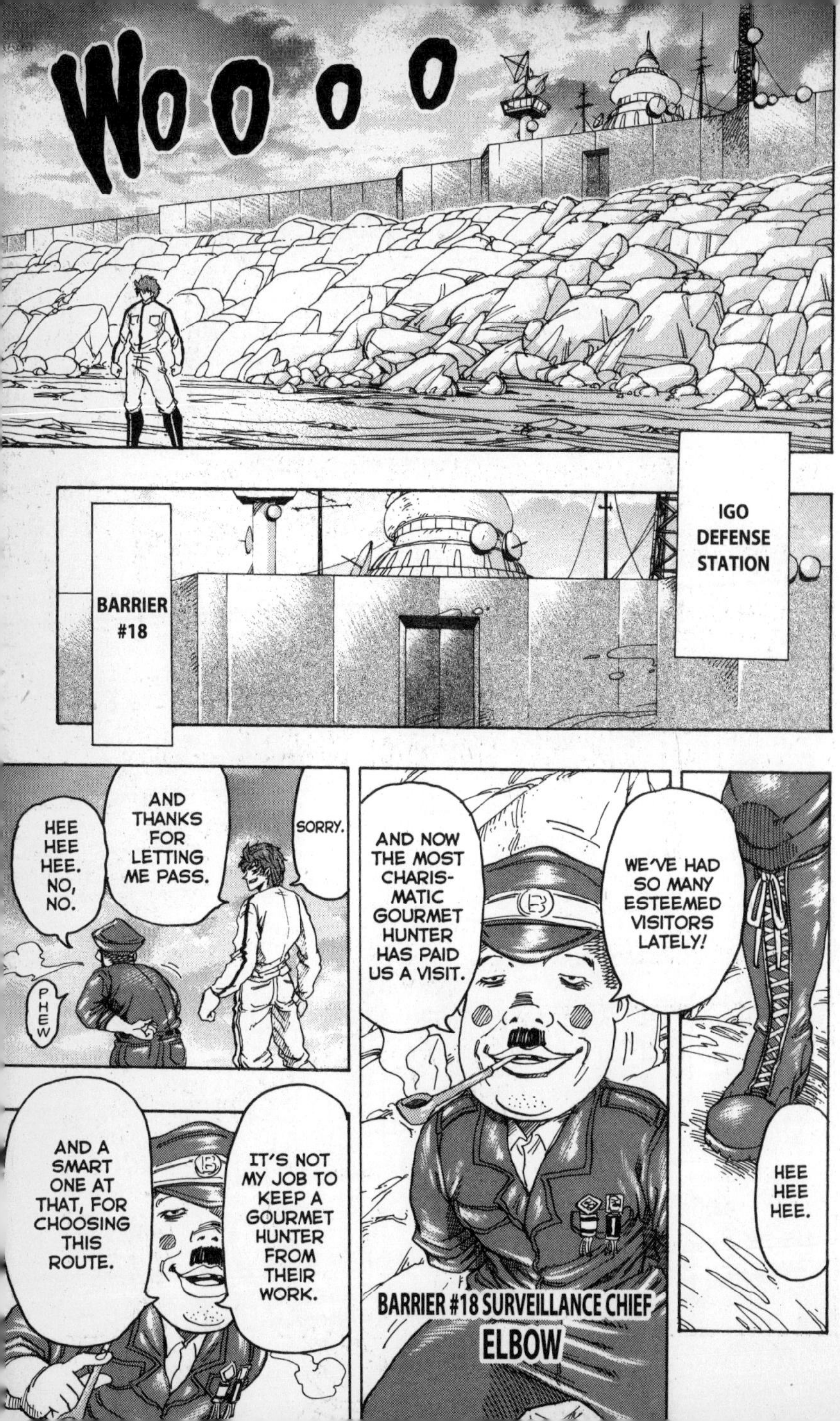
WOOOO
IGO DEFENSE STATION
BARRIER #18
WE'VE HAD SO MANY ESTEEMED VISITORS LATELY!
HEE HEE HEE.
AND NOW THE MOST CHARIS-MATIC GOURMET HUNTER HAS PAID US A VISIT.
BARRIER #18 SURVEILLANCE CHIEF
ELBOW
SORRY.
AND THANKS FOR LETTING ME PASS.
HEE HEE HEE. NO, NO.
PHEW
IT'S NOT MY JOB TO KEEP A GOURMET HUNTER FROM THEIR WORK.
AND A SMART ONE AT THAT, FOR CHOOSING THIS ROUTE.

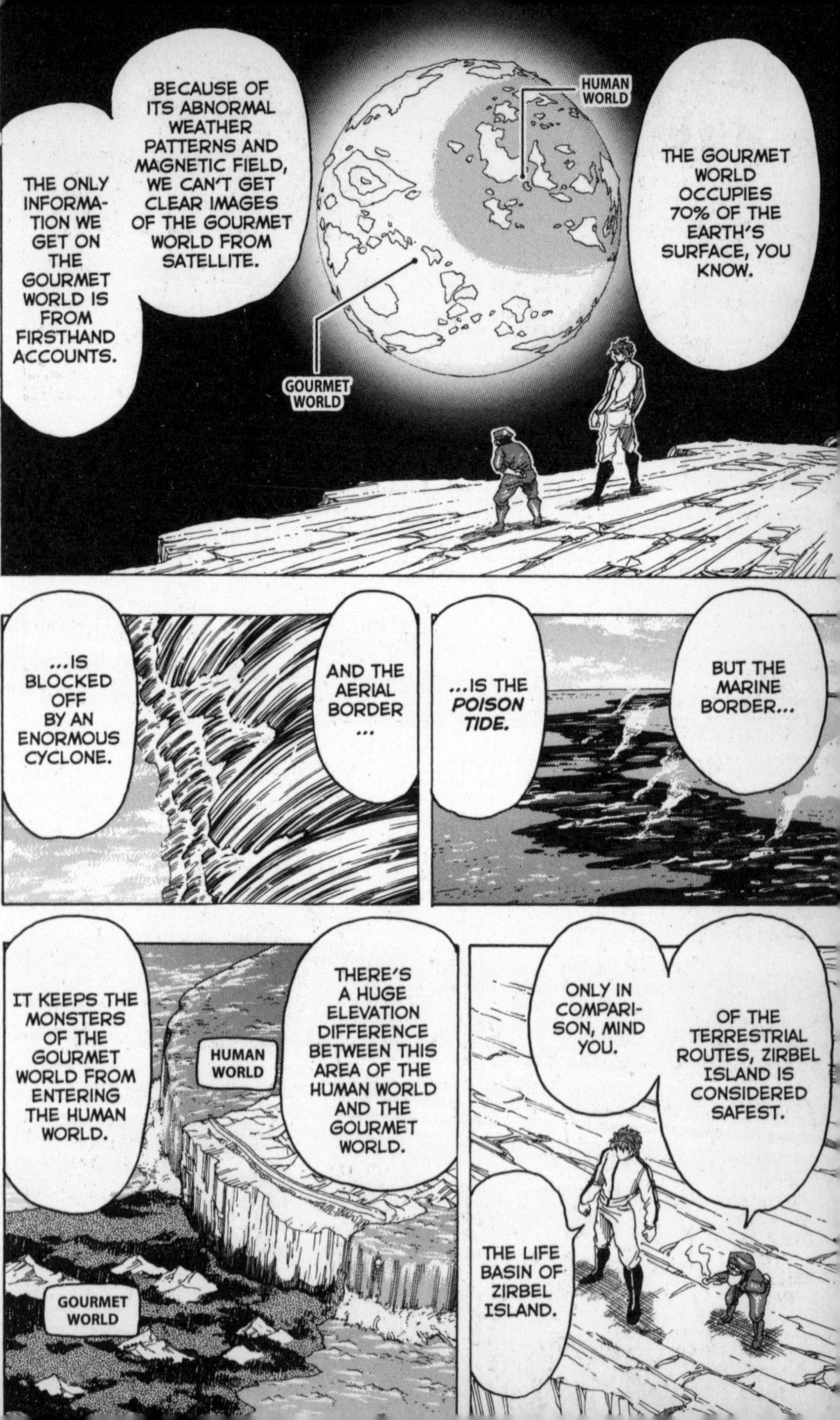
THE GOURMET WORLD OCCUPIES 70% OF THE EARTH'S SURFACE, YOU KNOW.
HUMAN WORLD
GOURMET WORLD
BECAUSE OF ITS ABNORMAL WEATHER PATTERNS AND MAGNETIC FIELD, WE CAN'T GET CLEAR IMAGES OF THE GOURMET WORLD FROM SATELLITE.
THE ONLY INFORMATION WE GET ON THE GOURMET WORLD IS FROM FIRSTHAND ACCOUNTS.
BUT THE MARINE BORDER...
...IS THE *POISON TIDE.*
AND THE AERIAL BORDER...
...IS BLOCKED OFF BY AN ENORMOUS CYCLONE.
OF THE TERRESTRIAL ROUTES, ZIRBEL ISLAND IS CONSIDERED SAFEST.
ONLY IN COMPARISON, MIND YOU.
THE LIFE BASIN OF ZIRBEL ISLAND.
THERE'S A HUGE ELEVATION DIFFERENCE BETWEEN THIS AREA OF THE HUMAN WORLD AND THE GOURMET WORLD.
HUMAN WORLD
IT KEEPS THE MONSTERS OF THE GOURMET WORLD FROM ENTERING THE HUMAN WORLD.
GOURMET WORLD

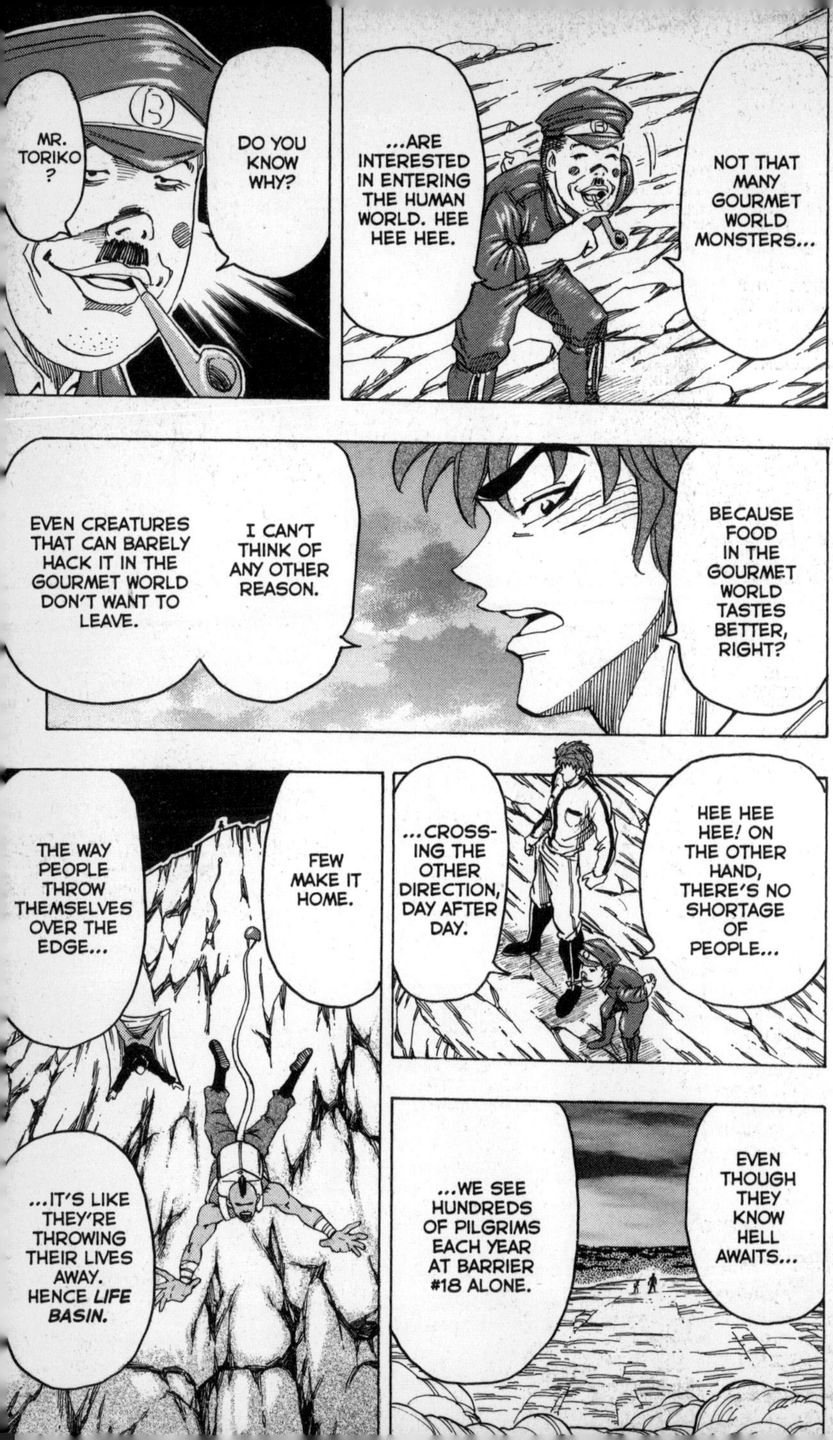
NOT THAT MANY GOURMET WORLD MONSTERS...
...ARE INTERESTED IN ENTERING THE HUMAN WORLD. HEE HEE HEE.
DO YOU KNOW WHY?
MR. TORIKO?
BECAUSE FOOD IN THE GOURMET WORLD TASTES BETTER, RIGHT?
I CAN'T THINK OF ANY OTHER REASON.
EVEN CREATURES THAT CAN BARELY HACK IT IN THE GOURMET WORLD DON'T WANT TO LEAVE.
HEE HEE HEE! ON THE OTHER HAND, THERE'S NO SHORTAGE OF PEOPLE...
...CROSSING THE OTHER DIRECTION, DAY AFTER DAY.
EVEN THOUGH THEY KNOW HELL AWAITS...
...WE SEE HUNDREDS OF PILGRIMS EACH YEAR AT BARRIER #18 ALONE.
FEW MAKE IT HOME.
THE WAY PEOPLE THROW THEMSELVES OVER THE EDGE...
...IT'S LIKE THEY'RE THROWING THEIR LIVES AWAY. HENCE *LIFE BASIN.*

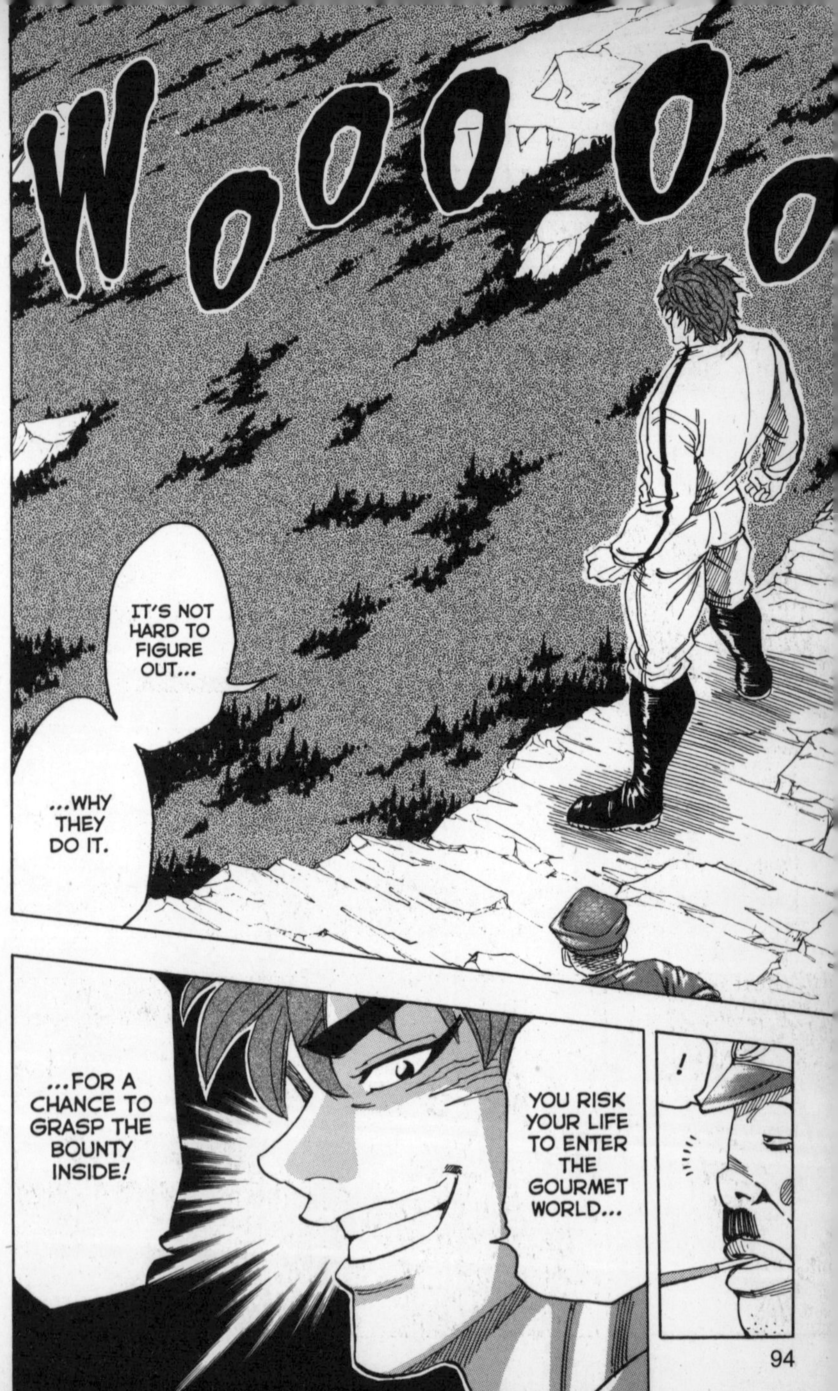
WOOOOOO
IT'S NOT HARD TO FIGURE OUT...
...WHY THEY DO IT.
!
YOU RISK YOUR LIFE TO ENTER THE GOURMET WORLD...
...FOR A CHANCE TO GRASP THE BOUNTY INSIDE!

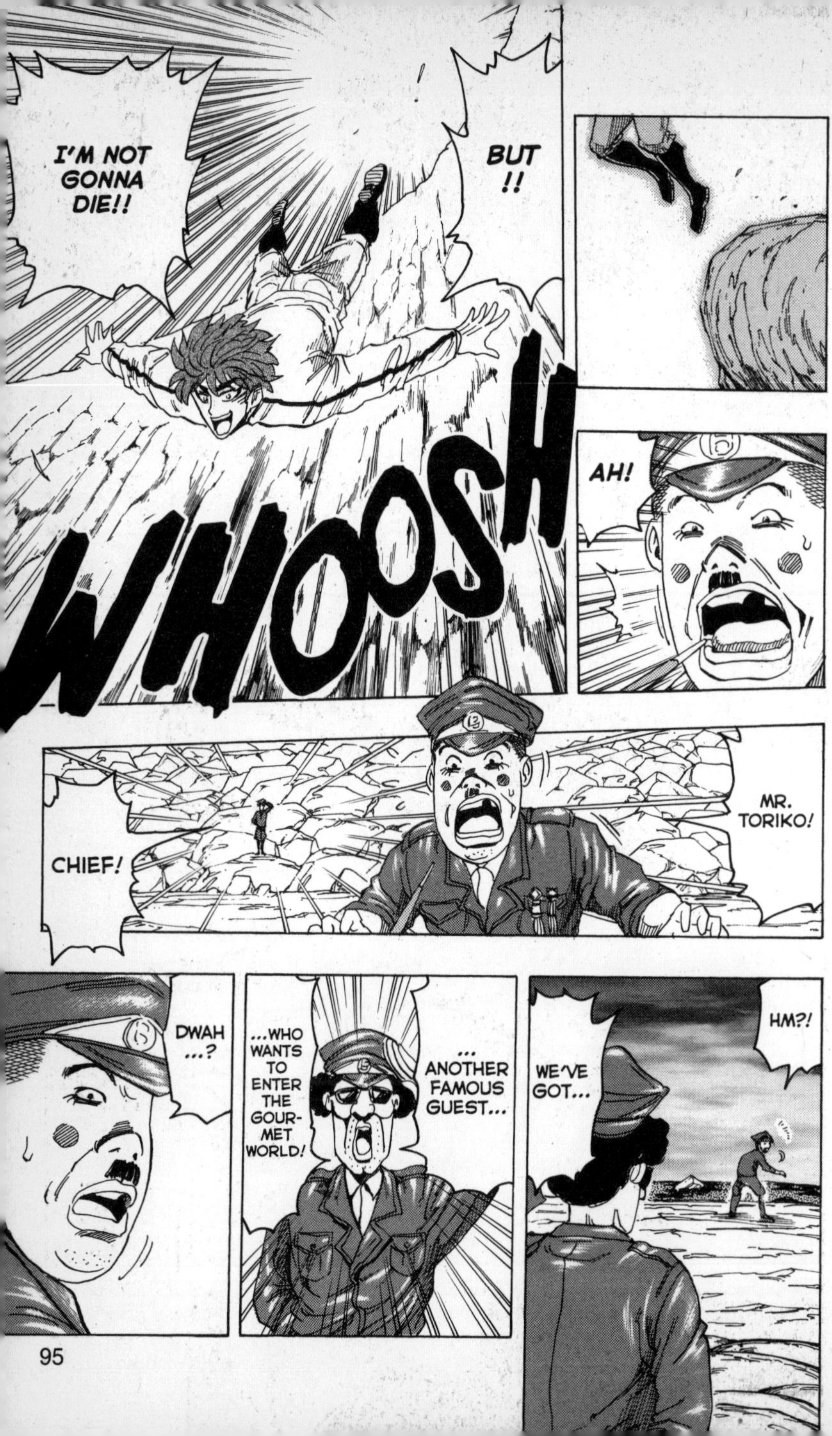
AH!
BUT!!
I'M NOT GONNA DIE!!
WHOOSH
MR. TORIKO!
CHIEF!
HM?!
WE'VE GOT...
... ANOTHER FAMOUS GUEST...
...WHO WANTS TO ENTER THE GOUR-MET WORLD!
DWAH ...?

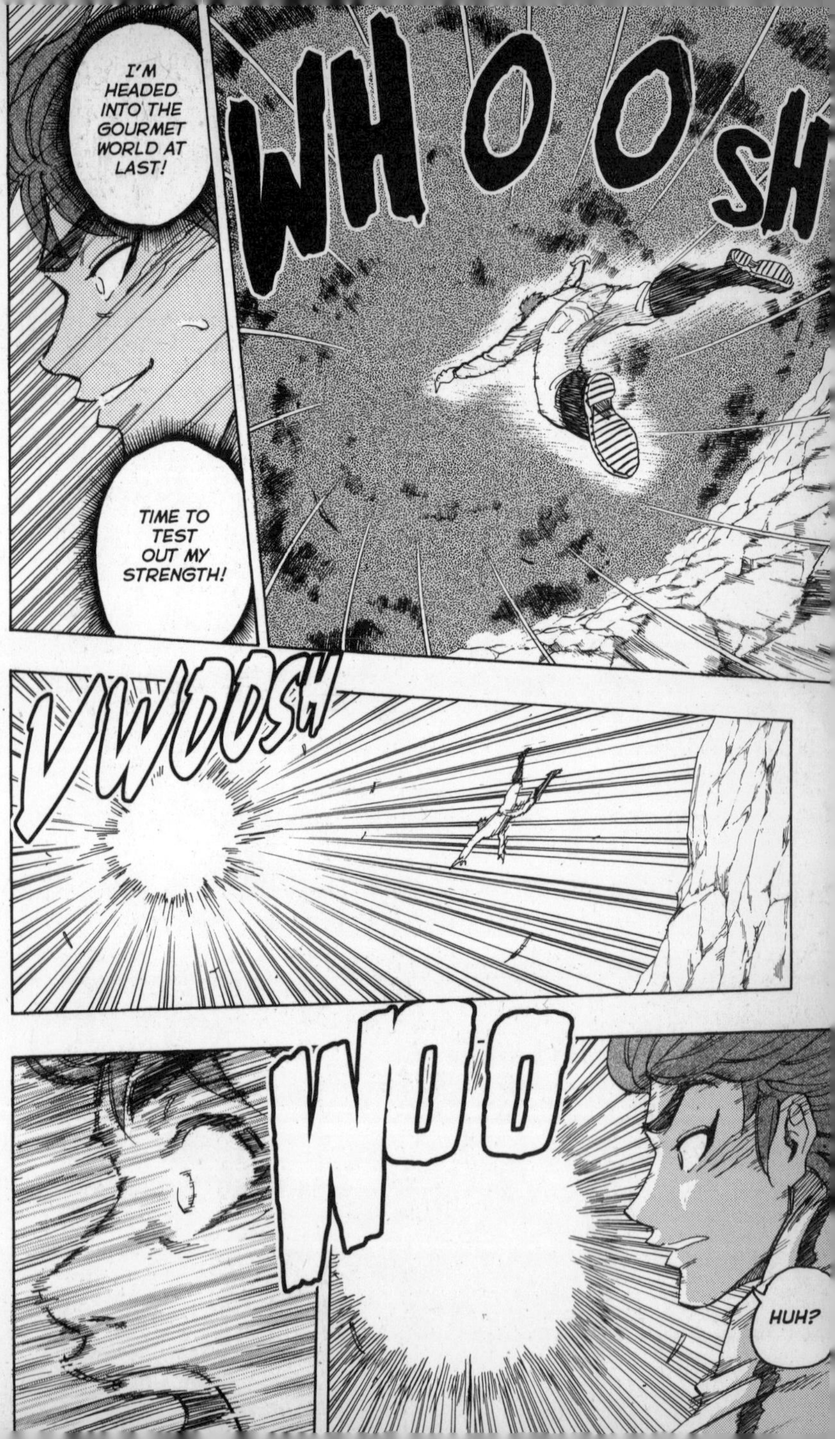
WHOOSH
I'M HEADED INTO THE GOURMET WORLD AT LAST!
TIME TO TEST OUT MY STRENGTH!
VWOOSH
WOO
HUH?

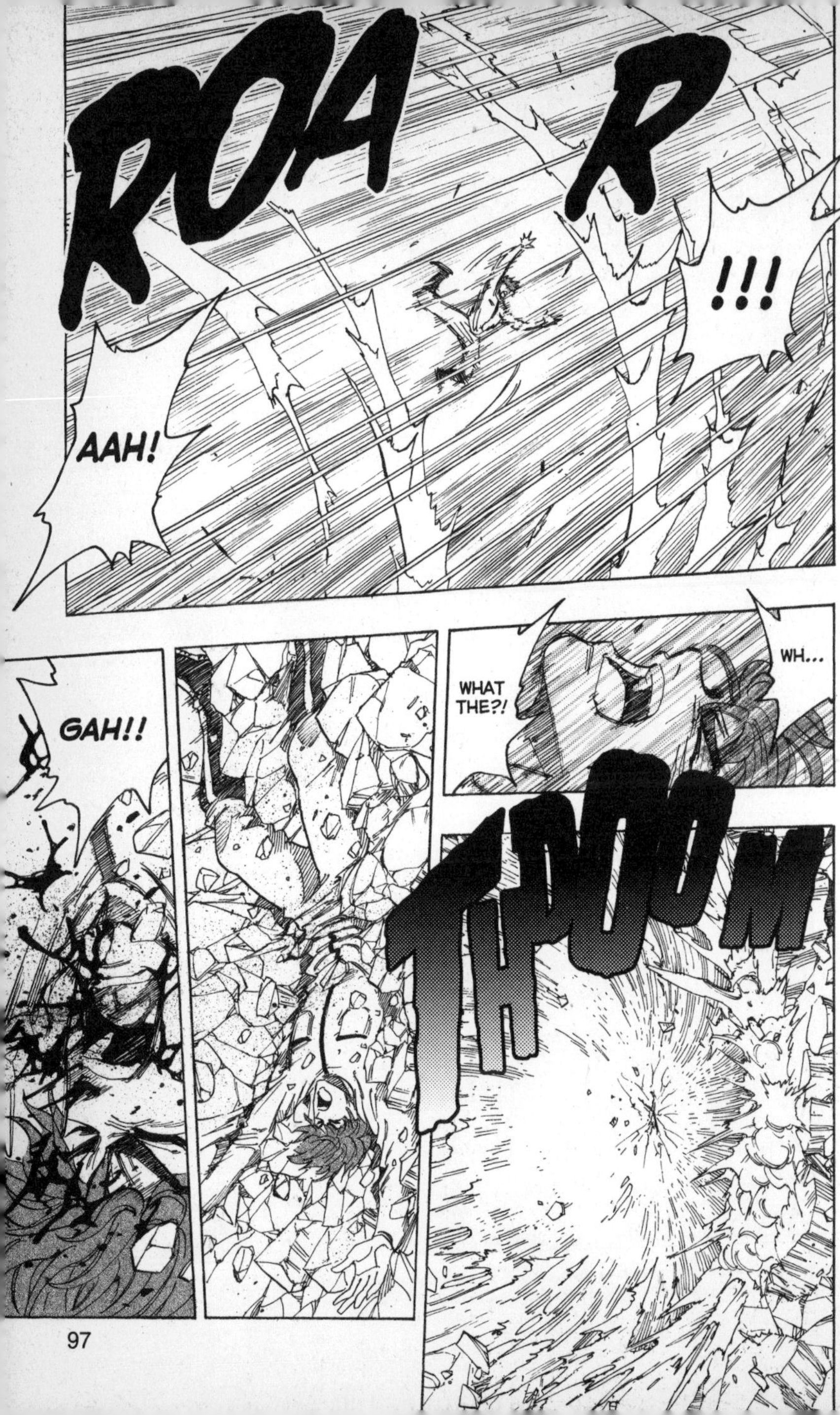
ROAR!!!
AAH!
WH...
WHAT THE?!
THOOM
GAH!!

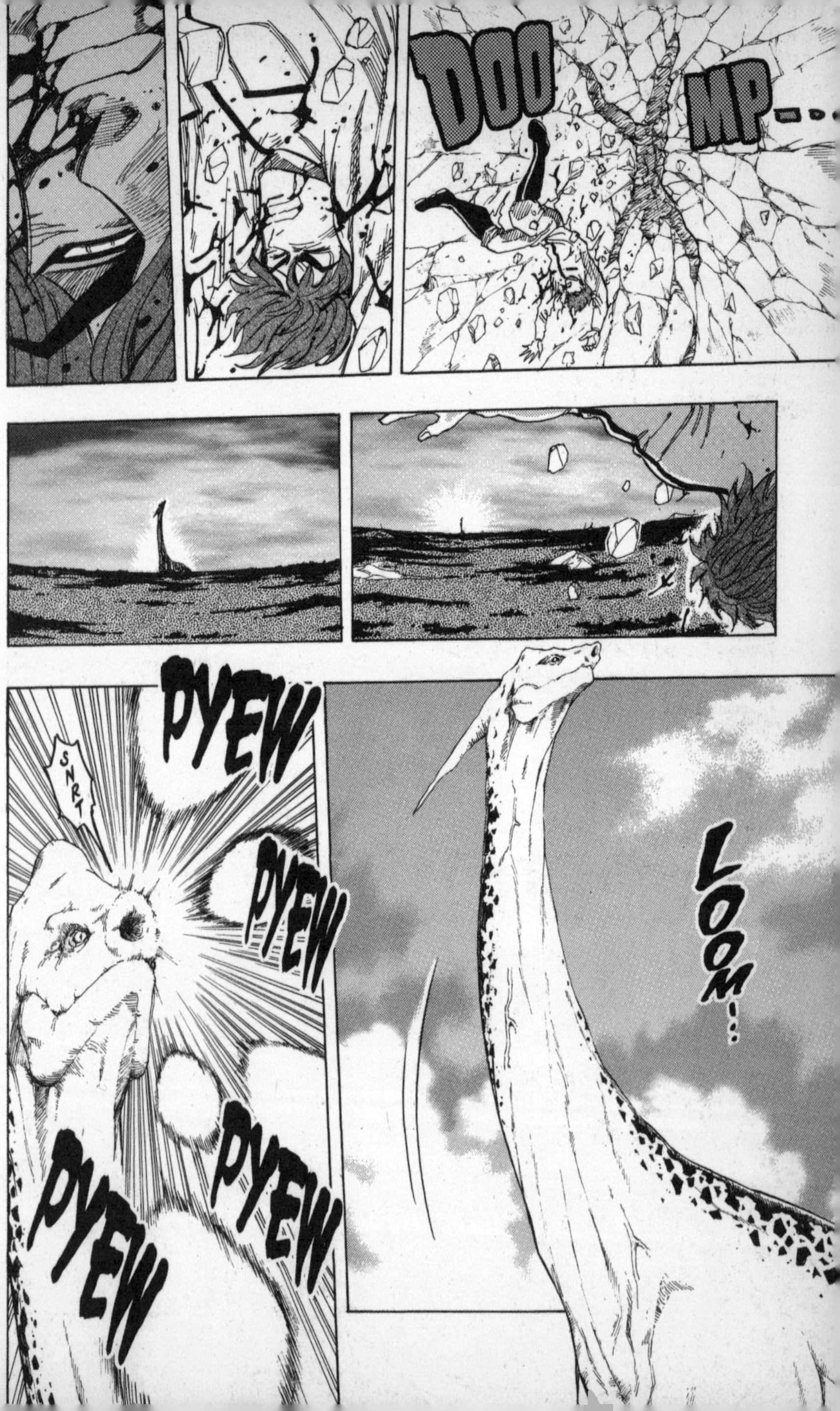

DOO
MP...
LOOM...
PYEW
SNRT
PYEW
PYEW
PYEW

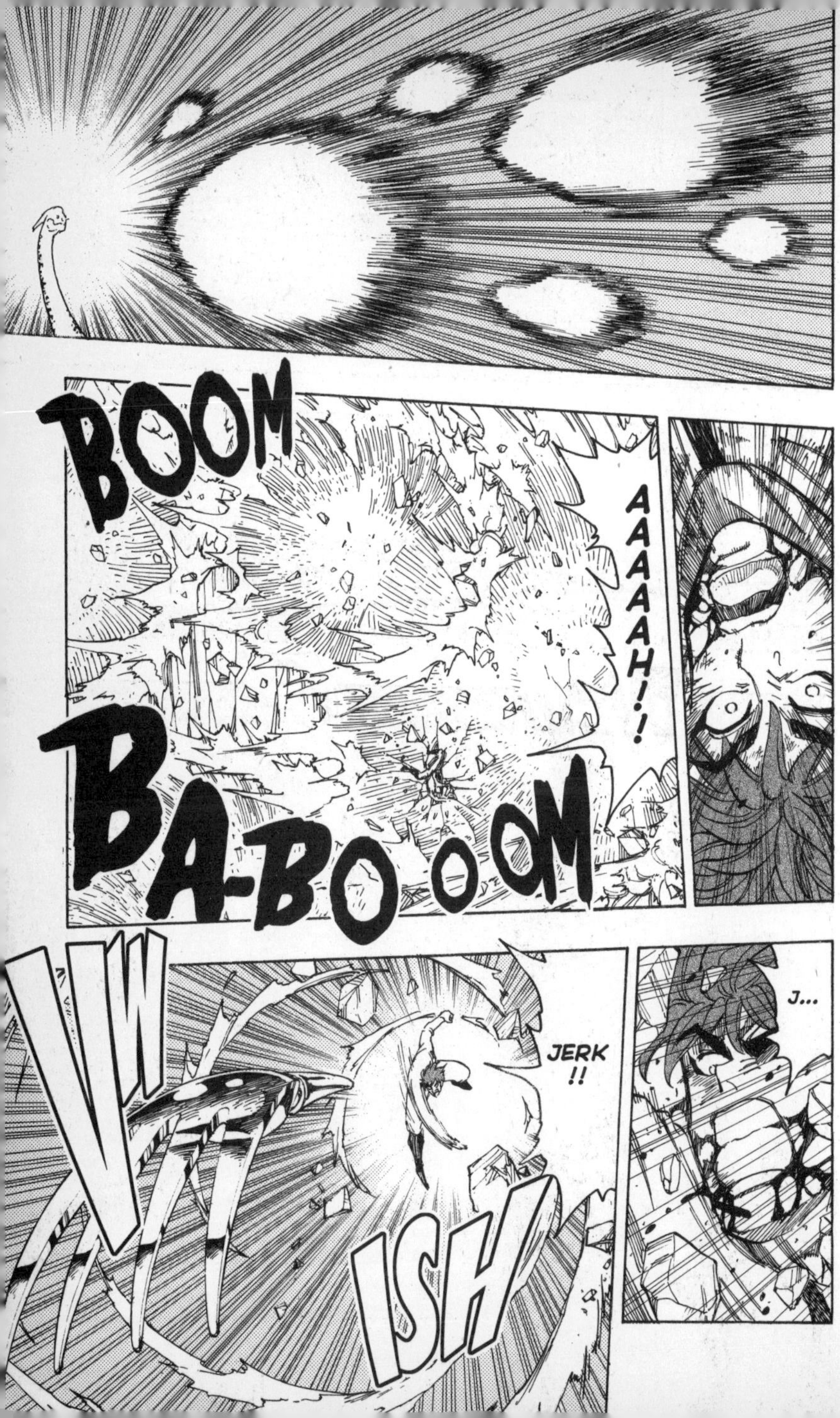
AAAAAAH!!
BOOM
BA-BO-O-OM
J...
JERK !!
VWISH

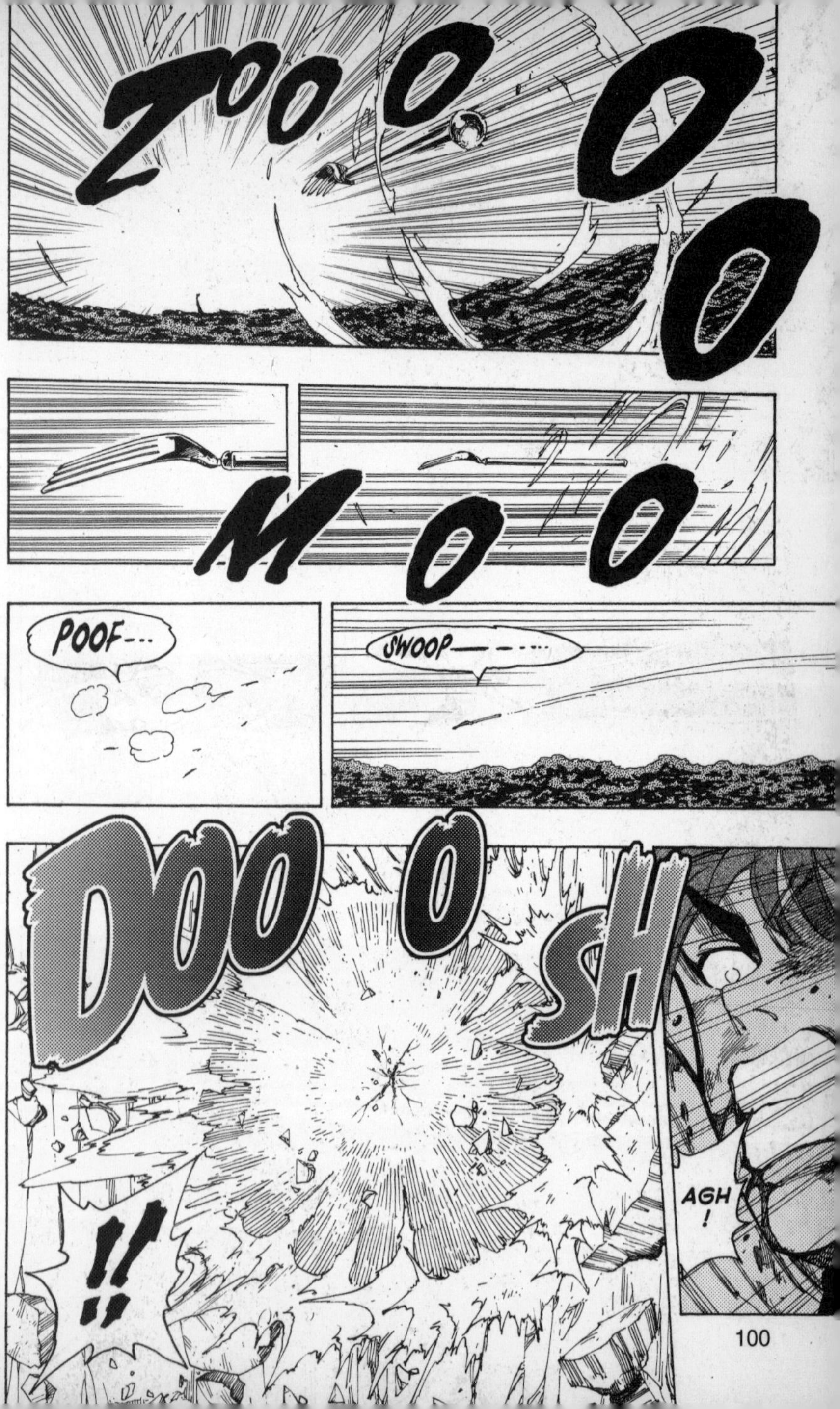
ZOOOOOO
MOO
SWOOP
POOF...
DOOOSH
AGH!
!!

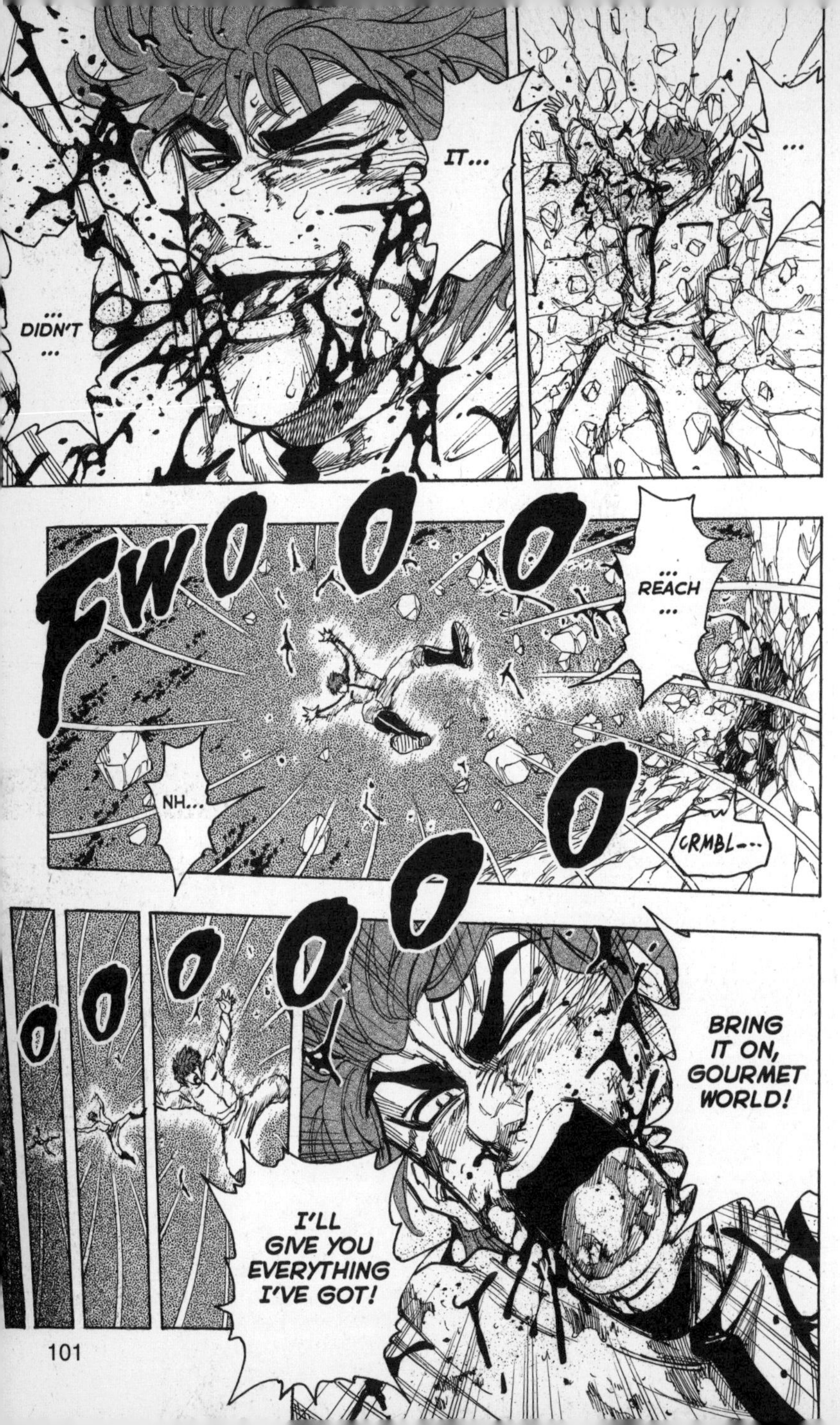
...
IT...
... DIDN'T ...
FWOOOOOOOOOOOOO
... REACH ...
CRMBL...
NH...
BRING IT ON, GOURMET WORLD!
I'LL GIVE YOU EVERYTHING I'VE GOT!

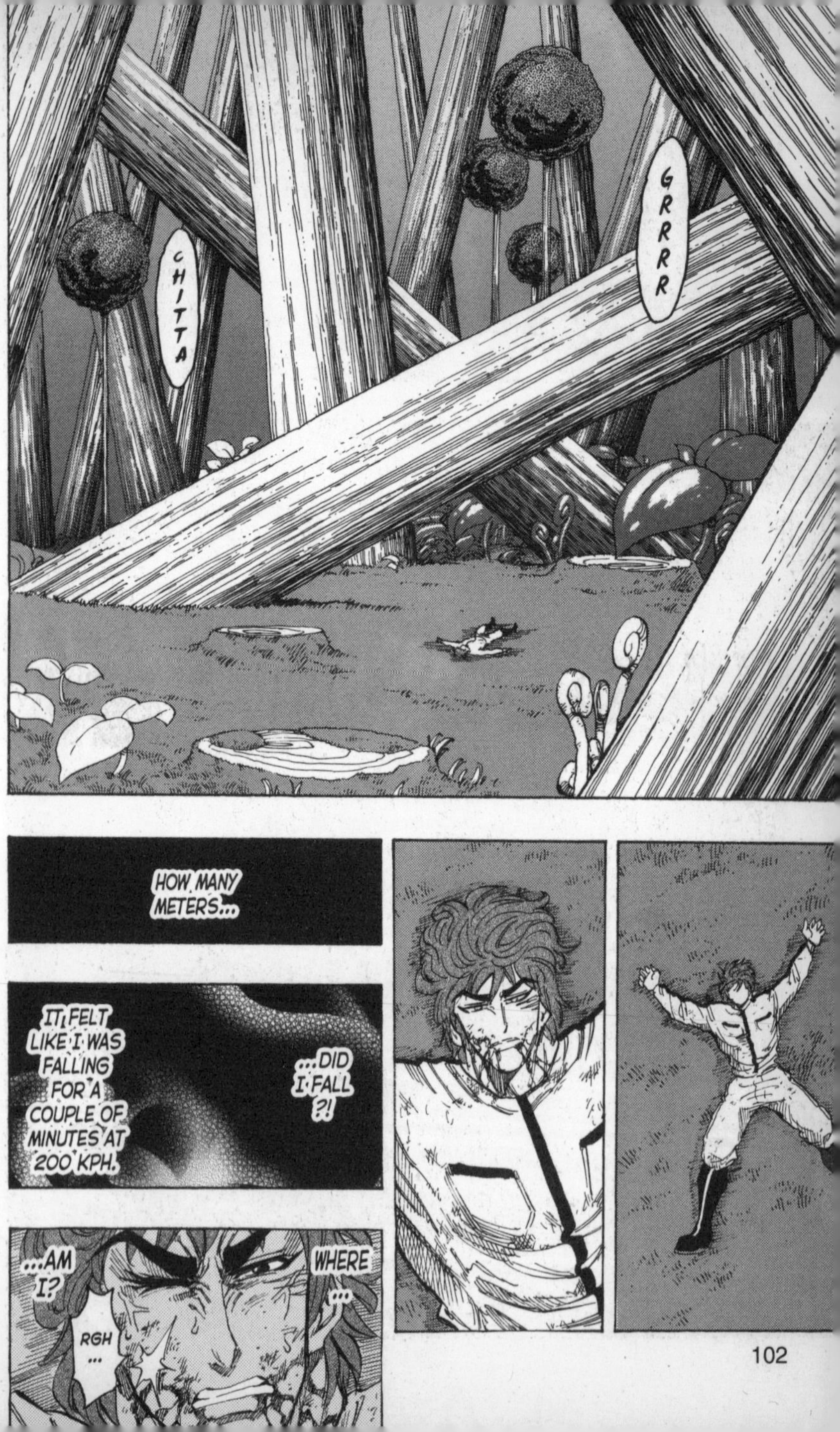
GRRRR
CHITTA
HOW MANY METERS...
...DID I FALL?!
IT FELT LIKE I WAS FALLING FOR A COUPLE OF MINUTES AT 200 KPH.
WHERE...
...AM I?
RGH...

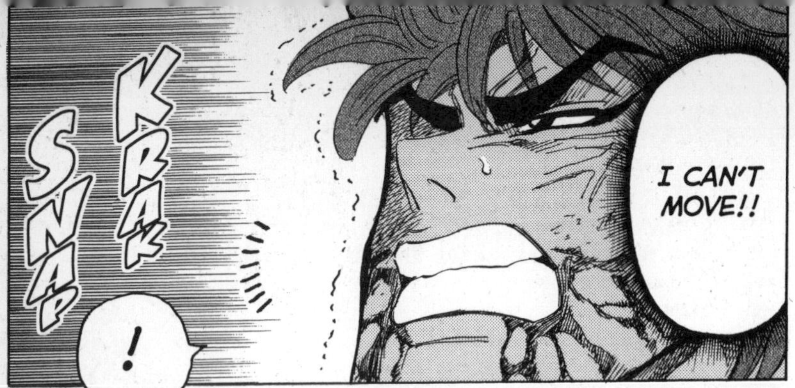
I CAN'T MOVE!!
!
KRAK
SNAP
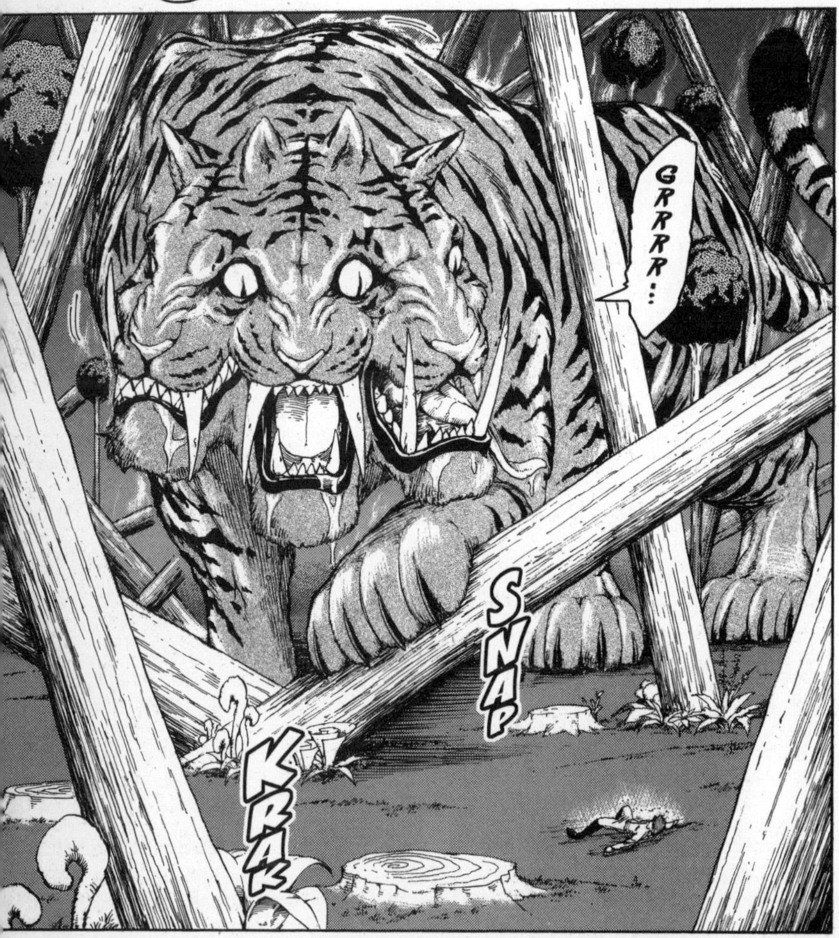
GRRRR...
SNAP
KRAK

TORIKO

GOURMET CHECKLIST

Vol. 125

 ### REGENERATION SEED
(YOSAKU SIGNATURE ITEM)

CAPTURE LEVEL: ---

HABITAT: YOSAKU'S REVIVAL LAB

LENGTH: ---

HEIGHT: ---

WEIGHT: ---

PRICE: 100,000,000 YEN PER SEED

SCALE

THIS PLANT, CREATED BY YOSAKU, ABSORBS THE DNA OF WHATEVER IT'S PLANTED IN. IT BLOSSOMS WITH A SEED CONTAINING THAT SAME DNA, WHICH CAN BE IMPLANTED IN A TARGET'S BODY TO REGROW TISSUES. BUT CAREFUL! THE REGENERATION SEED IS AS FRAGILE AS A BUBBLE, AND ON TOP OF THAT, IT MUST BE COMPATIBLE WITH THE HOST BODY. A FURTHER WORD OF CAUTION—THE SEED WILL ABSORB THE NUTRIENTS IT NEEDS TO GROW, EVEN IF THAT MEANS SUCKING YOU DRY. SO YOU BETTER HAVE CONSIDERABLE FORTITUDE, OR THE MEDICAL PROCEDURE SPELLS CERTAIN DEATH. THINK TWICE BEFORE USING THIS DOUBLE-EDGED SWORD.

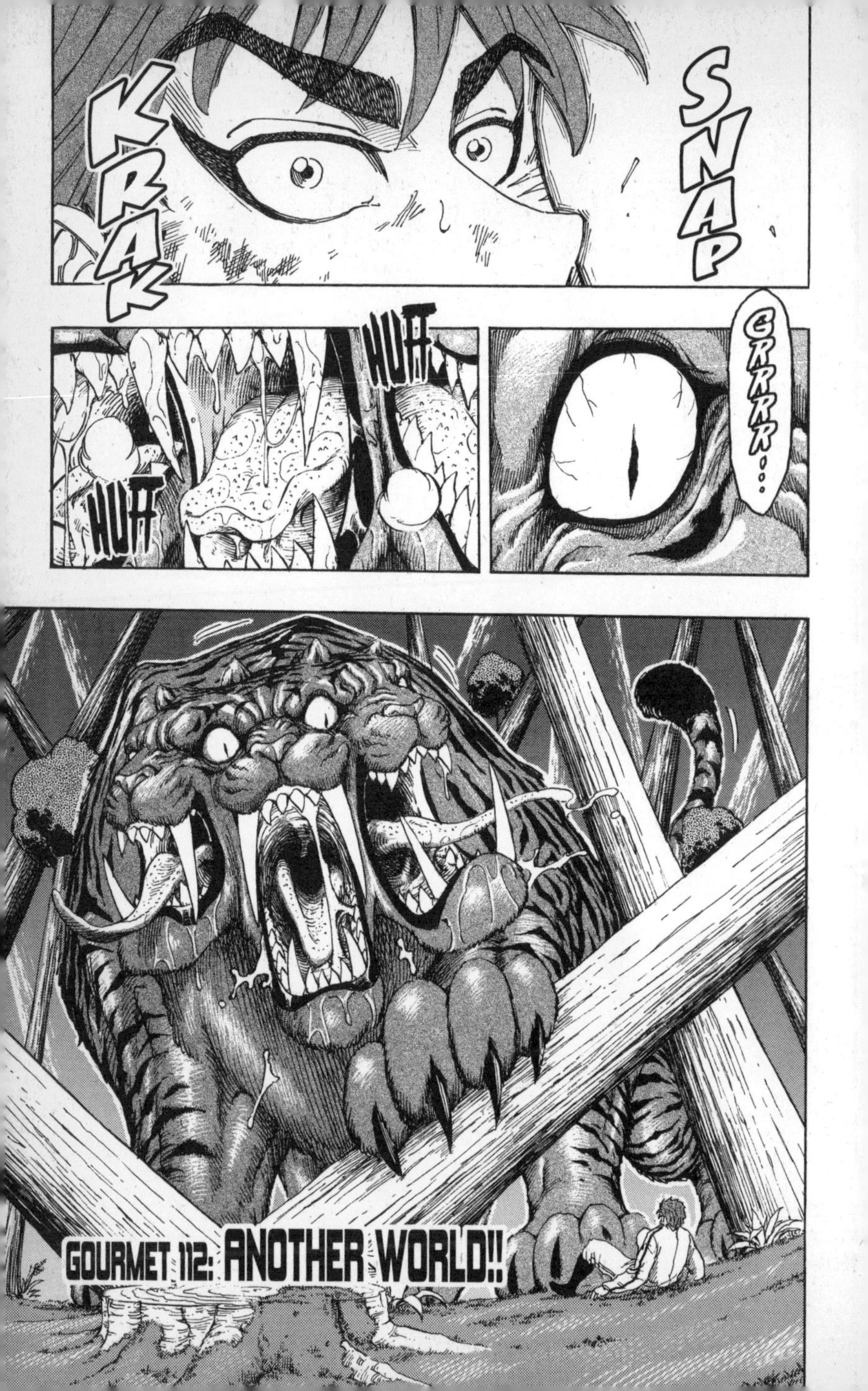
SNAP
KRAK
GRRRR...
HUFF
HUFF
GOURMET 112: ANOTHER WORLD!!

*SUBMITTED BY HAGANAIL MURATA FROM HYOGO!

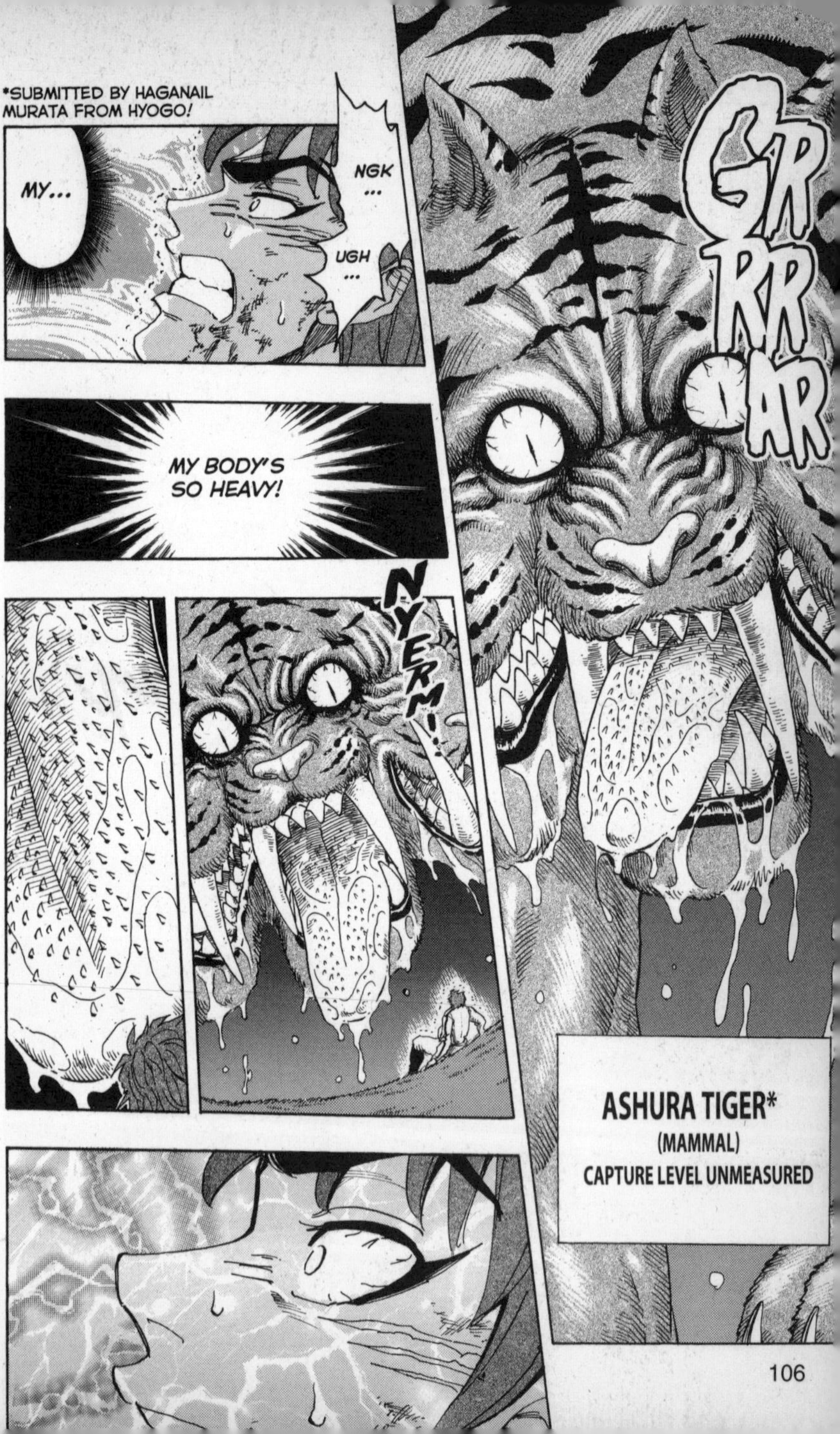
GRRROAR
ASHURA TIGER*
(MAMMAL)
CAPTURE LEVEL UNMEASURED
NGK ...
UGH ...
MY...
MY BODY'S SO HEAVY!
NYERM!

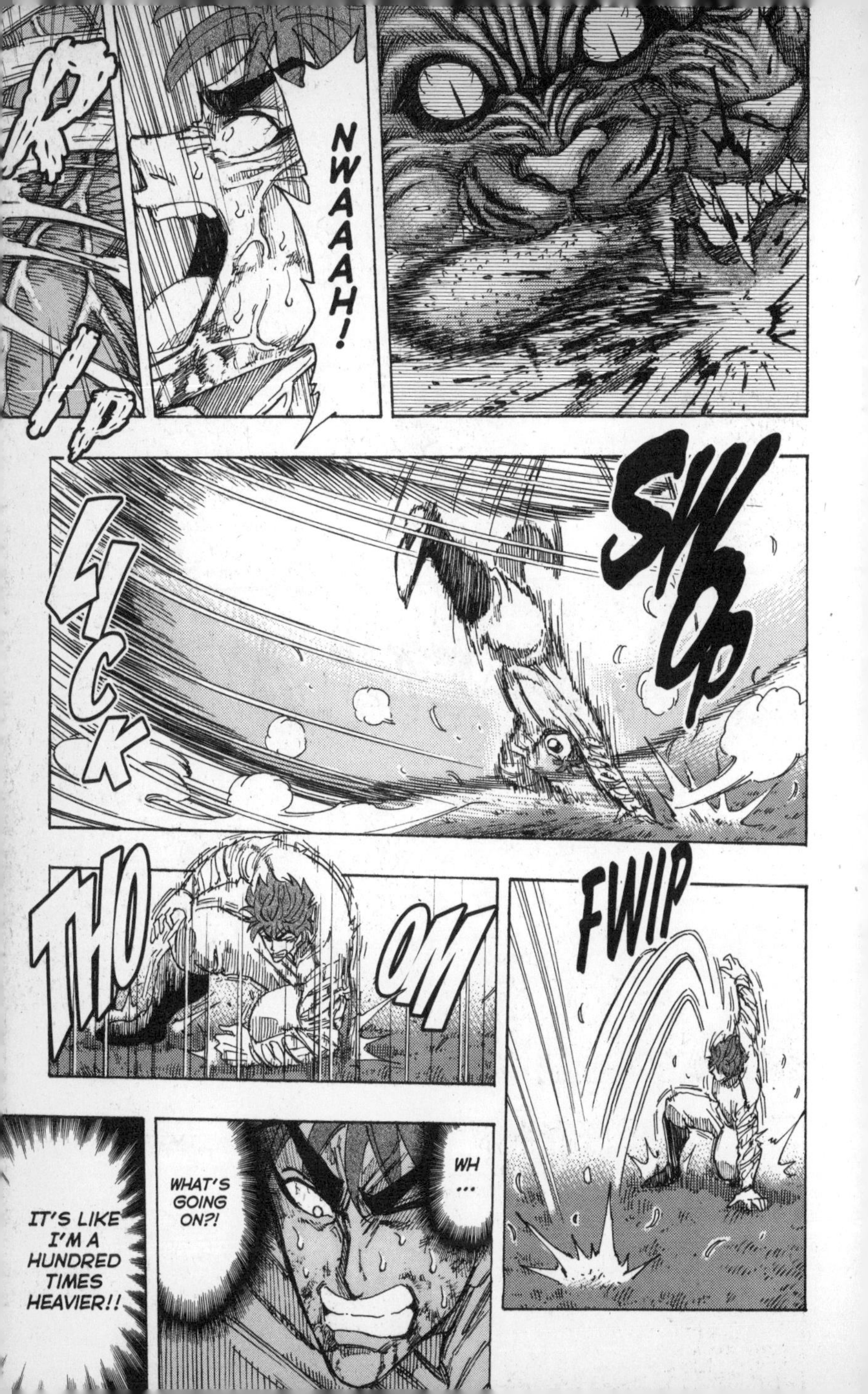
NWAAAAH!
RIP
SHLOP
LICK
FWIP
THOOM
WH...
WHAT'S GOING ON?!
IT'S LIKE I'M A HUNDRED TIMES HEAVIER!!

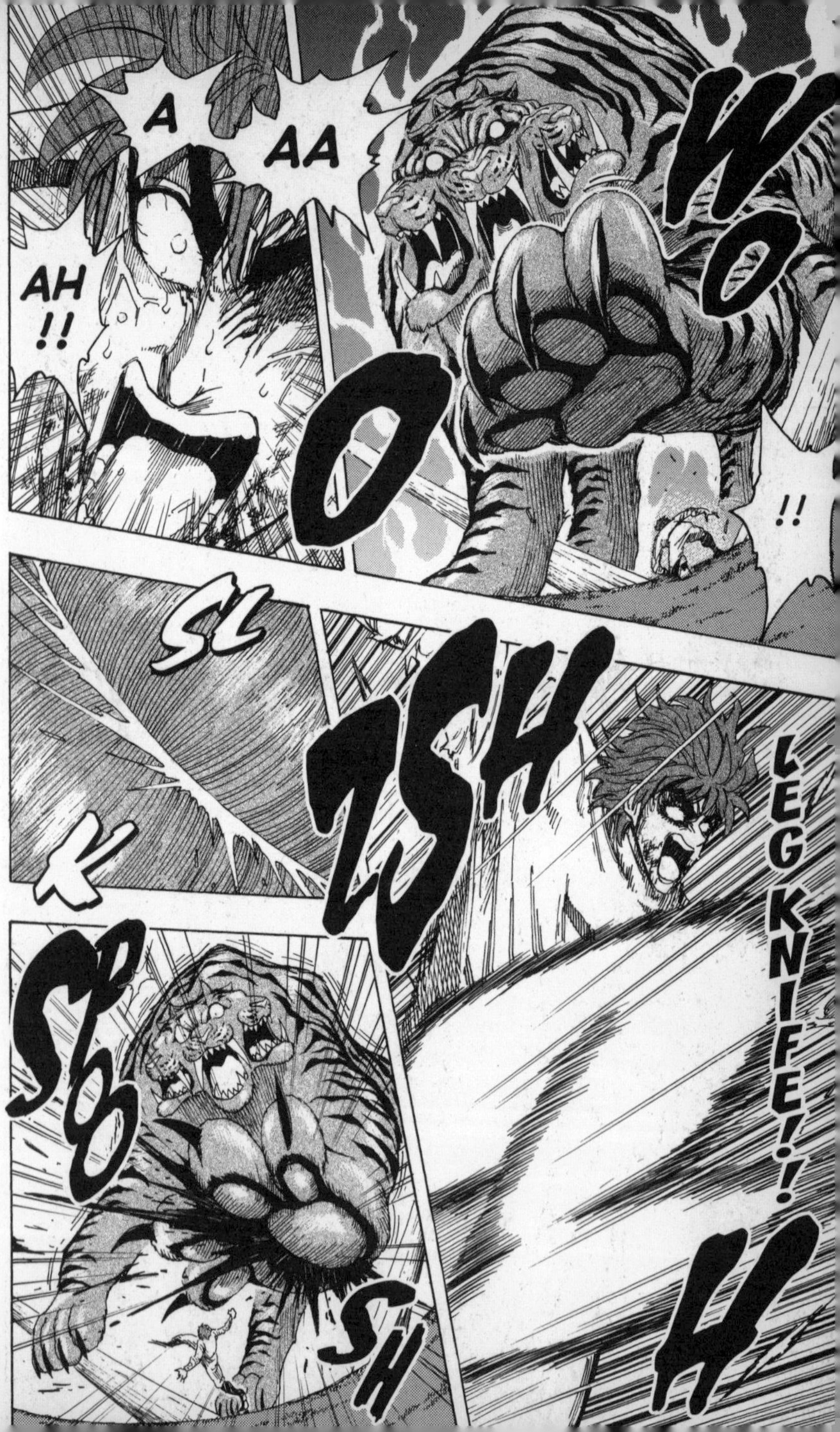
WHO
O
!!
A
AA
AH !!
LEG KNIFE!!
ZSH
SL
SH
H

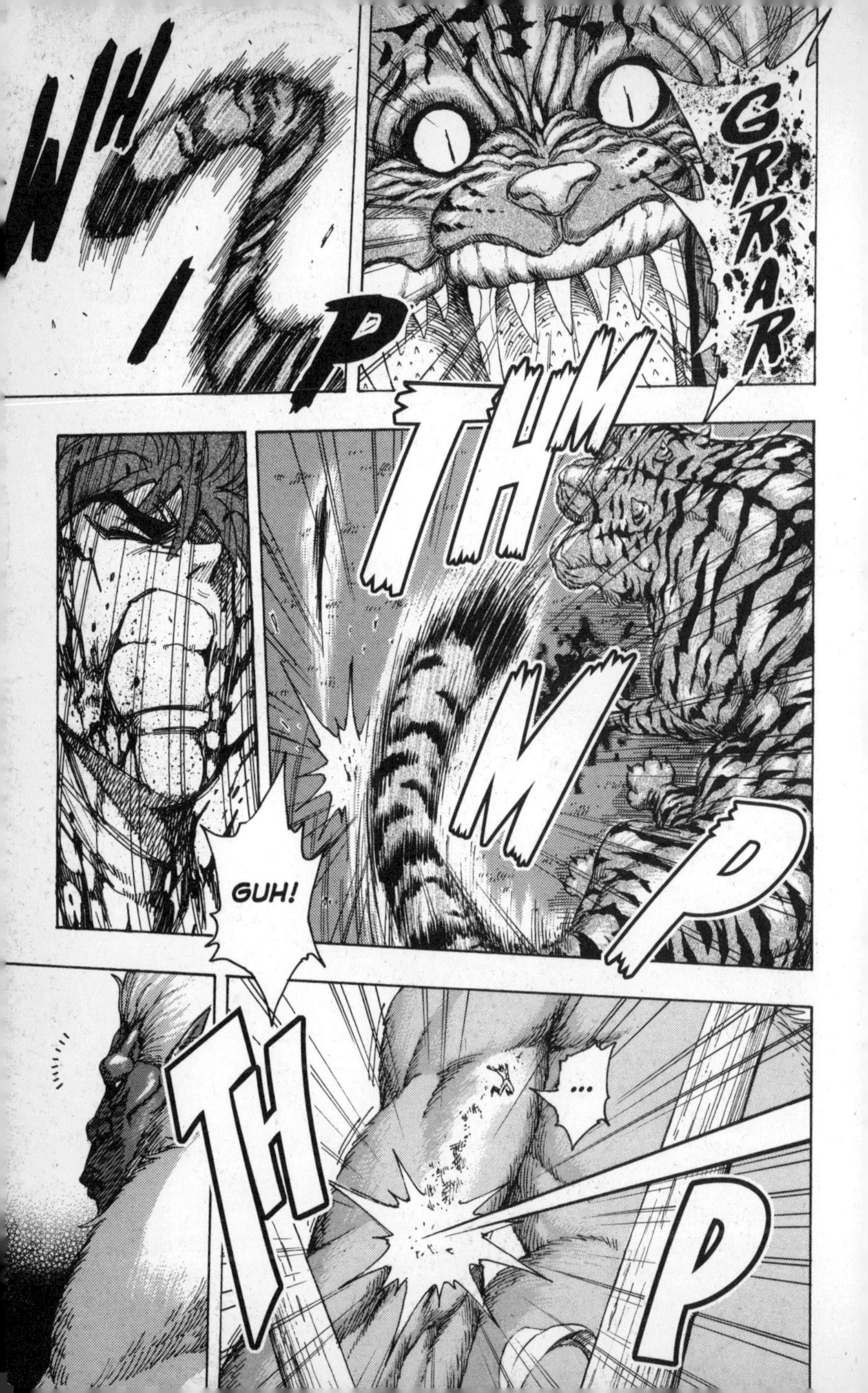
GRRAR
WHIP
THUMP
GUH!
...
THP

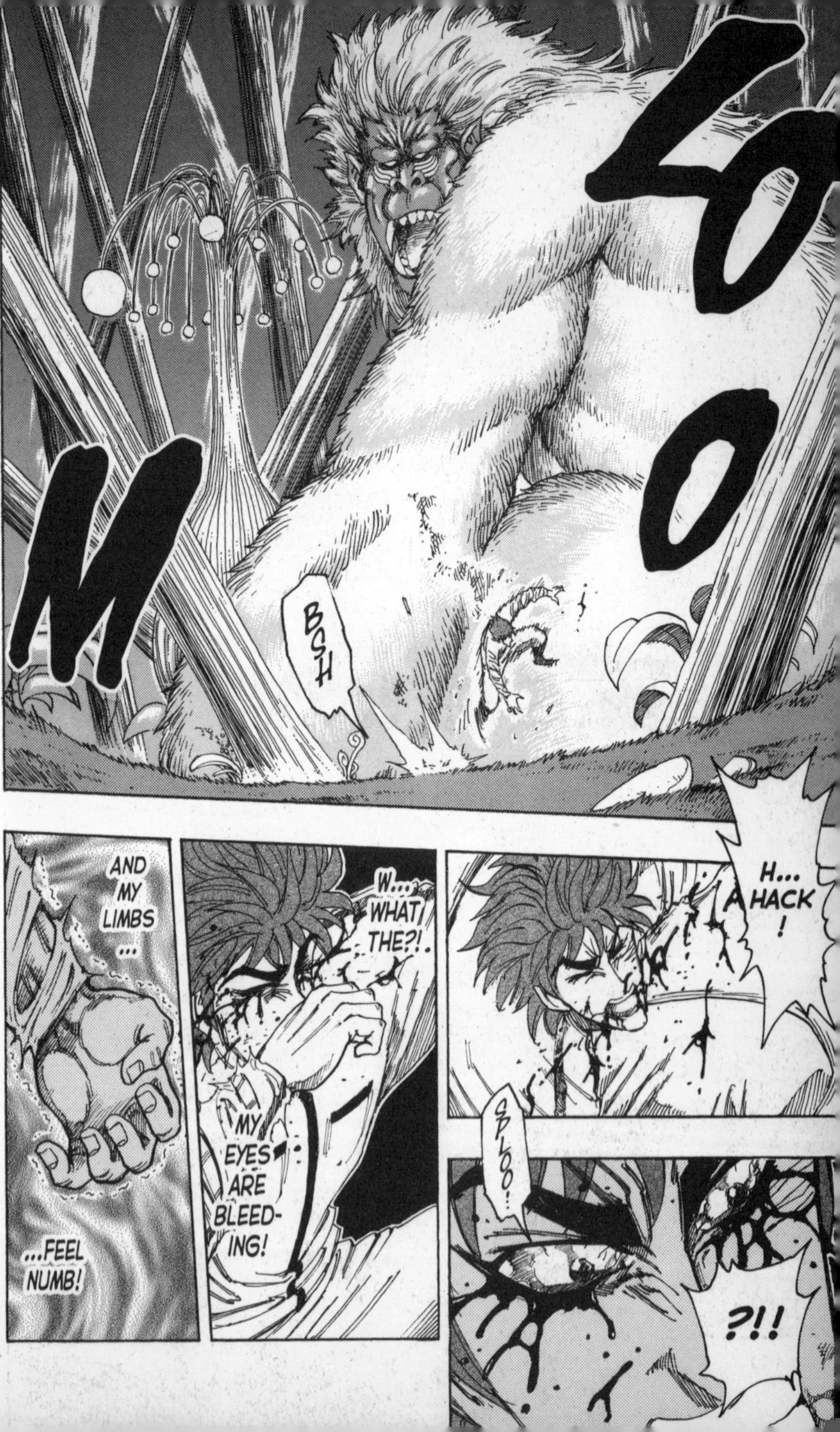
ZOOM
BSH
H... A HACK!
W... WHAT THE?!
MY EYES ARE BLEEDING!
AND MY LIMBS...
...FEEL NUMB!
SPLOO...
?!!

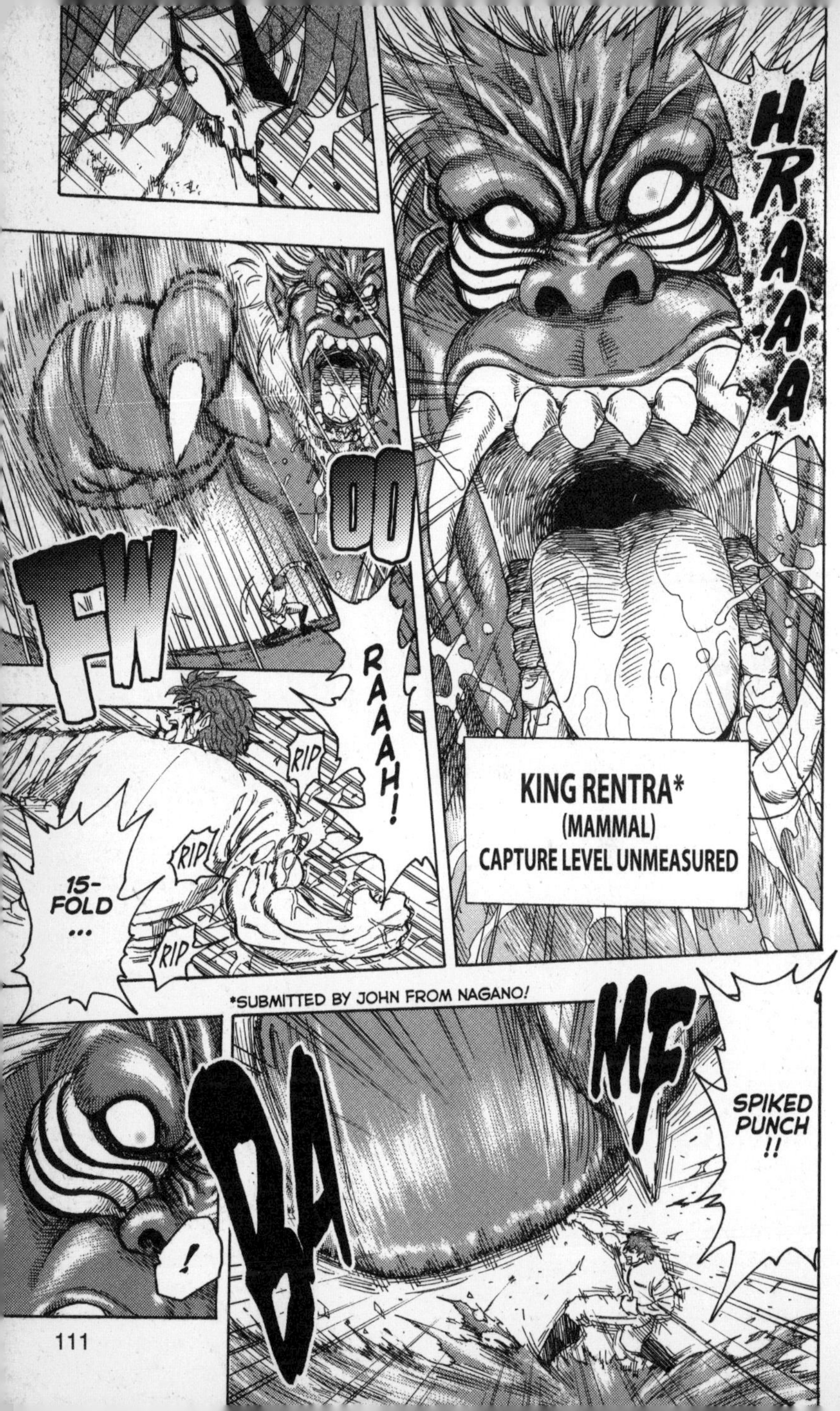
HRAAAA
KING RENTRA*
(MAMMAL)
CAPTURE LEVEL UNMEASURED
FWOO
RAAAAH!
RIP
RIP
RIP
15-FOLD ...
*SUBMITTED BY JOHN FROM NAGANO!
MF
SPIKED PUNCH !!
BA
!

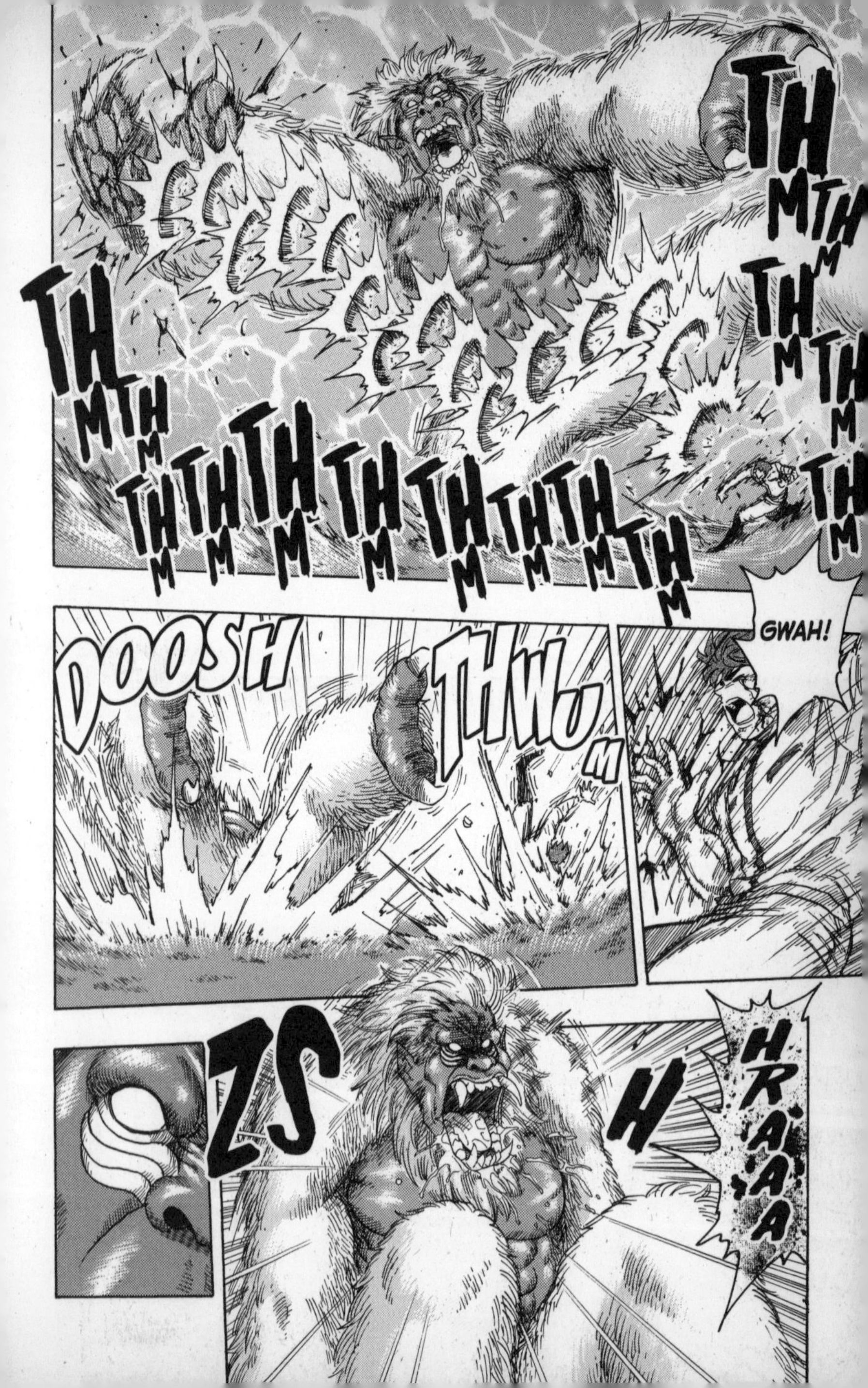
THMTHM
THMTHMTHM
THMTHM
THMTHMTHMTHMTHMTHMTHMTHMTHM
GWAH!
THWUM
DOOSH
HRAAAA
H
ZS

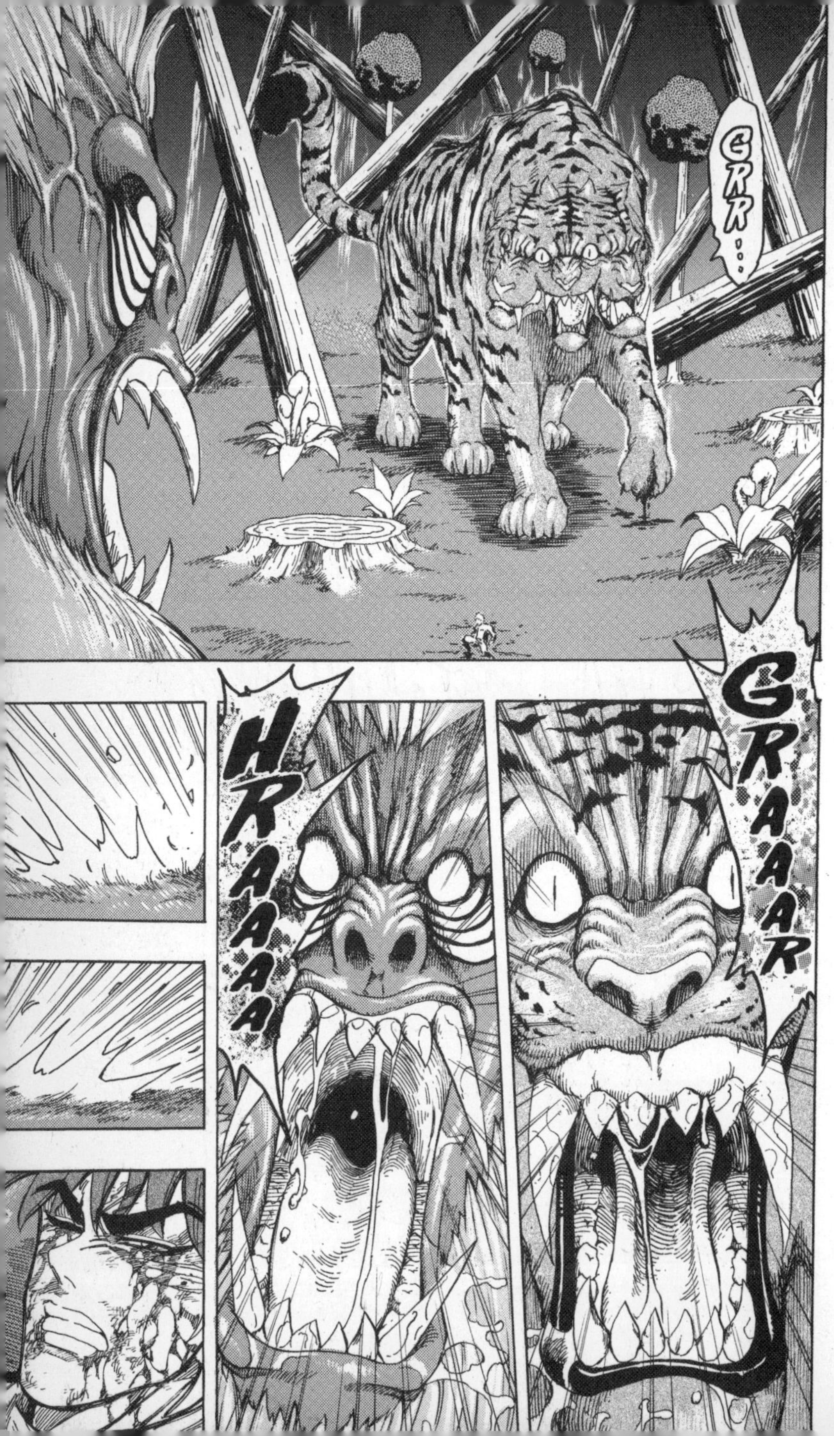
GRR...
GRAAAAR
HRAAAAA

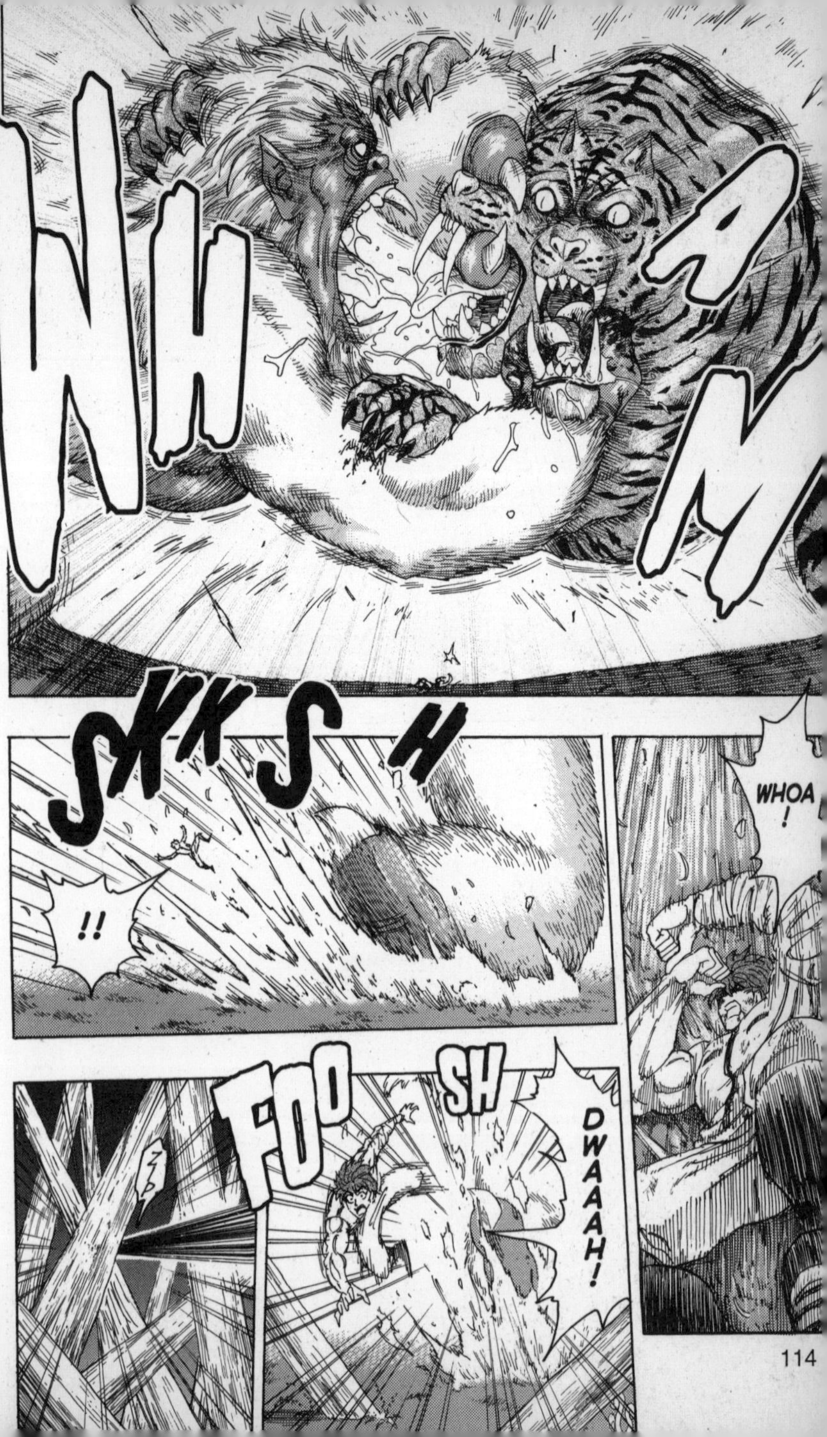
WHAM
WHOA!
SKKSH
!!
FOOSH
ZIP
DWAAAAH!

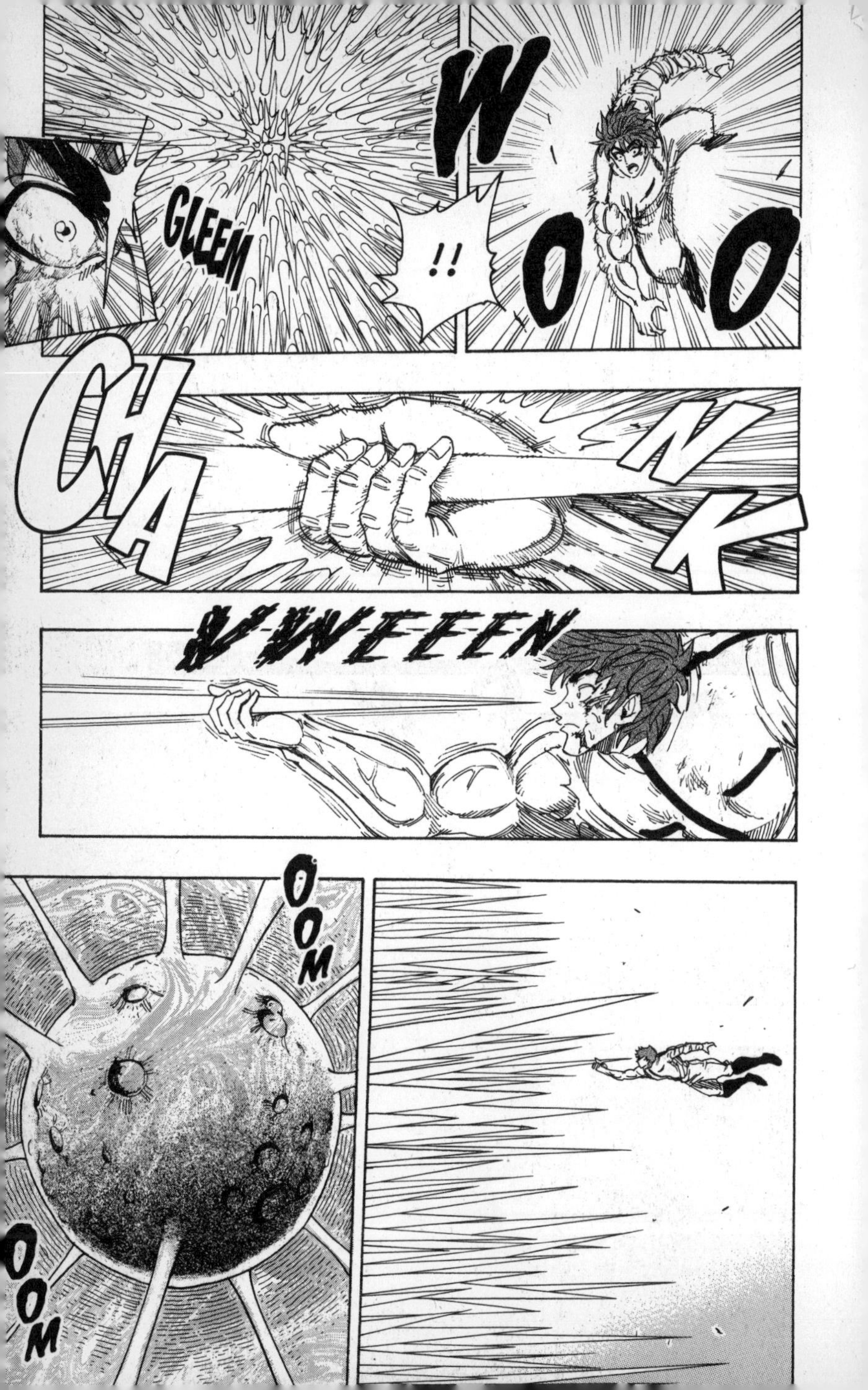
WOO
!!
GLEEM
CHANK
VVWEEEN
OOM
OOM

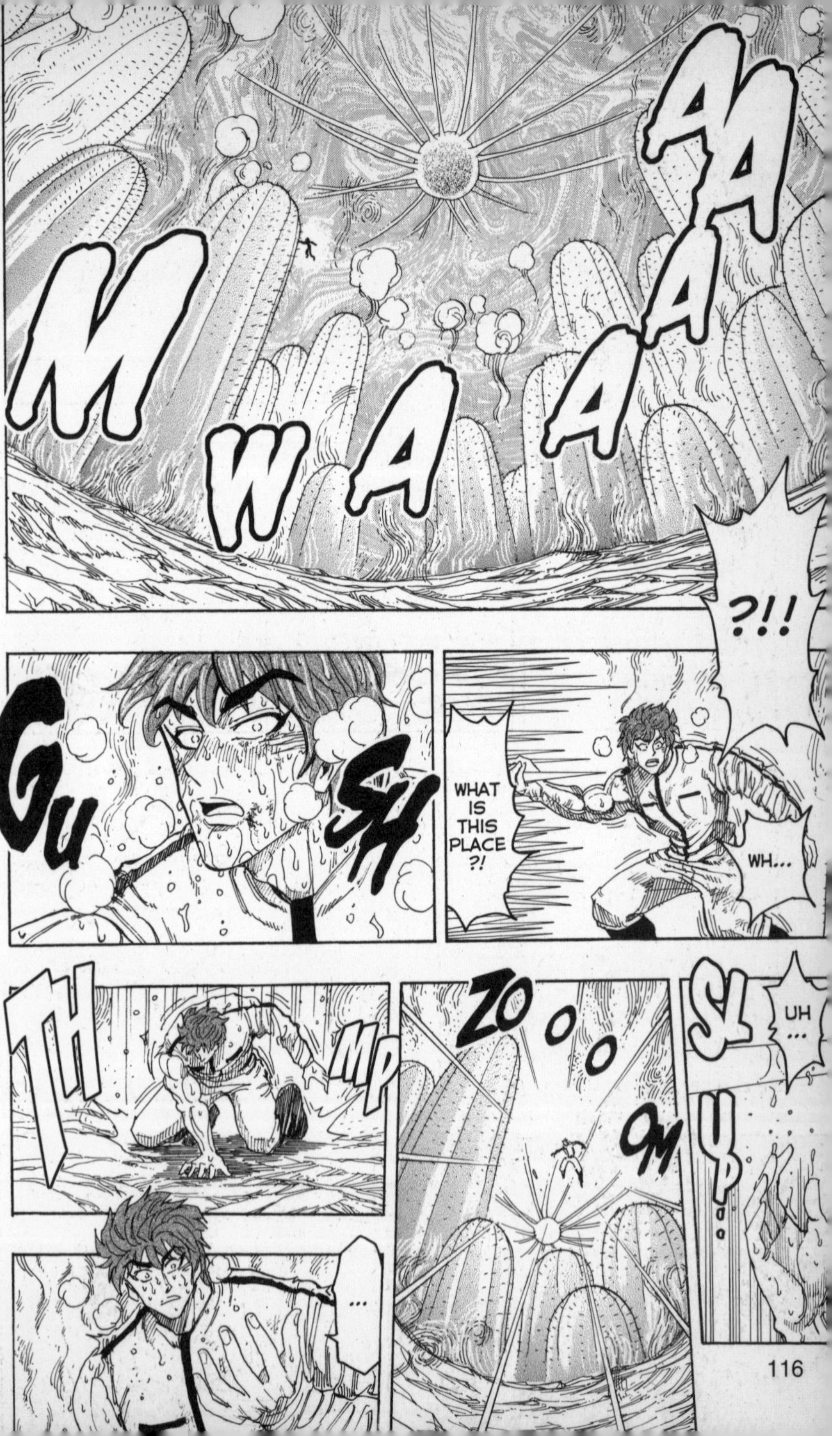

MWAAAAAA
?!!
WH...
WHAT IS THIS PLACE ?!
GUSH
UH ...
SLUP
ZOOOOM
THUMP
...

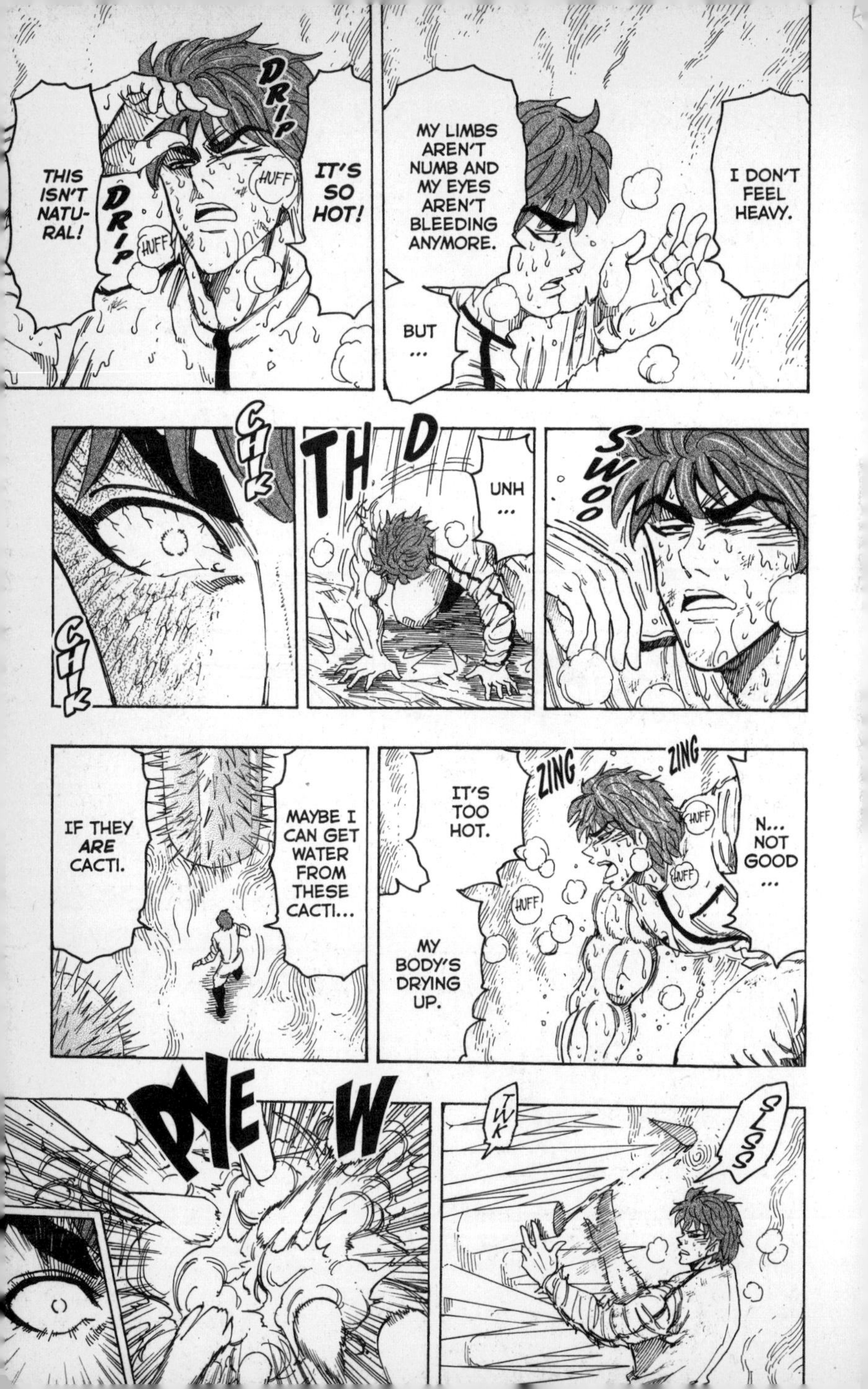
I DON'T FEEL HEAVY.
MY LIMBS AREN'T NUMB AND MY EYES AREN'T BLEEDING ANYMORE.
BUT ...
DRIP
IT'S SO HOT!
HUFF
DRIP
HUFF
THIS ISN'T NATU-RAL!
SWOO
THD
UNH ...
CHIK
CHIK
ZING
ZING
N... NOT GOOD ...
HUFF
HUFF
IT'S TOO HOT.
HUFF
MY BODY'S DRYING UP.
MAYBE I CAN GET WATER FROM THESE CACTI...
IF THEY *ARE* CACTI.
TWK
PYEW

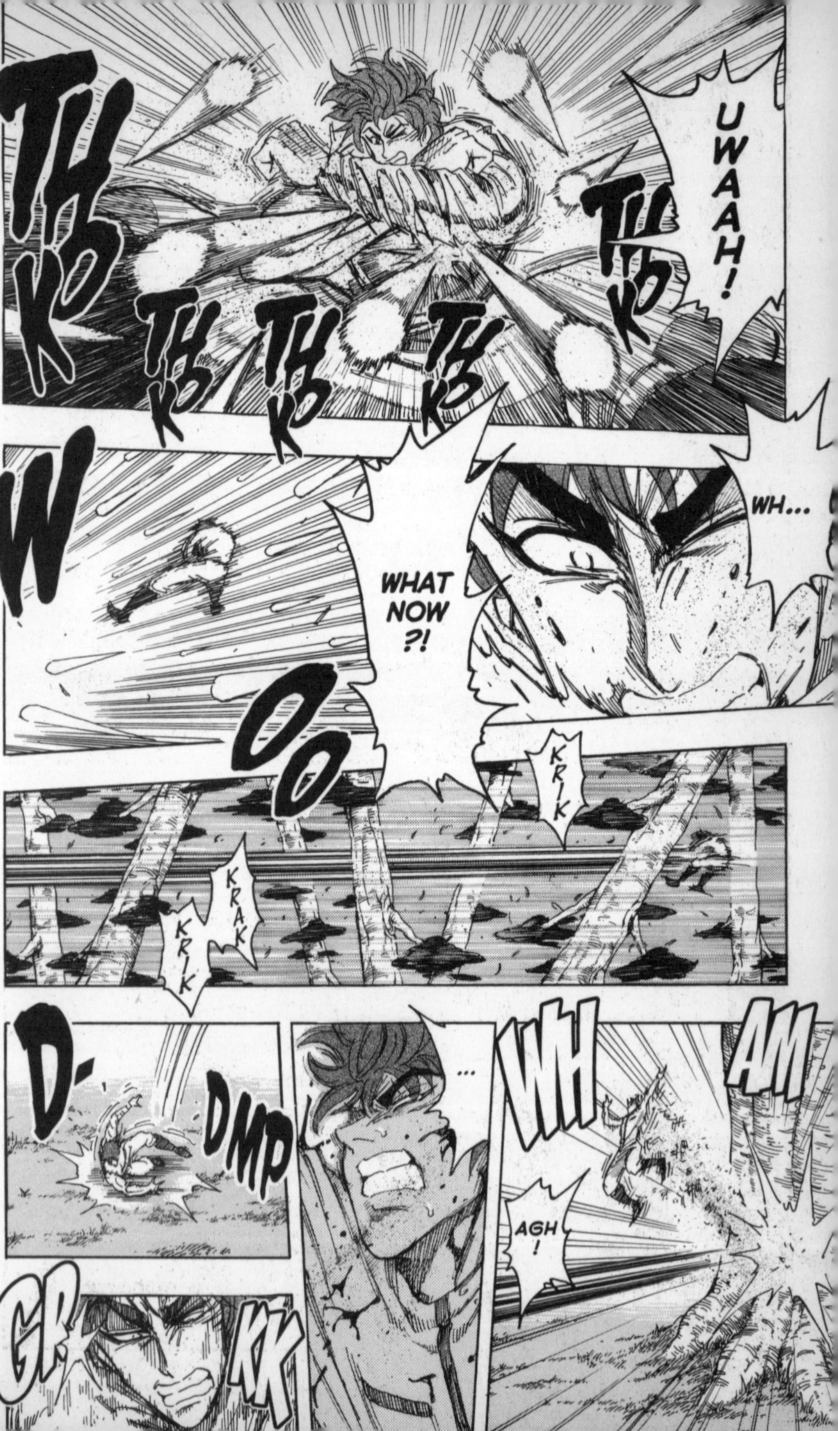
UWAAH!
THKO
THKO
THKO
THKO
THKO
WH...
WHAT NOW ?!
WOO
KRIK
KRAK
KRIK
WHAM
AGH!
...
D-DMP
GR KK

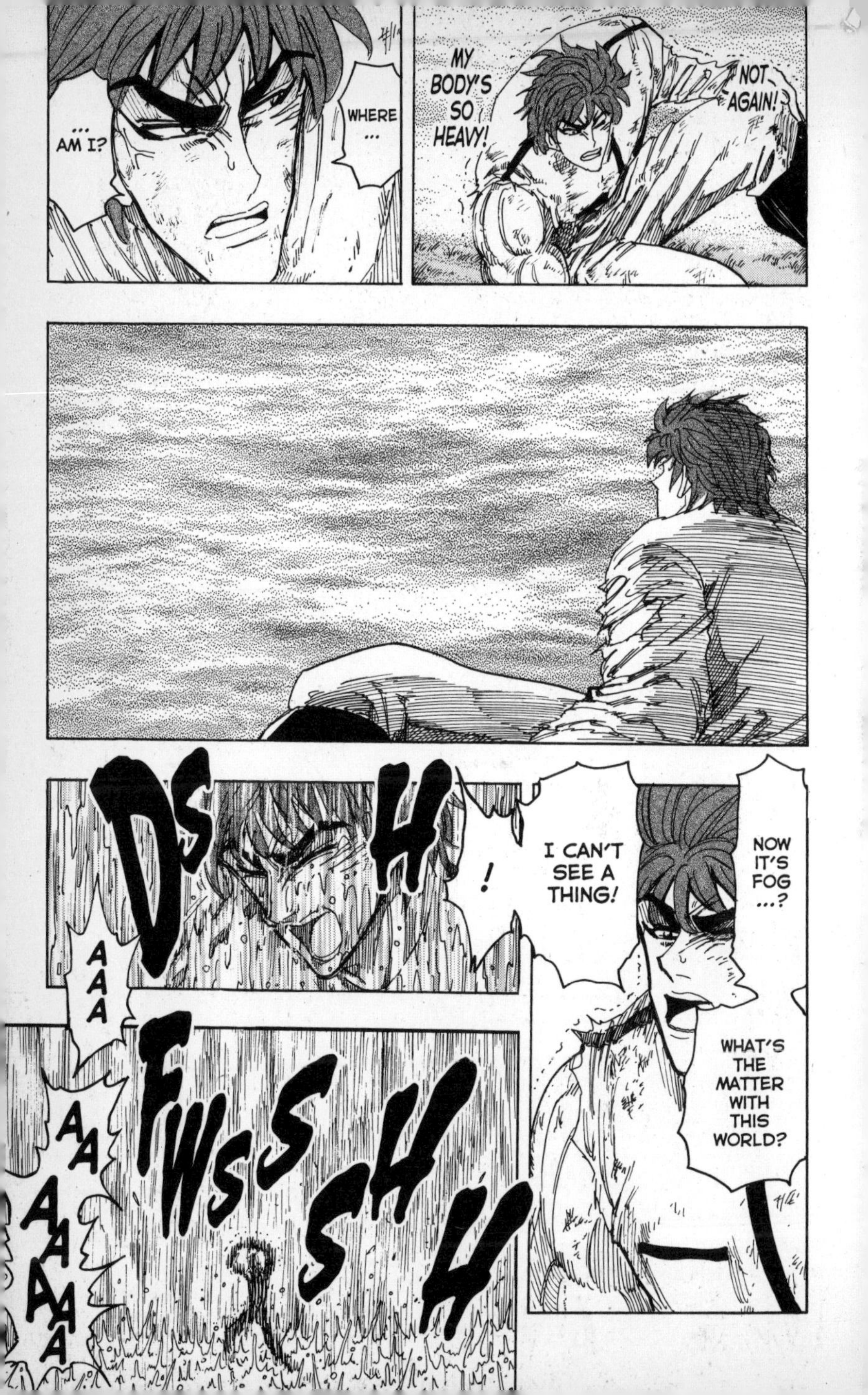
NOT AGAIN!
MY BODY'S SO HEAVY!
WHERE ...
... AM I?
NOW IT'S FOG ...?
WHAT'S THE MATTER WITH THIS WORLD?
I CAN'T SEE A THING!
!
DSH
AAA
AAAAAAAA
FWSSSHSHH

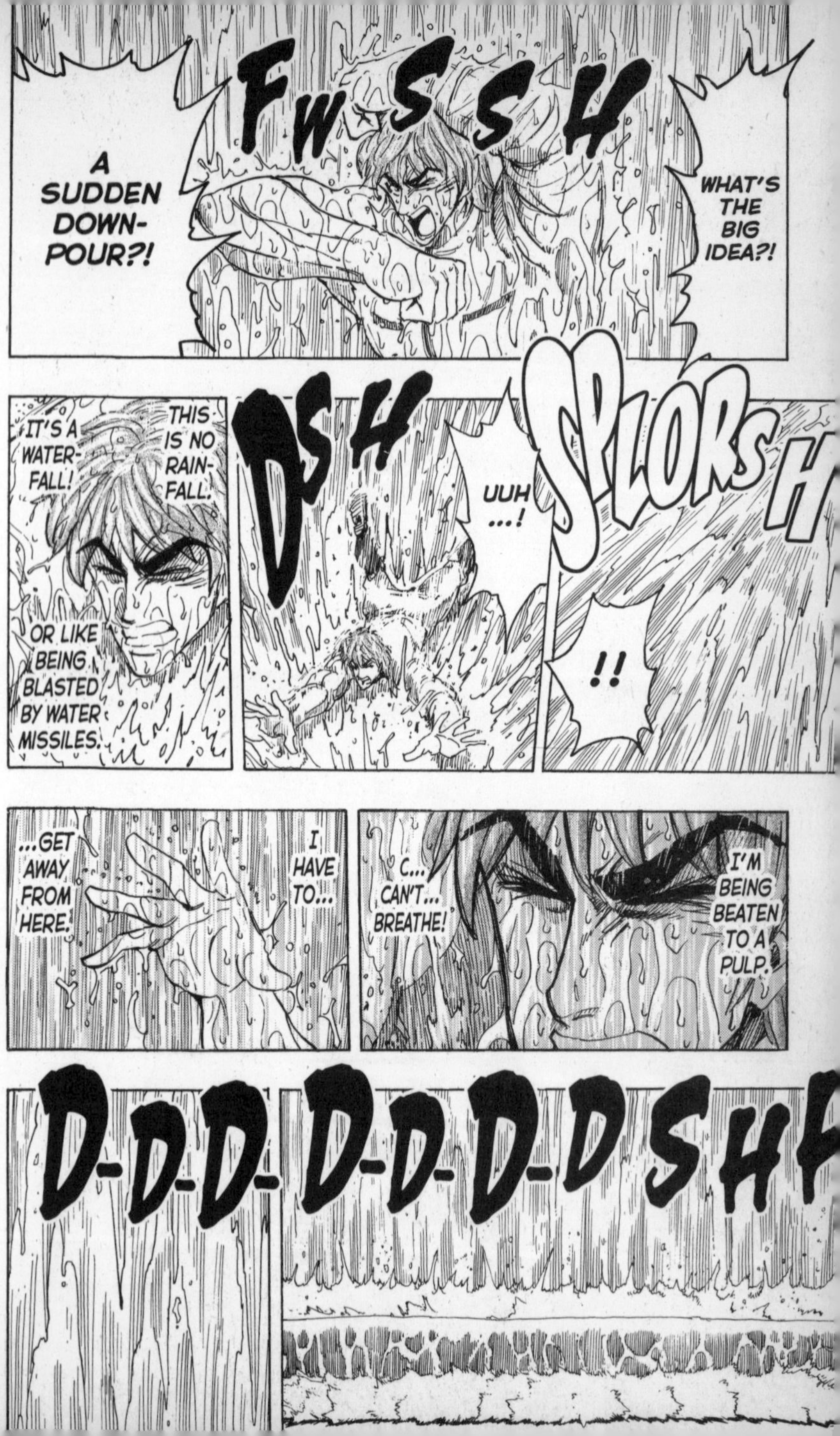
FWSSH
WHAT'S THE BIG IDEA?!
A SUDDEN DOWN-POUR?!
SPLORSH
!!
DSH
UUH ...!
THIS IS NO RAIN-FALL.
IT'S A WATER-FALL!
OR LIKE BEING BLASTED BY WATER MISSILES.
I'M BEING BEATEN TO A PULP.
C... CAN'T... BREATHE!
I HAVE TO...
...GET AWAY FROM HERE.
D-D-D-D-D-D-D-DSH

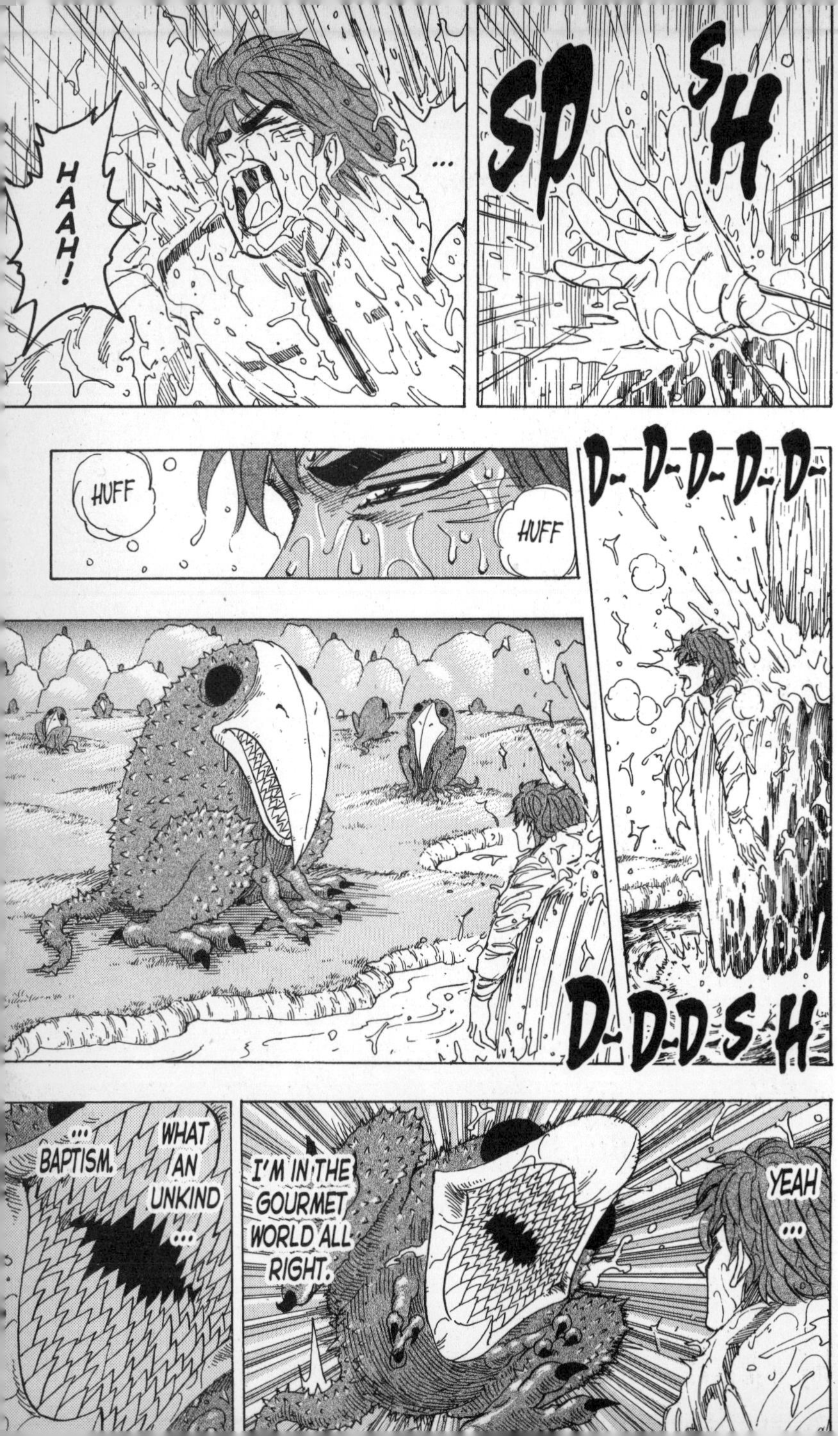
SP SH
...
HAAAH!
D- D- D- D- D-
HUFF
HUFF
D-D-D-S-H
YEAH ...
I'M IN THE GOURMET WORLD ALL RIGHT.
WHAT AN UNKIND ...
... BAPTISM.

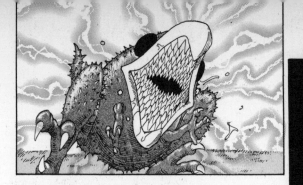

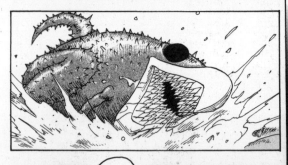

EVEN *I* GO WITHOUT A DRINK...

...HERE IN THE GOURMET WORLD.

SH F

SHUNK

122

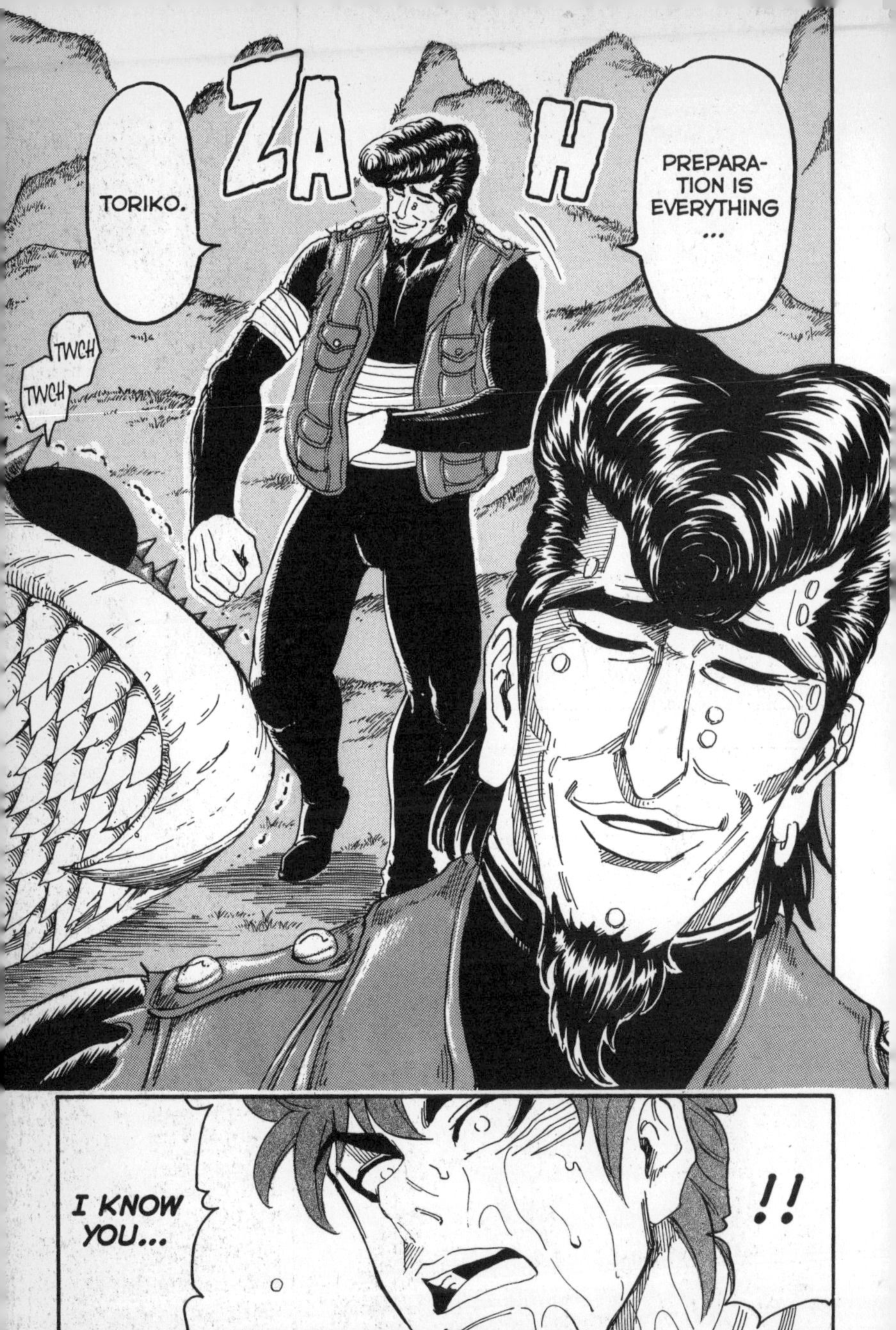
PREPARATION IS EVERYTHING ...
ZAH
TORIKO.
TWCH
TWCH
!!
I KNOW YOU...

TORIKO

GOURMET CHECKLIST

Vol. 126

HEALING JELLY
(YOSAKU SIGNATURE ITEM)

CAPTURE LEVEL: ---

HABITAT: YOSAKU'S REVIVAL LAB

LENGTH: ---

HEIGHT: ---

WEIGHT: ---

PRICE: 30,000 YEN PER LITER

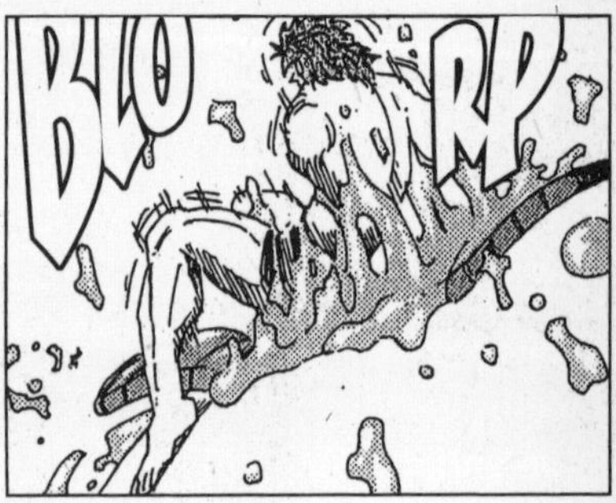
BLOORP

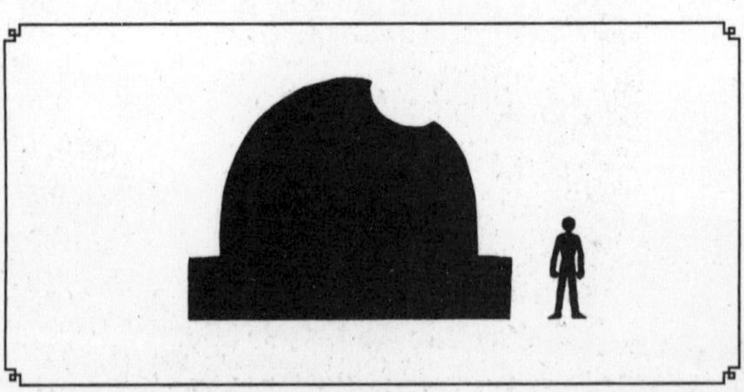

SCALE

YOSAKU CREATED THIS JELLY BY COMBINING MEDICINE BEE WORKER SALIVA, MEDICINE BEE ROYAL JELLY, AND VARIOUS HERBAL MEDICINES. IT'S A STRONG TONIC CHOCK FULL OF VITAMINS AND CAN ACTUALLY BE INGESTED, THOUGH SOAKING YOUR WHOLE BODY IN THE JELLY IS THE MOST EFFECTIVE MEANS OF BENEFITTING FROM ITS HEALING PROPERTIES.

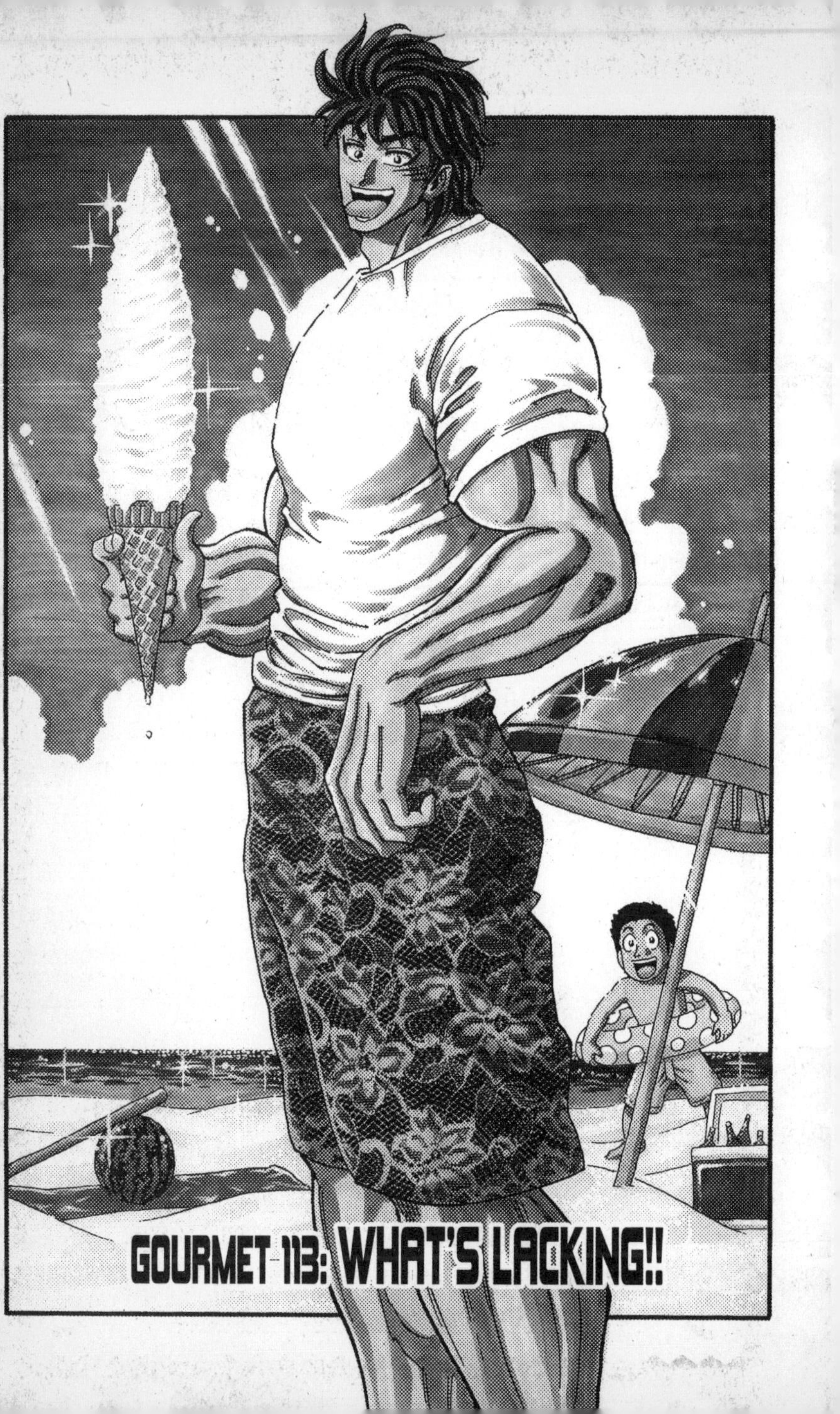
GOURMET 113: WHAT'S LACKING!!

TORIKO

GOURMET CHECKLIST

Vol. 127

SPINY EEL
(FISH)

CAPTURE LEVEL: 13

HABITAT: RELATIVELY LARGE OCEANS

LENGTH: 1 METER

HEIGHT: ---

WEIGHT: 12 KG

PRICE: 15,000 YEN PER FISH

SCALE

DID THIS END UP IN KOMATSU'S RECIPE FOR CENTURY SOUP? A LONG, SLENDER FISH FROM THE EEL FAMILY, THE SPINY EEL HATCHES IN THE DEEP SEAS, LIVES IN OPEN WATERS AS A JUVENILE, AND THEN SPENDS ITS ADULT LIFE IN LAKES AND RIVERS. TRUE TO ITS NAME, THE SPINY EEL IS ALMOST ALL SPINES AND NO MEAT. HOWEVER, THOSE SPINES PRODUCE A SUPERB SOUP STOCK. CHEFS WILL SHELL OUT TOP DOLLAR FOR THE BEST SPINY EELS.

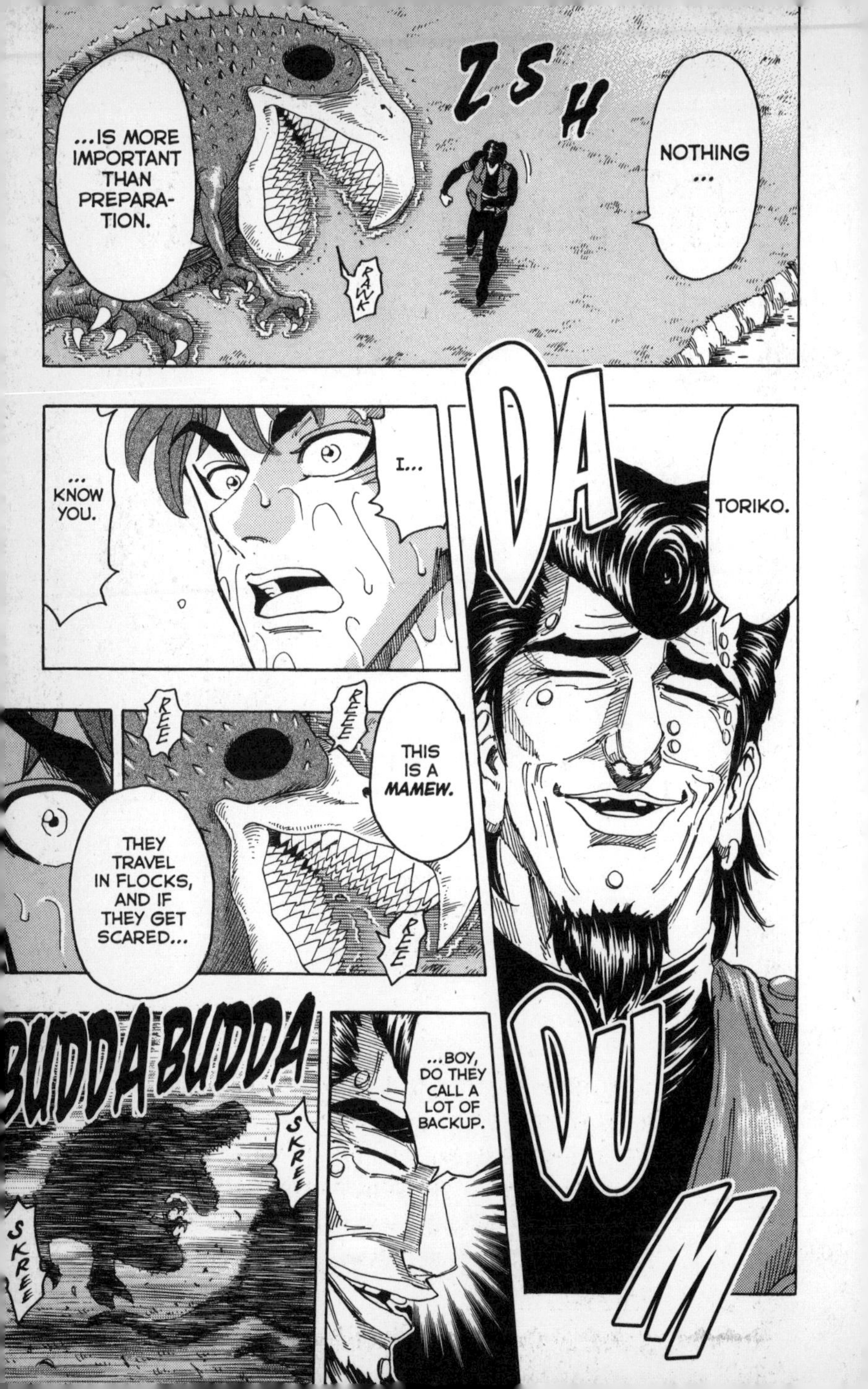
NOTHING ...
ZSH
...IS MORE IMPORTANT THAN PREPARATION.
PAWK
I...
... KNOW YOU.
TORIKO.
DA
OU
M
REE
REE
THIS IS A *MAMEW.*
THEY TRAVEL IN FLOCKS, AND IF THEY GET SCARED...
REE
...BOY, DO THEY CALL A LOT OF BACKUP.
BUDDA BUDDA
SKREE
SKREE

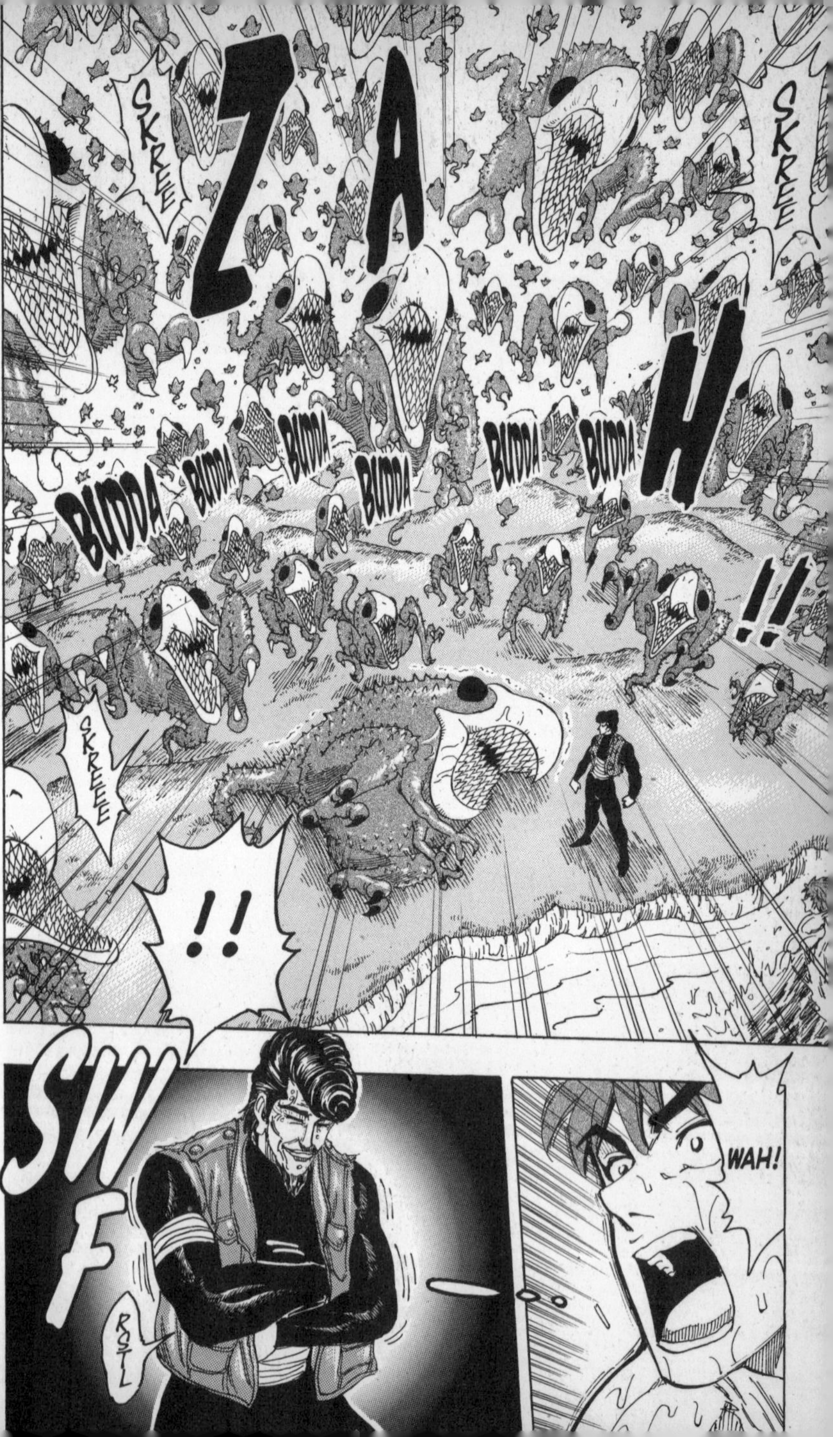
SKREE
ZA
SKREE
H
!!
BUDDA
BUDDA
BUDDA
BUDDA
BUDDA
BUDDA
SKREEEE
!!
WAH!
SW
F
RSTL

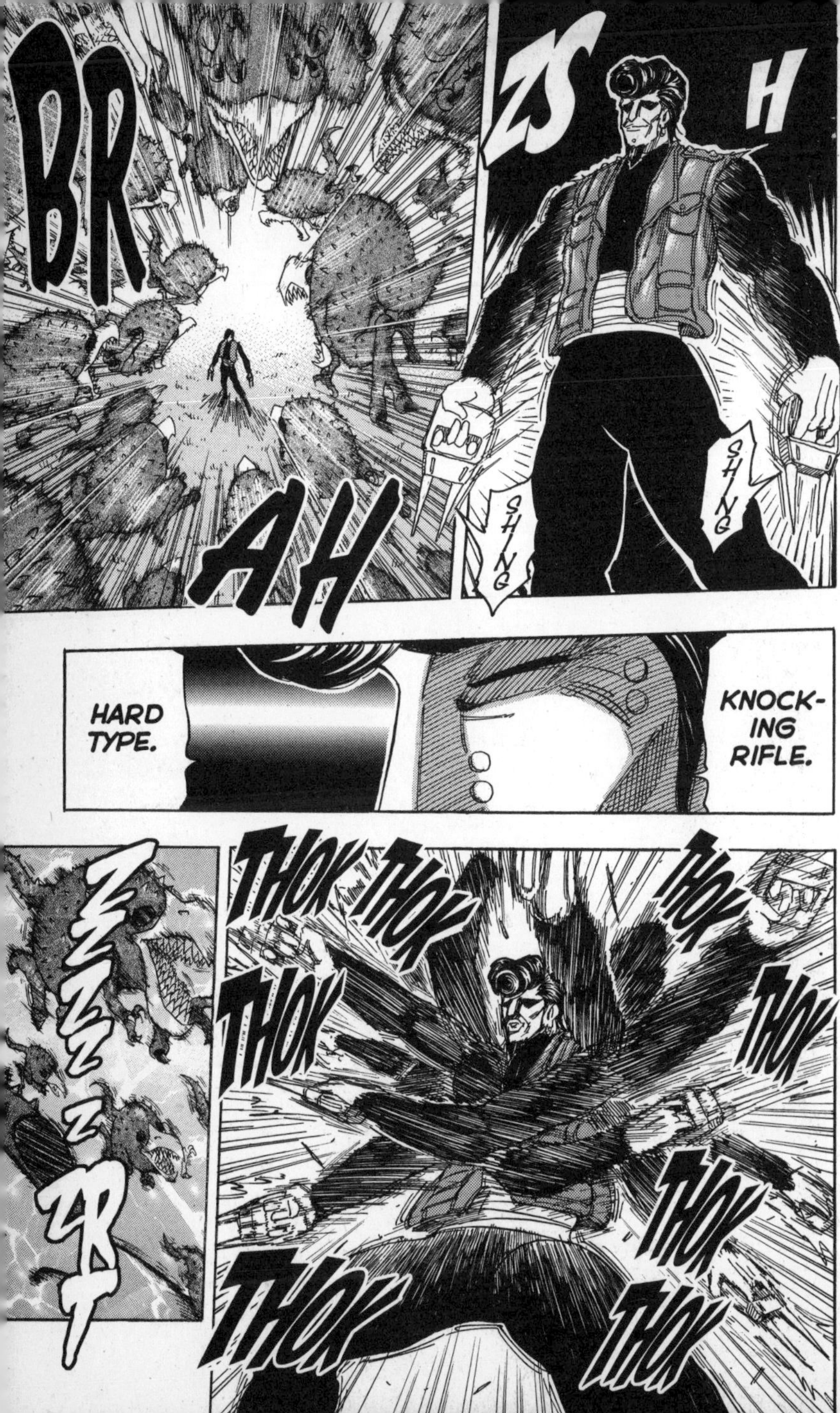
ZSH
SHING
SHING
BR
AH
KNOCKING-ING RIFLE.
HARD TYPE.
THOK
THOK
THOK
THOK
THOK THOK
THOK
THOK

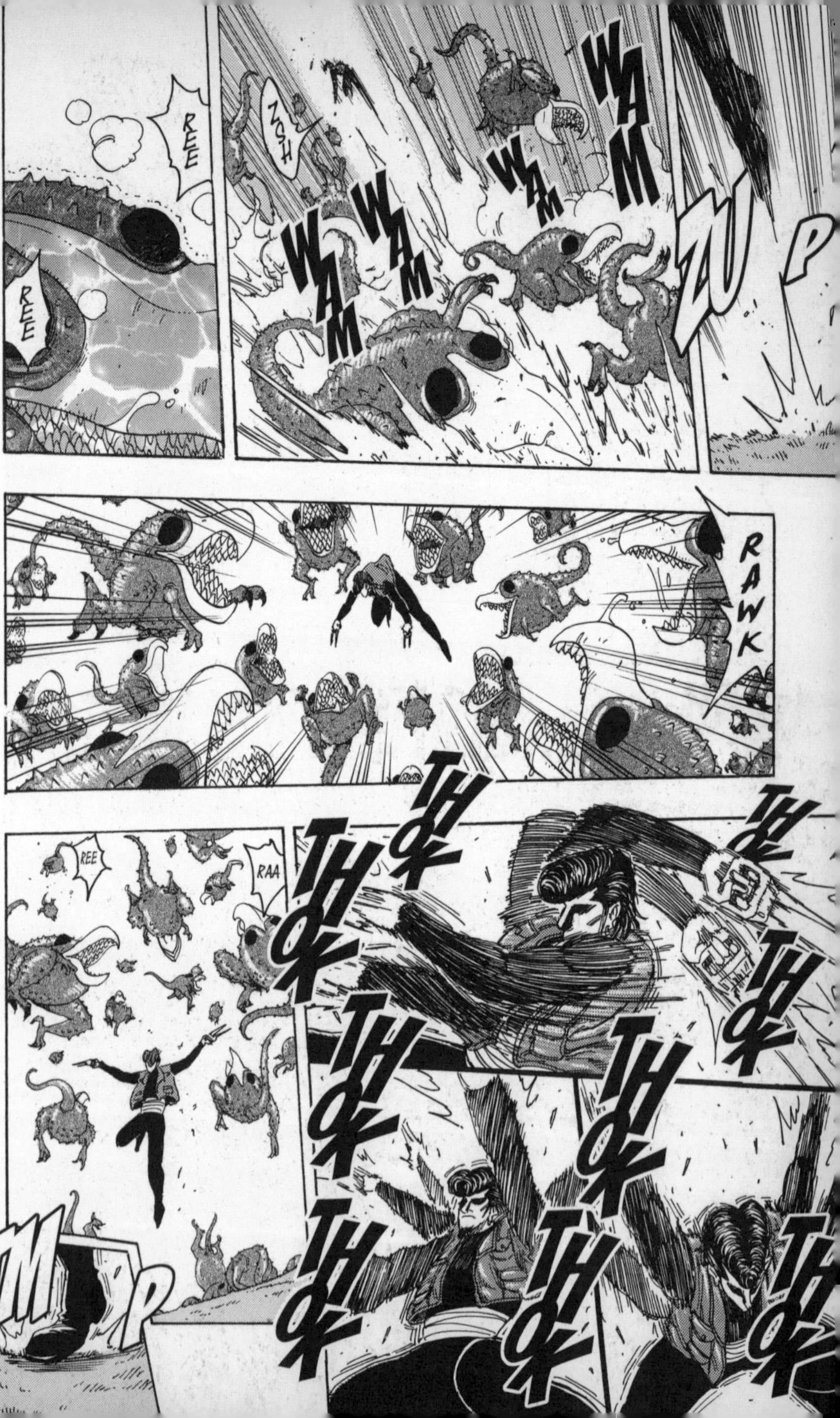
ZUP
WAM WAM
WAM
WAM
ZASH
REE
REE
RAWK
THOK THOK
THOK
THOK THOK
THOK THOK THOK
THOK
RAA
REE
TMP

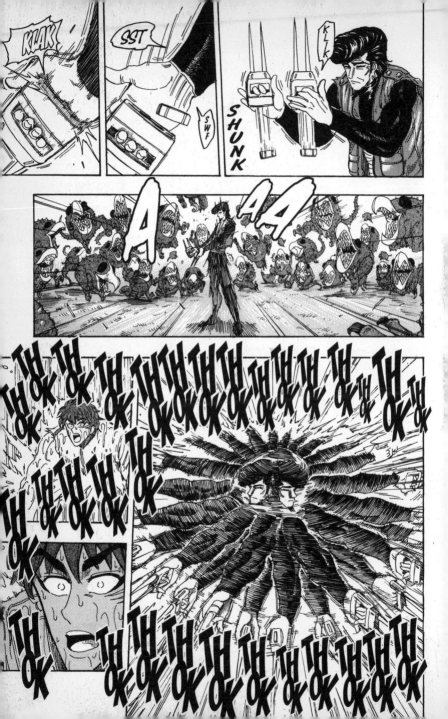

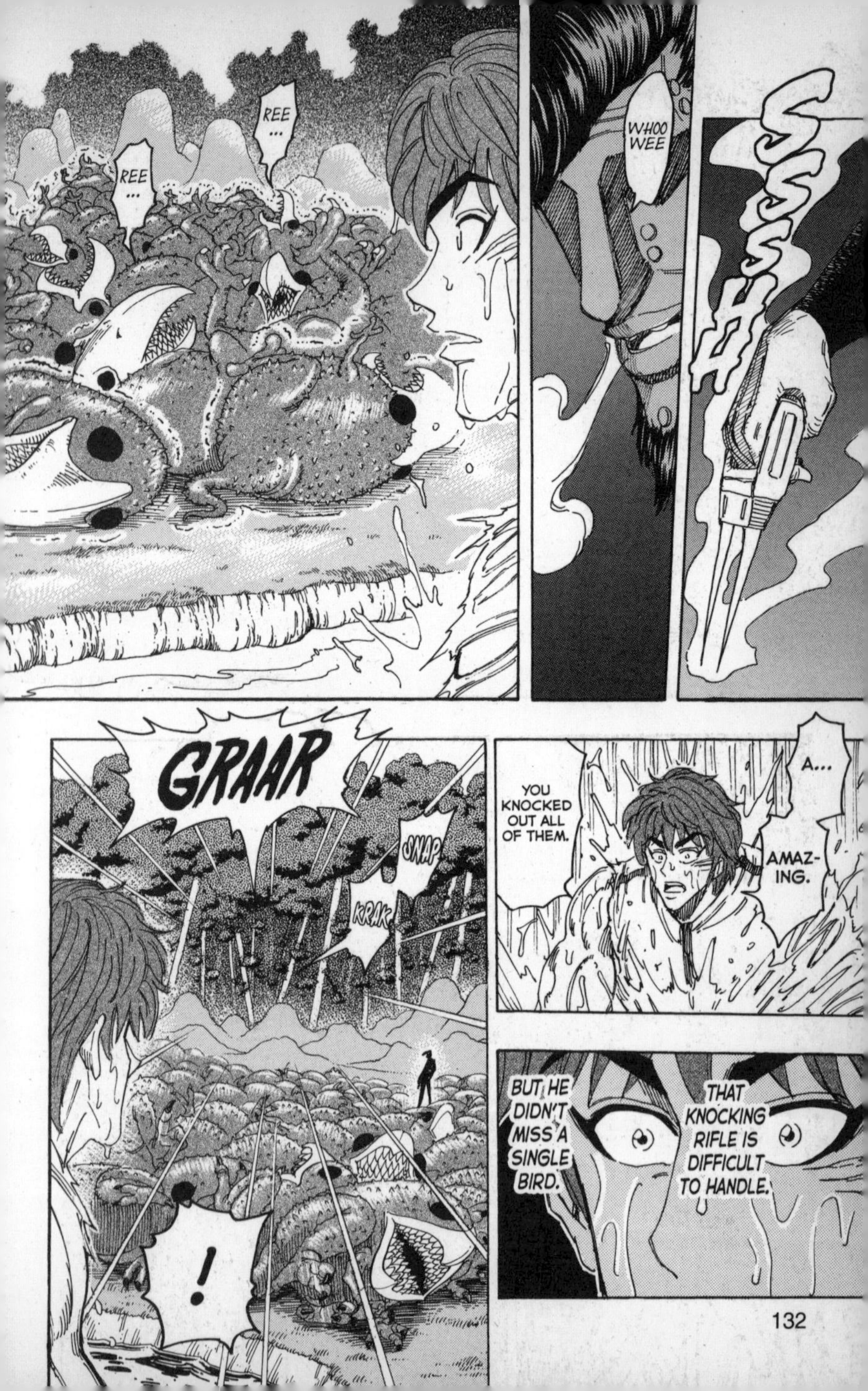
SSSHH
WHOO WEE
REE...
REE...
A...
AMAZ-ING.
YOU KNOCKED OUT ALL OF THEM.
THAT KNOCKING RIFLE IS DIFFICULT TO HANDLE.
BUT HE DIDN'T MISS A SINGLE BIRD.
GRAAR
SNAP
KRAK
!

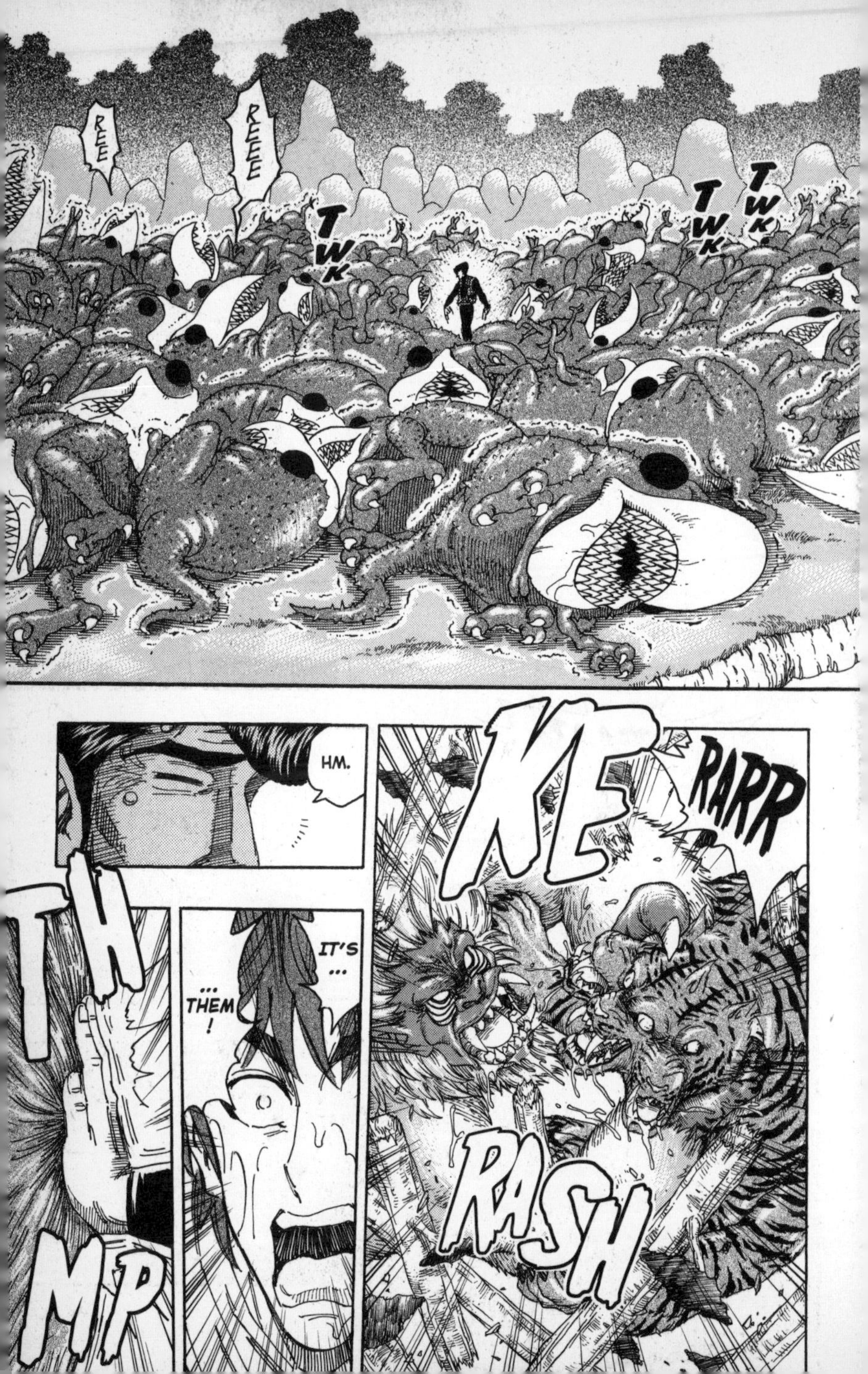
REEE
REE
TWK
TWK
TWK
KERASH
RARRR
HM.
IT'S ...
... THEM!
THMP

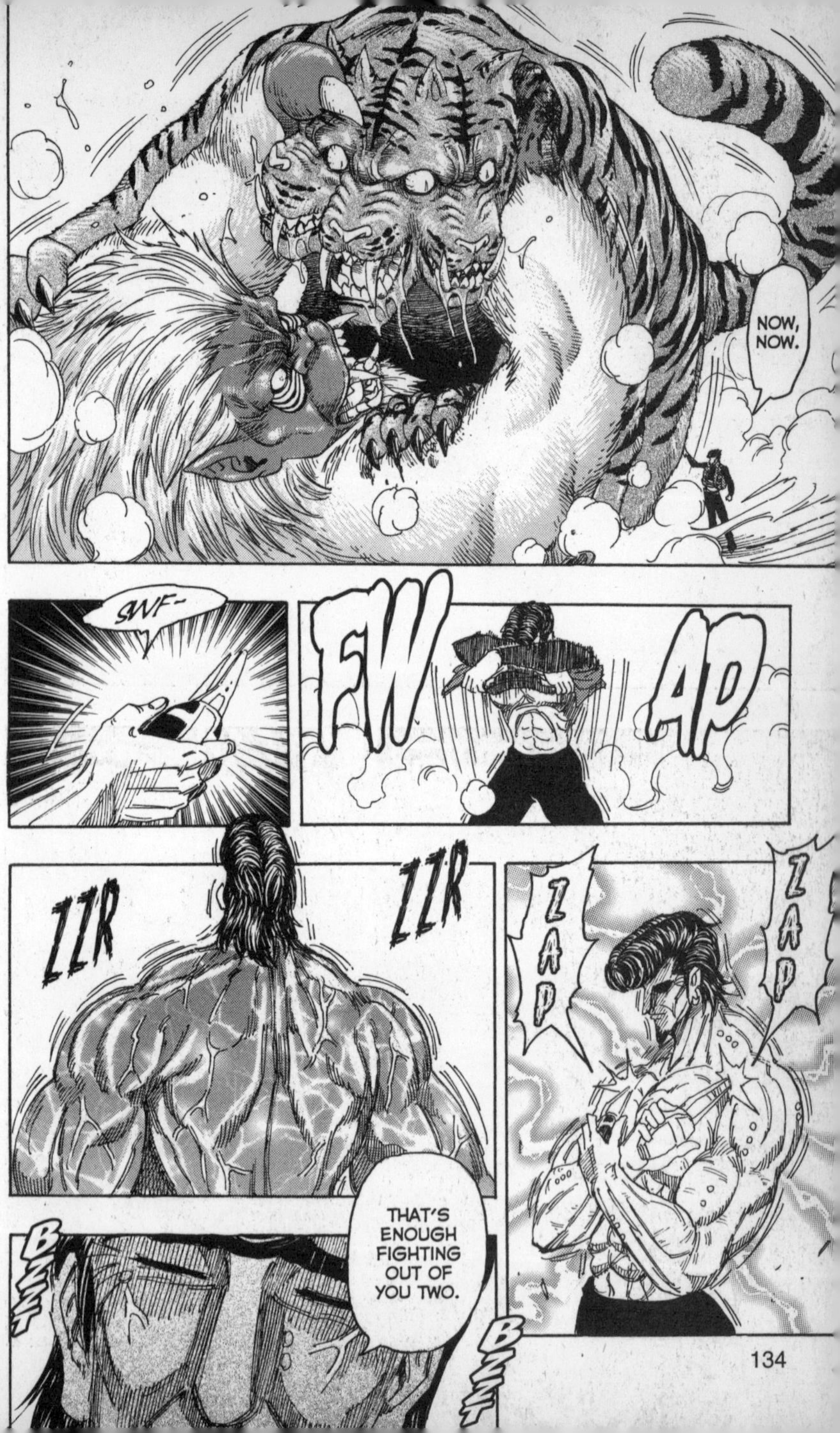
NOW, NOW.
FW
AP
SNF-
ZAP
ZAP
ZZR
ZZR
THAT'S ENOUGH FIGHTING OUT OF YOU TWO.
BZZT
BZZT

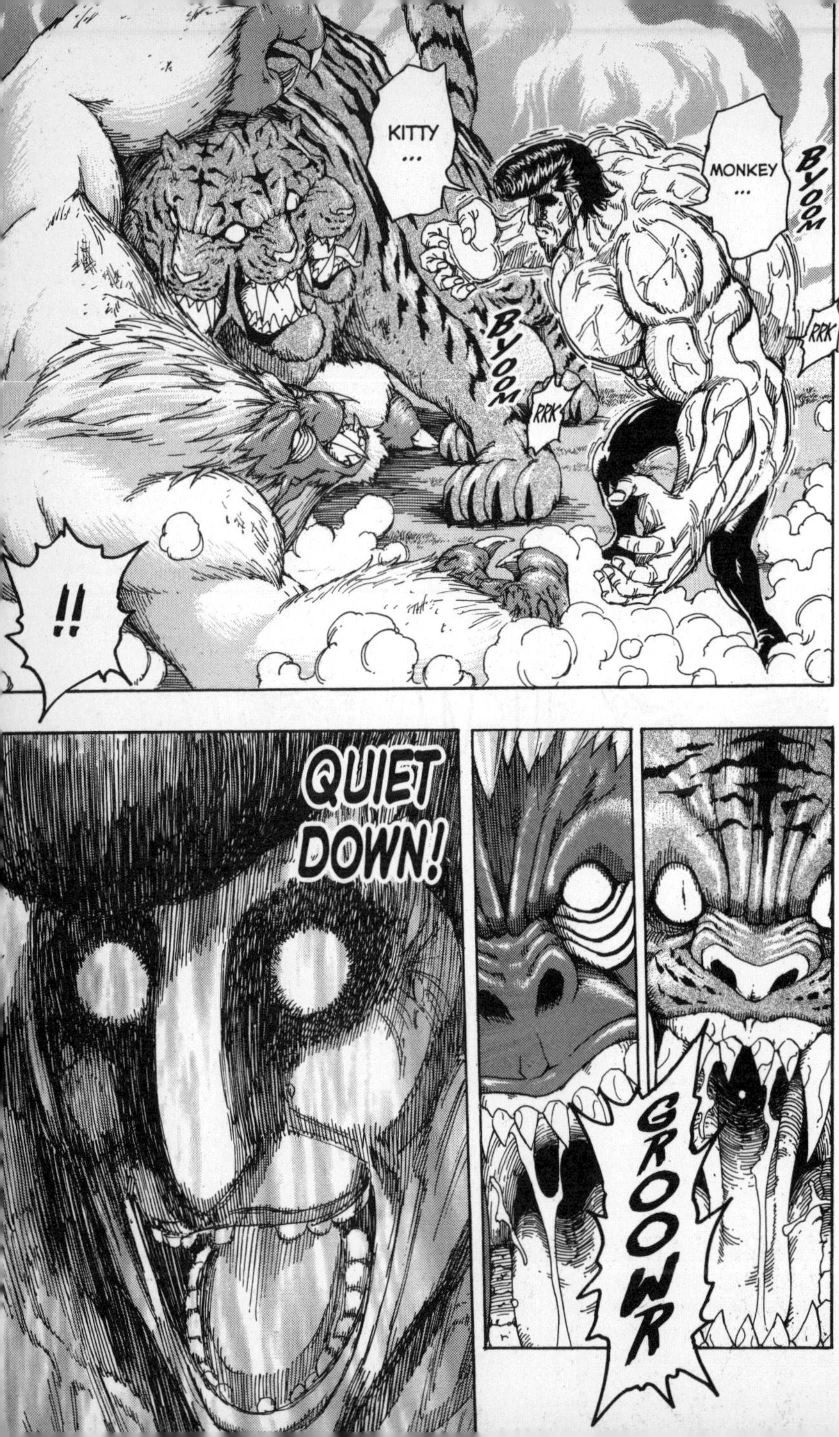
MONKEY ...
BYOOM
RRK
KITTY ...
BYOOM
RRK
!!
GROOOWR
QUIET DOWN!

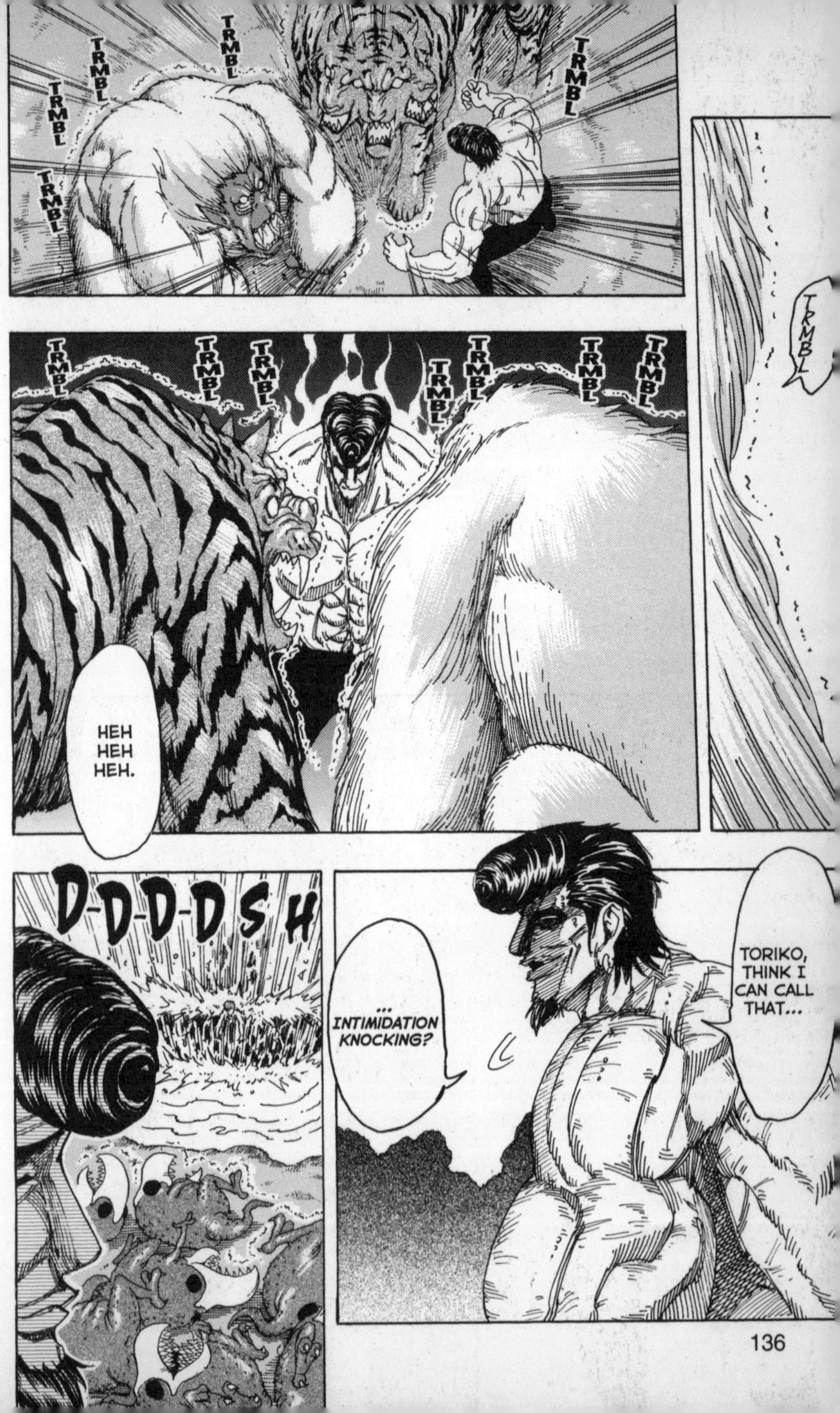
TRMBL
TRMBL
TRMBL
TRMBL
TRMBL
TRMBL
TRMBL
TRMBL
TRMBL
TRMBL
TRMBL
TRMBL
TRMBL
HEH HEH HEH.
TORIKO, THINK I CAN CALL THAT...
...INTIMIDATION KNOCKING?
D-D-D-DSH

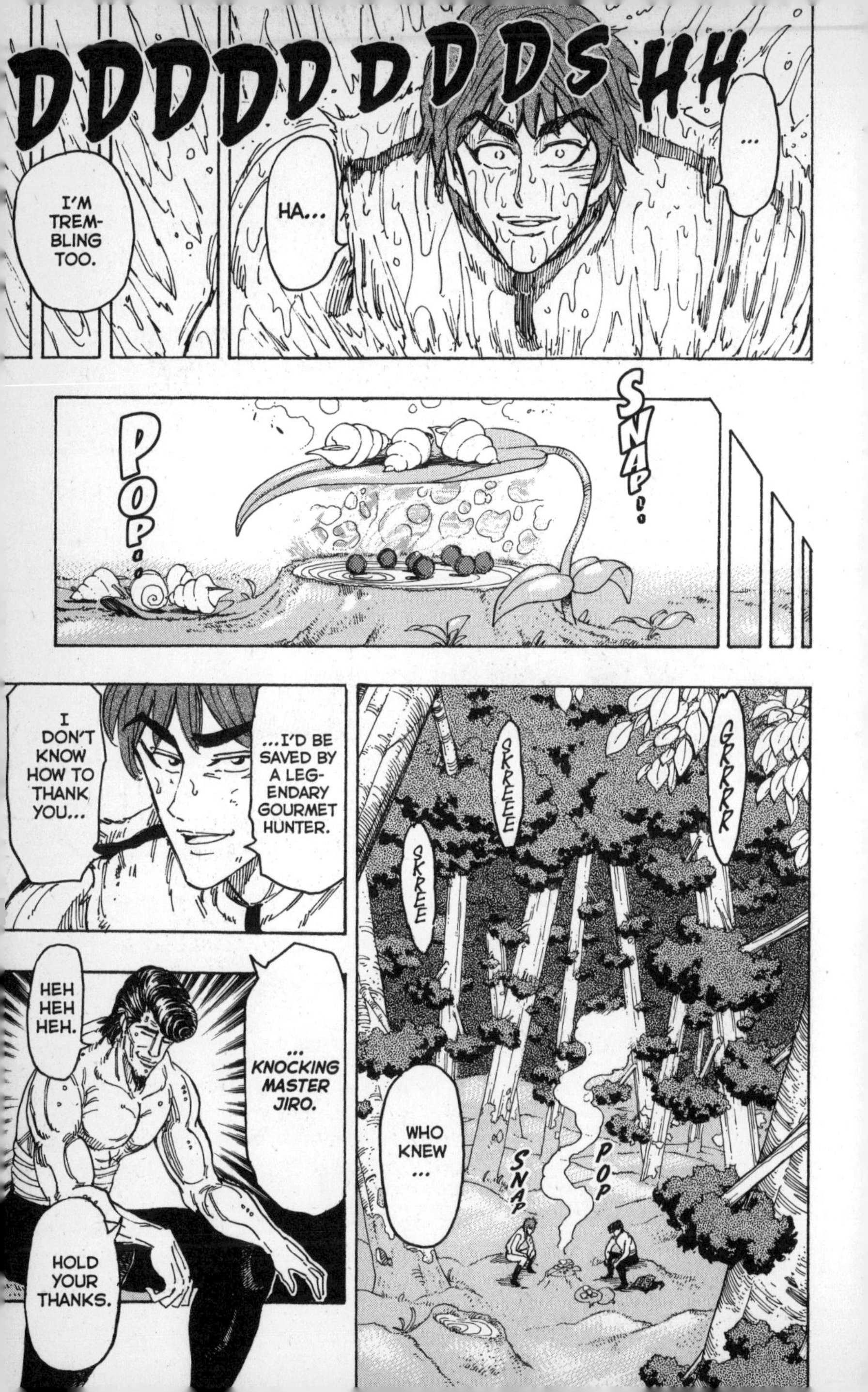
DDDDDDDDSHH
...
HA...
I'M TREMBLING TOO.
POP
SNAP
GRRRR
SKREEE
SKREE
WHO KNEW...
SNAP
POP
...I'D BE SAVED BY A LEGENDARY GOURMET HUNTER.
I DON'T KNOW HOW TO THANK YOU...
...KNOCKING MASTER JIRO.
HEH HEH HEH.
HOLD YOUR THANKS.

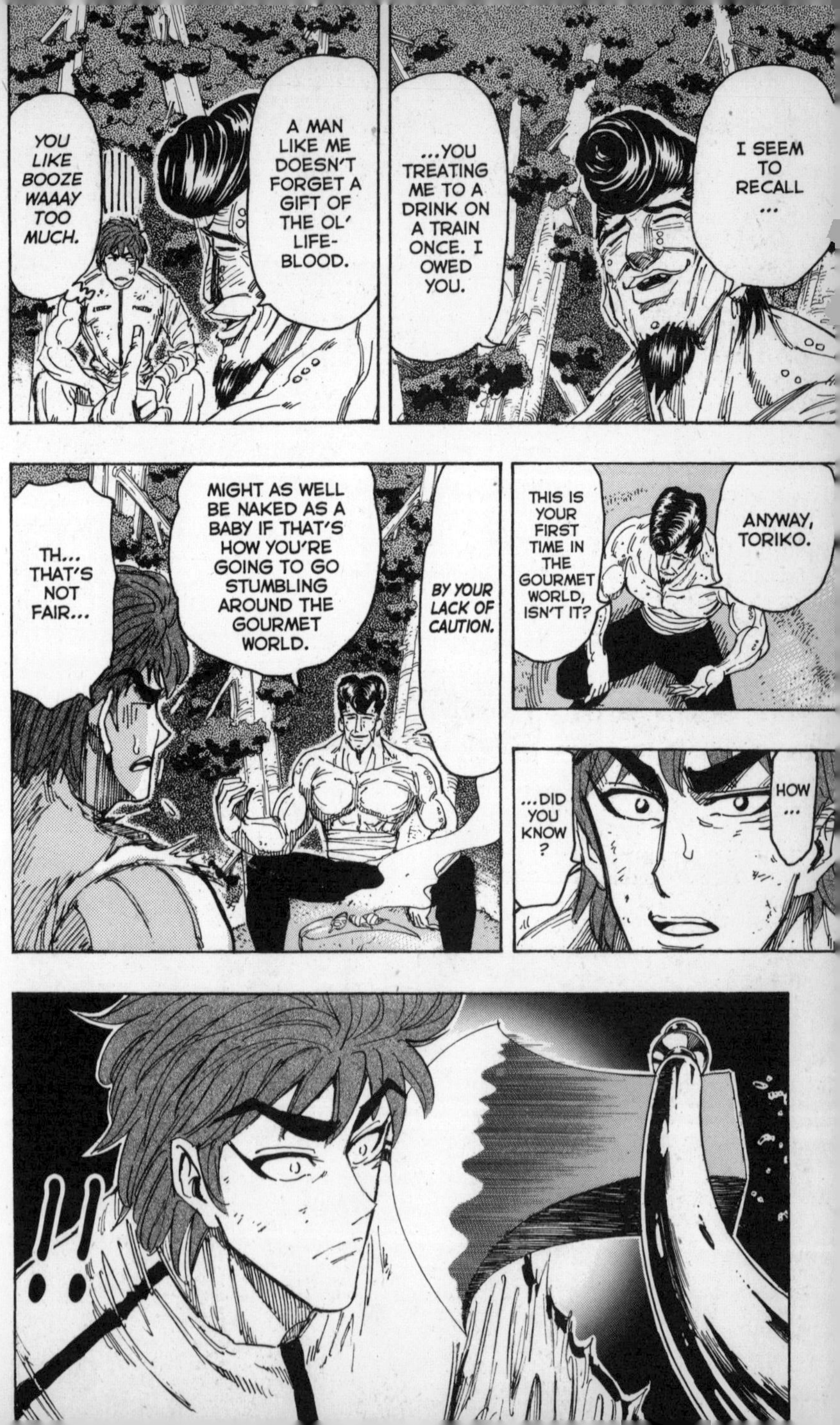
I SEEM TO RECALL...
...YOU TREATING ME TO A DRINK ON A TRAIN ONCE. I OWED YOU.
A MAN LIKE ME DOESN'T FORGET A GIFT OF THE OL' LIFE-BLOOD.
YOU LIKE BOOZE WAAAY TOO MUCH.
ANYWAY, TORIKO.
THIS IS YOUR FIRST TIME IN THE GOURMET WORLD, ISN'T IT?
HOW...
...DID YOU KNOW?
BY YOUR LACK OF CAUTION.
MIGHT AS WELL BE NAKED AS A BABY IF THAT'S HOW YOU'RE GOING TO GO STUMBLING AROUND THE GOURMET WORLD.
TH... THAT'S NOT FAIR...

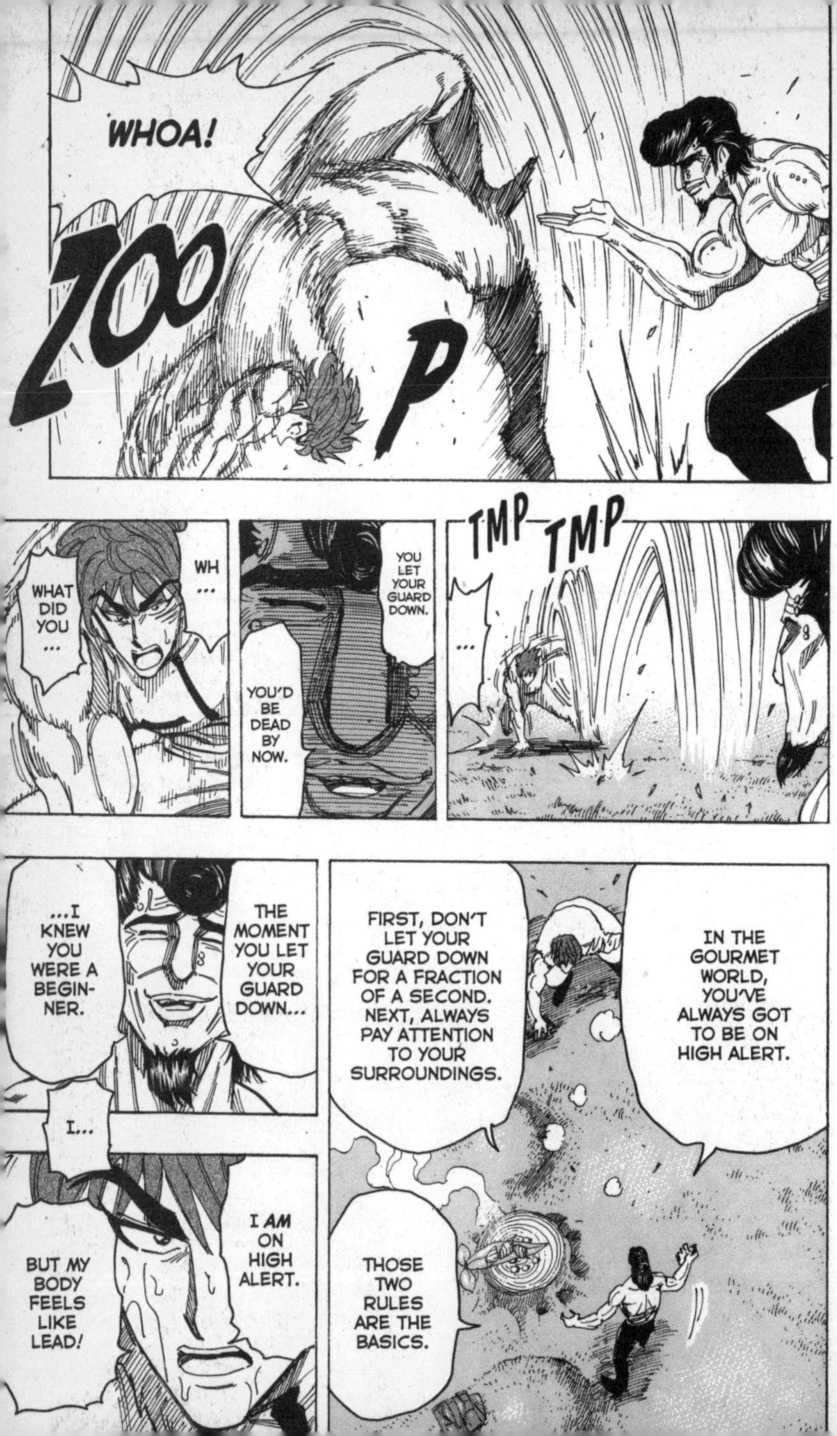
WHOA!
ZOOOP
TMP TMP
...
YOU LET YOUR GUARD DOWN.
YOU'D BE DEAD BY NOW.
WH...
WHAT DID YOU ...
IN THE GOURMET WORLD, YOU'VE ALWAYS GOT TO BE ON HIGH ALERT.
FIRST, DON'T LET YOUR GUARD DOWN FOR A FRACTION OF A SECOND. NEXT, ALWAYS PAY ATTENTION TO YOUR SURROUNDINGS.
THOSE TWO RULES ARE THE BASICS.
THE MOMENT YOU LET YOUR GUARD DOWN...
...I KNEW YOU WERE A BEGINNER.
I...
I AM ON HIGH ALERT.
BUT MY BODY FEELS LIKE LEAD!

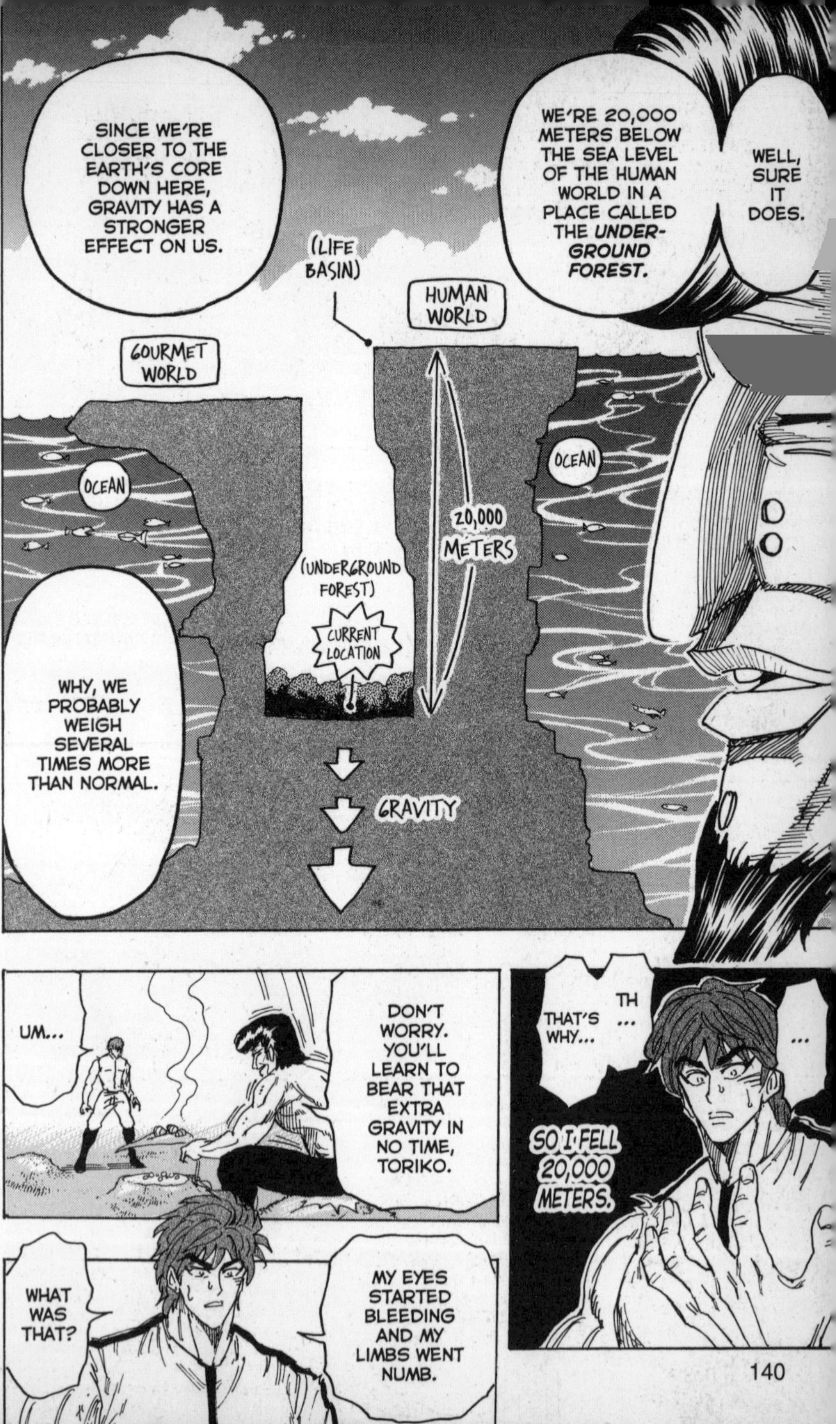
WELL, SURE IT DOES.
WE'RE 20,000 METERS BELOW THE SEA LEVEL OF THE HUMAN WORLD IN A PLACE CALLED THE *UNDER-GROUND FOREST.*
SINCE WE'RE CLOSER TO THE EARTH'S CORE DOWN HERE, GRAVITY HAS A STRONGER EFFECT ON US.
(LIFE BASIN)
HUMAN WORLD
GOURMET WORLD
OCEAN
OCEAN
20,000 METERS
(UNDERGROUND FOREST)
CURRENT LOCATION
GRAVITY
WHY, WE PROBABLY WEIGH SEVERAL TIMES MORE THAN NORMAL.
TH...
THAT'S WHY...
...
SO I FELL 20,000 METERS.
UM...
DON'T WORRY. YOU'LL LEARN TO BEAR THAT EXTRA GRAVITY IN NO TIME, TORIKO.
WHAT WAS THAT?
MY EYES STARTED BLEEDING AND MY LIMBS WENT NUMB.

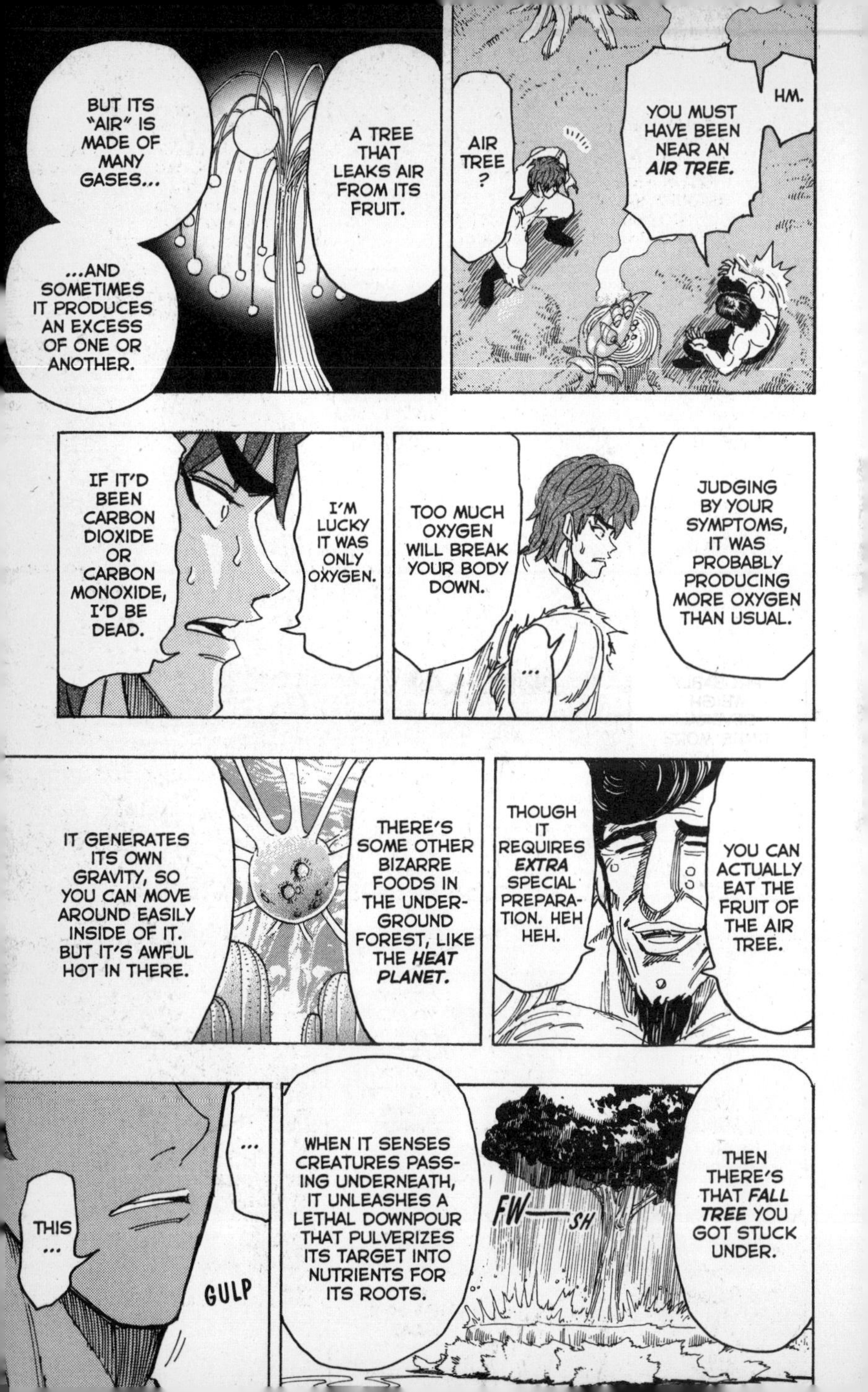
HM.
YOU MUST HAVE BEEN NEAR AN ***AIR TREE.***
AIR TREE ?
A TREE THAT LEAKS AIR FROM ITS FRUIT.
BUT ITS "AIR" IS MADE OF MANY GASES...
...AND SOMETIMES IT PRODUCES AN EXCESS OF ONE OR ANOTHER.
JUDGING BY YOUR SYMPTOMS, IT WAS PROBABLY PRODUCING MORE OXYGEN THAN USUAL.
TOO MUCH OXYGEN WILL BREAK YOUR BODY DOWN.
...
I'M LUCKY IT WAS ONLY OXYGEN.
IF IT'D BEEN CARBON DIOXIDE OR CARBON MONOXIDE, I'D BE DEAD.
YOU CAN ACTUALLY EAT THE FRUIT OF THE AIR TREE.
THOUGH IT REQUIRES ***EXTRA*** SPECIAL PREPARA-TION. HEH HEH.
THERE'S SOME OTHER BIZARRE FOODS IN THE UNDER-GROUND FOREST, LIKE THE ***HEAT PLANET.***
IT GENERATES ITS OWN GRAVITY, SO YOU CAN MOVE AROUND EASILY INSIDE OF IT. BUT IT'S AWFUL HOT IN THERE.
THEN THERE'S THAT ***FALL TREE*** YOU GOT STUCK UNDER.
FW—SH
WHEN IT SENSES CREATURES PASS-ING UNDERNEATH, IT UNLEASHES A LETHAL DOWNPOUR THAT PULVERIZES ITS TARGET INTO NUTRIENTS FOR ITS ROOTS.
...
THIS ...
GULP

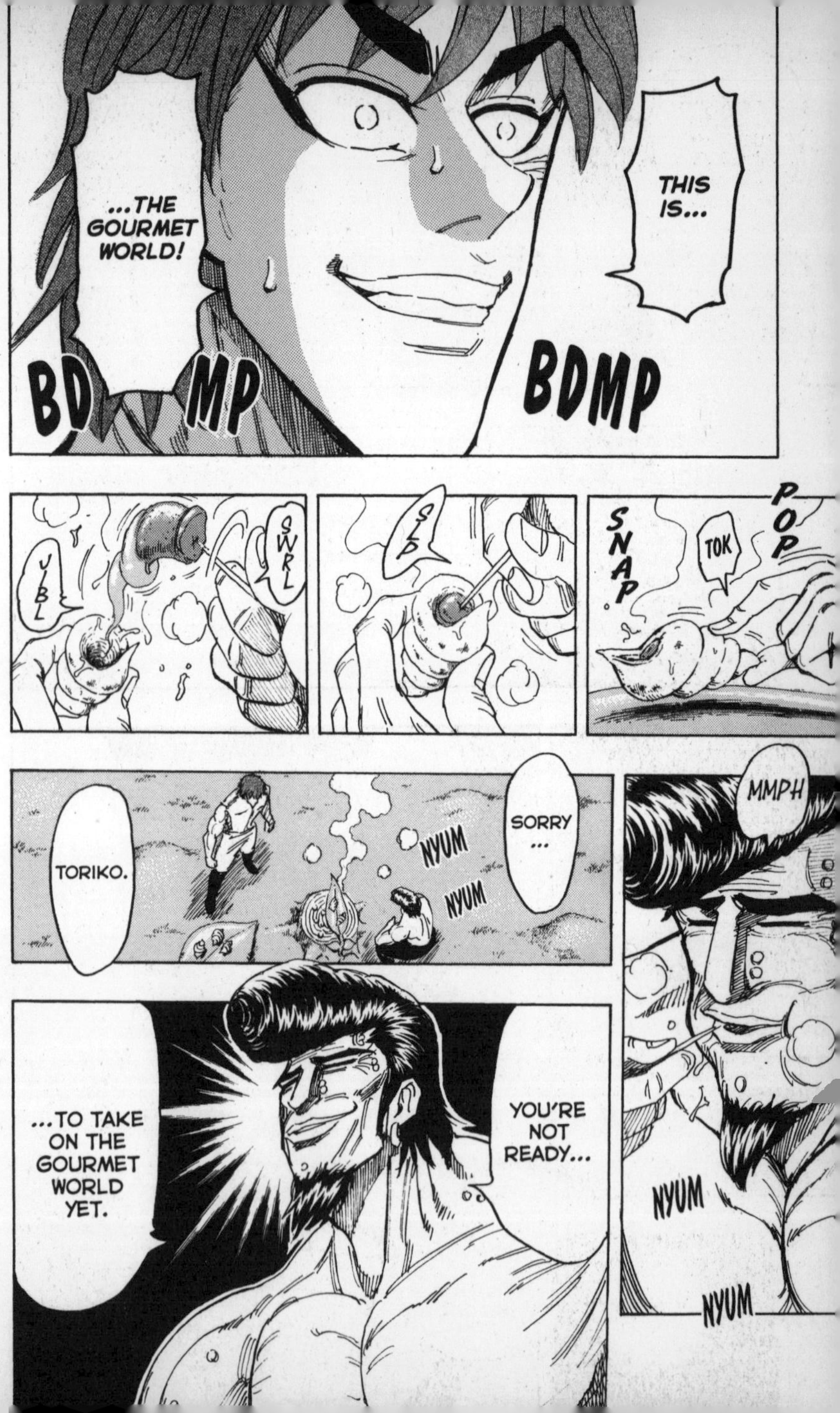
THIS IS...
...THE GOURMET WORLD!
BDMP
BDMP
POP
TOK
SNAP
SLP
SWRL
JIBL
MMPH
NYUM
NYUM
SORRY...
NYUM
NYUM
TORIKO.
YOU'RE NOT READY...
...TO TAKE ON THE GOURMET WORLD YET.

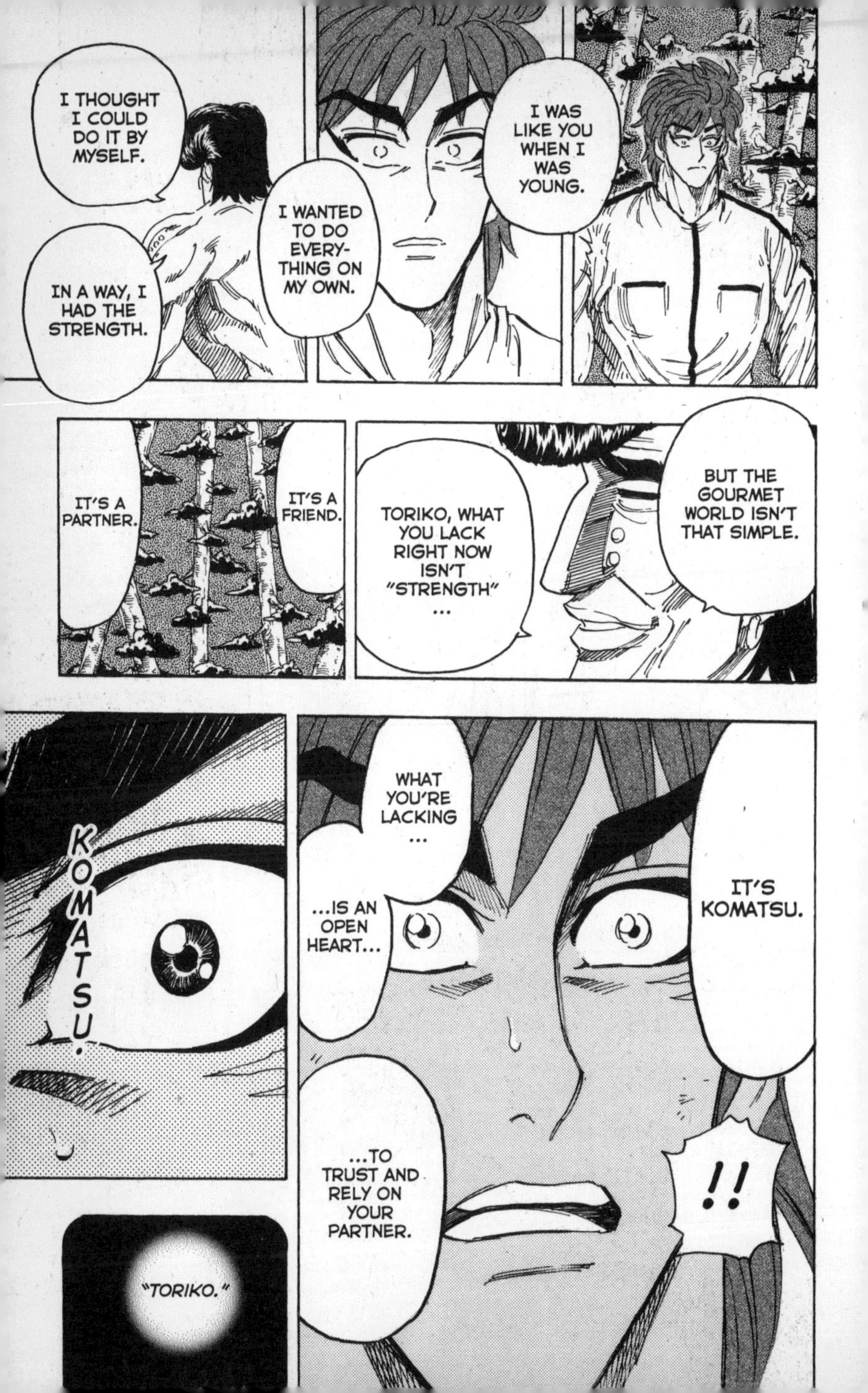
I WAS LIKE YOU WHEN I WAS YOUNG.
I WANTED TO DO EVERY-THING ON MY OWN.
I THOUGHT I COULD DO IT BY MYSELF.
IN A WAY, I HAD THE STRENGTH.
BUT THE GOURMET WORLD ISN'T THAT SIMPLE.
TORIKO, WHAT YOU LACK RIGHT NOW ISN'T "STRENGTH"...
IT'S A FRIEND.
IT'S A PARTNER.
WHAT YOU'RE LACKING...
...IS AN OPEN HEART...
...TO TRUST AND RELY ON YOUR PARTNER.
IT'S KOMATSU.
!!
KOMATSU!
"TORIKO."

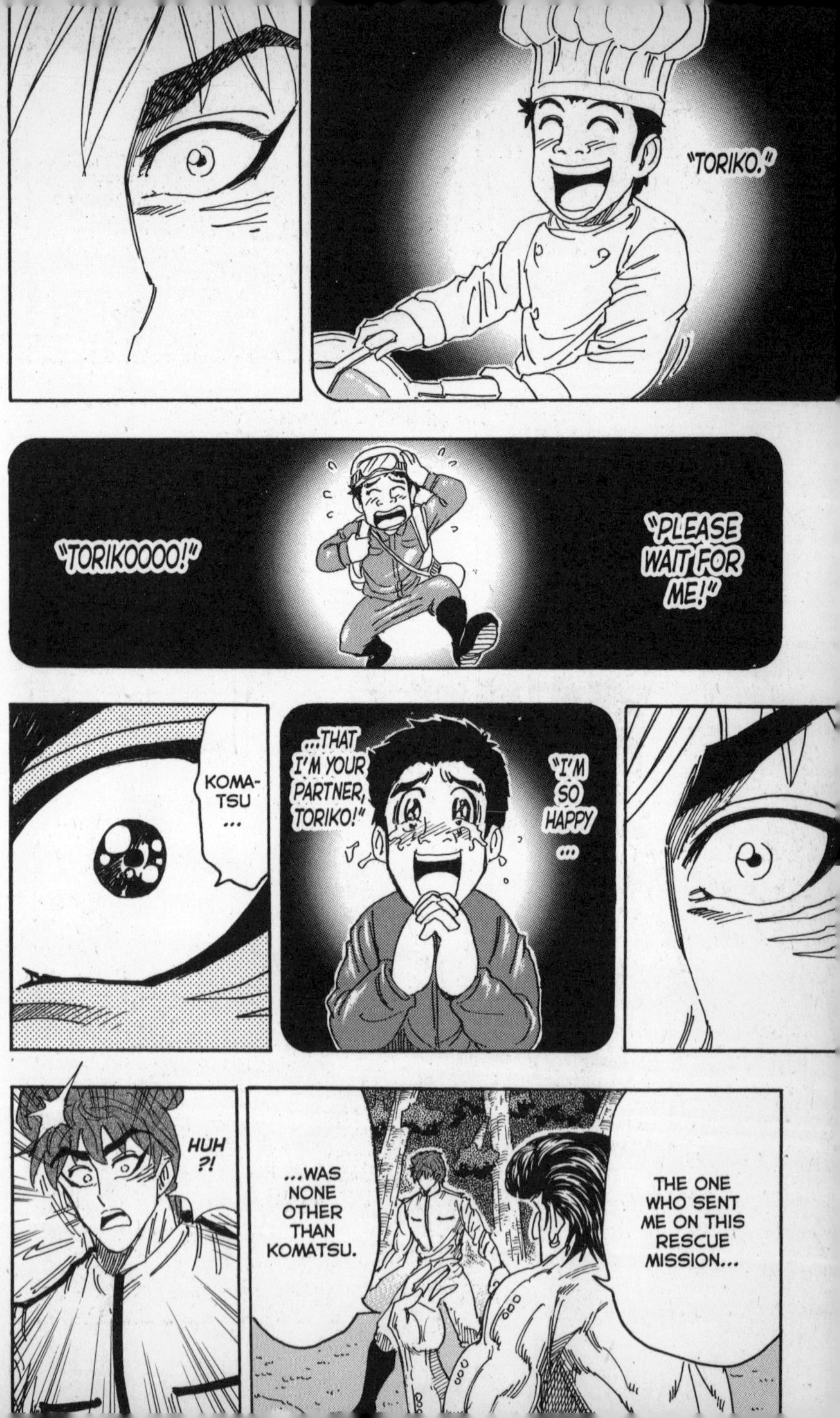
"TORIKO."
"PLEASE WAIT FOR ME!"
"TORIKOOOO!"
"I'M SO HAPPY...
...THAT I'M YOUR PARTNER, TORIKO!"
KOMA-TSU...
THE ONE WHO SENT ME ON THIS RESCUE MISSION...
...WAS NONE OTHER THAN KOMATSU.
HUH?!

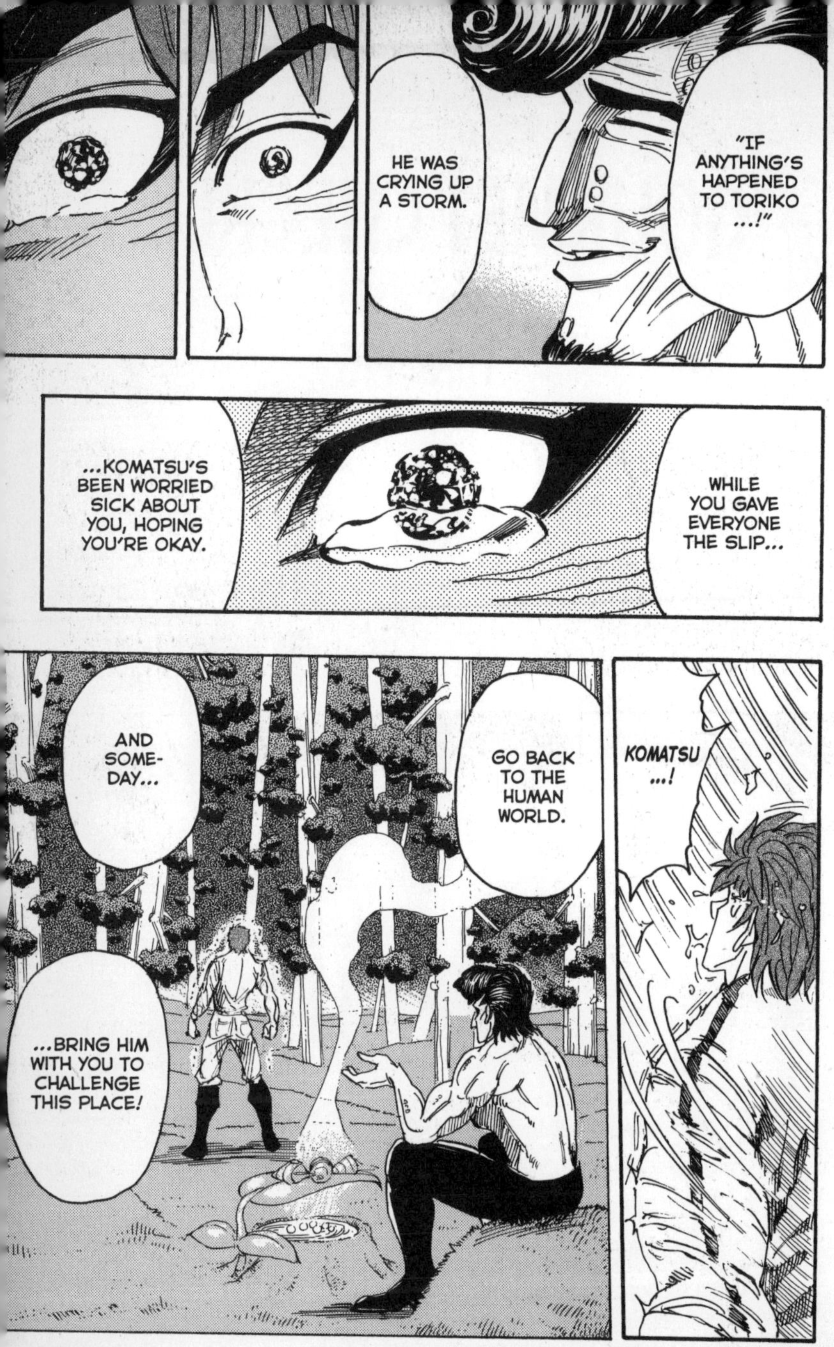
"IF ANYTHING'S HAPPENED TO TORIKO ...!"
HE WAS CRYING UP A STORM.
WHILE YOU GAVE EVERYONE THE SLIP...
...KOMATSU'S BEEN WORRIED SICK ABOUT YOU, HOPING YOU'RE OKAY.
KOMATSU ...!
GO BACK TO THE HUMAN WORLD.
AND SOME-DAY...
...BRING HIM WITH YOU TO CHALLENGE THIS PLACE!

TORIKO

GOURMET CHECKLIST

Vol. 128

TUNA PIG

(MAMMAL)

CAPTURE LEVEL: 10

HABITAT: OPEN SPACES (DIFFICULT TO
BREED IN CAPTIVITY)

LENGTH: 150 CM

HEIGHT: 60 CM

WEIGHT: 100 KG

PRICE: TUNA PORTION GOES FOR
100 G / 8,000 YEN; PORK PORTION GOES FOR
100 G / 2,500 YEN

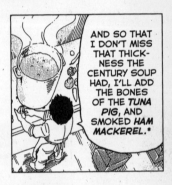

AND SO THAT I DON'T MISS THAT THICK-NESS THE CENTURY SOUP HAD, I'LL ADD THE BONES OF THE *TUNA PIG*, AND SMOKED *HAM MACKEREL.**

SCALE

DID THIS END UP IN KOMATSU'S RECIPE FOR CENTURY SOUP?
A PIG WHOSE LOWER HALF IS TUNA. THE TUNA PART TASTES
LIKE REAL TUNA! THE PIG PART ISN'T HALF BAD FOR PORK
EITHER, BEING REASONABLY JUICY AND FATTY. TUNA PIG
BONES ALSO MAKE AN EXCELLENT SOUP STOCK THAT
BLENDS BOTH PORK AND TUNA FLAVORS.

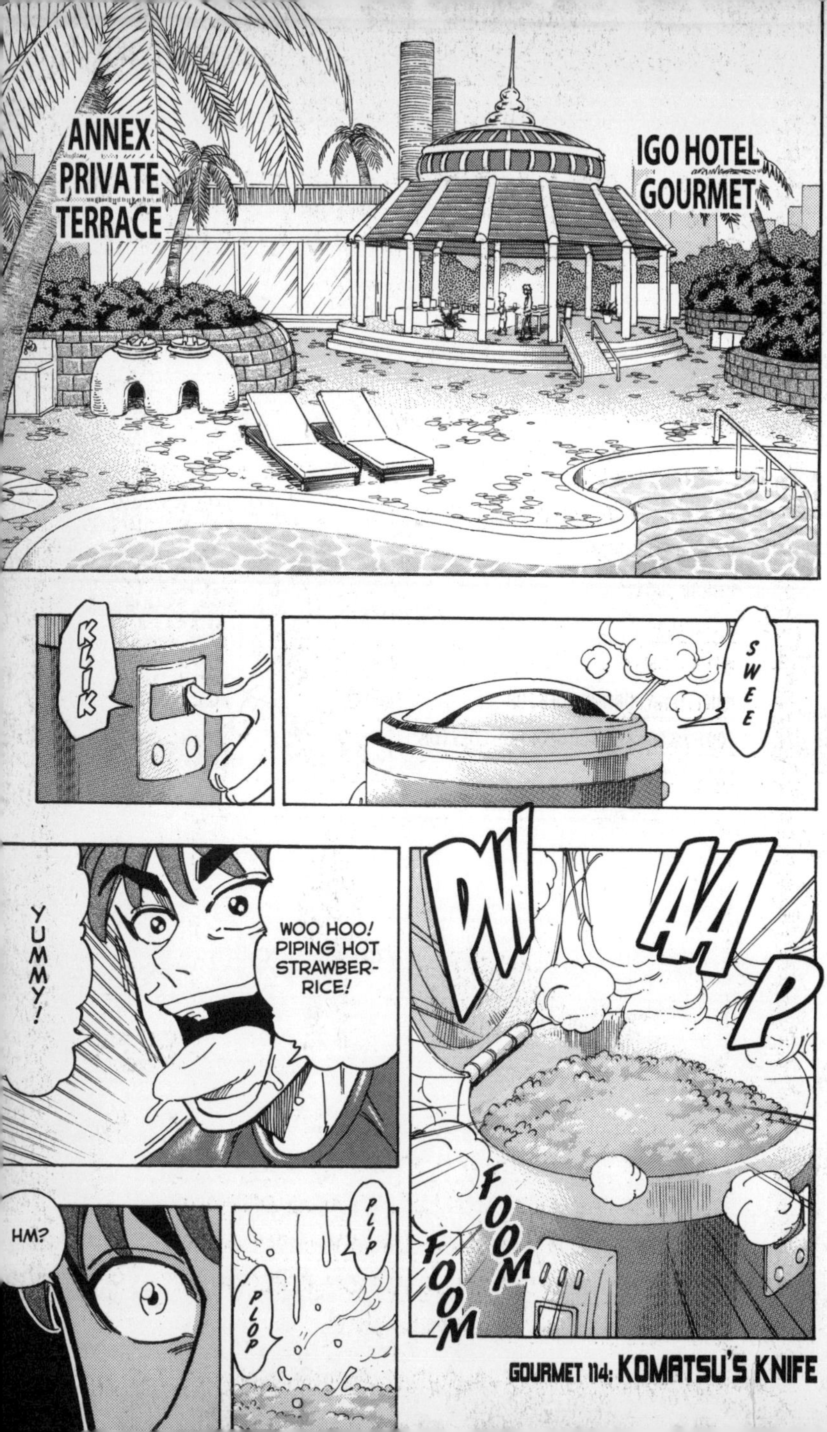
IGO HOTEL GOURMET
ANNEX PRIVATE TERRACE
SWEE
KLIK
DWAAP
FOOM FOOM
WOO HOO! PIPING HOT STRAWBER-RICE!
YUMMY!
PLIP
PLOP
HM?

GOURMET 114: KOMATSU'S KNIFE

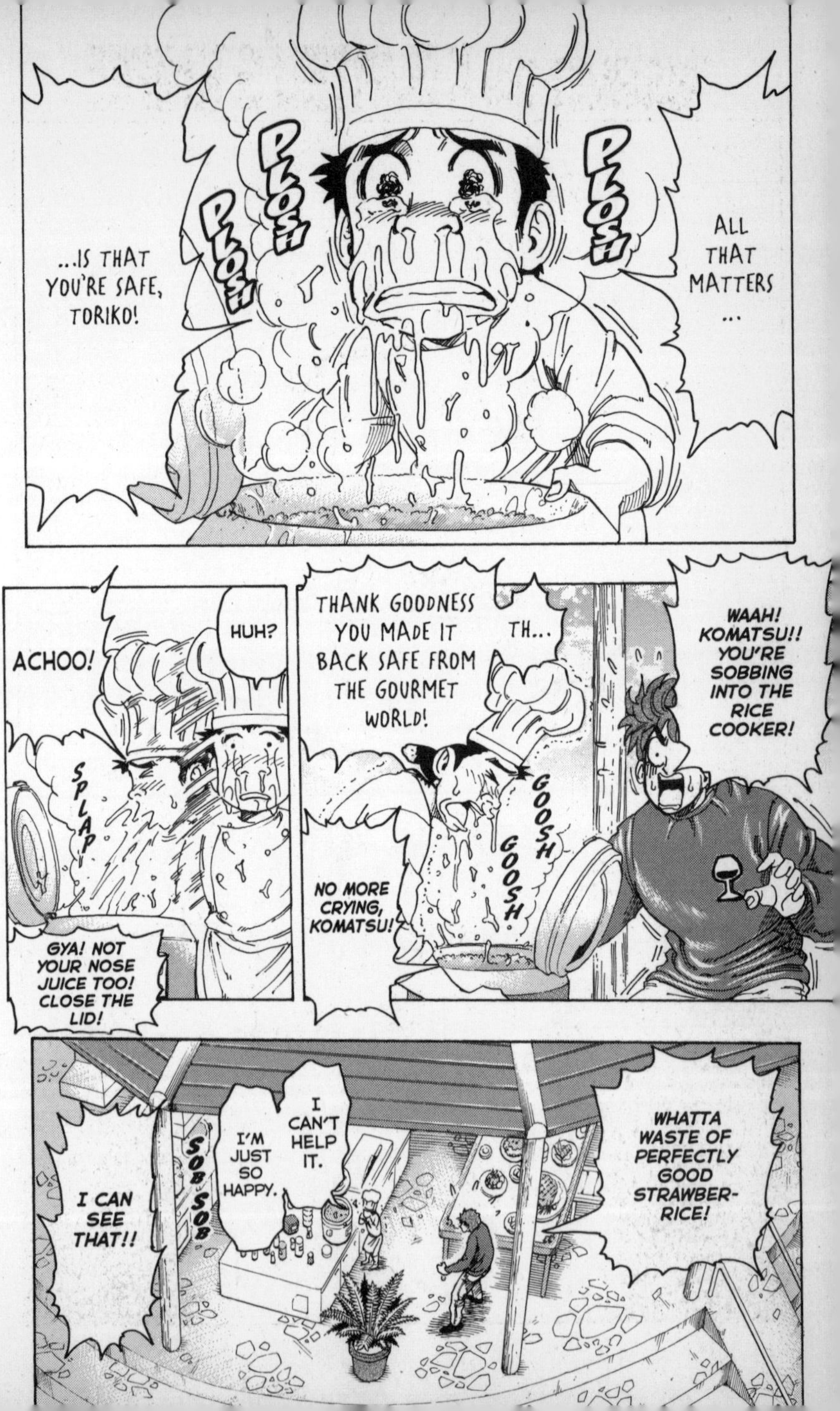
PLOSH
PLOSH
PLOSH
ALL THAT MATTERS ...
...IS THAT YOU'RE SAFE, TORIKO!
WAAH! KOMATSU!! YOU'RE SOBBING INTO THE RICE COOKER!
TH...
THANK GOODNESS YOU MADE IT BACK SAFE FROM THE GOURMET WORLD!
GOOSH GOOSH
NO MORE CRYING, KOMATSU!
HUH?
ACHOO!
SPLAP
GYA! NOT YOUR NOSE JUICE TOO! CLOSE THE LID!
WHATTA WASTE OF PERFECTLY GOOD STRAWBER-RICE!
I CAN'T HELP IT.
I'M JUST SO HAPPY.
SOB SOB
I CAN SEE THAT!!

GOURMET 114: KOMATSU'S KNIFE!!

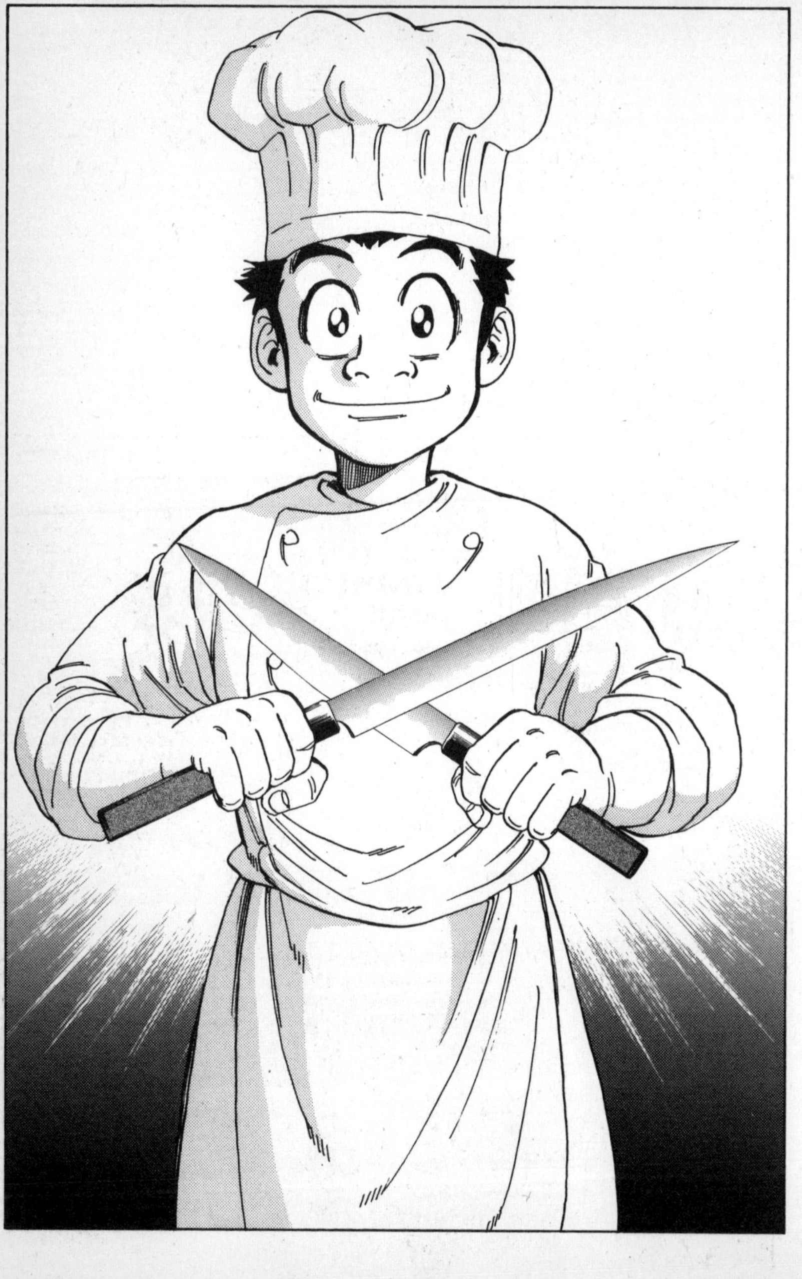

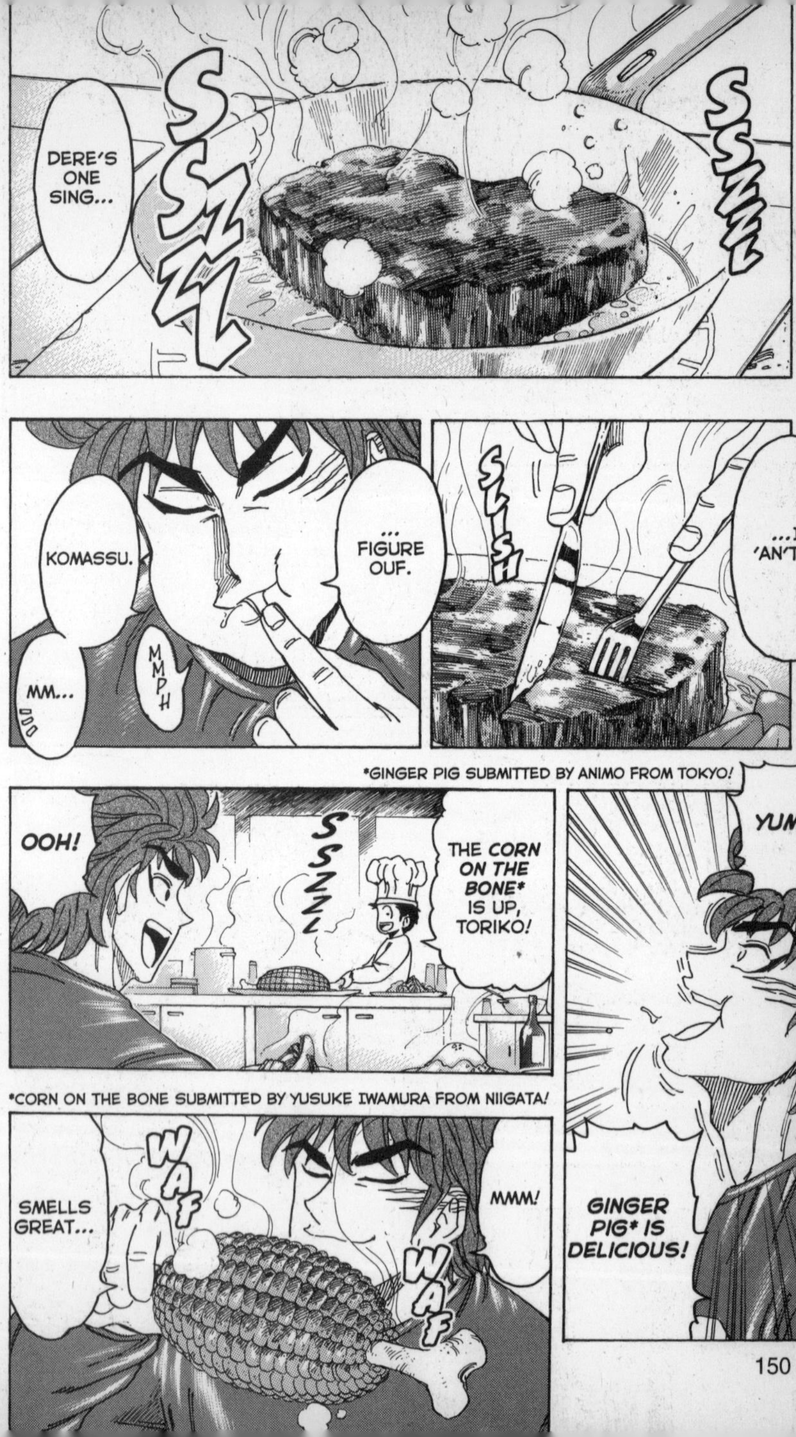
SSSZZZL
SSZZZL
DERE'S ONE SING...
...I 'AN'T...
SLISH
... FIGURE OUF.
KOMASSU.
MMPH
MM...
*GINGER PIG SUBMITTED BY ANIMO FROM TOKYO!
YUM!
GINGER PIG* IS DELICIOUS!
THE CORN ON THE BONE* IS UP, TORIKO!
SSZZZ
OOH!
*CORN ON THE BONE SUBMITTED BY YUSUKE IWAMURA FROM NIIGATA!
MMM!
WAF
WAF
SMELLS GREAT...

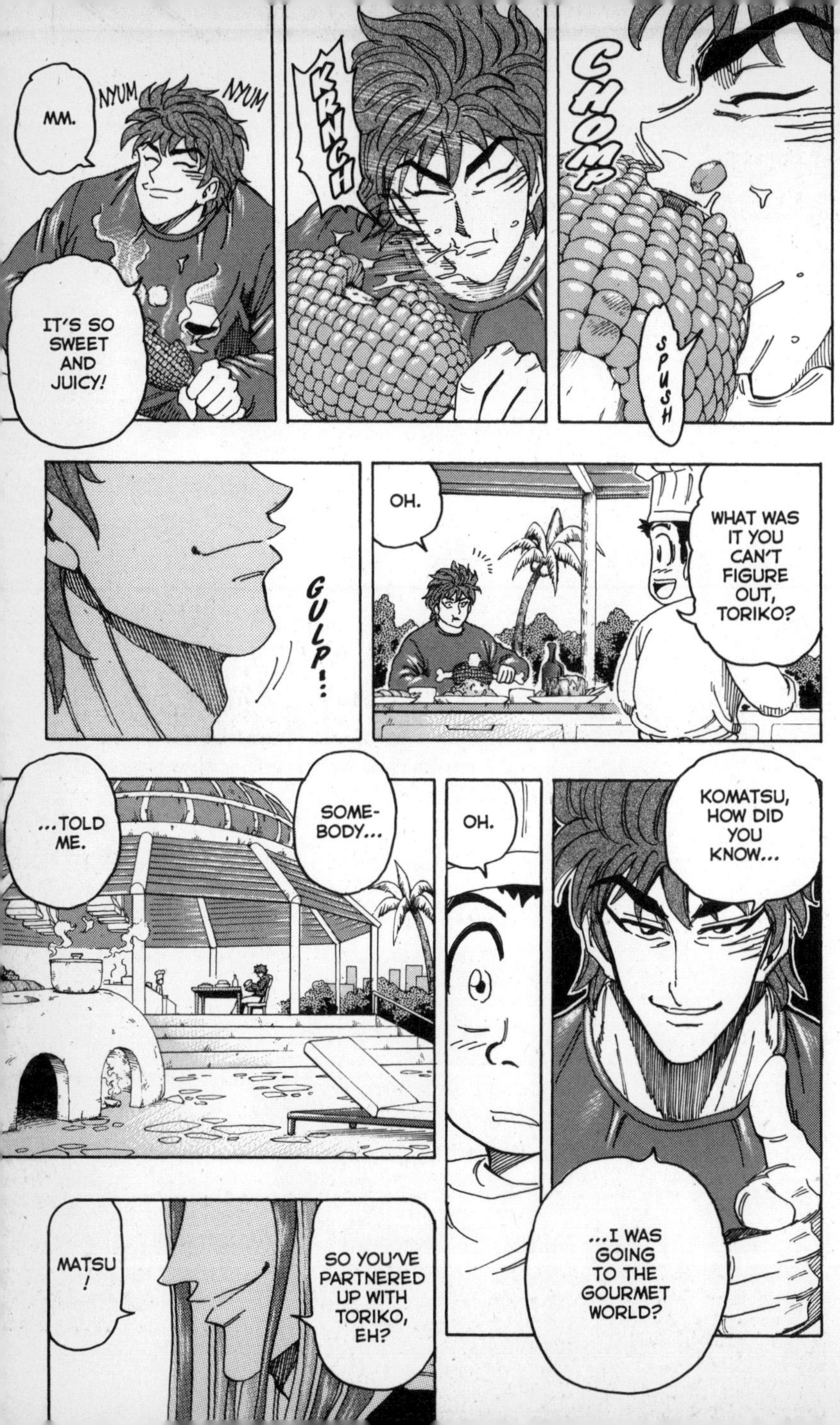
CHOMP
SPUSH
KRNCH
MM.
NYUM
NYUM
IT'S SO SWEET AND JUICY!
WHAT WAS IT YOU CAN'T FIGURE OUT, TORIKO?
OH.
GULP!!
KOMATSU, HOW DID YOU KNOW...
...I WAS GOING TO THE GOURMET WORLD?
OH.
SOME-BODY...
...TOLD ME.
SO YOU'VE PARTNERED UP WITH TORIKO, EH?
MATSU!

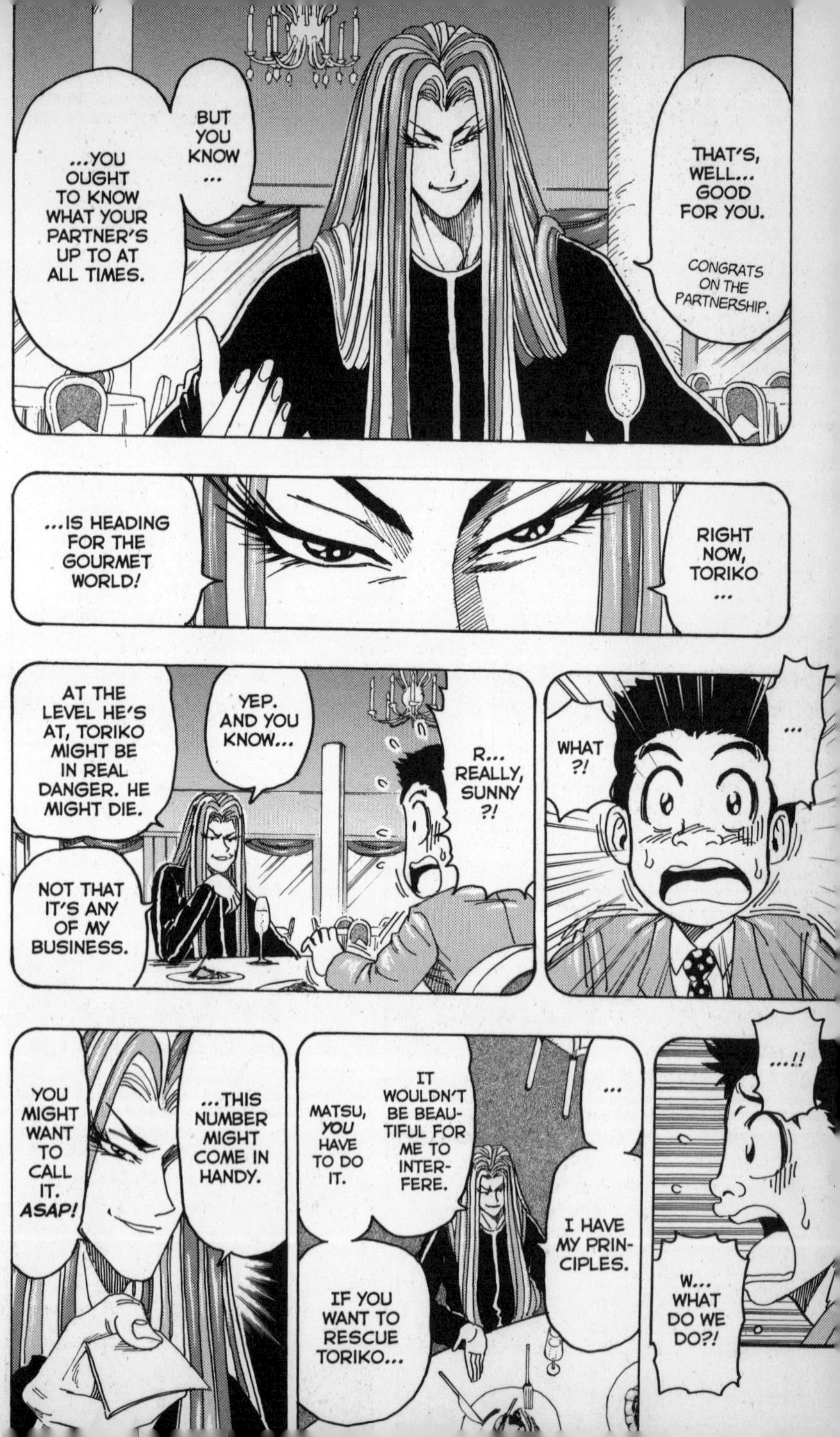
THAT'S, WELL... GOOD FOR YOU.
CONGRATS ON THE PARTNERSHIP.
BUT YOU KNOW...
...YOU OUGHT TO KNOW WHAT YOUR PARTNER'S UP TO AT ALL TIMES.
RIGHT NOW, TORIKO...
...IS HEADING FOR THE GOURMET WORLD!
...
WHAT?!
R... REALLY, SUNNY?!
YEP. AND YOU KNOW...
AT THE LEVEL HE'S AT, TORIKO MIGHT BE IN REAL DANGER. HE MIGHT DIE.
NOT THAT IT'S ANY OF MY BUSINESS.
...!!
W... WHAT DO WE DO?!
...
IT WOULDN'T BE BEAU-TIFUL FOR ME TO INTER-FERE.
I HAVE MY PRIN-CIPLES.
MATSU, *YOU* HAVE TO DO IT.
IF YOU WANT TO RESCUE TORIKO...
...THIS NUMBER MIGHT COME IN HANDY.
YOU MIGHT WANT TO CALL IT. *ASAP!*

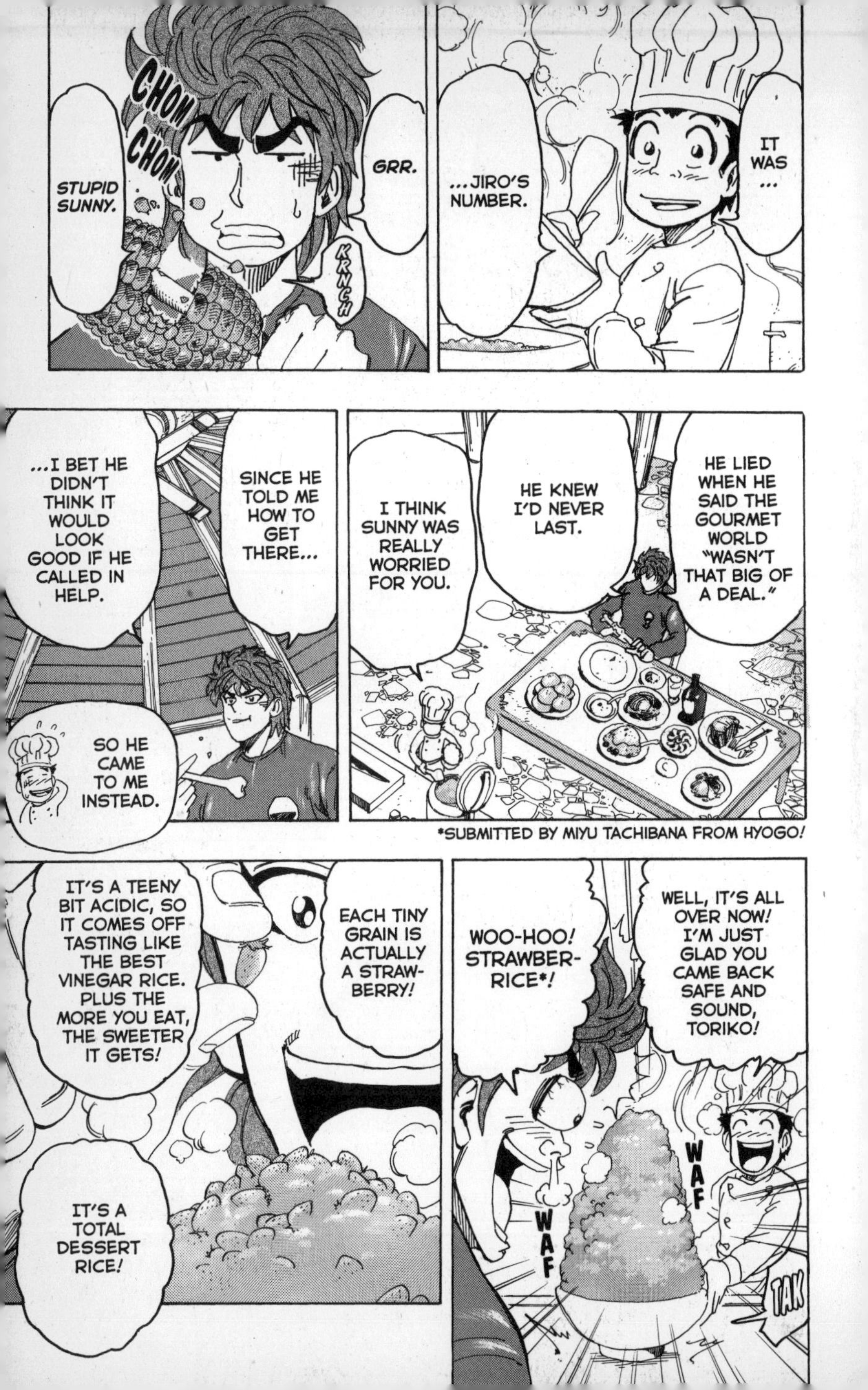
IT WAS ...
...JIRO'S NUMBER.
GRR.
CHOM CHOM
STUPID SUNNY.
KRNCH
HE LIED WHEN HE SAID THE GOURMET WORLD "WASN'T THAT BIG OF A DEAL."
HE KNEW I'D NEVER LAST.
I THINK SUNNY WAS REALLY WORRIED FOR YOU.
SINCE HE TOLD ME HOW TO GET THERE...
...I BET HE DIDN'T THINK IT WOULD LOOK GOOD IF HE CALLED IN HELP.
SO HE CAME TO ME INSTEAD.
WELL, IT'S ALL OVER NOW! I'M JUST GLAD YOU CAME BACK SAFE AND SOUND, TORIKO!
WOO-HOO! STRAWBER-RICE*!
WAF
WAF
TAK
EACH TINY GRAIN IS ACTUALLY A STRAW-BERRY!
IT'S A TEENY BIT ACIDIC, SO IT COMES OFF TASTING LIKE THE BEST VINEGAR RICE. PLUS THE MORE YOU EAT, THE SWEETER IT GETS!
IT'S A TOTAL DESSERT RICE!

*SUBMITTED BY MIYU TACHIBANA FROM HYOGO!

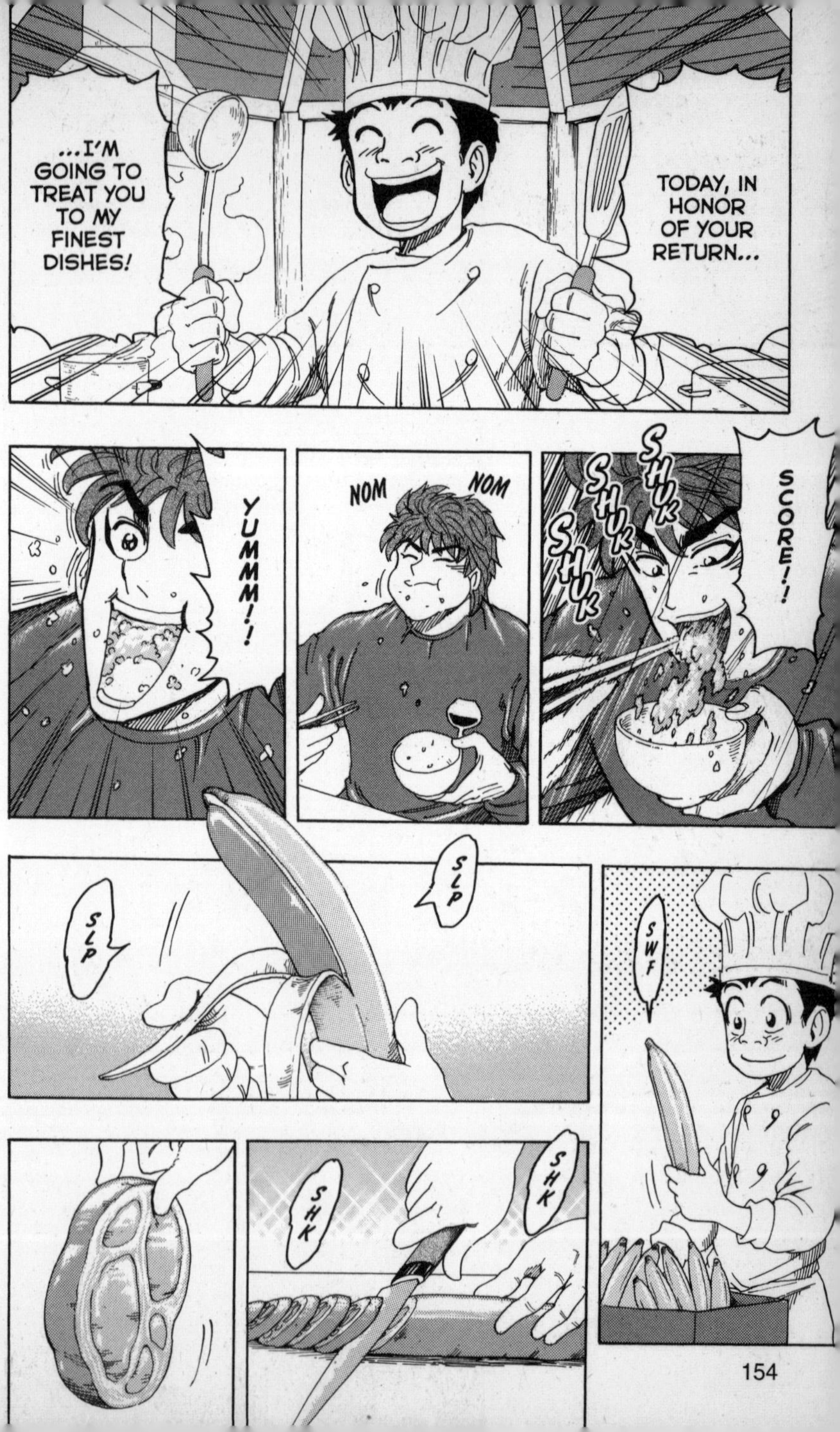
TODAY, IN HONOR OF YOUR RETURN...
...I'M GOING TO TREAT YOU TO MY FINEST DISHES!
SCORE!!
SHUK
SHUK
SHUK
NOM
NOM
YUMMM!!
SWF
SLP
SLP
SHK
SHK

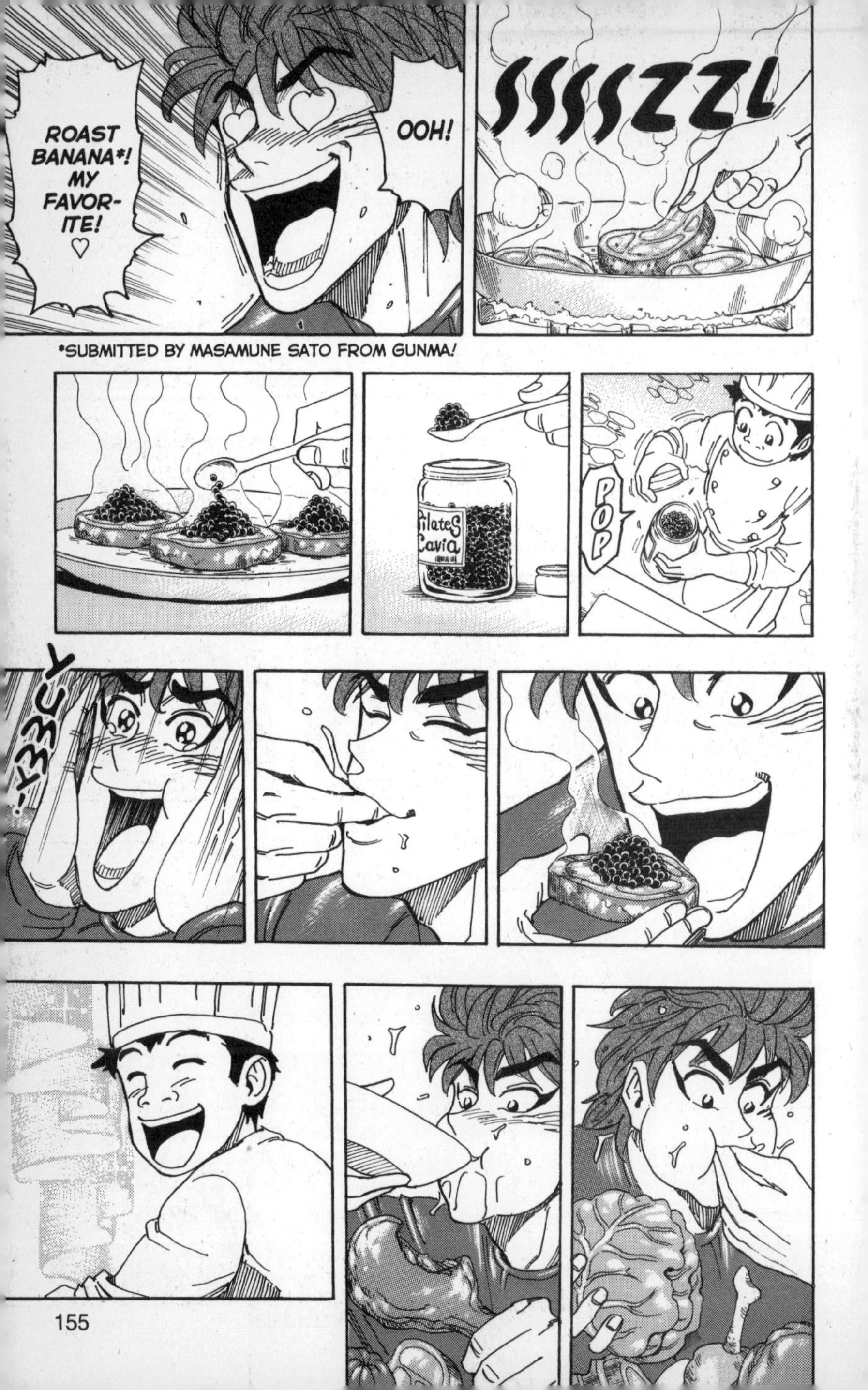
SSSSZZL
OOH!
ROAST BANANA*! MY FAVOR-ITE! ♡
POP POP
Pilates Cavia

*SUBMITTED BY MASAMUNE SATO FROM GUNMA!

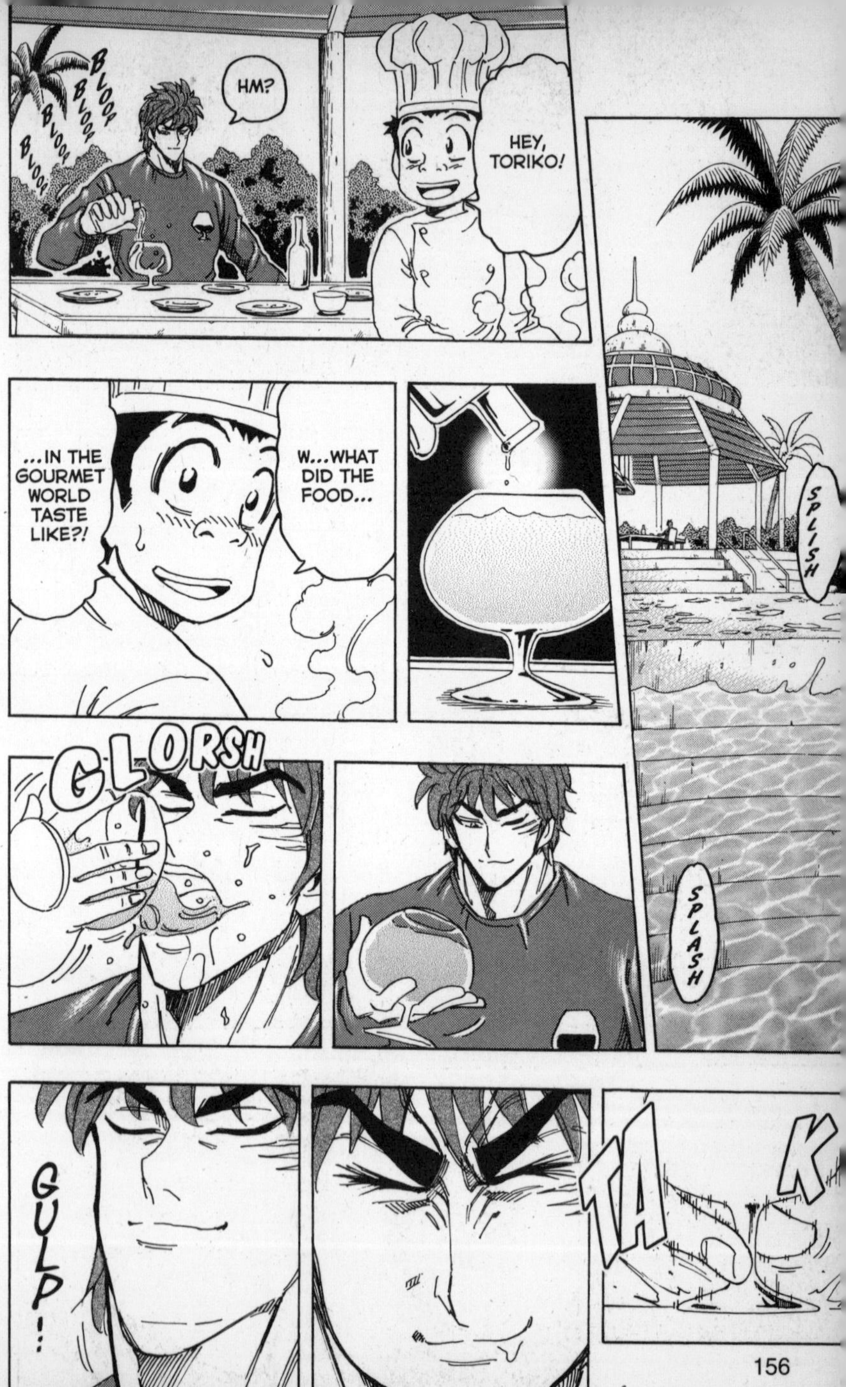
HEY, TORIKO!
HM?
BLOOP
BLOOP
BLOOP
BLOOP
SPLISH
SPLASH
W...WHAT DID THE FOOD...
...IN THE GOURMET WORLD TASTE LIKE?!
GLORSH
TAK
GULP!!

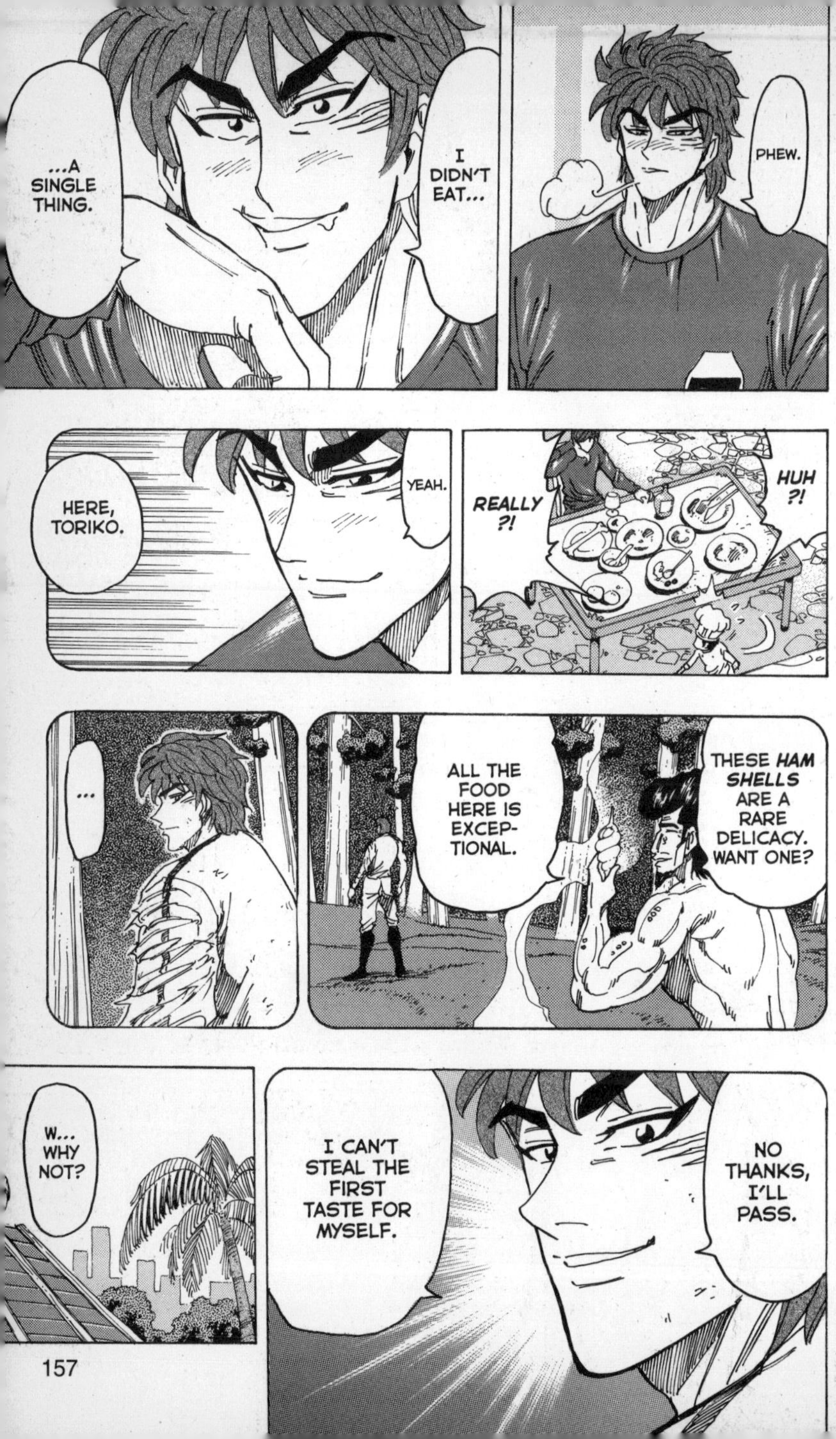
PHEW.
I DIDN'T EAT...
...A SINGLE THING.
HUH?!
REALLY?!
YEAH.
HERE, TORIKO.
THESE *HAM SHELLS* ARE A RARE DELICACY. WANT ONE?
ALL THE FOOD HERE IS EXCEPTIONAL.
...
NO THANKS, I'LL PASS.
I CAN'T STEAL THE FIRST TASTE FOR MYSELF.
W... WHY NOT?

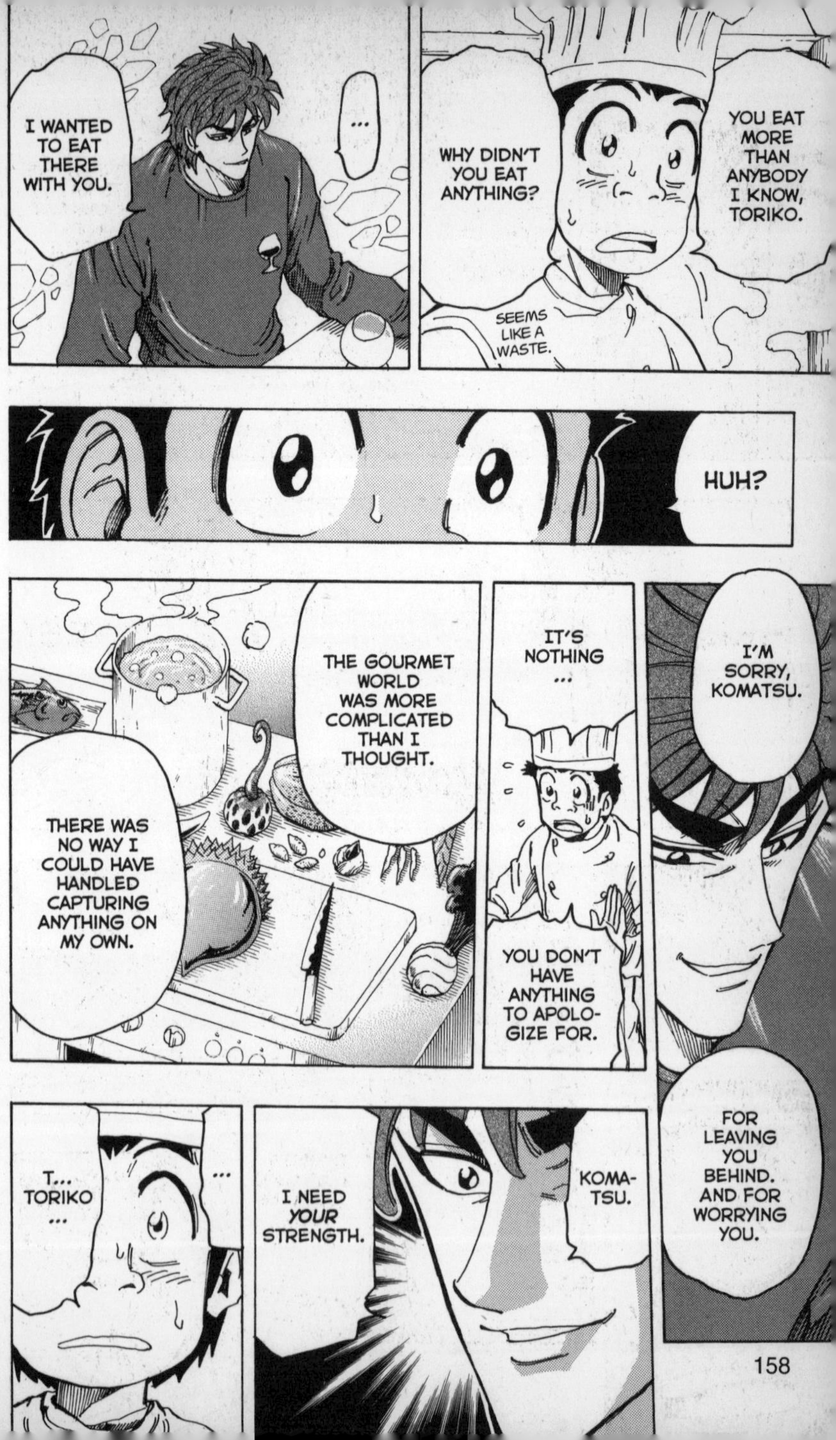
YOU EAT MORE THAN ANYBODY I KNOW, TORIKO.
WHY DIDN'T YOU EAT ANYTHING?
SEEMS LIKE A WASTE.
...
I WANTED TO EAT THERE WITH YOU.
HUH?
I'M SORRY, KOMATSU.
FOR LEAVING YOU BEHIND. AND FOR WORRYING YOU.
IT'S NOTHING ...
YOU DON'T HAVE ANYTHING TO APOLOGIZE FOR.
THE GOURMET WORLD WAS MORE COMPLICATED THAN I THOUGHT.
THERE WAS NO WAY I COULD HAVE HANDLED CAPTURING ANYTHING ON MY OWN.
KOMATSU.
I NEED *YOUR* STRENGTH.
...
T... TORIKO ...

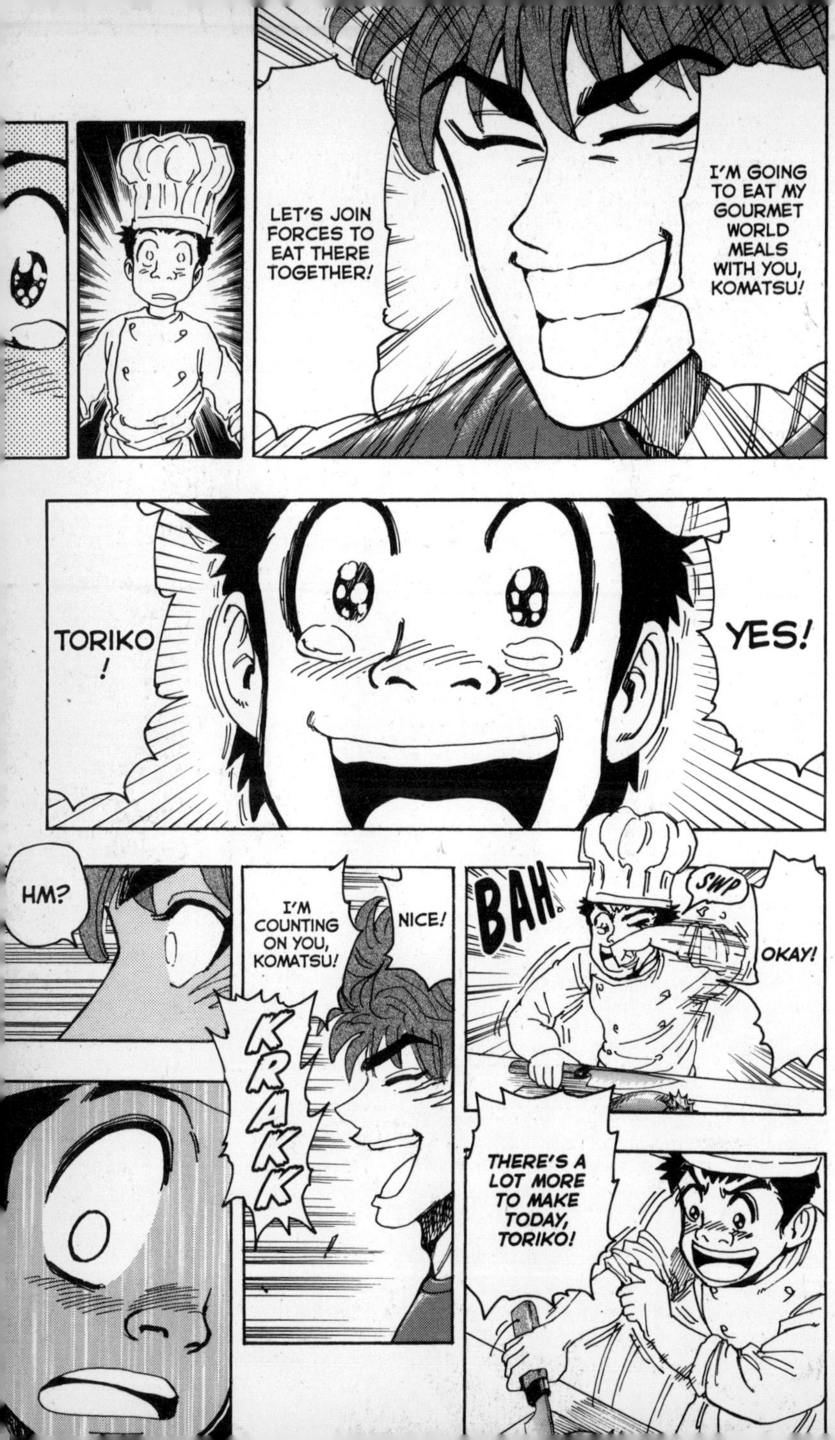
I'M GOING TO EAT MY GOURMET WORLD MEALS WITH YOU, KOMATSU!
LET'S JOIN FORCES TO EAT THERE TOGETHER!
YES!
TORIKO!
BAH
SWP
OKAY!
NICE!
I'M COUNTING ON YOU, KOMATSU!
HM?
THERE'S A LOT MORE TO MAKE TODAY, TORIKO!
KRAKK

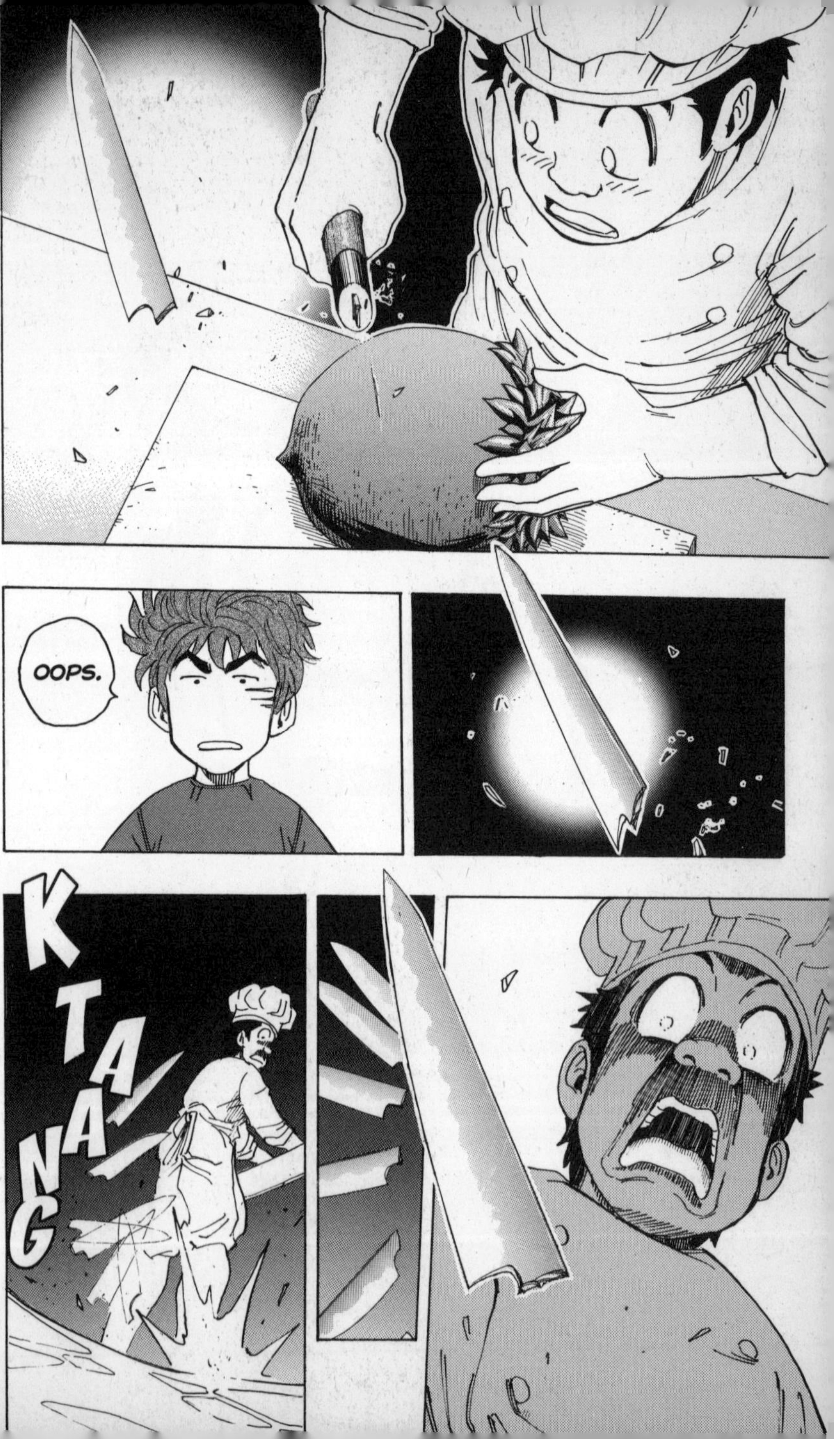
OOPS.
KTANANG

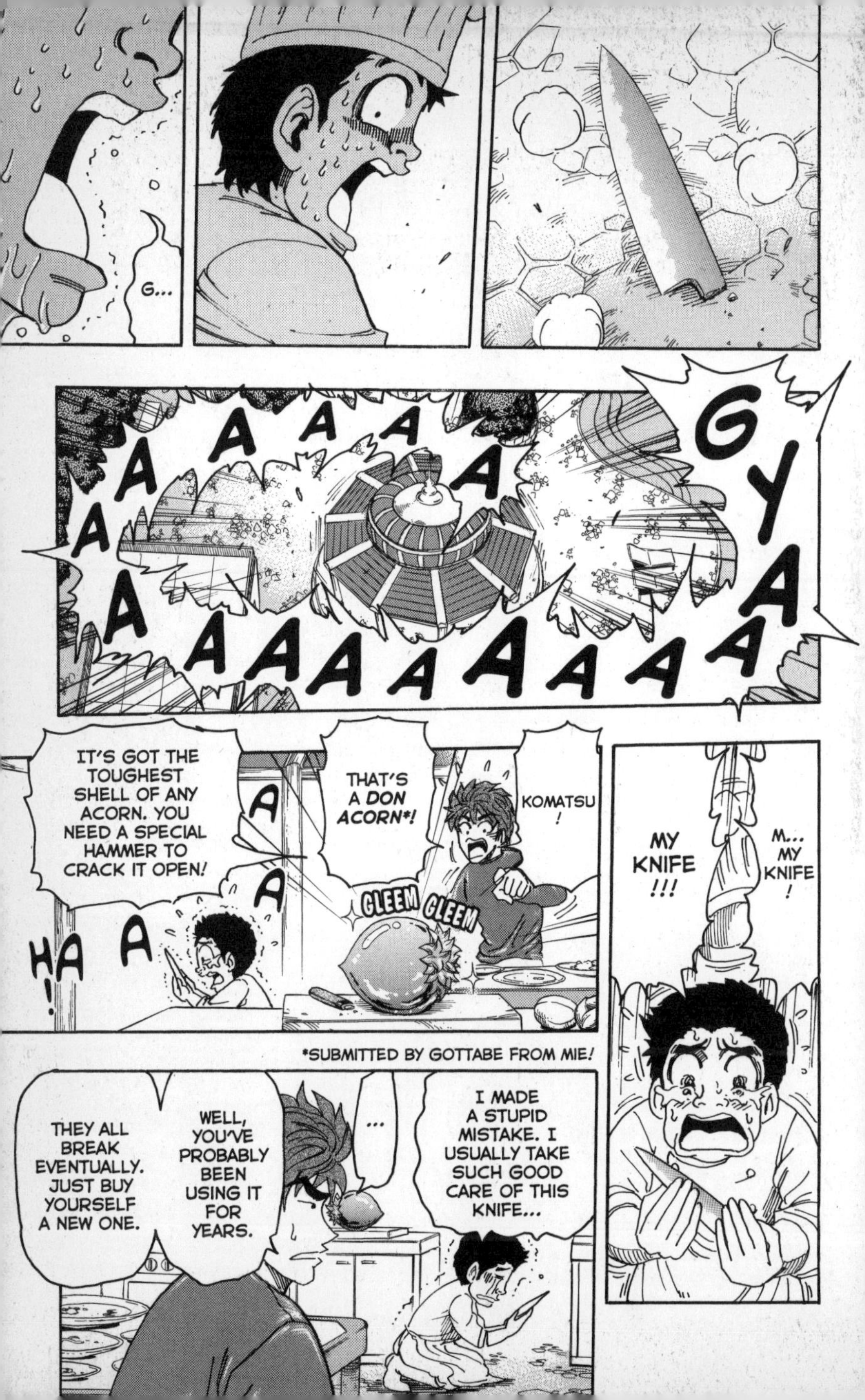
G...
GYAAAAAAAAAAAAAAAAAAA
M... MY KNIFE!
MY KNIFE!!!
KOMATSU!
THAT'S A *DON ACORN**!
IT'S GOT THE TOUGHEST SHELL OF ANY ACORN. YOU NEED A SPECIAL HAMMER TO CRACK IT OPEN!
GLEEM GLEEM
HAAAA!
*SUBMITTED BY GOTTABE FROM MIE!
I MADE A STUPID MISTAKE. I USUALLY TAKE SUCH GOOD CARE OF THIS KNIFE...
...
WELL, YOU'VE PROBABLY BEEN USING IT FOR YEARS.
THEY ALL BREAK EVENTUALLY. JUST BUY YOURSELF A NEW ONE.

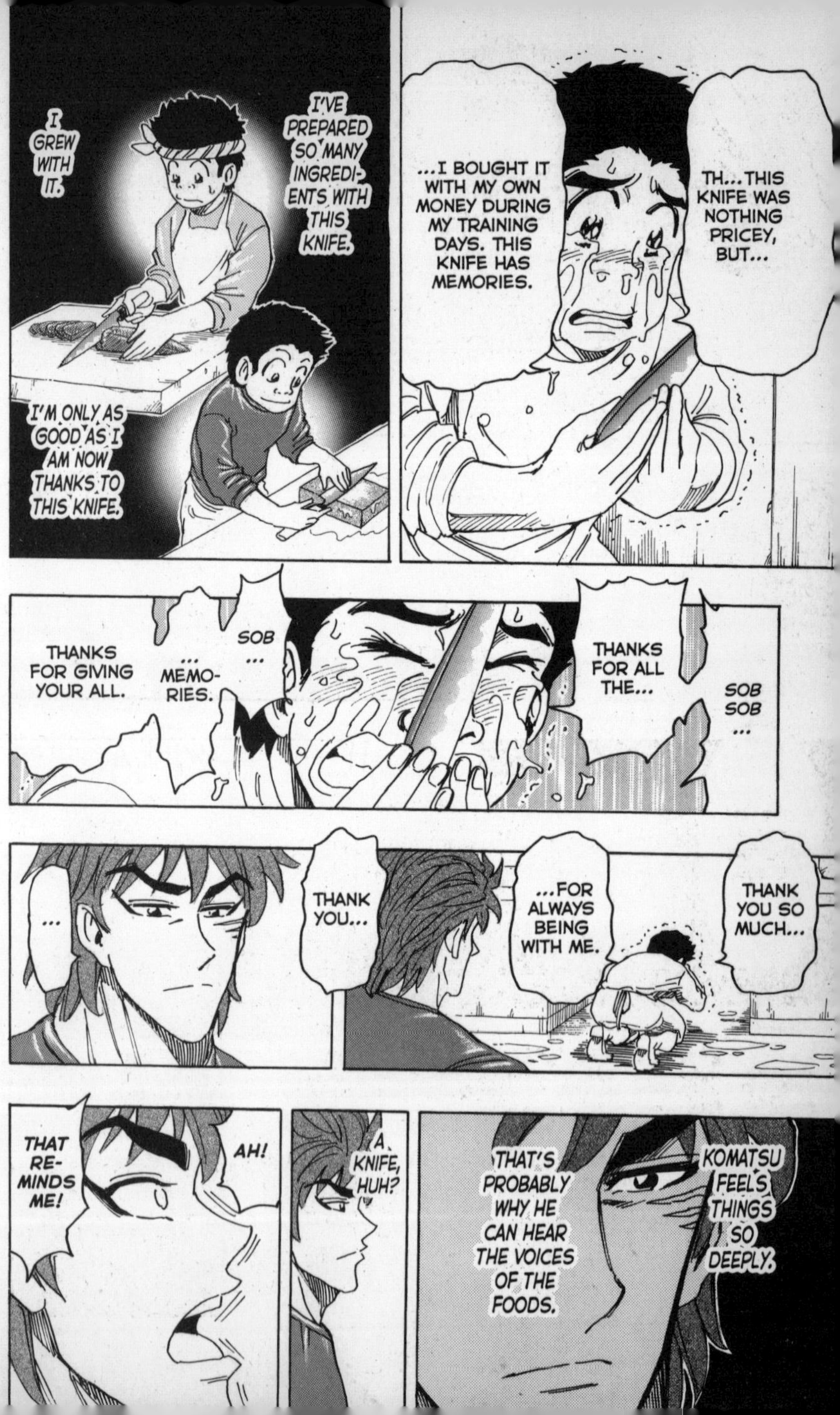
TH... THIS KNIFE WAS NOTHING PRICEY, BUT...
...I BOUGHT IT WITH MY OWN MONEY DURING MY TRAINING DAYS. THIS KNIFE HAS MEMORIES.
I'VE PREPARED SO MANY INGREDIENTS WITH THIS KNIFE.
I GREW WITH IT.
I'M ONLY AS GOOD AS I AM NOW THANKS TO THIS KNIFE.
SOB SOB...
THANKS FOR ALL THE...
SOB...
...MEMORIES.
THANKS FOR GIVING YOUR ALL.
THANK YOU SO MUCH...
...FOR ALWAYS BEING WITH ME.
THANK YOU...
...
KOMATSU FEELS THINGS SO DEEPLY.
THAT'S PROBABLY WHY HE CAN HEAR THE VOICES OF THE FOODS.
A KNIFE, HUH?
AH!
THAT REMINDS ME!

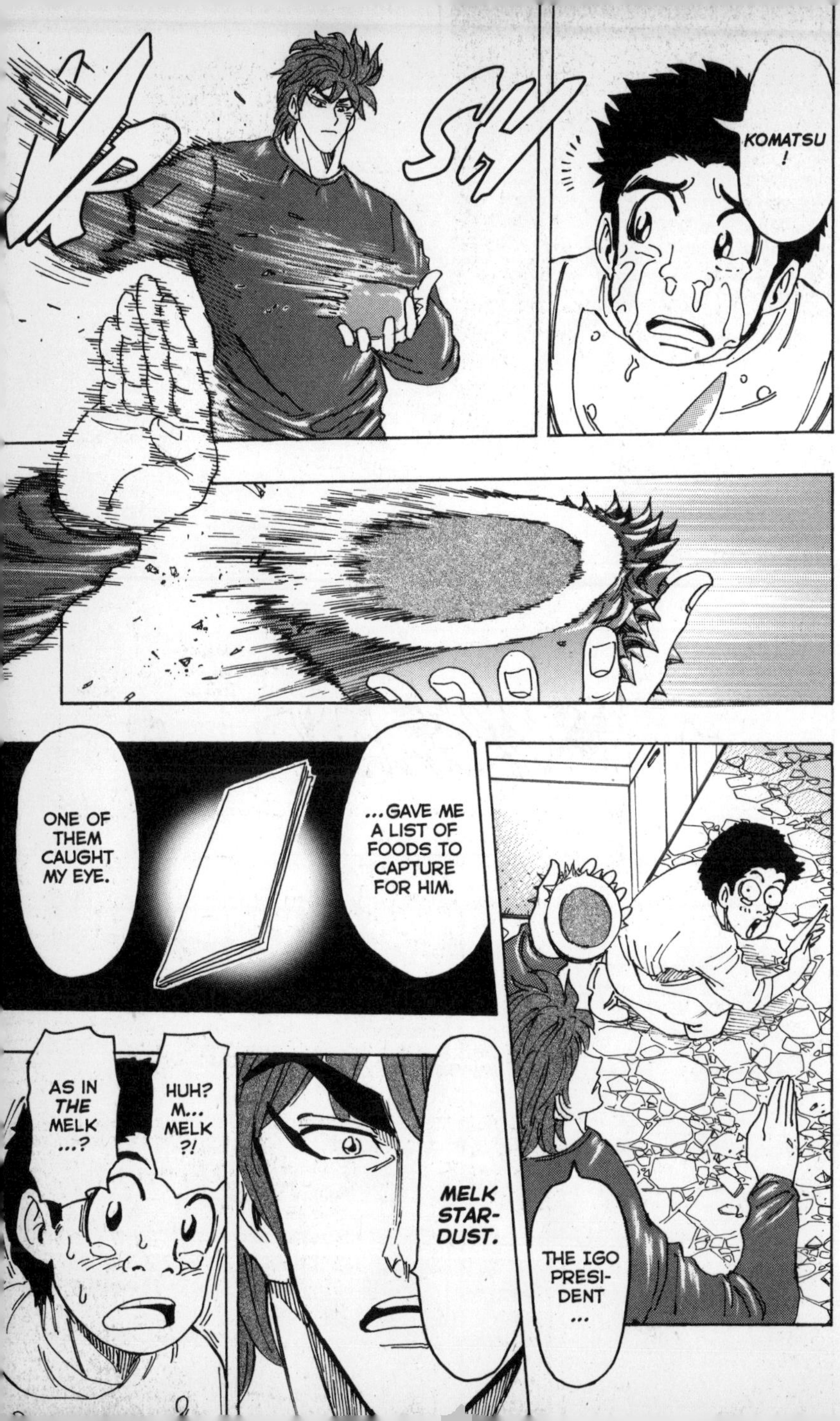
KOMATSU!
SH
THE IGO PRESIDENT...
...GAVE ME A LIST OF FOODS TO CAPTURE FOR HIM.
ONE OF THEM CAUGHT MY EYE.
MELK STARDUST.
HUH? M... MELK?!
AS IN THE MELK...?

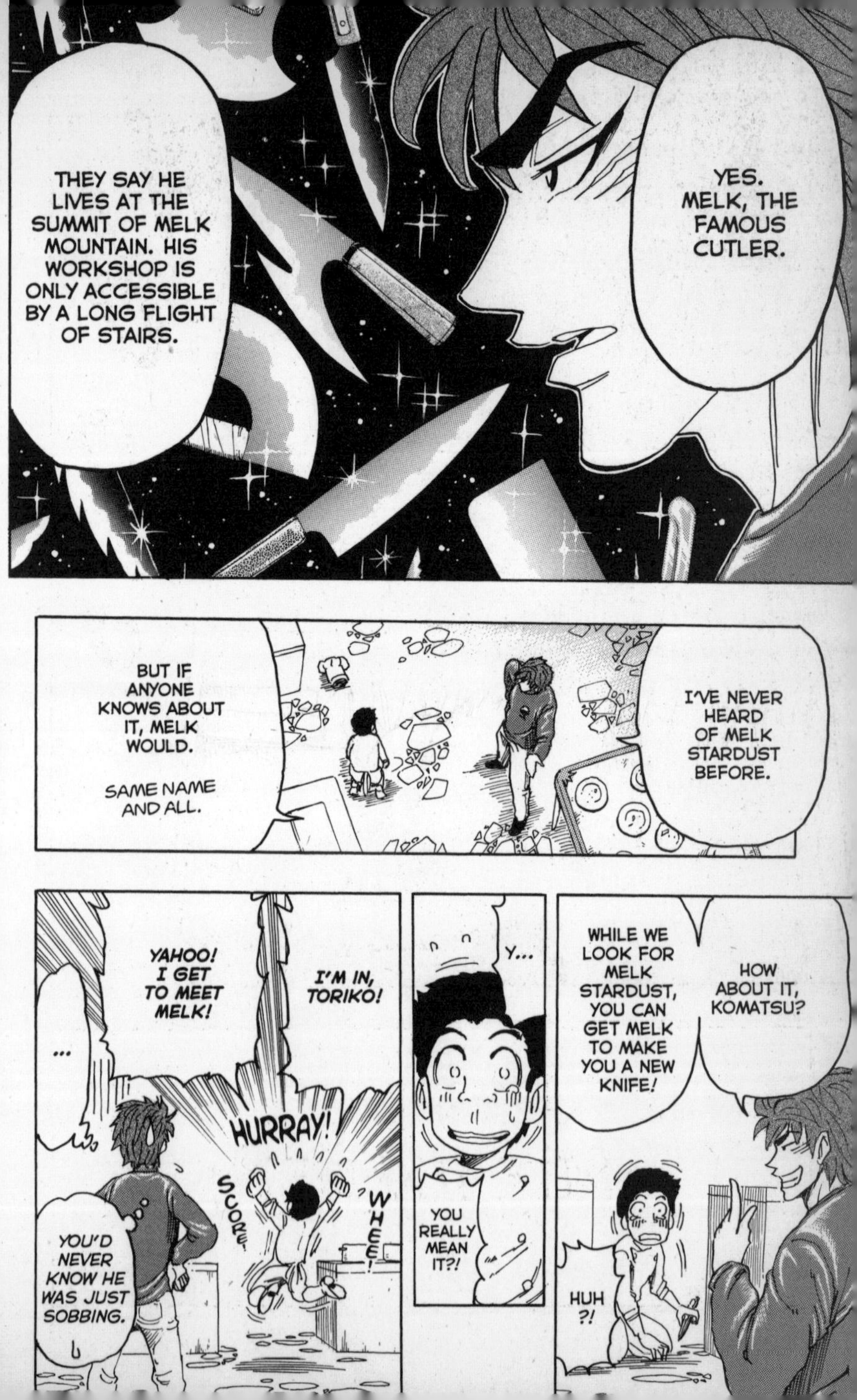
YES. MELK, THE FAMOUS CUTLER.
THEY SAY HE LIVES AT THE SUMMIT OF MELK MOUNTAIN. HIS WORKSHOP IS ONLY ACCESSIBLE BY A LONG FLIGHT OF STAIRS.
I'VE NEVER HEARD OF MELK STARDUST BEFORE.
BUT IF ANYONE KNOWS ABOUT IT, MELK WOULD.
SAME NAME AND ALL.
HOW ABOUT IT, KOMATSU?
WHILE WE LOOK FOR MELK STARDUST, YOU CAN GET MELK TO MAKE YOU A NEW KNIFE!
HUH ?!
Y...
YOU REALLY MEAN IT?!
I'M IN, TORIKO!
YAHOO! I GET TO MEET MELK!
HURRAY!
WHEE!
SCORE!
...
YOU'D NEVER KNOW HE WAS JUST SOBBING.

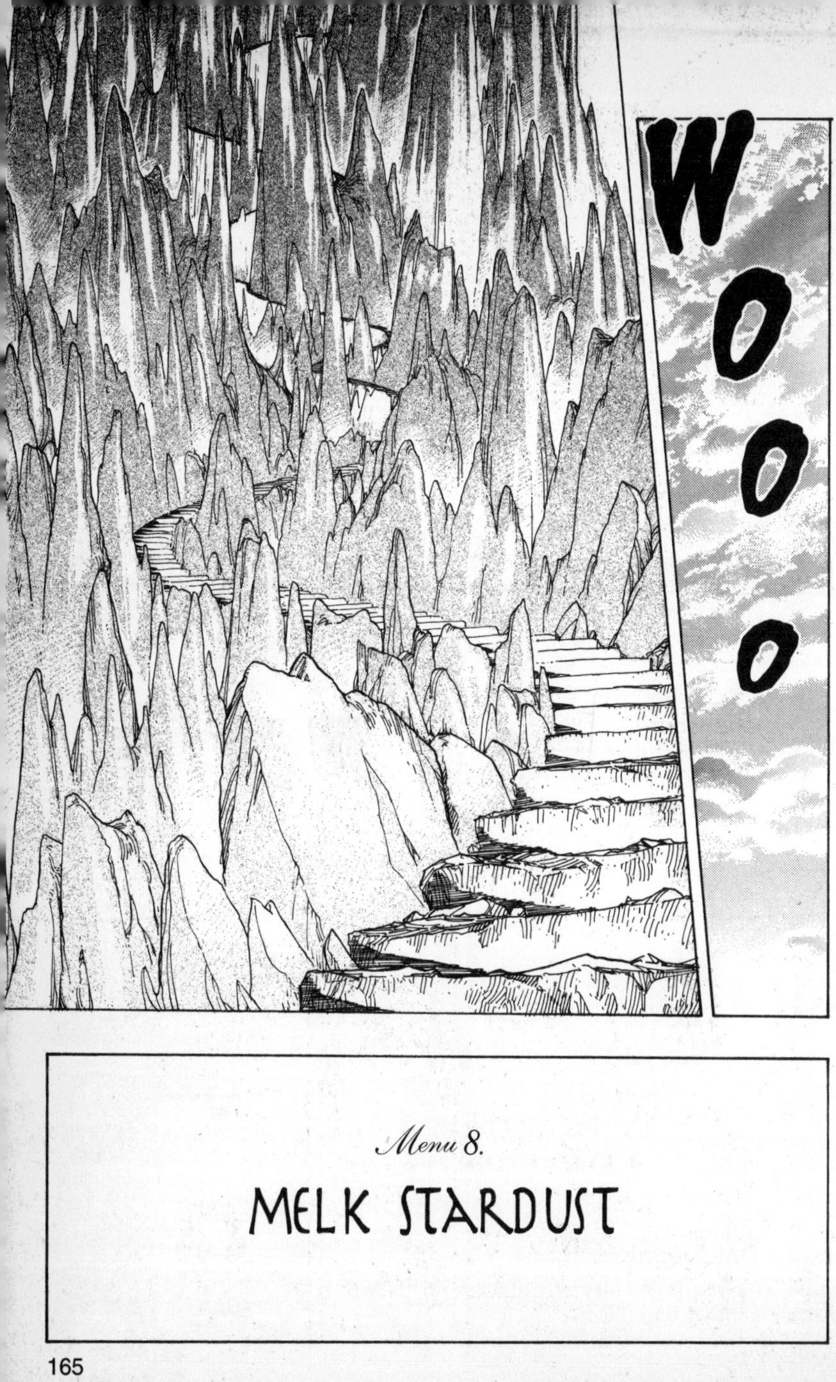
WOOO

Menu 8.

MELK STARDUST

TORIKO

GOURMET CHECKLIST

Vol. 129

BLOOD BUG

(INSECT)

CAPTURE LEVEL: 8

HABITAT: HEALING FOREST NEAR LIFE

LENGTH: 7 CM

HEIGHT: ---

WEIGHT: 100 G AT MAXIMUM CAPACITY

PRICE: 90,000 YEN PER BUG

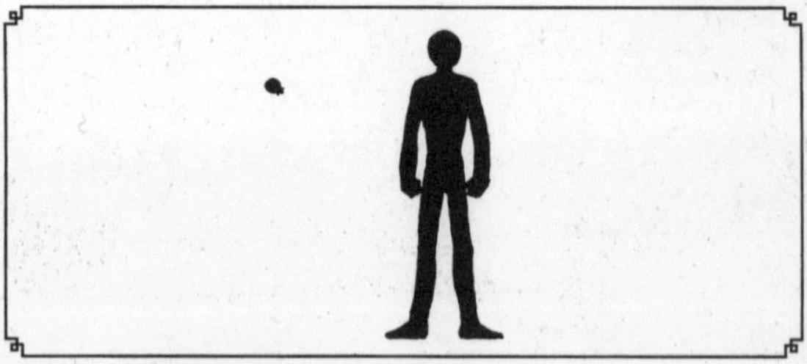

SCALE

A BUG THAT STORES HUMAN BLOOD IN ITS STOMACH. LIKE A MOSQUITO, A BLOOD BUG WILL SUCK UP YOUR BLOOD (BUT IT DOESN'T HURT). THEY WILL SLURP UP BLOOD TOXINS TOO, SO PLENTY OF PEOPLE PURPOSELY GET BITTEN. BLOOD BUGS' STOMACHS PURIFY THE BLOOD, MAKING IT SAFE FOR HUMAN USE ONCE AGAIN.

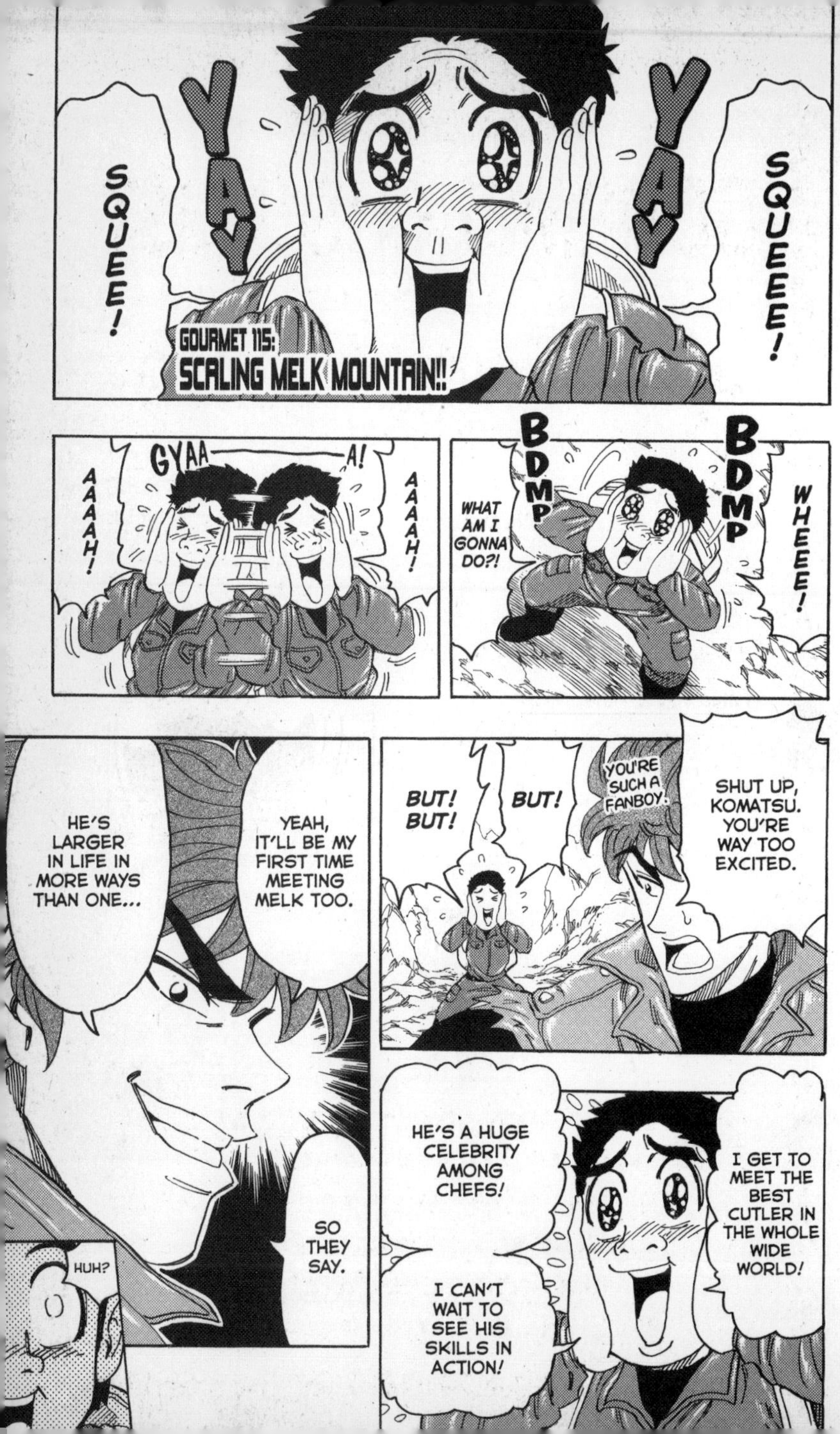
YAY
SQUEEE!
YAY
SQUEE!
GOURMET 115: SCALING MELK MOUNTAIN!!
WHEEE!
BDMP
BDMP
WHAT AM I GONNA DO?!
AAAAAH!
GYAA—A!
AAAAAH!
SHUT UP, KOMATSU. YOU'RE WAY TOO EXCITED.
YOU'RE SUCH A FANBOY.
BUT!
BUT! BUT!
I GET TO MEET THE BEST CUTLER IN THE WHOLE WIDE WORLD!
HE'S A HUGE CELEBRITY AMONG CHEFS!
I CAN'T WAIT TO SEE HIS SKILLS IN ACTION!
YEAH, IT'LL BE MY FIRST TIME MEETING MELK TOO.
HE'S LARGER IN LIFE IN MORE WAYS THAN ONE...
SO THEY SAY.
HUH?

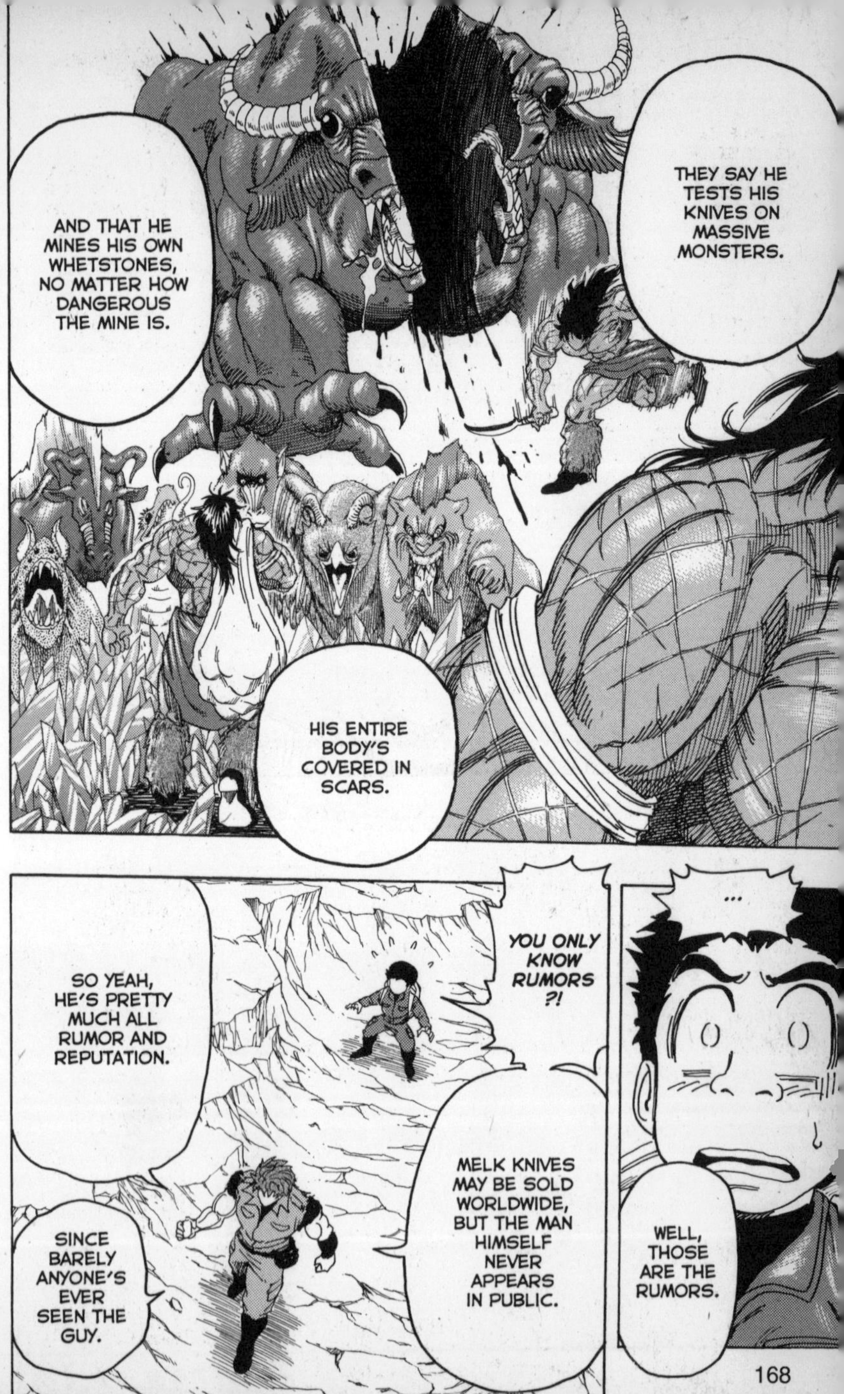
THEY SAY HE TESTS HIS KNIVES ON MASSIVE MONSTERS.
AND THAT HE MINES HIS OWN WHETSTONES, NO MATTER HOW DANGEROUS THE MINE IS.
HIS ENTIRE BODY'S COVERED IN SCARS.
...
WELL, THOSE ARE THE RUMORS.
YOU ONLY KNOW RUMORS ?!
MELK KNIVES MAY BE SOLD WORLDWIDE, BUT THE MAN HIMSELF NEVER APPEARS IN PUBLIC.
SO YEAH, HE'S PRETTY MUCH ALL RUMOR AND REPUTATION.
SINCE BARELY ANYONE'S EVER SEEN THE GUY.

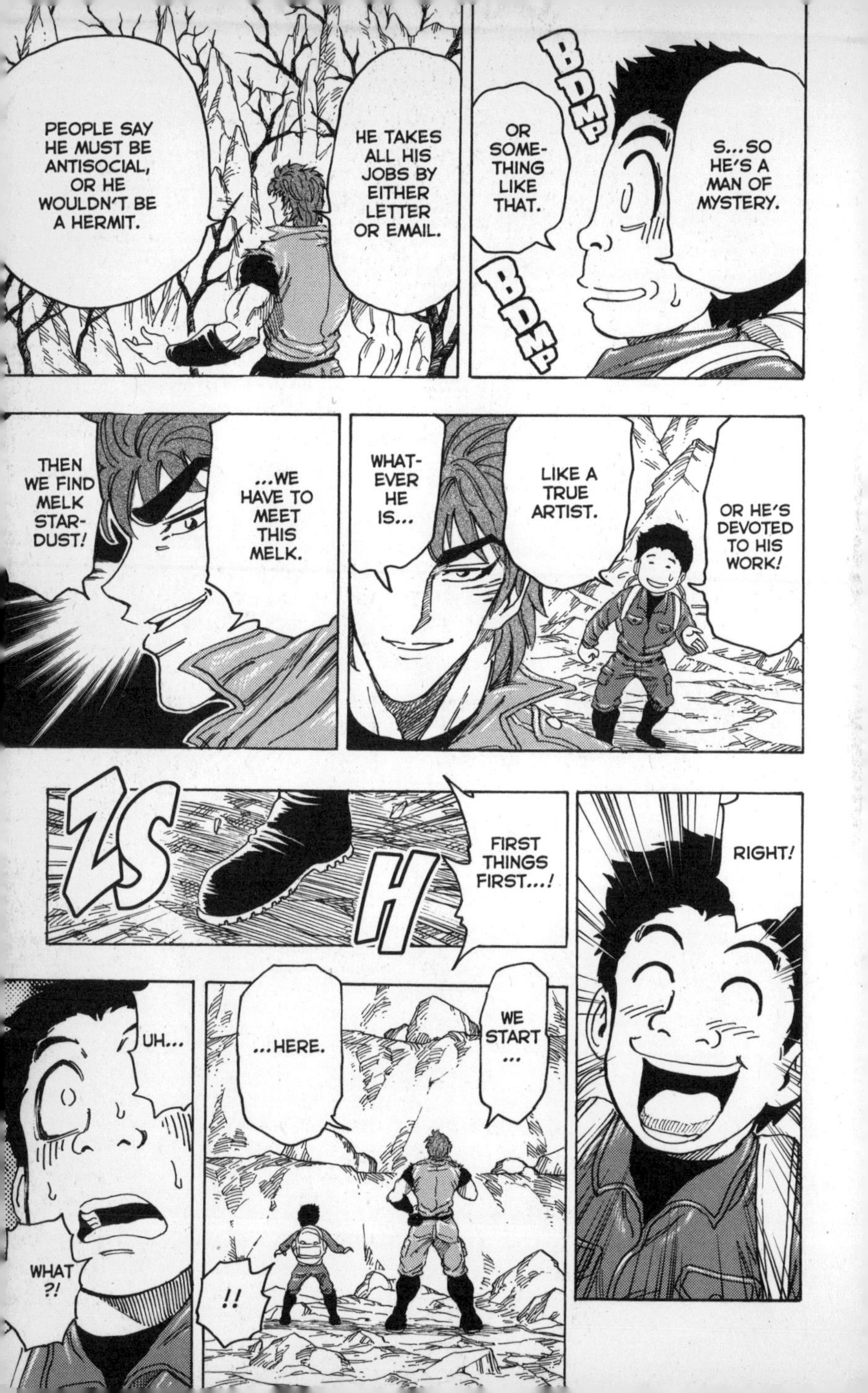
S...SO HE'S A MAN OF MYSTERY.
BDMP
BDMP
OR SOMETHING LIKE THAT.
HE TAKES ALL HIS JOBS BY EITHER LETTER OR EMAIL.
PEOPLE SAY HE MUST BE ANTISOCIAL, OR HE WOULDN'T BE A HERMIT.
OR HE'S DEVOTED TO HIS WORK!
LIKE A TRUE ARTIST.
WHATEVER HE IS...
...WE HAVE TO MEET THIS MELK.
THEN WE FIND MELK STARDUST!
RIGHT!
FIRST THINGS FIRST...!
ZSH
WE START...
...HERE.
!!
UH...
WHAT?!

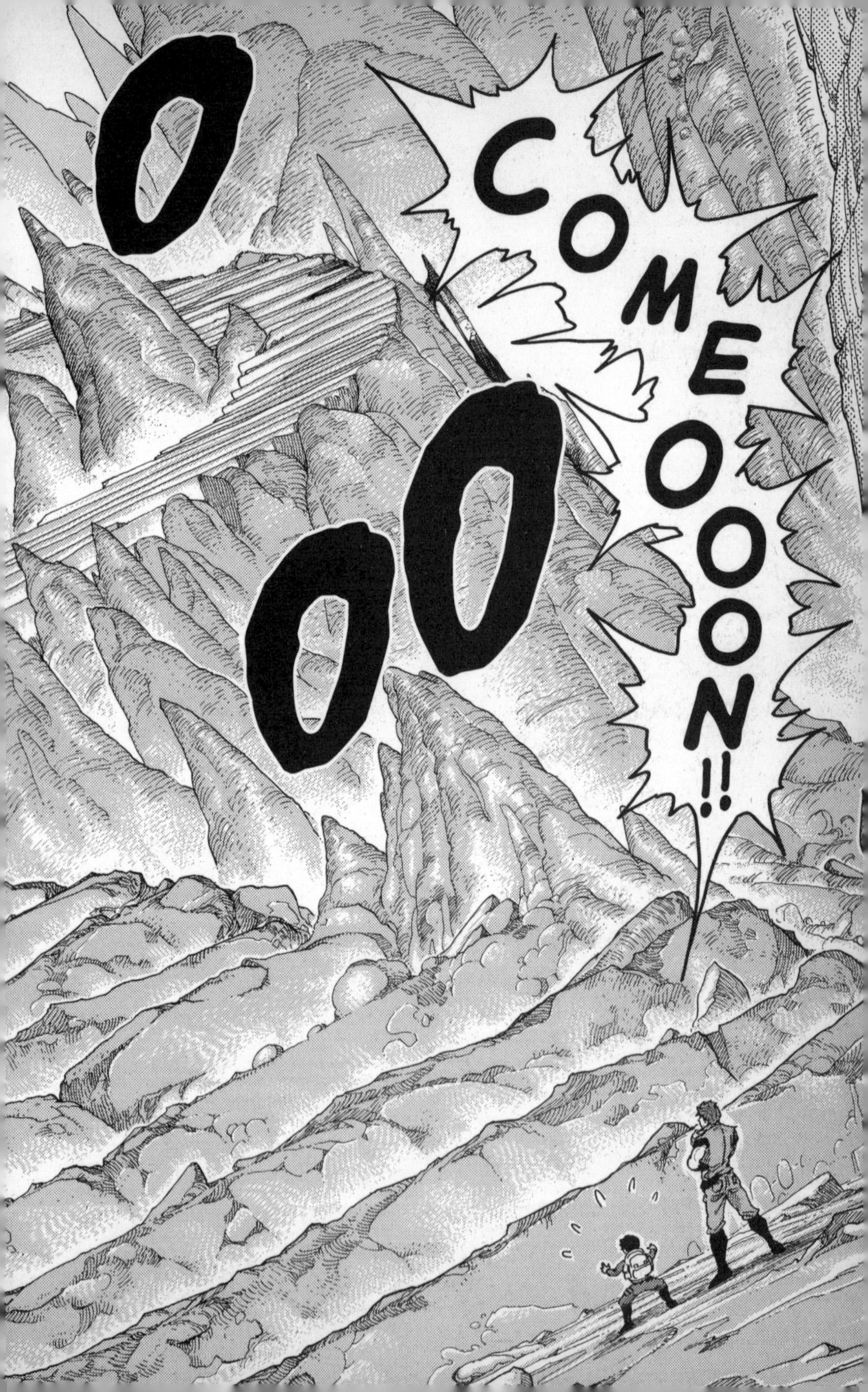
COME OOOON!!
OOO

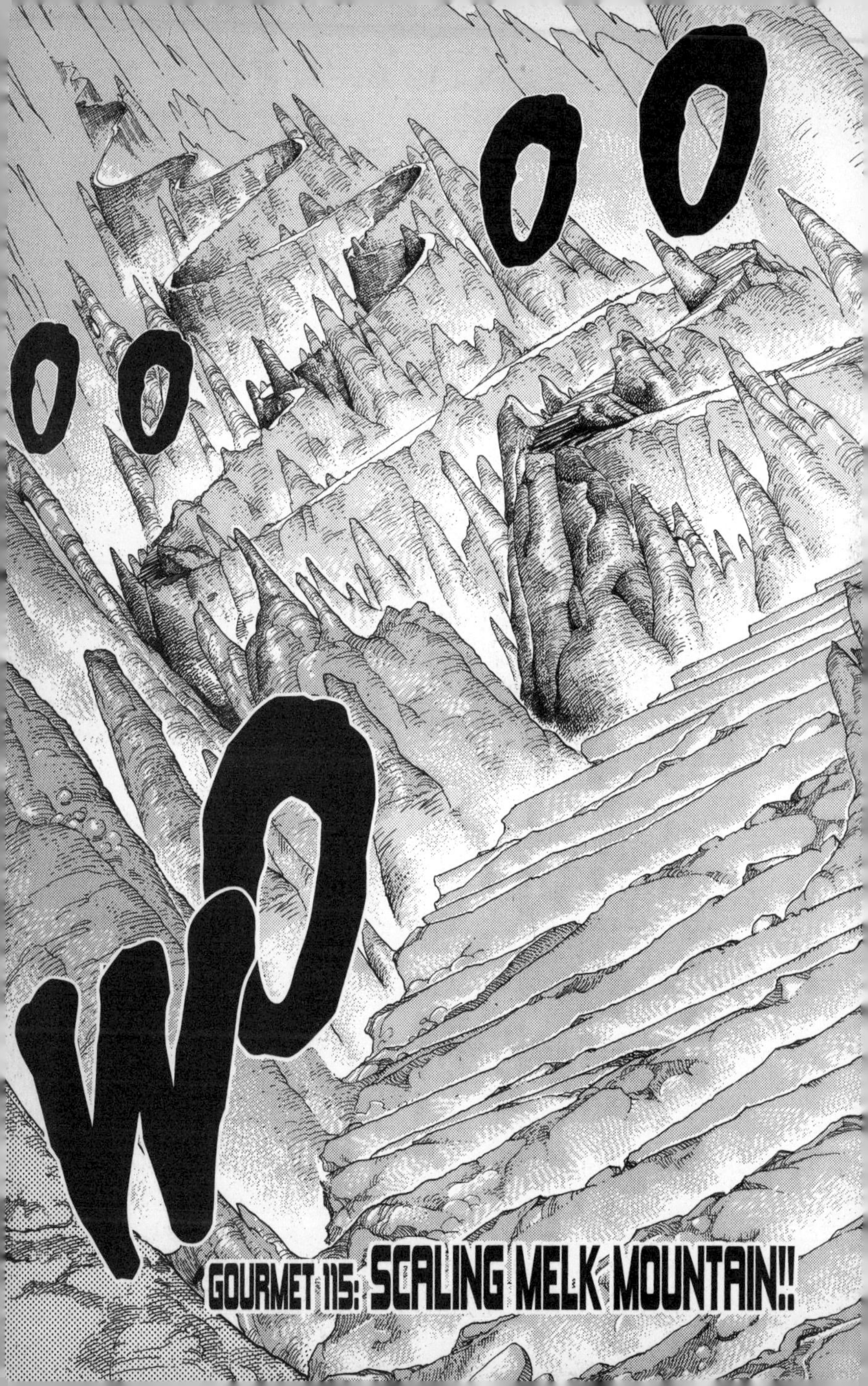
WOOOOO
GOURMET 115: SCALING MELK MOUNTAIN!!

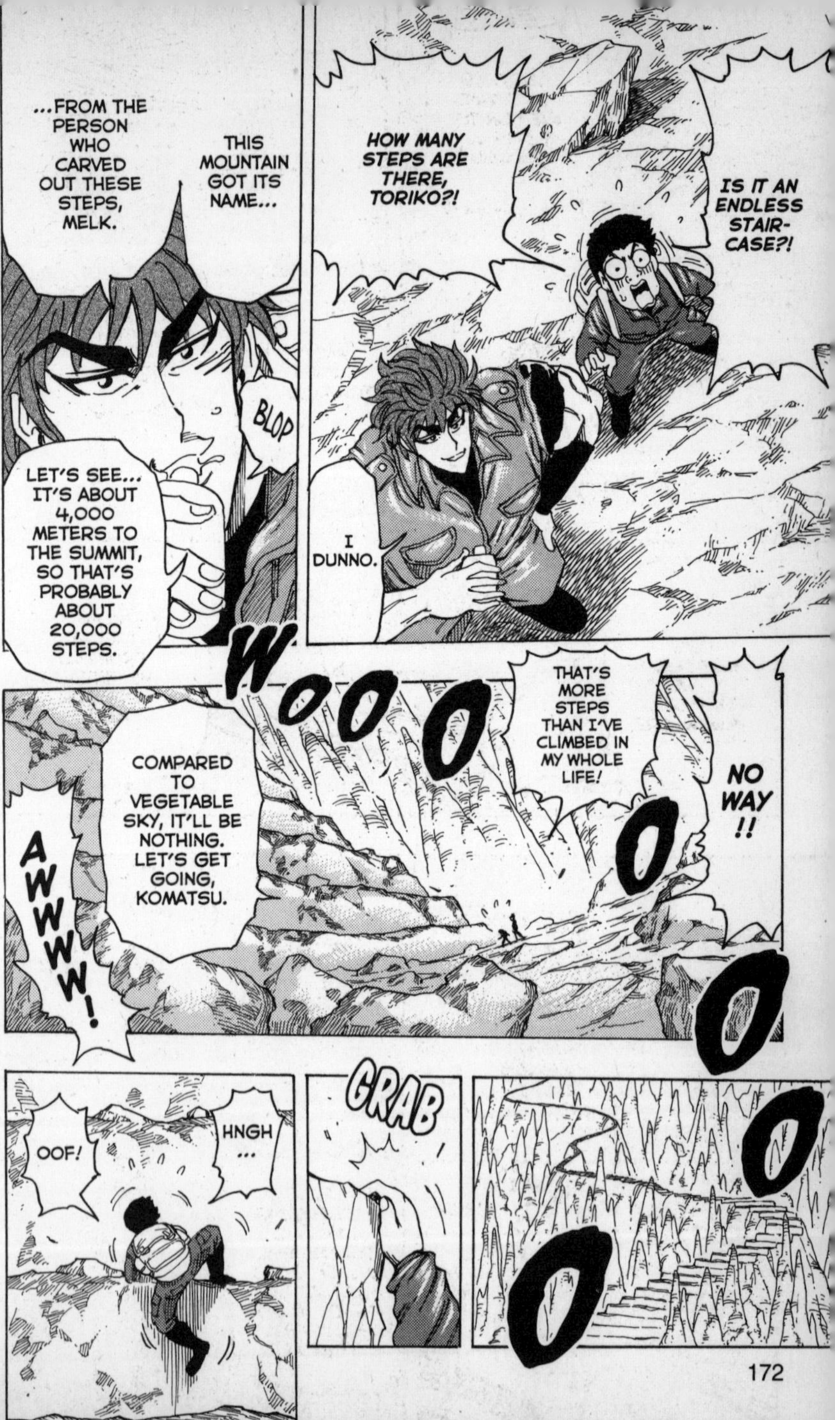
IS IT AN ENDLESS STAIR-CASE?!
HOW MANY STEPS ARE THERE, TORIKO?!
I DUNNO.
THIS MOUNTAIN GOT ITS NAME...
...FROM THE PERSON WHO CARVED OUT THESE STEPS, MELK.
BLOP
LET'S SEE... IT'S ABOUT 4,000 METERS TO THE SUMMIT, SO THAT'S PROBABLY ABOUT 20,000 STEPS.
NO WAY!!
THAT'S MORE STEPS THAN I'VE CLIMBED IN MY WHOLE LIFE!
COMPARED TO VEGETABLE SKY, IT'LL BE NOTHING. LET'S GET GOING, KOMATSU.
AWWWW!
WOOOOOOOO
GRAB
HNGH...
OOF!

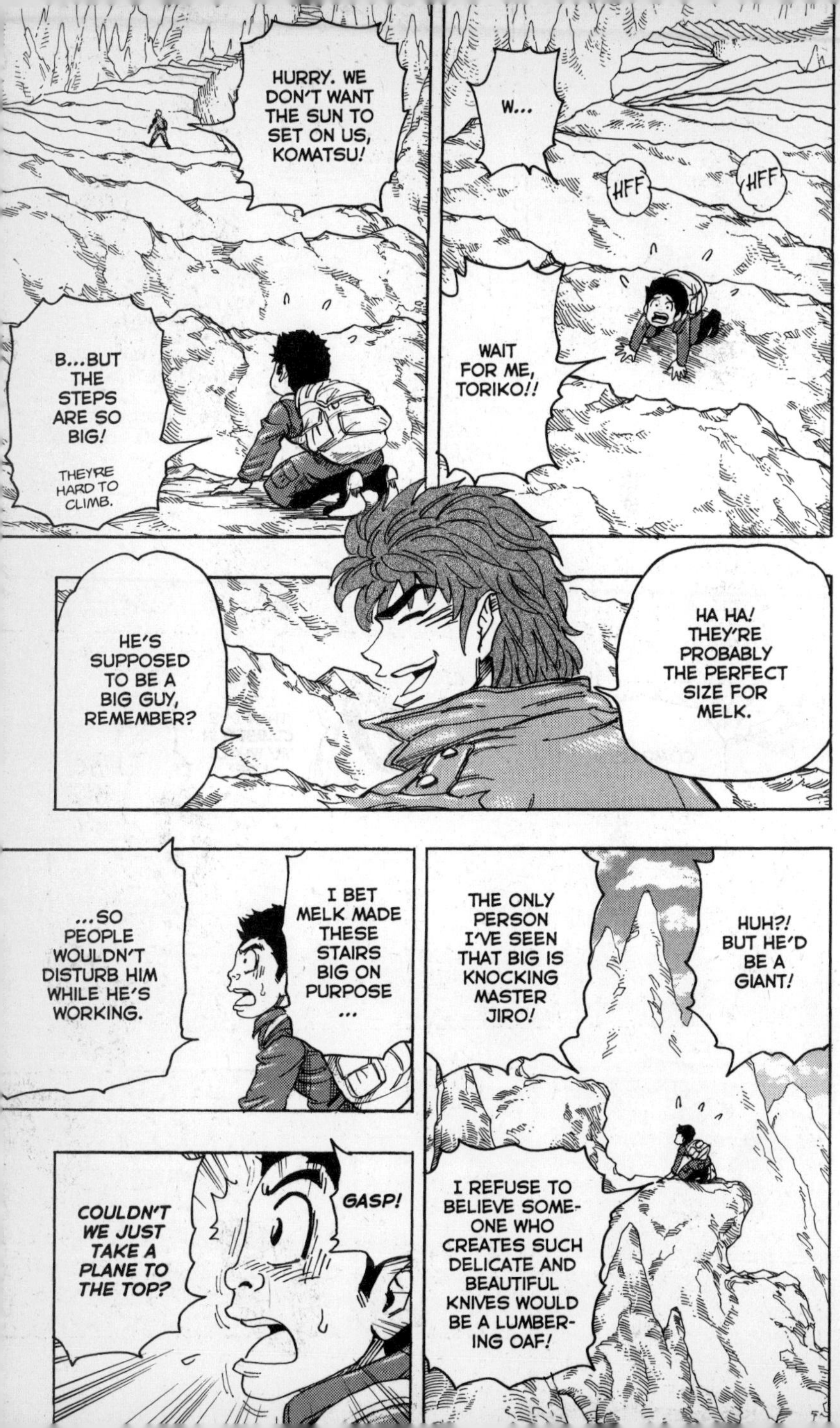

W...
HFF
HFF
WAIT FOR ME, TORIKO!!
HURRY. WE DON'T WANT THE SUN TO SET ON US, KOMATSU!
B...BUT THE STEPS ARE SO BIG!
THEY'RE HARD TO CLIMB.
HA HA! THEY'RE PROBABLY THE PERFECT SIZE FOR MELK.
HE'S SUPPOSED TO BE A BIG GUY, REMEMBER?
HUH?! BUT HE'D BE A GIANT!
THE ONLY PERSON I'VE SEEN THAT BIG IS KNOCKING MASTER JIRO!
I REFUSE TO BELIEVE SOME-ONE WHO CREATES SUCH DELICATE AND BEAUTIFUL KNIVES WOULD BE A LUMBER-ING OAF!
I BET MELK MADE THESE STAIRS BIG ON PURPOSE...
...SO PEOPLE WOULDN'T DISTURB HIM WHILE HE'S WORKING.
GASP!
COULDN'T WE JUST TAKE A PLANE TO THE TOP?

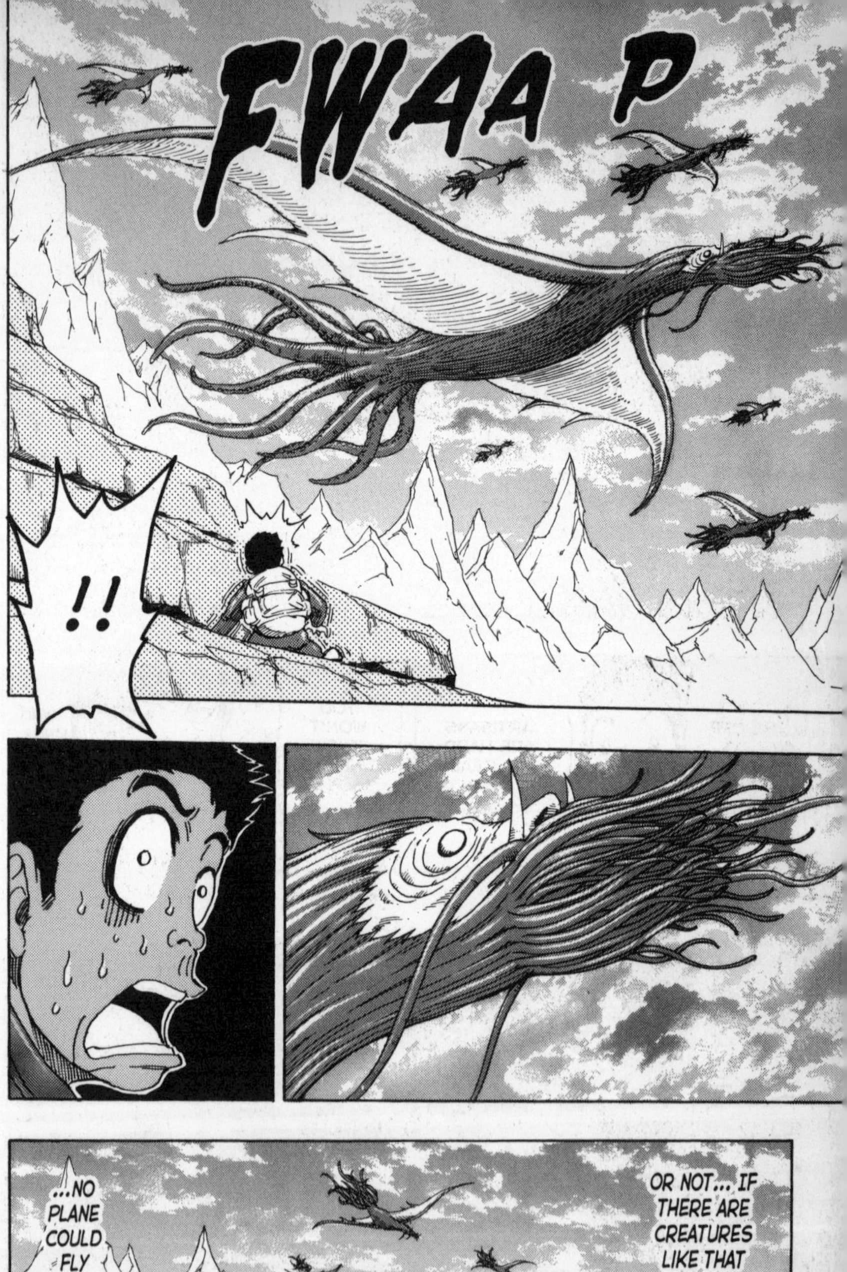
FWAA P
!!
OR NOT... IF THERE ARE CREATURES LIKE THAT AROUND...
...NO PLANE COULD FLY HERE.

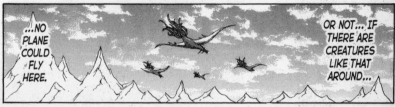

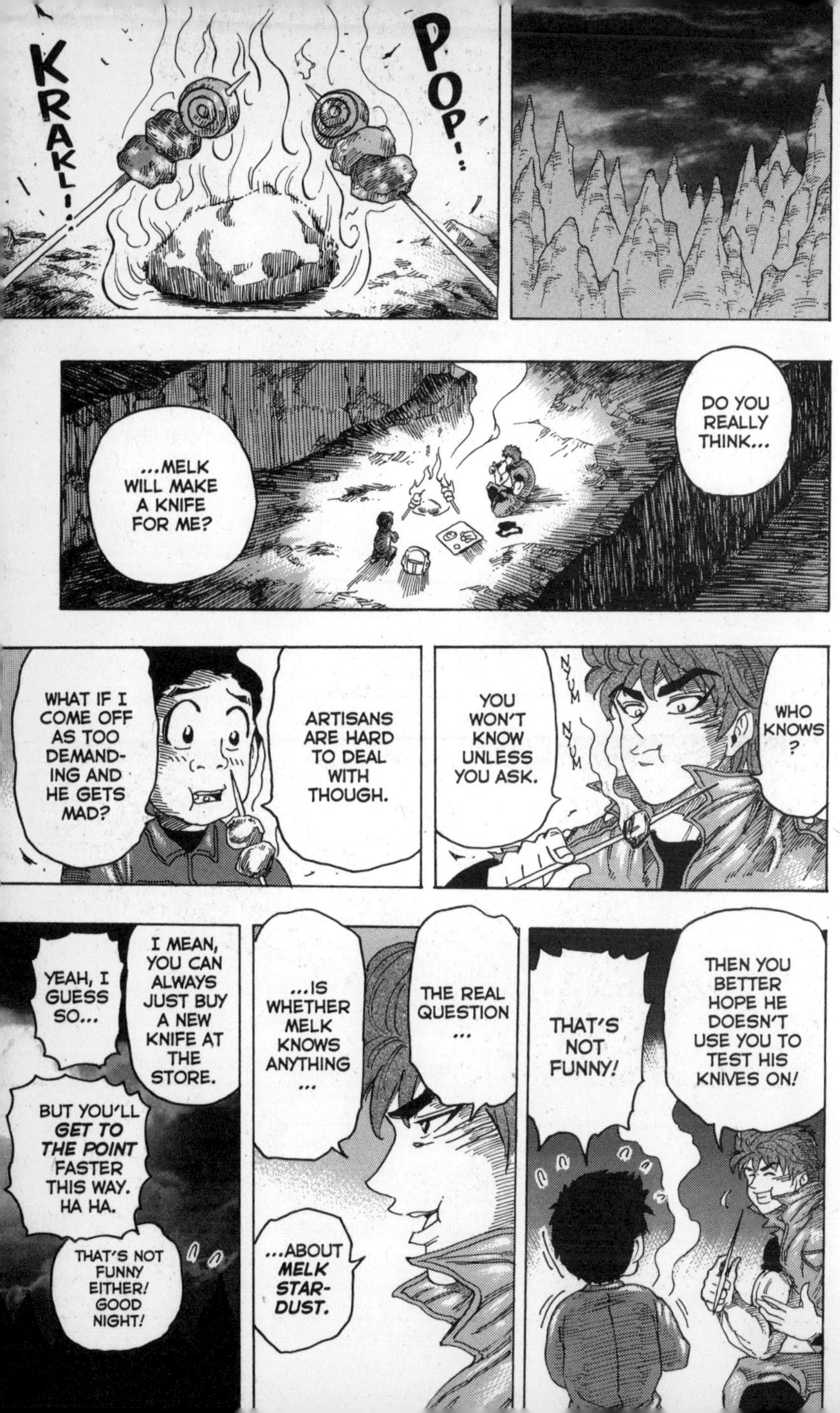
POP!!
KRAKL!!
DO YOU REALLY THINK...
...MELK WILL MAKE A KNIFE FOR ME?
WHO KNOWS?
NYUM NYUM
YOU WON'T KNOW UNLESS YOU ASK.
ARTISANS ARE HARD TO DEAL WITH THOUGH.
WHAT IF I COME OFF AS TOO DEMANDING AND HE GETS MAD?
THEN YOU BETTER HOPE HE DOESN'T USE YOU TO TEST HIS KNIVES ON!
THAT'S NOT FUNNY!
THE REAL QUESTION...
...IS WHETHER MELK KNOWS ANYTHING...
...ABOUT MELK STARDUST.
YEAH, I GUESS SO...
I MEAN, YOU CAN ALWAYS JUST BUY A NEW KNIFE AT THE STORE.
BUT YOU'LL GET TO THE POINT FASTER THIS WAY. HA HA.
THAT'S NOT FUNNY EITHER! GOOD NIGHT!

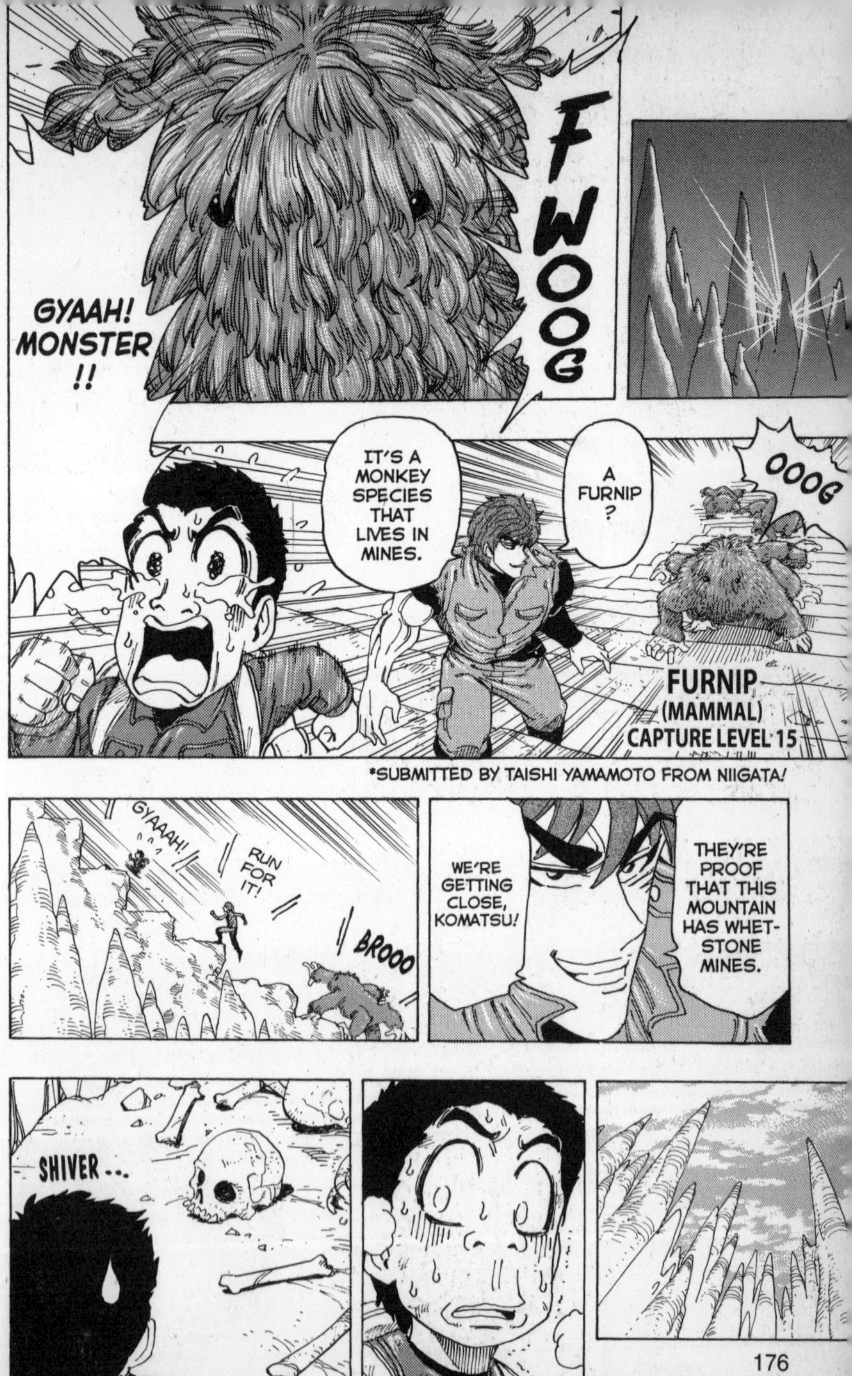
FWOOG
GYAAH! MONSTER !!
OOOG
A FURNIP ?
IT'S A MONKEY SPECIES THAT LIVES IN MINES.
FURNIP (MAMMAL) CAPTURE LEVEL 15
*SUBMITTED BY TAISHI YAMAMOTO FROM NIIGATA!
THEY'RE PROOF THAT THIS MOUNTAIN HAS WHET-STONE MINES.
WE'RE GETTING CLOSE, KOMATSU!
GYAAAH!
RUN FOR IT!
BROOO
SHIVER...

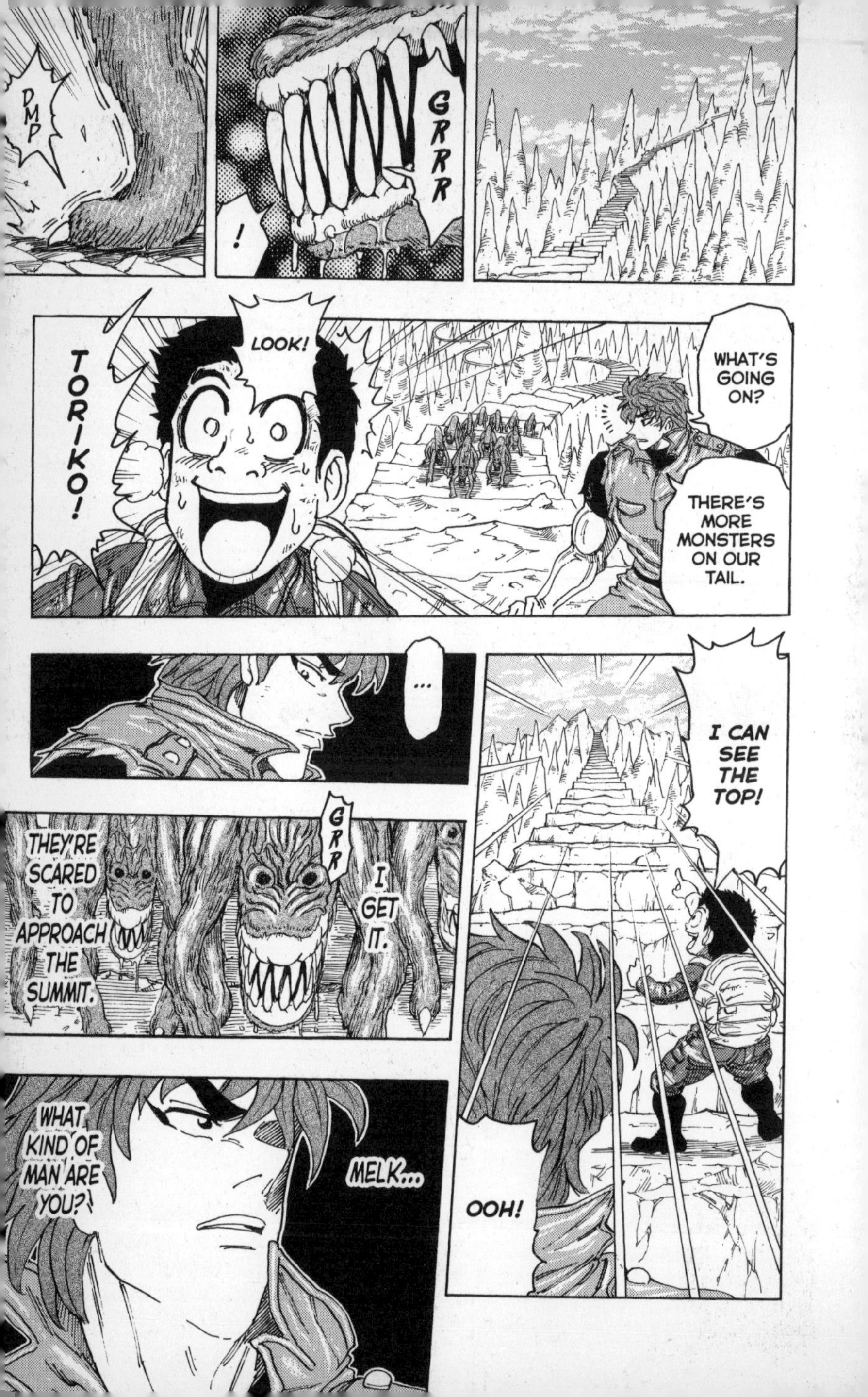
GRRR
!
DMP
WHAT'S GOING ON?
THERE'S MORE MONSTERS ON OUR TAIL.
LOOK!
TORIKO!
I CAN SEE THE TOP!
OOH!
...
GRR
I GET IT.
THEY'RE SCARED TO APPROACH THE SUMMIT.
MELK...
WHAT KIND OF MAN ARE YOU?

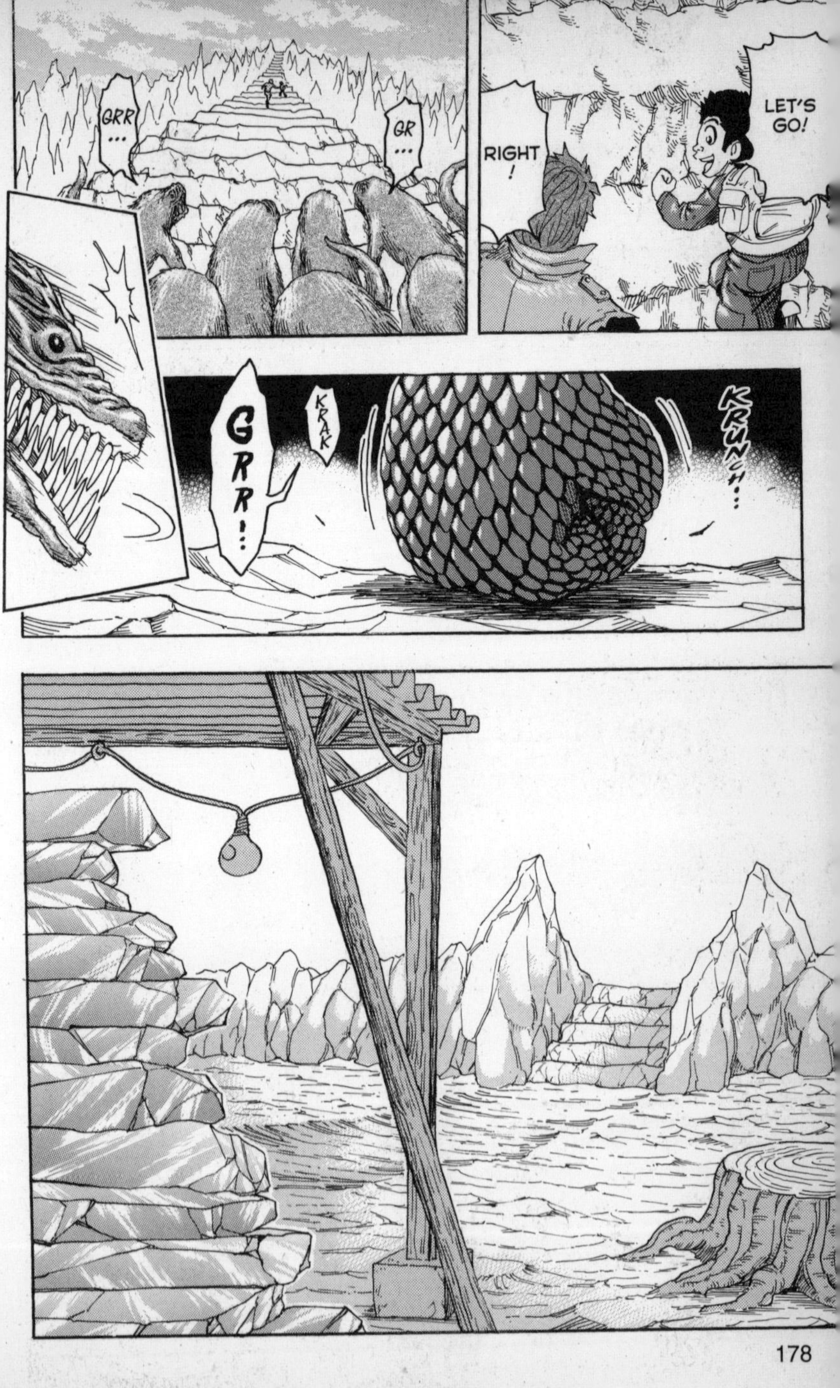
LET'S GO!
RIGHT!
GR...
GRR...
KRUNCH...
KRAK
GRR!!

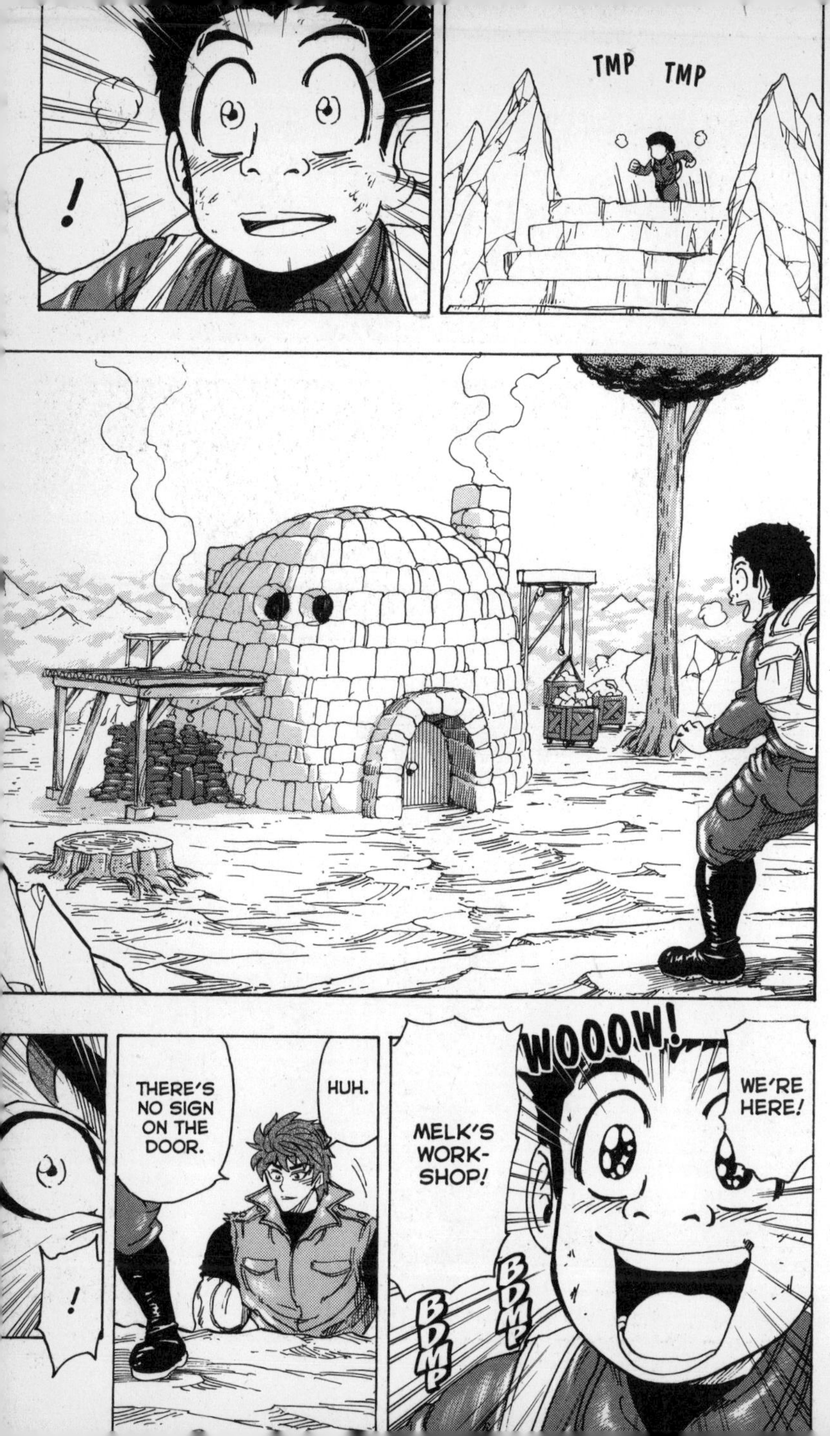
TMP TMP
!
WOOOW!
WE'RE HERE!
MELK'S WORK-SHOP!
BDMP
BDMP
HUH.
THERE'S NO SIGN ON THE DOOR.
!

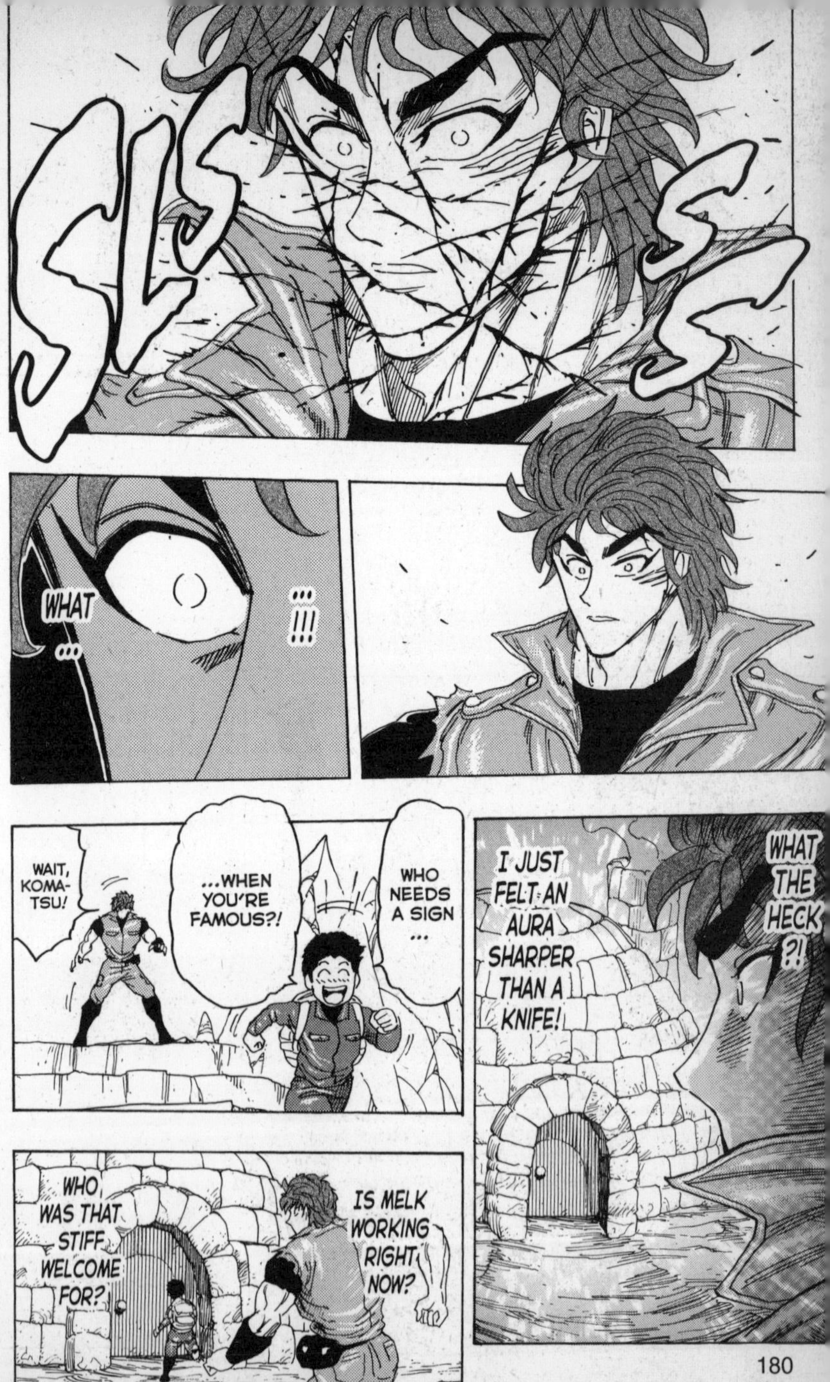
...!!!
WHAT ...
WHAT THE HECK ?!
I JUST FELT AN AURA SHARPER THAN A KNIFE!
WHO NEEDS A SIGN ...
...WHEN YOU'RE FAMOUS?!
WAIT, KOMA-TSU!
IS MELK WORKING RIGHT NOW?
WHO WAS THAT STIFF WELCOME FOR?

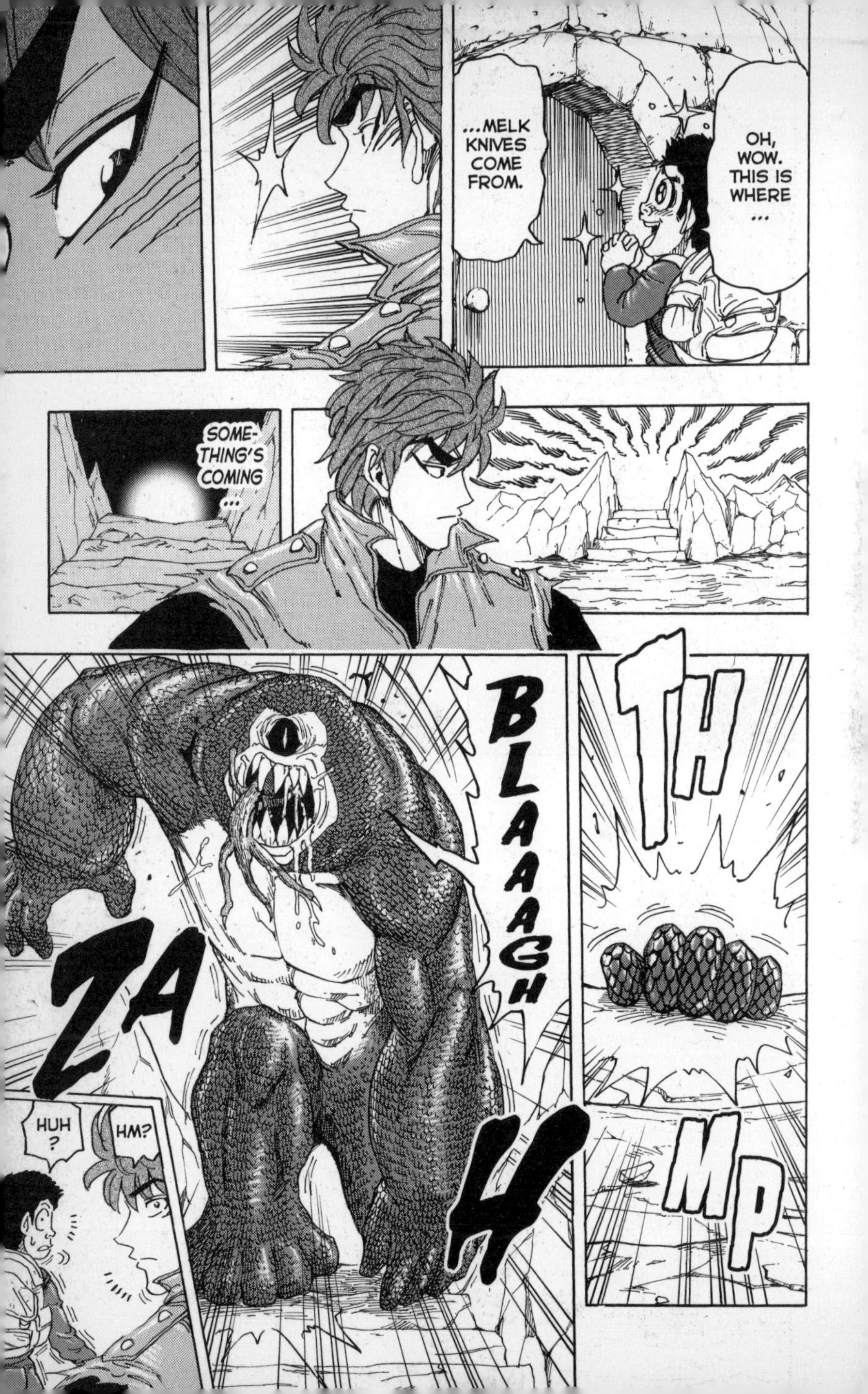
OH, WOW. THIS IS WHERE ...
...MELK KNIVES COME FROM.
SOME-THING'S COMING ...
TH
MP
BLAAAAGH
ZA
H
HM?
HUH ?

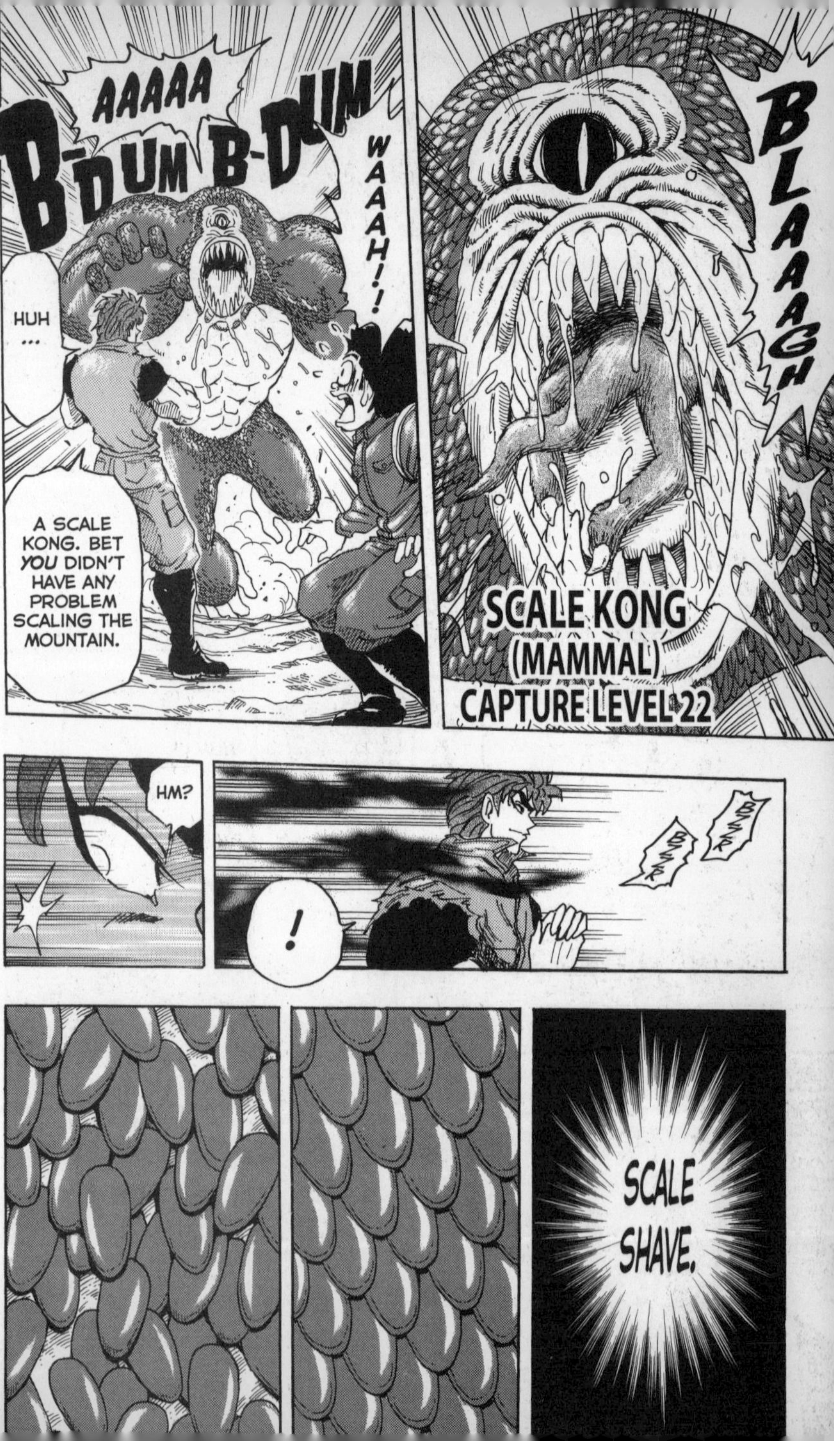
BLAAAAGH
SCALE KONG
(MAMMAL)
CAPTURE LEVEL 22
AAAAA
B-DUM B-DUM
WAAAAH!!
HUH ...
A SCALE KONG. BET *YOU* DIDN'T HAVE ANY PROBLEM SCALING THE MOUNTAIN.
BZZR
BZZR
!
HM?
SCALE SHAVE.

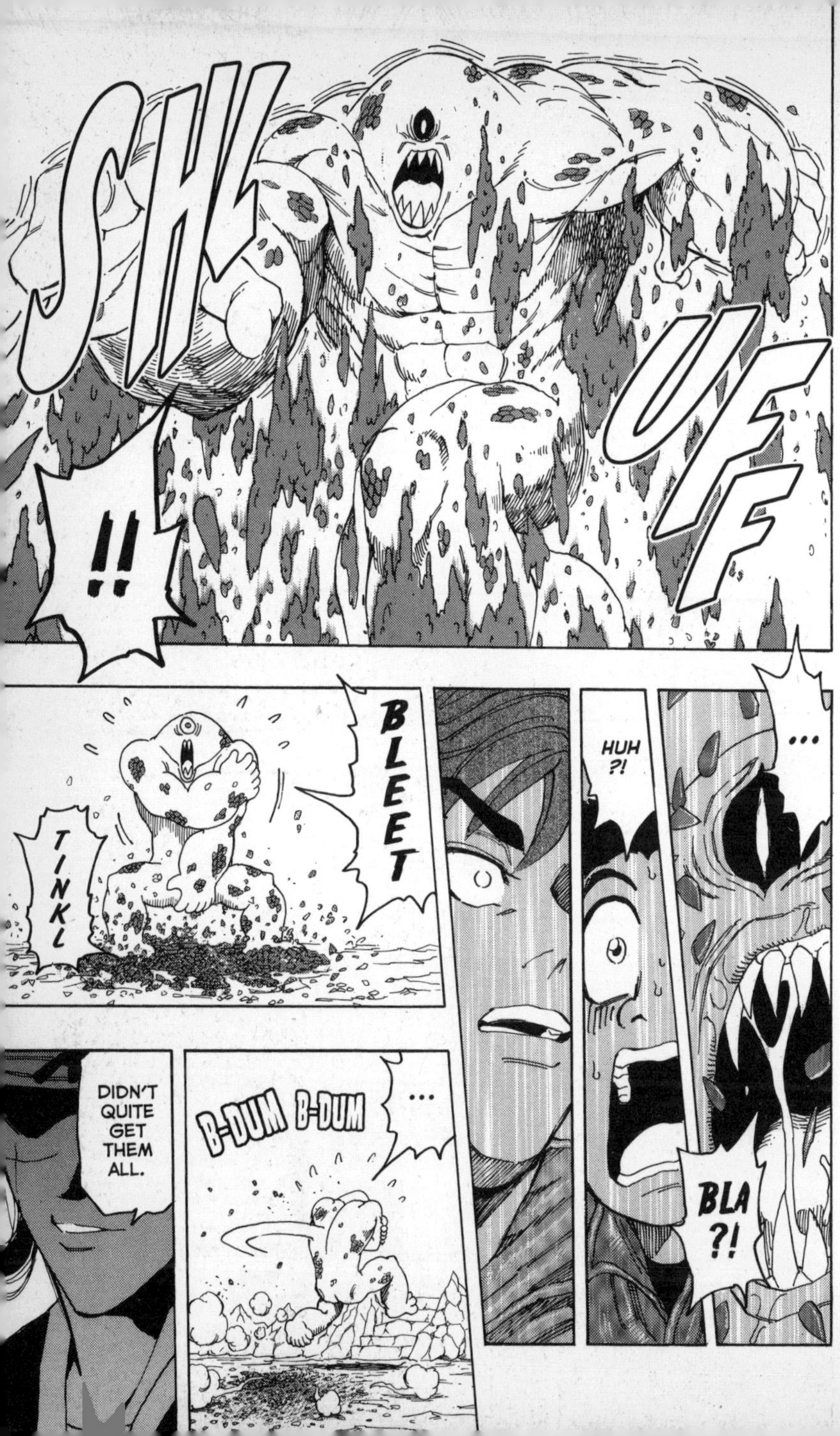
SHUFF
!!
...
HUH ?!
BLEEET
TINKL
BLA ?!
...
B-DUM B-DUM
DIDN'T QUITE GET THEM ALL.

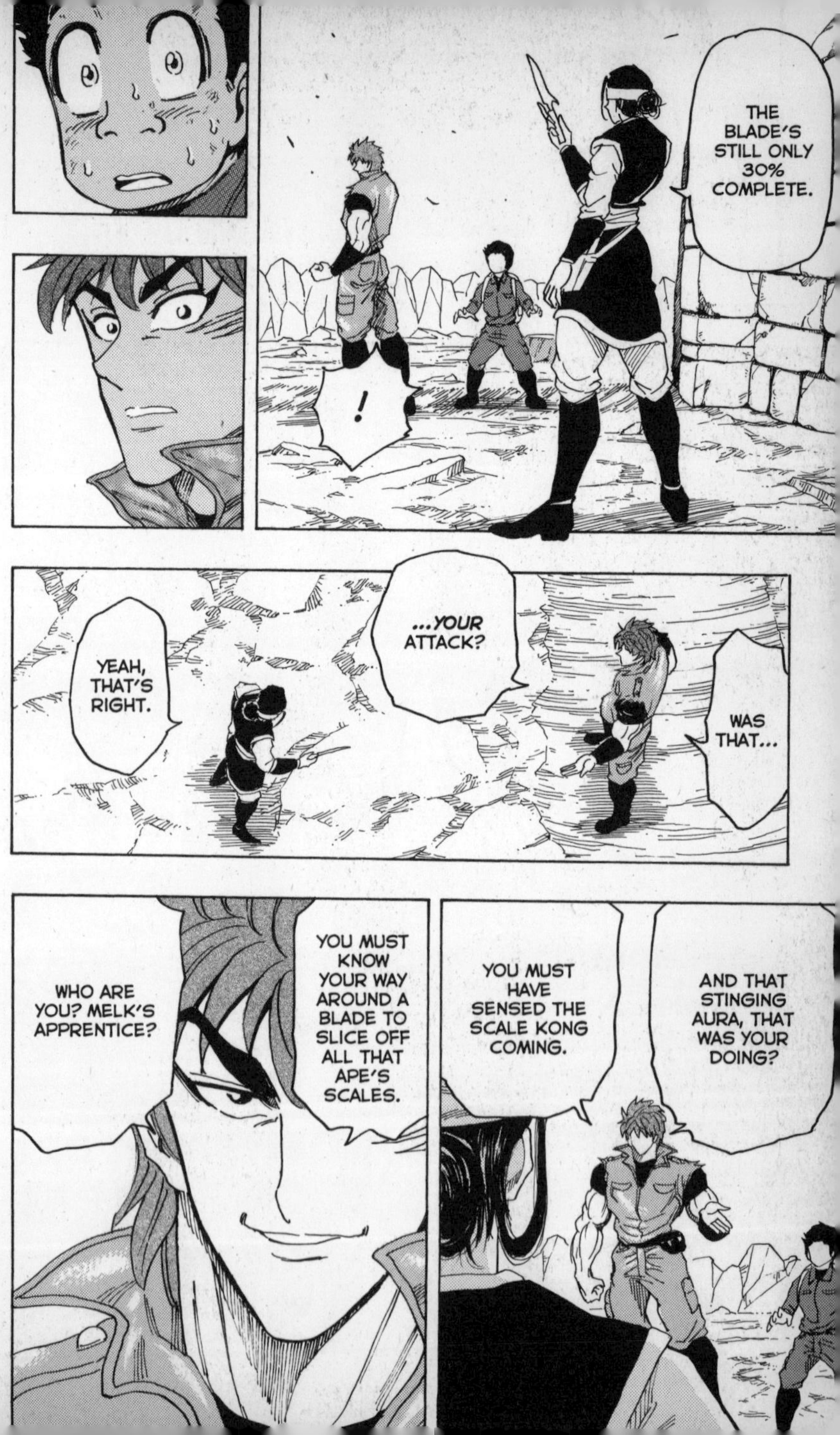
THE BLADE'S STILL ONLY 30% COMPLETE.
!
WAS THAT...
...YOUR ATTACK?
YEAH, THAT'S RIGHT.
AND THAT STINGING AURA, THAT WAS YOUR DOING?
YOU MUST HAVE SENSED THE SCALE KONG COMING.
YOU MUST KNOW YOUR WAY AROUND A BLADE TO SLICE OFF ALL THAT APE'S SCALES.
WHO ARE YOU? MELK'S APPRENTICE?

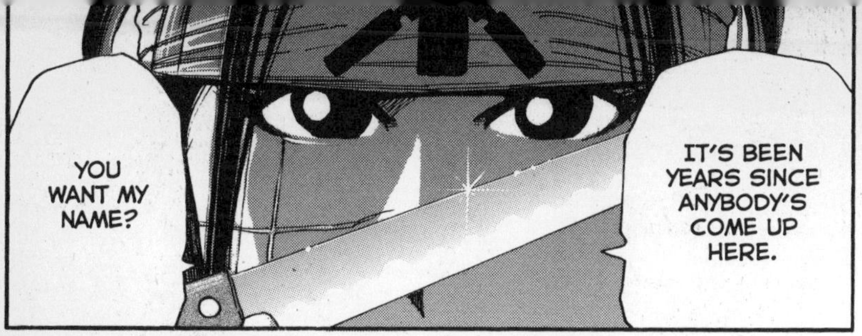
IT'S BEEN YEARS SINCE ANYBODY'S COME UP HERE.
YOU WANT MY NAME?

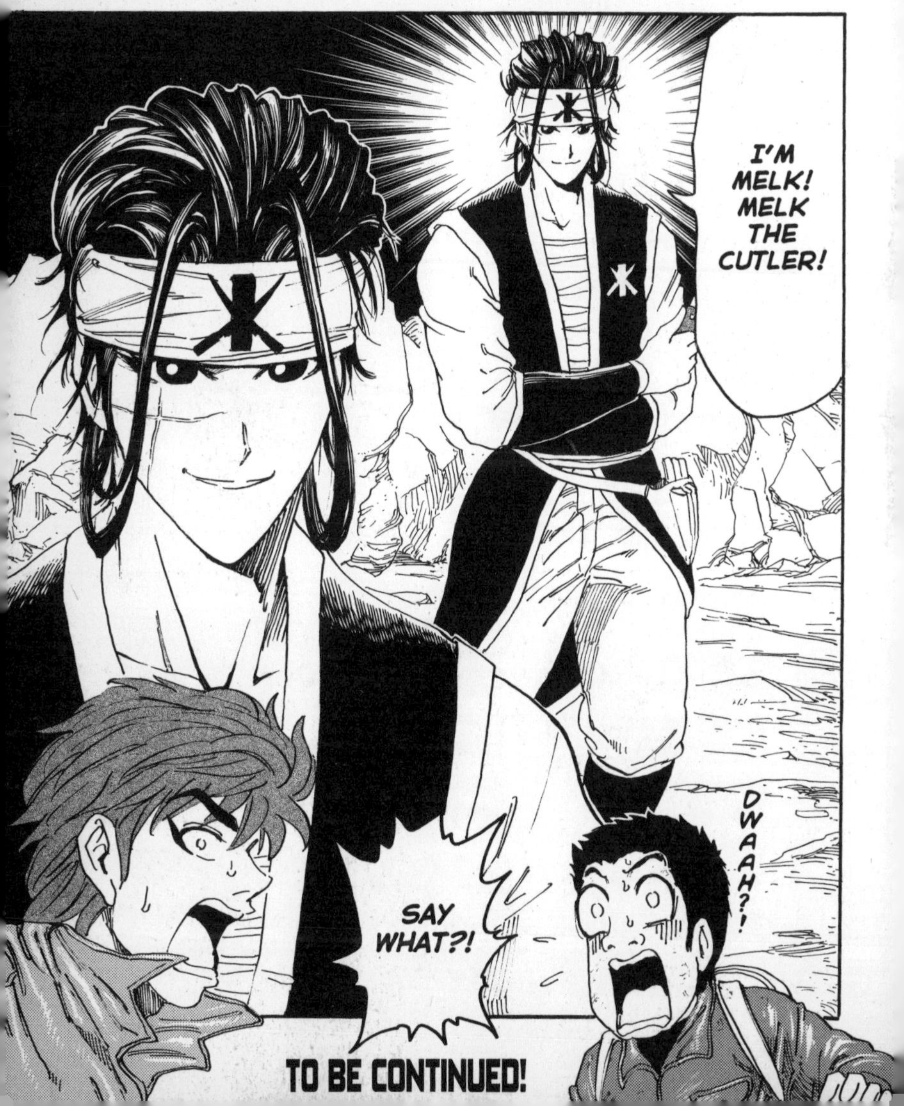
I'M MELK! MELK THE CUTLER!
DWAAAH?!
SAY WHAT?!

TO BE CONTINUED!

CHARACTER PROFILE

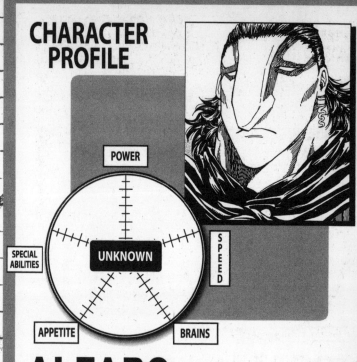

POWER

SPECIAL ABILITIES

UNKNOWN

SPEED

APPETITE

BRAINS

ALFARO

AGE:	UNKNOWN	**BIRTHDAY:**	UNKNOWN
BLOOD TYPE:	UNKNOWN	**SIGN:**	UNKNOWN
HEIGHT:	217 CM	**WEIGHT:**	275 KG
EYESIGHT:	20/4	**SHOE SIZE:**	38 CM

SPECIAL MOVES/ABILITIES:

● Throwing Plates

The garçon of Gourmet Corp. As the boss's right-hand man, he carries out all manner of duties and serves as the de facto reserve force for Gourmet Corp. His true potential is still unknown, but his battle skills are more highly regarded than the Head Chef's. Currently, he is one of the few people able to freely travel to and from the Gourmet World.

CHARACTER PROFILE

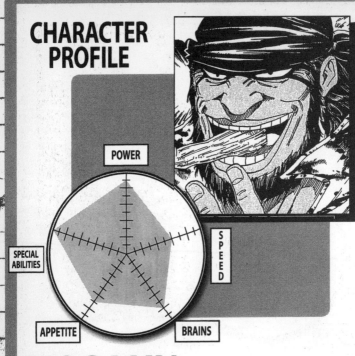

POWER

SPEED

SPECIAL
ABILITIES

APPETITE

BRAINS

YOSAKU

AGE:	55	**BIRTHDAY:**	DEC 8
BLOOD TYPE:	AB	**SIGN:**	SAGITTARIUS
HEIGHT:	195 CM	**WEIGHT:**	140 KG
EYESIGHT:	20/10	**SHOE SIZE:**	30 CM

SPECIAL MOVES/ABILITIES:

● Rousing Shock, Paste Spittle

The Red Reviver, known more commonly as "Bloodstained Yosaku." He's Teppei's master and a very capable Reviver. Despite plentiful failures, he's successfully revived a number of rare specimens, even creating a regenerative plant through genetic manipulation. He is also said to have played a role in reviving the legendary Gourmet Hunter Acacia's dessert, Earth. He loves to bend traditions and break rules, but his promises are unwavering.

COMING NEXT VOLUME

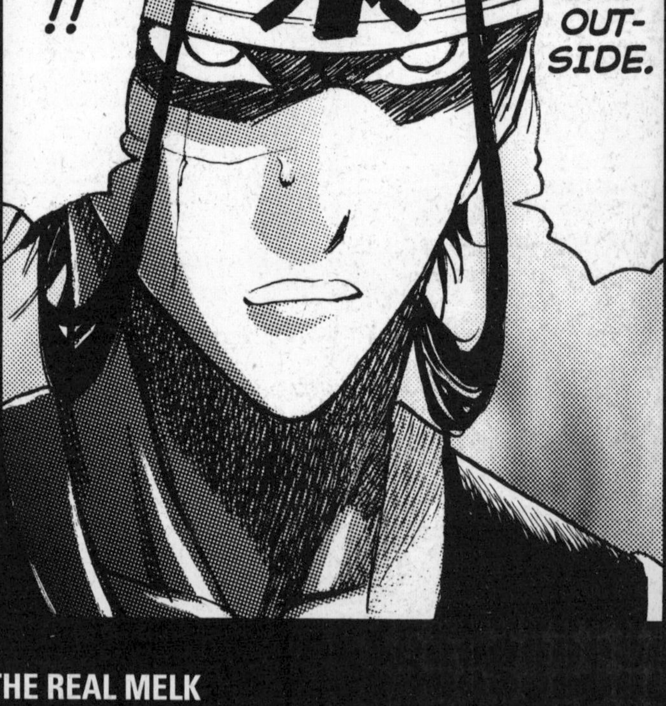
STEP OUT-SIDE.
NOW !!

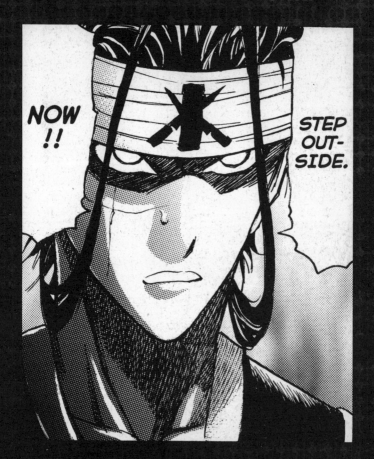

THE REAL MELK

Before the world's best cutler, Melk, will agree to fix Komatsu's broken kitchen knife, he demands that Toriko get him a superior whetstone that lies within the deepest cave in the world, guarded by terrifying subterranean creatures. Why did Melk drive such a hard bargain? Could he be hiding something?

AVAILABLE FEBRUARY 2013!

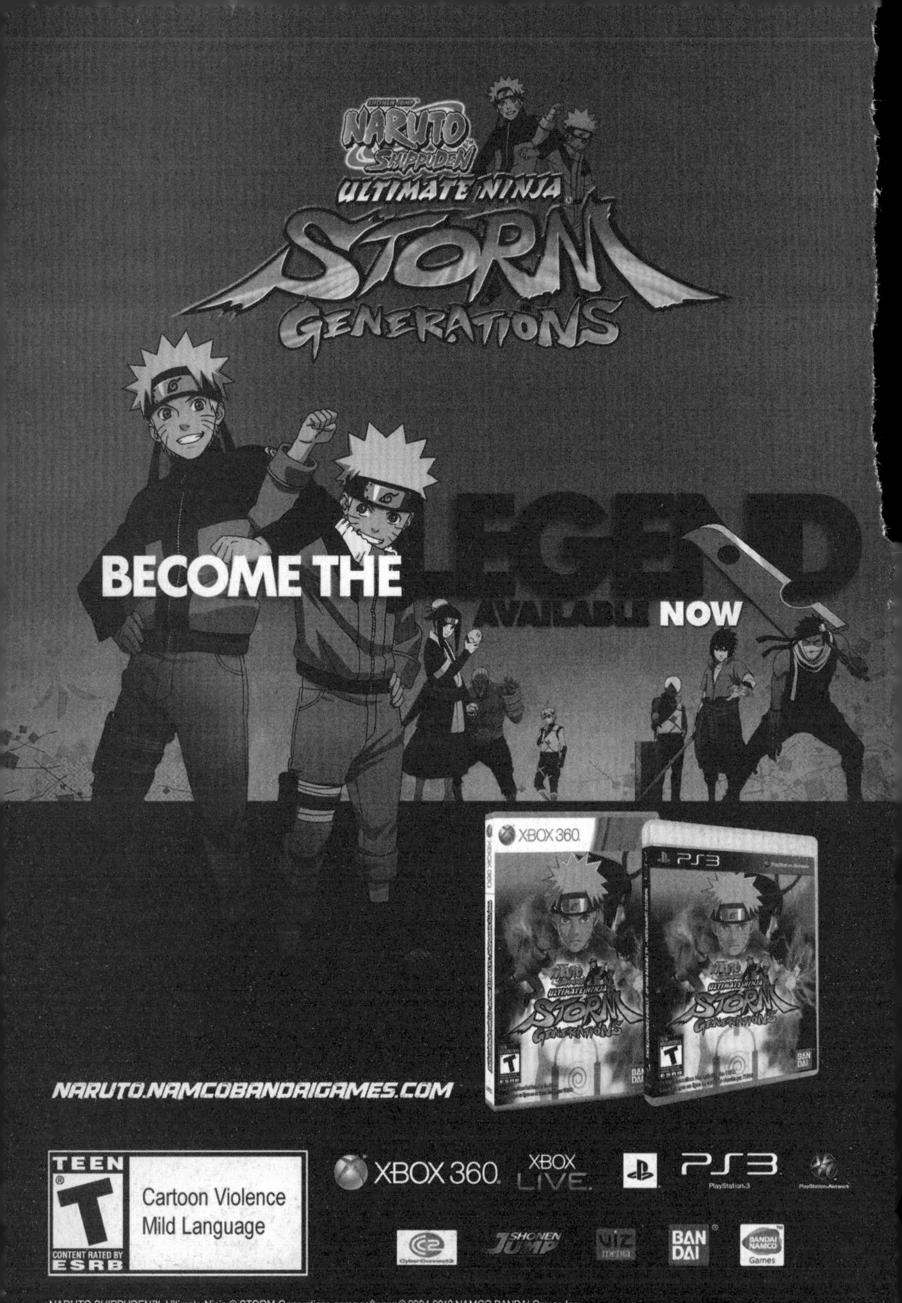
NARUTO SHIPPUDEN
ULTIMATE NINJA
STORM
GENERATIONS
BECOME THE LEGEND
AVAILABLE NOW
XBOX 360
PS3
NARUTO.NAMCOBANDAIGAMES.COM
TEEN
T
CONTENT RATED BY
ESRB
Cartoon Violence
Mild Language
XBOX 360
XBOX LIVE
PS3
PlayStation 3
SHONEN JUMP
BANDAI
BANDAI NAMCO Games

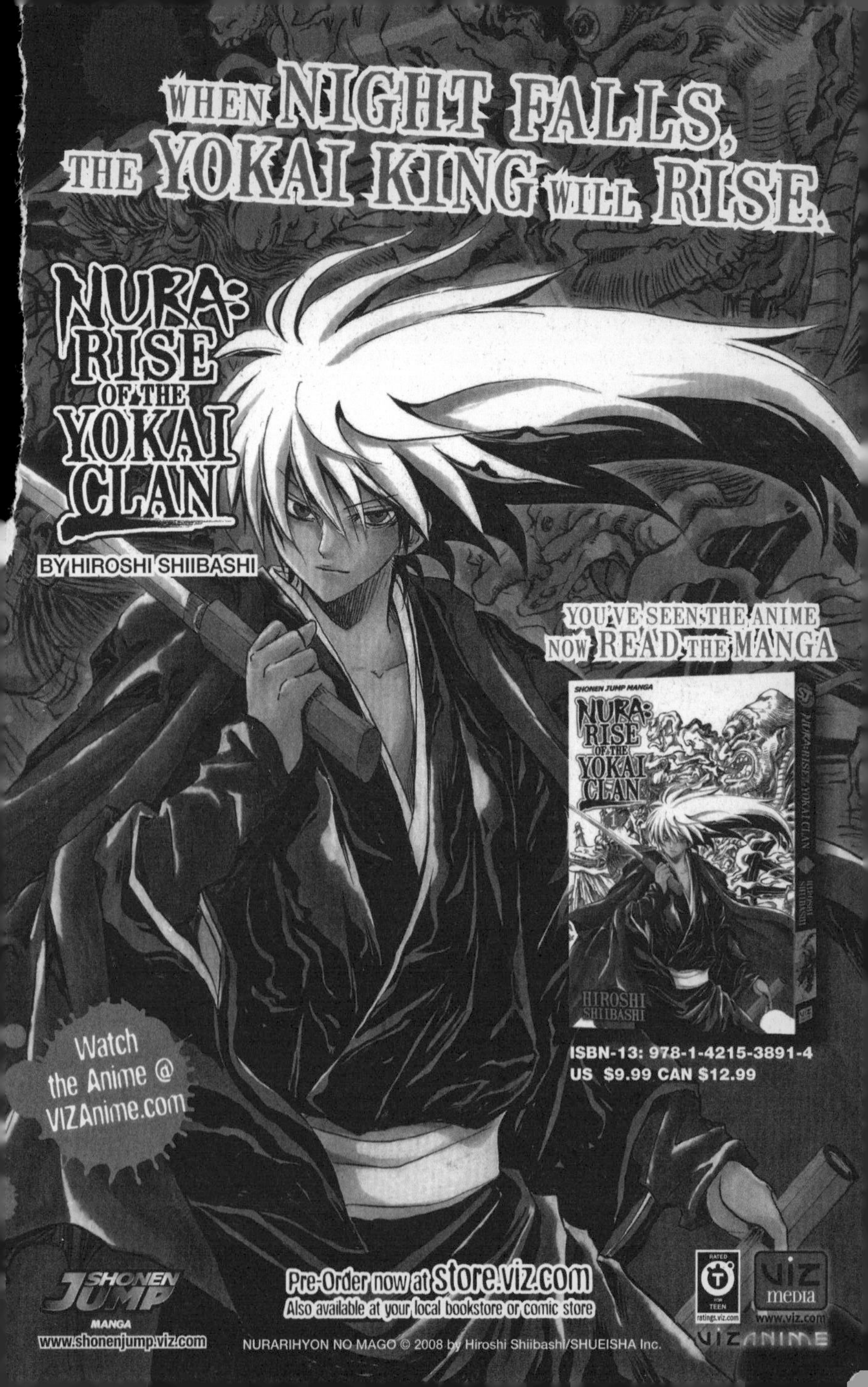
WHEN NIGHT FALLS, THE YOKAI KING WILL RISE.
NURA: RISE OF THE YOKAI CLAN
BY HIROSHI SHIIBASHI
YOU'VE SEEN THE ANIME NOW READ THE MANGA
SHONEN JUMP MANGA
NURA: RISE OF THE YOKAI CLAN
HIROSHI SHIIBASHI
ISBN-13: 978-1-4215-3891-4
US $9.99 CAN $12.99
Watch the Anime @ VIZAnime.com
SHONEN JUMP MANGA
www.shonenjump.viz.com
Pre-Order now at Store.viz.com
Also available at your local bookstore or comic store
RATED T FOR TEEN ratings.viz.com
VIZ media www.viz.com
VIZANIME
NURARIHYON NO MAGO © 2008 by Hiroshi Shiibashi/SHUEISHA Inc.

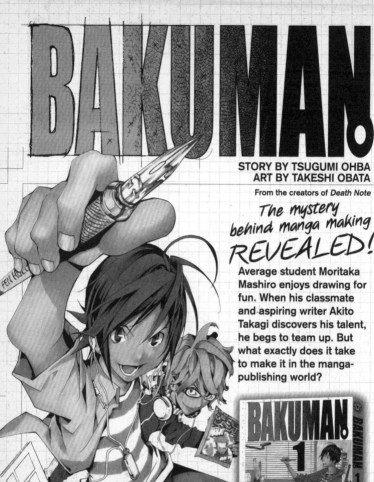

BAKUMAN。

STORY BY TSUGUMI OHBA
ART BY TAKESHI OBATA

From the creators of *Death Note*

The mystery behind manga making REVEALED!

Average student Moritaka Mashiro enjoys drawing for fun. When his classmate and aspiring writer Akito Takagi discovers his talent, he begs to team up. But what exactly does it take to make it in the manga-publishing world?

Bakuman。Vol. 1
ISBN: 978-1-4215-3513-5
$9.99 US / $12.99 CAN *

Manga on sale at store.viz.com
Also available at your local bookstore or comic store

You're Reading in the Wrong Direction!!

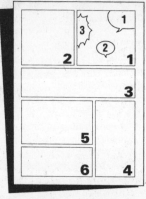

Whoops! Guess what? You're starting at the wrong end of the comic!

...It's true! In keeping with the original Japanese format, **Toriko** is meant to be read from right to left, starting in the upper-right corner.

Unlike English, which is read from left to right, Japanese is read from right to left, meaning that action, sound effects and word-balloon order are completely reversed... something which can make readers unfamiliar with Japanese feel pretty backwards themselves. For this reason, manga or Japanese comics published in the U.S. in English have sometimes been published "flopped"— that is, printed in exact reverse order, as though seen from the other side of a mirror.

By flopping pages, U.S. publishers can avoid confusing readers, but the compromise is not without its downside. For one thing, a character in a flopped manga series who once wore in the original Japanese version a T-shirt emblazoned with "M A Y" (as in "the merry month of") now wears one which reads "Y A M"! Additionally, many manga creators in Japan are themselves unhappy with the process, as some feel the mirror-imaging of their art skews their original intentions.

We are proud to bring you Mitsutoshi Shimabukuro's **Toriko** in the original unflopped format. For now, though, turn to the other side of the book and let the adventure begin...!

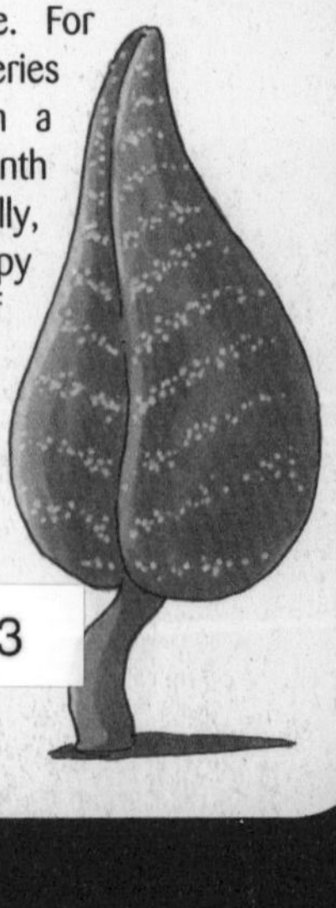

—Editor